The Parties Respond

TRANSFORMING AMERICAN POLITICS

Lawrence C. Dodd, Series Editor

Dramatic changes in political institutions and behavior over the past three decades have underscored the dynamic nature of American politics, confronting political scientists with a new and pressing intellectual agenda. The pioneering work of early postwar scholars, while laying a firm empirical foundation for contemporary scholarship, failed to consider how American politics might change or recognize the forces that would make fundamental change inevitable. In reassessing the static interpretations fostered by these classic studies, political scientists are now examining the underlying dynamics that generate transformational change.

Transforming American Politics brings together texts that address four closely related aspects of change. A first concern is documenting and explaining recent changes in American politics—in institutions, processes, behavior, and policy making. A second is reinterpreting classic studies and theories to provide a more accurate perspective on postwar politics. The series will look at historical change to identify recurring patterns of political transformation within and across the distinctive eras of American politics. Last and perhaps most important, the series presents new theories and interpretations that explain the dynamic processes at work and thus clarify the direction of contemporary politics. All of the books focus on the central theme of transformation—transformation in both the conduct of American politics and in the way we study and understand its many aspects.

BOOKS IN THIS SERIES

The Parties Respond

CHANGES IN AMERICAN PARTIES AND CAMPAIGNS

FIFTH EDITION

Mark D. Brewer

University of Maine

L. Sandy Maisel

Colby College

WESTVIEW
PRESS
A Member of the Perseus Books Group

Westview Press was founded in 1975 in Boulder, Colorado, by notable publisher
and intellectual Fred Praeger. Westview Press continues to publish scholarly titles
and high-quality undergraduate- and graduate-level textbooks in core social science
disciplines. With books developed, written, and edited with the needs of serious
nonfiction readers, professors, and students in mind, Westview Press honors its
long history of publishing books that matter.

Find us on the World Wide Web at www.westviewpress.com.

Every effort has been made to secure required permissions for all text, images, maps,
and other art reprinted in this volume.

Westview Press books are available at special discounts for bulk purchases in the
United States by corporations, institutions, and other organizations. For more
information, please contact the Special Markets Department at the Perseus Books
Group, 2300 Chestnut Street, Suite 200, Philadelphia, PA 19103, or call (800) 810-4145,
ext. 5000, or e-mail special.markets@perseusbooks.com.

Library of Congress Cataloging-in-Publication Data

The parties respond : changes in American parties and campaigns / [edited by] Mark D.
Brewer, L. Sandy Maisel. — 5th ed.
      p.   cm.
   Includes bibliographical references and index.
   ISBN 978-0-8133-4600-7 (pbk. : alk. paper) — ISBN 978-0-8133-4601-4 (e-book)
1. Political parties—United States. I. Brewer, Mark D. II. Maisel, Louis Sandy, 1945–
JK2261.P29 2012
324.273—dc23   2012004008

10 9 8 7 6 5 4 3 2

To Mark's children, Megan, Jack, David, and Gabriel,
the first one of these to you as a group, and to Sandy's
grandchildren, Conrad, Weber, Gus, Tyler, and Leo, hopefully
the next generation to carry on a tradition of interest in
and dedication to the principles of American politics.

Contents

List of Figures and Tables

Figures

Tables

Prologue

The first edition of this compilation was published in 1990, with the contributors focused on the 1988 presidential election and its aftermath. At that time one of the dominant themes in the academic literature on American political parties was the idea of party decline. The guts of this idea entailed the belief that for a variety of reasons—the increased use of television advertising in election campaigns, the institution of direct primaries and caucuses to select presidential candidates, the advantages of incumbency in congressional elections, the rise of candidate-centered campaigns, to name but a few—political parties in the United States were, to put it simply, not what they used to be. The days of parties being central players in American politics—channeling and managing political conflict, mobilizing and educating voters, structuring individual vote choice, dominating policy making in Congress—were over, and in the eyes of more than a few were unlikely to ever return. Given that such a view represented the dominant paradigm of the time, it is not surprising that the first edition of *The Parties Respond* reflected this perspective, at least to a certain extent.

As we write this in late 2011 the belief that this concept of party decline was at best overstated and at worst illusory is slowly but seemingly steadily gaining support among those who study political parties in the American context. The key to making sense of apparently reinvigorated political parties lies in the title of this anthology: *The Parties Respond*. Throughout the now 200-plus years of their existence in the United States, political parties have been faced with a seemingly endless array of challenges, obstacles, and opportunities. The one constant in this dynamic has been that the parties respond, and that they do so in a strategic manner, at least some of the time. This characteristic resembles perhaps the defining feature of The Dude in the Coen Brothers' classic film *The Big Lebowski*. In the film, The Dude, played by Jeff Bridges, always manages to "abide," no matter what confronts him. American political parties are the same way; they always manage to respond, no matter what confronts them.

This view of resurgent parties comes through in many, although not all, of the chapters contained in this volume. There is a reason for this variation; the power and relevance of political parties vary among the many different areas of American politics. The role of parties in Congress, for example, may be (and in fact is) very different from the role parties play in the presidential nominating process. But from our perspective one thing is clear: political parties remain vital and central actors in the American polity, and, in the spirit of Schattschneider (1942), understanding contemporary American politics would be impossible without an understanding of the place of parties in these politics.

The chapters in this collection represent our attempt to further this understanding. Jeff Stonecash opens the volume with a chapter examining how political scientists have studied political parties, and what this can tell us about partisan change. Nicol Rae follows with a discussion of the place of parties in American history, a discussion that concludes with an insightful presentation of where our parties are today. In Chapter 3, Mark Brewer looks at how the Democratic and Republican Parties attempt to build winning electoral coalitions, and in Chapter 4 Marjorie Randon Hershey, Nathaniel Birkhead, and Beth Easter examine the place of party activists in American politics, and how these activists contribute to party polarization.

Chapters 5 through 8 analyze parties as institutional actors. First, Dan Shea, J. Cherie Strachan, and Michael Wolf turn their view to a far too often ignored element of American parties—party organization at the local level. Paul Herrnson then shifts to party organizations at the national level in Chapter 6. In Chapter 7, Barbara Norrander walks readers through the role parties play in the presidential nominating contests. Diana Dwyre concludes this section with an up-to-the-minute tutorial on the role political parties play in financing American campaigns in Chapter 8.

Moving from parties as institutional actors, Chapters 9 through 12 deal with how parties relate to governing institutions themselves. In Chapter 9 Walt Stone, Sandy Maisel, and Trevor Lowman examine the place of parties in congressional elections through the lens of the Tea Party movement and the Republican Party in 2010. Diana Owen tackles the ever-changing area of parties and the media in Chapter 10, paying particular attention to how parties have responded to technological innovation. In Chapter 11 Sean Theriault and Jonathan Lewallen devote their attention to the role of parties in the congressional policy process, and in Chapter 12 Cal Mackenzie examines the place of parties in the executive branch. Finally, Alan Abramowitz deftly closes the volume with an almost real-time snapshot of the place of parties in contemporary American political life on the grand scale.

We believe that the chapters contained in this collection present readers with an accessible and thorough account of what they need to know about political parties in order to understand contemporary American politics. It was a joy for us to put together. We hope you find it as enjoyable to read.

Acknowledgments

As the editor of any anthology knows all too well, the success, or lack thereof, of any edited volume lies with the authors of the pieces selected for inclusion in the compilation. In this case we are extremely fortunate to have been graced with a group of extremely bright, insightful, prestigious, and, perhaps best of all, diligent and attentive contributors. We chose to aim high in our initial list of desired contributors, and we were successful in this attempt. The top shelf scholars of American political parties whose work is presented here are far and away the most important element of the text you see before you. Many of these contributors graciously made time in already busy schedules and/or temporarily set aside other projects to prepare their chapters for this volume. For that, and all of their efforts, we are unendingly thankful.

A number of other people were instrumental in bringing this collection together. At Westview Press, we want to first thank Larry Dodd, in whose series this book appears. We especially want to thank Toby Wahl, the Senior Editor for Politics at Westview, whose interest in and push for a new edition provided the initial spark for the revival of this text, and whose guidance was instrumental in bringing the project to a successful conclusion. We also need to thank Brooke Kush, Associate Development Editor at Westview, for providing useful assessment information of the previous edition, Victoria Henson, Toby's Editorial Assistant, for her work on various tasks, and to Anais Scott, who did an excellent job in copyediting this text. Melissa Veronesi, our Production Editor at Perseus Books, smoothly guided the book to completion. Danielle Hansen quickly and skillfully completed a number of tasks as

Mark's research assistant during the process of completing this book, a fact which made his life much easier.

Finally, we want to thank our respective families, who are always patient and unceasingly understanding as book deadlines approach. For Mark, this means his wife, Tammy, and his four children, Megan, Jack, David, and Gabriel, who all had a little less husband and daddy time due to this collection. Tammy is to be particularly commended for putting up with this as the final, frantic push for completion was taking place in mid-to-late December. For Sandy, this means his wife, Patrice, to whom his debt grows with each passing year and each new enterprise. And in closing, Mark wants to thank Sandy for suggesting to Westview that he come onboard as editor for the fifth edition. This suggestion was and is much appreciated.

Mark D. Brewer, Orono, Maine
L. Sandy Maisel, Rome, Maine

1

Political Science and the Study of Parties

Sorting Out Interpretations of Party Response

JEFFREY M. STONECASH
Maxwell School, Syracuse University

Political parties play a central role in the democratic process. They seek to win elections by representing voter concerns, which makes those concerns central to political decision making. When social change occurs parties serve as the organization most sensitive to representing emerging public concerns so they can secure the votes of affected constituents. The last several decades provide an important test to whether parties are playing out this role. Remarkable social change has occurred. The parties have steadily diverged in the policies they advocate (McCarty et al. 2006). Do these diverging positions reflect the divisions of society? Are parties playing the responsive role we presume in representing differing concerns? If so, how has this occurred?

In seeking an answer we turn to the academic studies of political parties, and it is at that point that someone might become very puzzled. The academic literature contains two very different interpretations, derived from different notions of what constitutes a party and what we should examine to assess the state of parties. These lead to corresponding differences in interpretations of what role parties are playing in responding to voters and changing social conditions. These affect the assessment of whether and how different concerns are being represented in American politics. The intent of this chapter is to provide an overview of the two very different interpretations of parties that exist in the literature. The goal is to sort out these differences and help anyone trying to wade through the voluminous literature on parties to understand the differences they will encounter and the notions of parties underlying these differing interpretations. The interpretations have considerable significance for our understanding of the interaction of social change and the representation process in American politics.

These differing interpretations emerged in an effort to understand trends developing in American politics. These trends provide the factual context, the changing political world that academics were seeking to understand. We begin with that political context—the trends—which people were seeking to understand. Once these trends and their significance are reviewed, we will move to the two interpretations that seek to explain those trends. The central question is: Are parties largely playing the role of supporting actors of candidates, or are they playing a central role in responding to social change? The dominant view among academics has been the former. Campaigns are widely seen as candidate centered, with parties playing a supporting role of providing services that assist candidates. The alternative interpretation is that parties have been central actors in driving change. They are playing this role as articulators of fundamentally different views of how society should work and the role government should play. They have sought to attract and represent the electoral bases that hold these differing views. In this second interpretation the process of trying to create majority coalitions created change that might have been seen as candidate centered, but it was not.

Political Trends

The political reality that academics seek to interpret has changed over time. The instigation to offer new interpretations began in response to changes emerging in the 1960s. In the 1950s there seemed to be a clear political situation. Most voters had strong affective or emotional attachments to political parties, and those attachments were stable (Campbell et al. 1960). States that voted for one party had generally been voting for that party for decades. Then evidence began to accumulate that indicated partisan loyalties were declining. Figures 1.1 and 1.2 provide evidence on the most important trends. These trends present two analytic challenges for students of political parties. First, why did the trends of the 1950s through the 1980s occur? Second, why did the trends generally reverse direction in the 1990s?

The first concern involves change from the 1950s through the 1980s. At the individual level (Figure 1.1) three trends were important. In national surveys respondents were asked if they were Democrat or Republican or did not identify with a party. Those replying independent are shown in the top line of Figure 1.1. Then those initially saying they were independent were asked if they lean to either party. Those indicating that they lean to a party are then assigned to that party and those left are called "pure independents." From 1952 through 1964 just over 20 percent indicated they were Independents or unattached. After 1964 this number increased to 35 percent and has remained high. The percentage of "pure" Independents also increased somewhat and then declined to close to the level of the 1950s. The third indicator is split-ticket voting, defined as a voter selecting presidential and House candidates of different parties. This increased in the 1970s and stayed relatively high through the 1980s.

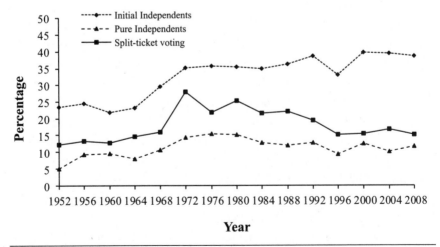

FIGURE 1.1 Independents and Split-Ticket Voting, 1952–2008

House district election results also suggested something was changing the relevance of political parties. The first matter involved an apparent increase in the security of incumbents. There was evidence that elections were resulting in less partisan turnover in control of seats (Jones 1964). Incumbents were experiencing rising vote percentages and more were deemed safe (Mayhew 1974a, 1974b). The ability of incumbents to raise their vote percentage during their career meant that when they retired there was now a greater decline in the vote for that party as the vote returned to some "normal" level (Payne 1980).

These changes coincided, and seemed compatible, with a second set of trends, shown in Figure 1.2. In each House district there is a partisan percentage for presidential and House candidates. These results can be correlated across districts. If the presidential and House results are essentially the same *within* districts but differ *across* districts, the correlation will be high. From 1900 through the 1950s it was high, suggesting that voters were voting for candidates of the same party within each district. Then in the 1960s it dropped and became erratic in subsequent years. As presidential and House results disconnected, there was an increase in the percentage of districts in which the winner of the presidential and House votes are of different parties. These are called split-outcome districts. Beginning in the 1950s, the presence of these outcomes began to increase and continued to increase through the 1980s. This prompted concern that House members were becoming insulated from swings in partisan support that occur in presidential elections (Burnham 1975).

These changes at the individual and district level suggested that something significant was happening to parties and to party loyalty within the electorate. The question was: What would explain these changes? Why were fewer voters identifying with parties, why were more splitting their ticket, and why were presidential and House results less associated?

Then most trends reversed. The percentages of pure Independents and ticket-splitting declined. The correlation between presidential and House results increased and the percentage of split outcomes decreased. The return of the presidential-House correlation, however, did not indicate a return to the past. The South had moved from being Democratic to predominantly Republican. The Northeast had moved from being heavily Republican to heavily Democratic. The renewed correlation reflected parties with very different geographical bases compared to the early 1900s. From the 1950s to the early

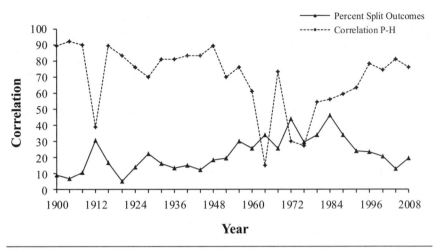

FIGURE 1.2 Correlation of Republican Presidential-House Election Results and Split Outcomes, 1900–2008

2000s major changes had occurred. What might explain all these changes? Two distinct explanations have emerged over time. Both focus on changes in society, candidate behavior, and the role of party organizations.

One interpretation is that the evidence indicates that campaigns have become more candidate centered, and that party organizations have declined as central actors. The result was that voting for parties was declining among individuals and across House districts. This view then faced the puzzle of why there was a decline in split-ticket voting and a return of a higher correlation between presidential and House voting. The answer, to be developed later, is that voters and candidates were making individual decisions to sort themselves out between the parties. Parties as organizations are not seen as central to the process of change, but in the background serving as supporting actors to candidates.

The alternative view places parties at the center of the process of change. Significant changes in society and the role of government were occurring. Voters were developing very different reactions to these changes. Parties recognized this and sought to represent these differences. Party officials responded and mobilized groups, raised money, recruited candidates, altered party images, and created parties with different electoral bases than had previously existed. They provided services but not just to keep some role in the process.

They were seeking to direct support to desired candidates to help create a unified majority. Sometimes the party had to accept less than ideologically pure candidates, but the goal was to build a coalition of elected officials with considerable unity on policy issues. This process of change was lengthy but eventually resulted in the partisan divisions that exist now.

The differences in these views are crucial for understanding how social change is responded to, how partisan change occurs, and what role political parties have played in change. The former interpretation defines parties as formal organizations that essentially must accept and work with the candidates that come to them. They can steer resources to the candidates, but there is little sense that a sort of organized effort is seeking to shape the candidates that comprise the party. Change occurs, but as the cumulative effect of many, many individual decisions. The latter defines parties as an inclusive network of actors, some formal leaders of the party and some not. This network wants to win elections, but the pursuit of a majority is inextricably tied to concern with ideas about what the party should be seeking in terms of policy. The concern about policy directions is a significant catalyst to organize, to recruit candidates, and to raise money to attain majorities. This network is actively responding to and creating partisan change. Perhaps most important, the two approaches differ in how electoral patterns of the last several decades are interpreted, a matter to be discussed at the end. The basis of the candidate-centered interpretation will first be presented, followed by the party-centered interpretation. Then the differences in how the two might explain electoral patterns will be discussed.

The Emergence of Candidate-Centered Politics

The trends displayed in Figures 1.1 and 1.2 presented an interpretative challenge to academics. What could explain them and what did they say about the state of political parties in America? The primary response among scholars was that these trends were the result of a combination of factors that were creating dealignment: the decline of party organizations and the emergence of candidates who were making themselves—not the party—the focus of campaigns.

This explanation of what was happening in the 1960s is built from two explanatory frameworks, one involving the nature of voter attachments of parties and the other involving an interpretation of how political change occurs. At any one time an alignment exists, with groups of voters identifying with a party. The attachments of voters to parties were seen as affective, based on social group identities—being Protestant, or Southern, or black—and not so much issues (Campbell et al. 1960; Green et al. 2002). Voters were resistant to change and parties represented a fairly stable set of concerns.

Given this stability, there was a need for an explanation of how change occurred. That was provided by critical realignment theory (Key 1955). In this interpretation, change happened periodically and relatively abruptly in American history. When social change occurred it created new issues. Parties might be uncertain about how to respond because taking a stance would alienate some of their existing base. As social change continued, concerns and needs were unmet, eventually resulting in a relatively abrupt disruption of existing alignments and the formation of new ones (Burnham 1970; Sundquist 1983). This cycle seemed to occur about every thirty-two years. That framework is used to organize American political history into eras in textbooks (Hershey 2009, 118–121).

Given this framework, some were expecting realignment in the 1960s, following the realignment of 1932–36 that created the New Deal coalition. The conditions seemed ripe for such a change to occur. It was roughly thirty years since the last realignment and there was a sense that the issues that had dominated since the 1930s—class, the role of labor, and industrial power—were fading in relevance. Inequality was declining (Danziger and Gottschalk 1995, 53) and class divisions were apparently declining in relevance as a source of political conflict (Alford 1963; Stonecash 2000, 1–8). New issues involving race, sex, and a variety of lifestyle choices were dominating, and political divisions had less structure (Ladd and Hadley 1975; Edsall and Edsall 1991). Some even argued the Western world was moving into a postmaterialist phase where the dominant concerns involved more amorphous issues of the quality of life (Inglehart 1971, 1977). It appeared to be a classic case of new issues disrupting old alignments.

The analytic difficulty was that it proved hard to find a critical realignment in the 1960s.[1] This prompted a search for another explanation of what could explain the trends of the 1960s and 1970s. The search for another explanation began with assessing changes in parties and the context within which they operated. Party leaders had once had significant power over nominations. In the early 1900s, many states adopted primaries, reducing the power of party leaders (Ware 2002). Elected officials once had numerous patronage positions to appoint, which gave them workers to call upon for campaign work. Civil service appointments by tests were gradually replacing patronage. Voters had once been required to select a party ballot, or one listing only candidates from one party. Gradually states had adopted ballots that presented all candidates, allowing voters to choose candidates from different parties. Party leaders had less influence and voters had more choice. The result was a lengthy decline in party organizations and an increase in split-ticket voting (Burnham 1965).

The decline in party organizations and the shift in the mix of issues were contributing to the growing independence of candidates in running campaigns. Candidates were enjoying an increase in the resources to run campaigns. These changes were giving them more autonomy from party organizations. Television was becoming more widespread and provided a means for candidates to present themselves to voters. Direct mail and polling were becoming available to individual candidates, who could raise their own funds to pay for and control these resources. Members of Congress were allocating themselves larger staff and travel allowances. The presumption was that the increase in access to incumbent and candidate-controlled resources was providing the means to create more of a personal image and diminish the extent to which a candidate was seen as reflective of a party. These changes explained the abrupt increase in the 1966 election in the percentage of House incumbents that received 60 percent of the vote, a level designated as "safe" (Mayhew 1974a, 1974b). Candidates, and particularly incumbents, were trying to build personal and enduring electoral bases to make their electoral fortunes independent of the regular swings in party fortunes that end many careers (Tufte 1973; Burnham 1975; Ferejohn 1977). The result was an increase in split-ticket voting, and election results for different offices were increasingly disconnected.

These historical changes provided a backdrop that explained the trends shown in Figures 1.1 and 1.2. In the first part of the century voting had been focused on parties, and parties had the resources to respond in order to maintain this situation. The change in the issue content of politics had disrupted political alignments. Candidates were now operating on their own and creating votes based on their personal image and their ability to deliver benefits to the district. The result was a decline in party voting within the electorate and a decline in the role of parties (Broder 1972; Crotty 1984; Wattenberg 1990, 1991, 1998).

This narrative of increasing candidate autonomy fit with what was happening to the unity of political parties in Congress. In the early 1900s Democrats regularly voted with Democrats and Republicans regularly voted with Republicans. Party unity was high. Over time party unity had steadily declined and by the 1970s it was at the lowest level ever recorded (Brady et al. 1979; Collie and Brady 1985). The parties were more diverse in their composition, with some Democrats more conservative than Republicans and some Republicans more liberal than Democrats. Members of Congress were seen as primarily concerned with reelection and catering to local constituencies. Party meant less than it had in earlier decades. The result was a sense that there was less responsiveness in American politics (Burnham 1975). Members of Congress were focused on serving disparate local concerns and not discussing national problems (Fiorina 1980).

This focus on Members of Congress as actors autonomous from parties and acting solely on their personal views fit with the interest in the rational-choice approach first presented by Anthony Downs (1957). Many academics were intrigued with the idea of taking actors as having set preferences (or "ideal points" in this approach (Poole and Rosenthal 1984, 1985)) and focusing on how agreements within institutions develop, given some distribution of preferences among members. Positing that candidates are essentially independent provides a basis for pursuing such an analytic approach (for reviews of this approach see Aldrich 1995, 2011). Some went so far as to suggest that Congress should be thought of as a set of independent actors with party meaning very little (Krehbiel 1993).

The culmination of these developments was an interpretation of American political parties as a loose coalition of independent actors who come together when it suits their individual agendas. America has "arguably the most radically candidate-centered system in the world" (McGhee 2008, 722). Elections are seen as focused on candidates (Menefee-Libey 2000; Herrnson 2008, 6–70). In this interpretation the role left for parties as organizations is to support candidates. Parties have lists of consultants, pollsters, direct mail vendors, and fund-raisers who can provide assistance to candidates (Herrnson 2009). In this interpretation parties play a role as service providers. This allows the party to adapt to a changing context and still be relevant by helping those candidates who emerge as interested in running within each party.

While candidates are seen as operating independently, the trends of the last two decades present a puzzle. If candidates are independent, why are the parties in Congress steadily moving further apart? In the last several decades party unity has increased (Polsby 2004). The average voting positions of members of each party are moving further apart. Among voters, more voters are identifying with a party (Hetherington 2001), and those identifying with a party are increasingly voting for it (Bartels 2000; Stonecash 2006). The correlation between presidential and House elections results across districts has increased and there are fewer split outcomes. It appears that partisanship has steadily grown in recent years. How could that occur if candidates operate independently?

The proposed answer is that a "sorting" process has occurred. Candidates are assessing the composition and concerns of parties and deciding with which party they wish to align. As conservatives drift to the Republican Party and liberals to the Democratic Party the composition of each party becomes clearer, resulting in more "sorting out" of candidates. At the individual level the same process is occurring as voters survey the political landscape (Fiorina and Abrams 2008). Those already within a party may change their views to stay in tune with party positions. Others with set views change their party identification (Levendusky 2009) or change their views to fit with their party identification (Layman and Carsey 2002a, 2002b; Carsey and Layman 2006). The result of all these decisions has been a sorting of conservatives into the Republican Party and liberals into the Democratic Party.

The role of parties in all these changes is somewhere between minimal and central. They have fewer financial resources and struggle to influence nominations. Candidates raise their own funds and seek to create their own image. Voters are seen as responding by basing their vote on the person more than the party. Parties exist as entities that seek to play a role in all this, but the general presumption is that they are not central to change.

Party-Centered Politics

There is an alternative interpretation of political trends and the role of political parties in creating change. This interpretation begins with an older and different sense of the relationship of constituents and parties, and with a more expansive notion of a party and of its role. This explanation begins with the simple notion that parties in American democracy represent interests and ideas, not just social groups (Turner 1951; Turner and Schneier 1970; Sanders 1999; Bensel 2000; Shafer and Johnston 2006). Parties are seen as vehicles to represent differences in interests and ideas about how society should work and what policies should be adopted to have a responsive democracy (White 2003; Brewer and Stonecash 2007). Each party wins votes and seats in some House districts and not in others because they represent different concerns (Froman 1963; Cummings 1966; Mayhew 1966; Shannon 1968; Stonecash, Brewer, and Mariani 2003). They may struggle with how much to retain an existing base versus responding to changing conditions and new groups, but the concern is not just affective bonds with social groups, but representing interests and ideas about what government should do (Black and Black 1987, 2002, 2007; Brewer and Stonecash 2009).

The notion of party underlying this is not limited to the formal organization and its legal ability to influence nominations and to raise and spend money on campaigns (Kolodny 1998; Kolodny and Dwyre 1998; Monroe 2001). The notion of party is more expansive and focuses on the informal network of those seeking to influence the direction of the party and those who represent it (Masket 2009). This can include party officials, activists, and interest groups who advocate for policies and candidates (Cohen et al. 2008; Layman et al. 2010). It can include donors who can have a significant impact by supporting some candidates and trying to discourage contributions to others. It is a loose network of actors seeking to shape the party (Dulio 2004, 2011; Grossman and Dominguez 2009; Koger, Masket, and Noel 2009, 2010; Skinner, Masket, and Dulio forthcoming). Together these diverse actors are seeking to shape the concerns and image of their party.

The important matter is just what policies are desired by this network of actors. Much of the literature sees the 1960s and 1970s as an era of dealignment, with parties having less clarity of policy concerns. The alternative view is that this was a time when parties were responding with great uncertainty to developing social and political concerns. They were driven by notions of what should be and seeking to shift the policy positions of their parties to represent those concerns and attract new constituents. The result was a lengthy process of pursuing and adding some constituents and shedding others. In this view the resulting change might have seemed to be dealignment, but it was really a shift in the primary concerns of each party. Election results and voter identifications took some time to catch up, but they eventually did, resulting in the trends of the 1990s and 2000s shown in Figures 1.1 and 1.2.

This process began in the 1950s and 1960s with discontent within each party about its positions. Within the Democratic Party there had been a longstanding tension between the southern and northern wings of the party. The southern wing wanted to retain segregation and opposed expanding social programs (Black and Black 1987). The northern wing wanted to eliminate segregation and supported expanding social programs (Carmines and Stimson 1989; Feinstein and Schickler 2008; Schickler et al. 2010). Liberal Democrats wanted to expand their electoral support in the North and were steadily pushing for more liberal policies to respond to northern concerns (Mackenzie and Weisbrot 2008). The Republican Party faced a different situation. It was the minority party in America and wanted to create a majority coalition. Conservatives wanted a more conservative party (Phillips 1969; Rusher 1984; McGirr 2002) and wanted to pursue conservative voters in the South (Hodgson 1996; Edwards 1999; Perlstein 2001, 2008; Critchlow 2007; Reiter and Stonecash 2011). The pursuit of a more conservative base was often difficult and resulted in some setbacks, but over time the party has created more of a conservative image, attracted more conservatives, and shifted the political debate in their direction (Mason 2004; Edsall 2006; Smith 2007; Hacker and Pierson 2011).

Each party was following a path of responding to new issues and pursuing voters it had not done well with in past elections (Klinkner 1994; Hillygus and Shields 2008). This meant risking losing their existing base. The lengthy process of change—known as secular realignment (Key 1959)—diminished the clarity of each party's image. It became less clear what each party stood for and who constituted the party. From the 1950s through the 1980s the Democratic Party had a base in the South (which opposed many government programs) and a base in the North (which wanted more programs). It was difficult for many voters to have a clear image of the Democratic Party. This created tensions about how liberal the party should be (Hale 1995). Eventually the party lost most of its seats in the South and became more homogeneous. It still struggled with how liberal it should be (Kuttner 1987; Kuhn 2007), but it was much less of a southern party (Edsall and Edsall 1991; Dionne 1997).

The efforts to produce clear results came later for Republicans. The party was able to win presidential contests, but they struggled to win the Senate and were out of the majority in the House from 1954 through 1993. Only in 1994 did the party gain a majority by winning more seats in the South. Gradually the party attracted more conservatives (Abramowtiz 1994; Abramowitz and Saunders 1998; Stonecash 2007; Abramowitz 2010a). As the majority of the party became conservative, the public saw the party as more conservative and it continued on the path to being the clear conservative alternative to the Democratic Party.

Eventually the concerns of each party were recognized and each party attracted more of those supportive of its agenda (Hetherington and Weiler 2009). Liberals, those with limited attachments to religion, minorities, and the less affluent were more likely to vote Democratic, while conservatives, those committed to religious principles, whites, and the more affluent were more likely to vote Republican Democratic (Abramowitz 2010b; Layman 2001; Olson 2010; Haynie and Watts 2010; Stonecash 2000, 2010).

These protracted changes fit with a party-driven explanation of the changes presented in Figures 1.1 and 1.2. As the parties began their process of change, three important matters occurred. First the image of each party became muddled. Any voter trying to assess the essential concerns of each party was likely to be less clear as the 1960s and 1970s unfolded. That would likely lead to fewer voters having strong attachments to parties and an increase in the percentage of those seeing themselves as Independents. Second, some people identifying with each party were likely to be uncomfortable with remaining in the party as it altered its composition and concerns. They were likely to be less attached to a party and more likely to split their ticket as they struggled with which party to identify with. Third, this process was likely to result in more split outcomes in House elections and a diminished correlation between presidential and House contests. Conservatives in the South voted for Republican presidential candidates before they voted for Republican House candidates. Liberals in the North were probably inclined to vote for Democratic presidential candidates before also voting for Democratic House candidates. The ability of each party to recruit House candidates in new areas was also erratic and altered the consistency of voting.

As the process unfolded each party attracted voters it wanted and lost those uncomfortable with the direction of the party. The Democratic Party lost seats in the South and gained in the North (Speel 1998). The Republican Party gradually lost the Northeast (Reiter and Stonecash 2011). There were internal debates as to whether each party was going in the right direction (Galston 1985; Rae 1989; Galston and Kamarck 1989; Brown 1991; Balz and Brownstein 1996; Greenberg 1996; Baer 2000; Busch 2005; Brownstein 2007; Gerson 2008). As each party's composition became more homogeneous and their images became more consistent voters perceived the changes and each party attracted more consistent loyalties (Bartels 2000). As incumbents retired from the House they were replaced by the same party that was winning presidential contests within the district.

The overall result was that partisanship increased (Jacobson 2000, 2003, 2007). As shown in Figure 1.1, the percentage of pure Independents declined in the 1990s and after, as did split-ticket voting. As shown in Figure 1.2, the percentage of split outcomes declined and the correlation between presidential and House results increased (Rohde 1991; Stonecash forthcoming). The process of change the parties had set in motion took time and patience, but the eventual result was a return to the level of party voting that had dominated in the 1950s.

Differing Interpretations of Party Change and the Evidence

These differences in interpretation of how change has come about are important for three reasons. First, there is a crucial difference in the notion of what constitutes party activity. The candidate-centered view is based on the formal role of parties in controlling nominations, raising money, and providing workers. The party-centered view presumes a party is a network of actors seeking to mobilize candidates, resources, and voter support. The former is limited and the latter is much more inclusive as to who is considered part of the party. This difference is important for what we look for when it comes to trying to discern the role and impact of "party" activity. The latter is much broader in scope and much harder to gather information about. Those embracing the former can send surveys to party organization offices and regard those responses as validly capturing the state of parties. The latter requires pursuing issues of who communicates with and supports others and how their efforts tie together to build support for candidates and positions. It is a far more demanding pursuit to understand parties.

Second, these differing views embody contrasting notions of what motivates and drives change. The former assumes, almost like the "invisible hand" of economics, that change evolves from a decentralized, somewhat spontaneous process of candidates and voters sorting themselves out between the two major parties. The image is of individualistic choices with no organizations seeking to persuade and move voters. Those who assemble in Congress have relatively set views and the challenge of leadership is to work with those set views. The latter assumes that actors see common themes and concerns and work to find others with common interests. They seek to work together to build support for positions, to create party images, and to attract voters. They are motivated by commonality of issues and are seeking to build a majority so they can enact policies that will support their notions of what should be. Those who assemble in Congress have clear policy views, but they also have a concern for party and may be amenable to shifting their positions as the collectivity of a party considers what strategy will advance their party (Mellow 2008; Karol 2009; Lee 2009).

Third, and perhaps most important for understanding parties and their evolution, the two differ in their ability to explain changes over time in indicators of partisanship. The former presents us with a portrait of Members of Congress acting independently. They presumably wish to buffer themselves from the fluctuations in partisan support that presidents experience, so efforts to build their vote percentage and insulate themselves from fluctuations should result in sustained separation of House and presidential results. If Members of Congress create personal votes, distinct from party, then presumably partisanship in the electorate would also remain somewhat subdued. The increase in split outcomes and the decline in straight-ticket voting that began to develop in the 1960s should persist as congressional candidates have more and more experience and assistance in creating personal votes.

In contrast, if parties are steadily recruiting candidates compatible with party interests, and losing those who are less supportive of the direction the party is going, the pattern should be very different. The results for House and presidential results should become very much the same over time as candidate recruitment succeeds and incumbents representing the past of the party retire. The correlation between the two sets of results should return to a high level. As this process continues the image of the party should become clearer. The party should attract those who are sympathetic and lose those who are uncomfortable with the direction the party is taking. These supporters should be more inclined to vote for the candidates of their party.

The Evidence

Many theories or interpretations emerge from deductive thinking about the world. The interpretations about the role of parties developed inductively. Political trends developed in the 1960s and 1970s and academics began a search for an explanation of change. The dominant view has been that issues changed, parties declined, candidates became more independent, and voters were less partisan. The difficulty that explanation faces is that as Figures 1.1 and 1.2 indicate, district and individual level trends have reversed course. A reexamination of the evidence about the ability of incumbents in Congress to increase their vote percentages indicates that there was no increase (Stonecash 2008). Further, the candidate-centered interpretation seems to be of less relevance at a time when the parties in Washington are lining up and voting together and against the other party with greater and greater frequency.

Some of those perhaps seeking to save the candidate-centered interpretation have proposed the argument that candidates and people are sorting themselves out, with parties serving as the background context actors are responding to (Levendusky 2009). Others have suggested that politicians are simply disconnected from the public and pursuing their own agendas (Fiorina et al. 2006; Fiorina 2009). Parties are not seen as organizers of this process or as representing real substantive and differing interests of the American public.

The alternative explanation is that these changes were organized and shaped by party activism. If this interpretation is valid, then we should expect to see gradual changes as incumbents retire and are replaced, and as voters perceive the shifting focus of each party. We should also see partisanship increasing over time, and a closer fit between presidential and House results. In fact we do see both gradual movement and a return to greater partisanship at the individual and district level. The patterns in the data suggest the latter interpretation is a more plausible explanation of the changes over the last fifty years. It is also difficult to ignore the remarkable efforts that parties are now making to recruit candidates (Ruthenberg and Zeleny 2011) with the presumption, or at least the hope, that they will vote with the party in Congress when they arrive (Brady, MacGillis, and Montgomery 2011). While there may be two strong traditions of interpretation in the discipline, the evidence appears to tilt significantly to the party-centered one to explain the trends of recent decades.

References

Abramowitz, Alan I. 1994. "Issue Evolution Reconsidered: Racial Attitudes and Partisanship in the US Electorate." *American Journal of Political Science* 38, 1 (February): 1–24.

_____. 2010a. "Ideological Realignment Among Voters." In *New Directions in American Political Parties,* edited by Jeffrey M. Stonecash, 126–147. New York: Routledge.

_____. 2010b. *The Disappearing Center: Engaged Citizens, Polarization, and American Democracy.* New Haven: Yale University Press.

Abramowitz, Alan I., and Kyle L. Saunders. 1998. "Ideological Realignments in the US Electorate." *Journal of Politics* 60, 3 (August): 634–652.

Aldrich, John. 1995. *Why Parties?* Chicago: University of Chicago Press.

_____. 2011. *Why Parties? A Second Look.* Chicago: University of Chicago Press.

Alford, Robert R. 1963. *Party and Society: The Anglo-American Democracies.* Westport, CT: Greenwood Press.

Baer, Kenneth S. 2000. *Reinventing Democrats: The Politics of Liberalism from Reagan to Clinton.* Lawrence, KS: University Press of Kansas.

Balz, Daniel J., and Ronald Brownstein. 1996. *Storming the Gates: Protest Politics and the Republican Revival.* Boston: Little, Brown, and Company.

Bartels, Larry M. 1998. "Electoral Continuity and Change, 1868–1996." *Electoral Studies* 17, 3 (September): 301–326.

_____. 2000. "Partisanship and Voting Behavior, 1952–1996." *American Journal of Political Science* 44, 1 (January): 35–49.

Bensel, Richard F. 2000. *The Political Economy of American Industrialism, 1877–1900.* New York: Cambridge University Press.

Black, Earl, and Merle Black. 1987. *Politics and Society in the South.* Cambridge, MA: Harvard University Press.

_____. 2002. *The Rise of Southern Republicans.* Cambridge, MA: Harvard University Press.

_____. 2007. *Divided America: The Ferocious Power Struggle in American Politics.* New York: Simon and Schuster.

Brady, David W., Joseph Cooper, and Patricia A. Hurley. 1979. "The Decline of Party in the US House of Representatives, 1887–1968." *Legislative Studies Quarterly* 4, 3 (August): 381–407.

Brady, Dennis, Alec MacGillis, and Lori Montgomery. 2011. "Origins of the Debt Showdown," *The Washington Post.* August 6. http://www.washingtonpost.com/business/economy/origins-of-the-debt-showdown/2011/08/03/gIQA9uqIzI_story.html.

Brewer, Mark D., and Jeffrey M. Stonecash. 2007. *Split: Class and Cultural Divides in American Politics.* Washington, DC: CQ Press.

_____. 2009. *The Dynamics of American Political Parties.* New York: Cambridge University Press.

Broder, David. 1972. *The Party's Over: The Failure of Politics in America.* New York: Harper and Row.

Brown, Peter. 1991. *Minority Party: Why the Democrats Face Defeat in 1992 and Beyond.* Washington, DC: Regenry Gateway.

Brownstein, Ronald. 2007. *The Second Civil War: How Extreme Partisanship Has Paralyzed Washington and Polarized America.* New York: Penguin Press.

Burnham, Walter Dean. 1965. "The Changing Shape of the American Political Universe." *American Political Science Review* 59, 1 (March): 7–28.

_____. 1970. *Critical Elections and the Mainsprings of American Politics.* New York: W. W. Norton.

_____. 1975. "Insulation and Responsiveness in Congressional Elections." *Political Science Quarterly* 90, 3 (Fall): 411–435.

Busch, Andrew E. 2005. *Reagan's Victory: The Presidential Election of 1980 and the Rise of the Right.* Lawrence, KS: University Press of Kansas.

Campbell, Angus, Philip Converse, Warren Miller, and Donald Stokes. 1960. *The American Voter.* New York: John Wiley and Sons.

Campbell, James E. 2006. "Party Systems and Realignments in the United States, 1868–2004." *Social Science History* 30 (Fall): 359–386.

Carmines, Edward G., and James A. Stimson. 1989. *Issue Evolution: Race and the Transformation of American Politics.* Princeton, NJ: Princeton University Press.

Carsey, Thomas M., and Geoffrey C. Layman. 2006. "Changing Sides or Changing Minds? Party Identification and Policy Preferences in the American Electorate." *American Journal of Political Science* 50 (April): 464–477.

Cohen, Marty, David Karol, Hans Noel, and John Zaller. 2008. *The Party Decides: Presidential Nominations Before and After Reform.* Chicago: University of Chicago Press.

Collie, Melissa P., and David W. Brady. 1985. "The Decline of Partisan Voting Coalitions in the House of Representatives." In *Congress Reconsidered,* edited by Lawrence C. Dodd and Bruce I. Oppenheimer, 272–287. 3rd ed. Washington, DC: CQ Press.

Critchlow, Donald. 2007. *The Conservative Ascendancy.* Cambridge, MA: Harvard University Press.

Crotty, William. 1984. *American Parties in Decline.* 2nd ed. Boston: Little, Brown, and Co.

Cummings, Milton C., Jr. 1966. *Congressmen and the Electorate.* New York: Free Press.

Danziger, Sheldon, and Peter Gottschalk. 1995. *American Unequal.* Cambridge, MA: Harvard University Press.

Dionne, E. J., Jr. 1997. *They Only Look Dead.* New York: Touchstone.

Downs, Anthony. 1957. *An Economic Theory of Democracy.* New York: Harper and Row.

Dulio, David A. 2004. *For Better or Worse: How Political Consultants Are Changing Elections in the United States.* Albany: SUNY Press.

_____. 2011. "The Impact of Political Consultants." In *Electoral Challenge: Theory Meets Practice,* edited by Stephen C. Craig and David B. Hills, 243–270. 2nd ed. Washington, DC: CQ Press.

Edsall, Thomas B. 2006. *Building Red America: The Conservative Coalition and the Drive for Permanent Power.* New York: Basic Books.

Edsall, Thomas Byrne, and Mary D. Edsall. 1991. *Chain Reaction: The Impact of Race, Rights, and Taxes on American Politics.* New York: W. W. Norton.

Edwards, Lee. 1999. *The Conservative Revolution.* New York: Free Press.

Feinstein, Brian D., and Eric Schickler. 2008. "Platforms and Partners: The Civil Rights Realignment Reconsidered." *Studies in American Political Development* 22 (Spring): 115–116.

Ferejohn, John A. 1977. "On the Decline of Competition in Congressional Elections." *American Political Science Review* 71, 1 (March): 166–176.

Fiorina, Morris P. 1980. "The Decline of Collective Responsibility in American Politics." *Daedalus* 109 (Summer): 25–45.

Fiorina, Morris P., and Samuel J. Abrams. 2008. "Political Polarization in the American Public." *Annual Review of Political Science* 11: 563–588.

Fiorina, Morris P., with Samuel J. Abrams. 2009. *Disconnect: The Breakdown of Representation in American Politics.* Norman, OK: University of Oklahoma Press.

Fiorina, Morris P., with Samuel J. Abrams and Jeremy C. Pope. 2006. *Culture War? The Myth of a Polarized America,* 2nd ed. New York: Pearson/Longman.

Froman, Lewis A., Jr. 1963. *Congressmen and Their Constituencies.* Chicago: McNally.

Galston, William. 1985. "The Future of the Democratic Party." *The Brookings Review* (Winter): 16–24.

Galston, William, and Elaine C. Kamarck. 1989. "The Politics of Evasion: Democrats and the Presidency." *Progressive Policy Institute* 2 (May): 195–216.

Gerson, Michael. 2008. "How My Party Lost Its Way." *Newsweek.* January 28, 28.

Green, Donald P., Bradley Palmquist, and Eric Shickler. 2002. *Partisan Hearts and Minds: Political Parties and the Social Identities of Voters.* New Haven: Yale University Press.

Greenberg, Stanley B. 1996. *Middle Class Dreams: Politics and Power of the New American Majority.* New Haven, CT: Yale University Press.

Grossman, Matt, and Casey B. K. Dominguez. 2009. "Party Coalitions and Interest Group Networks." *American Politics Research* 37, 5 (September): 767–800.

Hacker, Jacob S., and Paul Pierson. 2011. *Winner-Take-All Politics: How Washington Made the Rich Richer–and Turned Its Back on the Middle Class.* New York. Simon and Schuster.

Hale, Jon F. 1995. "The Making of the New Democrats." *Political Science Quarterly* 110, 2: 207–232.

Haynie, Kerry L., and Candis S. Watts. 2010. "Blacks and the Democratic Party: A Resilient Coalition." In *New Directions in American Political Parties,* edited by Jeffrey M. Stonecash, 110–125. New York: Routledge.

Herrnson, Paul S. 2008. *Congressional Elections: Campaigning at Home and in Washington.* 5th ed. Washington, DC: Congressional Quarterly Press.

_____. 2009. "The Roles of Party Organization, Party-Connected Committees, and Party Allies in Elections." *Journal of Politics* 71, 4 (October): 1207–1224.

Hershey, Marjorie Randon. 2009. *Party Politics in America.* 13th ed. New York: Pearson/Longman.

Hetherington, Marc J. 2001. "Resurgent Mass Partisanship: The Role of Elite Polarization?" *American Political Science Review* 95, 3 (September): 619–632.

Hetherington, Marc J., and Jonathan D. Weiler. 2009. *Authoritarianism and Polarization in American Politics.* Cambridge: Cambridge University Press.

Hillygus, D. Sunshine, and Todd G. Shields. 2008. *The Persuadable Voter: Wedge Issues in Presidential Campaigns.* Princeton: Princeton University Press.

Hodgson, Godfrey. 1996. *The World Turned Right Side Up.* Boston: Mariner Books.

Inglehart, Ronald. 1971. "The Silent Revolution in Europe." *American Political Science Review* 65, 4 (December): 991–1017.

_____.1977. *Silent Revolution.* Princeton: Princeton University Press.

Jacobson, Gary C. 2000. "Party Polarization in National Politics: The Electoral Connection." In *Polarized Politics: Congress and the President in a Partisan Era,* edited by Jon R. Bond and Richard Fleisher, 9–30. Washington, DC: Congressional Quarterly Press.

_____. 2003. "Party Polarization in Presidential Support: The Electoral Connection." *Congress and The Presidency* 30, 1 (Spring): 1–36.

_____. 2007. *A Divider, Not a Uniter: George W. Bush and the American People.* New York: Pearson/Longman.

Jones, Charles O. 1964. "Inter-Party Competition in Congressional Seats." *Western Political Quarterly* 17, 3 (September): 461–476.

Karol, David. 2009. *Party Position Change in American Politics: Coalition Management.* New York: Cambridge University Press.

Key, V. O., Jr. 1955. "A Theory of Critical Elections." *Journal of Politics* 17, 1 (February): 3–18.

_____. 1959. "Secular Realignment and the Party System." 1959. *Journal of Politics* 21, 2 (May): 198–210.

Klinkner, Philip A. 1994. *The Losing Parties: Out-Party National Committees, 1956–1993.* New Haven: Yale University Press.

Koger, Gregory, Seth Masket, and Hans Noel. 2009. "Partisan Webs: Information Exchange and Party Networks." *British Journal of Political Science* 39, 3 (July): 633–653.

_____. 2010. "Cooperative Party Factions in American Politics." *American Politics Research* 38, 1 (January): 33–53.

Kolodny, Robin. 1998. *Pursuing Majorities: Congressional Campaign Committees in American Politics.* Norman, OK: University of Oklahoma Press.

Kolodny, Robin, and Diana Dwyre. 1998. "Party-Orchestrated Activities for Legislative Party Goals." *Party Politics* 4, 3: 275–295.

Krehbiel, Keith. 1993. "Where's the Party?" *British Journal of Political Science* 23, 2 (April): 235–266.

Kuhn, David Paul. 2007. *The Neglected Voter: White Men and the Democratic Dilemma.* New York: Palgrave Macmillan.

Kuttner, Robert. 1987. *The Life of the Party: Democratic Prospects in 1988 and Beyond.* New York: Penguin Books.

Ladd, Everett Carll, and Charles Hadley. 1975. *Transformations of the American Party System.* New York: W. W. Norton.

Layman, Geoffrey C. 2001. *The Great Divide: Religious and Cultural Conflict in American Party Politics.* New York: Columbia University Press.

Layman, Geoffrey C., and Thomas M. Carsey. 2002a. "Party Polarization and Party Structuring of Policy Attitudes: A Comparison of Three NES Panel Studies." *Political Behavior* 24, 3 (September): 199–236.

_____. 2002b. "Party Polarization and 'Conflict Extension' in the American Electorate." *American Journal of Political Science* 46, 4 (October): 786–802.

Layman, Geoffrey C., Thomas M. Carsey, John C. Green, Richard Herrera, and Rosalyn Cooperman. 2010. "Party Polarization, Party Commitment, and Conflict Extension Among American Party Activists." *American Political Science Review* 104, 2 (May): 324–346.

Lee, Frances E. 2009. *Beyond Ideology: Politics, Principles, and Partisanship in the US Senate.* Chicago: University of Chicago Press.

Levendusky, Matthew. 2009. *The Partisan Sort: How Liberals Became Democrats and Conservatives Became Republicans.* Chicago: University of Chicago Press.

Mackenzie, G. Calvin, and Robert Weisbrot. 2008. *The Liberal Hour: Washington and the Politics of Change in the 1960s.* New York: Penguin Press.

Masket, Seth E. 2009. *No Middle Ground: How Informal Party Organizations Control Nominations and Polarize Legislatures.* Ann Arbor: University of Michigan Press.

Mason, Robert. 2004. *Richard Nixon and the Quest for a New Majority.* Chapel Hill: The University of North Carolina Press.

Mayhew, David R. 1966. *Party Loyalty Among Congressmen: the Difference Between Demo-crats and Republicans, 1947–1962.* Cambridge: Harvard University Press.

———.1974a. *The Electoral Connection.* New Haven: Yale University Press.

———. 1974b. "Congressional Elections: The Case of the Vanishing Marginals." *Polity* 6: 295–317.

———. 2003. *Electoral Realignments: A Critique of an American Genre.* New Haven: Yale University Press.

McCarty, Nolan, Keith T. Poole, and Howard Rosenthal. 2006. *Polarized America: The Dance of Ideology and Unequal Riches.* Cambridge: M.I.T. Press.

McGhee, Eric. 2008. "National Tides and Local Results in US House Elections." *British Journal of Political Science* 38, 4 (October): 719–783.

McGirr, Lisa. 2002. *Suburban Warriors: the Origins of the New American Right.* Princeton, NJ: Princeton University Press.

Mellow, Nicole. 2008. *The State of Disunion: Regional Sources of Modern American Partisan-ship.* Baltimore: Johns Hopkins University Press.

Menefee-Libey, David. 2000. *The Triumph of Candidate-Centered Politics.* New York: Chatham House.

Merrill, Samuel, III, Bernard Grofman, and Thomas Brunell. 2008. "Cycles in American Na-tional Electoral Politics, 1854–2006: Statistical Evidence and an Explanatory Model." *American Political Science Review* 102, 1 (February): 1–17.

Monroe, J. P. 2001. *The Political Party Matrix: The Persistence of Organization.* Albany: State University of New York Press.

Olson, Laura R. 2010. "Religion, Moralism, and the Cultural Wars: Competing Moral Visions." In *New Directions in American Political Parties,* edited by Jeffrey M. Stonecash, 148–165. New York: Routledge.

Paulson, Arthur C. 2000. *Realignment and Party Revival: Understanding American Electoral Politics at the Turn of the Twenty-First Century.* Westport: Praeger.

———. 2007. *Electoral Realignment and the Outlook for American Democracy.* Boston: Northeastern University Press.

Payne, James L. 1980. "The Personal Electoral Advantage of House Incumbents, 1936–1976." *American Politics Quarterly* 8, 4 (October): 465–482.

Perlstein, Rick. 2001. *Before the Storm.* New York: Hill and Wang.

———. 2008. *Nixonland: The Rise of a President and the Fracturing of America.* New York: Scribner.

Phillips, Kevin P. 1969. *The Emerging Republican Majority.* New Rochelle, NY: Arlington House.

Polsby, Nelson. 2004. *How Congress Evolves: Social Bases of Institutional Change.* New York: Oxford University Press.

Poole, Keith T., and Howard Rosenthal. 1984. "The Polarization of American Politics." *Journal of Politics* 46, 4 (November): 1061–1079.

———. 1985. "A Spatial Model for Legislative Roll Call Analysis." *American Journal of Polit-ical Science* 29, 2 (May): 357–384.

Rae, Nicol C. 1989. *The Decline and Fall of the Liberal Republicans from 1952 to the Present.* New York: Oxford University Press.

Reiter, Howard L., and Jeffrey M. Stonecash. 2011. *Counter-Realignment: Political Change in the Northeast.* New York: Cambridge University Press.

Rohde, David W. 1991. *Parties and Leaders in the Postreform House.* Chicago: University of Chicago Press.

Rusher, William A. 1984. *The Rise of the Right*. New York: William Morrow and Company, Inc.

Ruthenberg, Jim, and Jeff Zeleny. 2011. "Democrats Outrun by a 2-Year G.O.P. Comeback Plan," *New York Times*. November 3. http://www.nytimes.com/2010/11/04/us/politics/04campaign.html?scp=37&sq=Republican%20political%20plan&st=cse.

Sanders, Elizabeth. 1999. *Roots of Reform: Farmers, Workers, and the American State*. Chicago: University of Chicago Press.

Schickler, Eric, Kathryn Pearson, and Brian Feinstein. 2010. "Congressional Parties and Civil Rights Politics from 1933 to 1972." *Journal of Politics* 72, 3 (July): 672–689.

Shafer, Byron E. ed. 1991. *The End of Realignment? Interpreting American Electoral Eras*. Madison, WI: University of Wisconsin Press.

Shafer, Byron E., and Richard Johnston. 2006. *The End of Southern Exceptionalism: Class, Race, and Partisan Change in the Postwar South*. Cambridge, MA: Harvard University Press.

Shannon, W. Wayne. 1968. *Party, Constituency and Congressional Voting*. Baton Rouge: Louisiana University Press.

Skinner, Richard M., Seth E. Masket, and David A. Dulio. Forthcoming. "527 Committees and the Political Party Network." *American Politics Research*.

Smith, Mark A. 2007. *Right Talk*. Princeton, NJ: Princeton University Press.

Speel, Robert W. 1998. *Changing Patterns of Voting in the Northern United States: Electoral Realignment, 1952–1996*. University Park, PA: Pennsylvania State University Press.

Stonecash, Jeffrey M. 2000. *Class and Party in American Politics*. Boulder, CO.: Westview Press.

_____. 2006. *Parties Matter: Realignment and the Return of Partisanship*. Boulder, CO: Lynne Rienner.

_____. 2007. "The Rise of the Right: More Conservatives or More Concentrated Conservatism." In *The State of the Parties*, edited by John C. Green and Daniel J. Coffey, 317–330. 5th ed. Lanham, MD: Rowman and Littlefield.

_____. 2008. *Reassessing the Incumbency Effect*. New York: Cambridge University Press.

_____. 2010. "Class in American Politics." In *New Directions in American Political Parties*, edited by Jeffrey M. Stonecash, 110–125. New York: Routledge.

_____. Forthcoming. Party Pursuits and the Presidential-House Election Connection, 1900–2008. New York: Cambridge University Press.

Stonecash, Jeffrey M., Mark D. Brewer, and Mack D. Mariani. 2003. *Diverging Parties: Social Change, Realignment, and Party Polarization*. Boulder, CO: Westview Press.

Stonecash, Jeffrey M., and Everita Silina. 2005. "Reassessing the 1896 Realignment." *American Political Research* 33, 1 (January): 3–32.

Sundquist, James L. 1983. *Dynamics of the Party System: Alignment and Realignment of Political Parties in the United States*. Rev. ed. Washington, DC: Brookings Institution.

Tufte, Edward R. 1973. "The Relationship Between Seats and Votes in Two-Party Systems." *American Political Science Review* 67, 2 (June): 540–554.

Turner, Julius. 1951. *Party and Constituency: Pressures on Congress*. Baltimore, MD: The Johns Hopkins Press.

Turner, Julius, and Edward V. Schneier. 1970. *Party and Constituency: Pressures on Congress*. Rev. ed. Baltimore: Johns Hopkins Press.

Ware, Alan. 2002. *The American Direct Primary: Party Institutionalization and Transformation in the North*. New York: Cambridge.

_____. 2006. *The Democratic Party Heads North, 1877–1962*. New York: Cambridge University Press.

Wattenberg, Martin P. 1990. *The Decline of American Political Parties, 1952-1988*. Cambridge, MA: Harvard University Press.

_____. 1991. *The Rise of Candidate-Centered Politics*. Cambridge, MA: Harvard University Press.

_____. 1998. *The Decline of American Political Parties, 1952-1996*. Cambridge, MA: Harvard University Press.

White, John K. 2003. *The Values Divide: American Politics and Culture in Transition*. New York: Chatham House Publishers.

Endnotes

1. As the search for realignment in the 1960s occurred there were also studies about whether there had even been major realignments in the past (Mayhew 2003; Stonecash and Silina 2005). The debate about this issue continues (Shafer 1991; Paulson 2000, 2007; Bartels 1998; Campbell 2006; Merrill et al. 2008).

2

The Diminishing Oddness of American Political Parties

NICOL C. RAE

Florida International University, Miami

The "Strangeness" of American Parties

Political parties are the most critical intermediary political institutions between citizens and government. Through competing for control of government in elections, the parties aggregate mass preferences in such a fashion that electoral outcomes become meaningful (what political scientists call "structuring the vote"). Parties also provide government accountability, since support or otherwise for the governing party (or combination of parties) allows citizens to exercise their fundamental democratic power: to "throw the rascals out." To date no mass democracy has been able to function in the absence of political parties.

In most contemporary democracies the parties are primarily defined by ideology, and since ideology defines parties it is generally emphasized and taken very seriously at both mass and elite levels. In the majority of democracies political parties are also highly centralized and vertically organized with the national party leadership being sovereign over regional or local units. In fact, as democracies in the modern world are largely parliamentary systems (where party cohesion is critical to maintaining a parliamentary majority and control of the government), the major parties tend to be highly

25

disciplined, with the party leadership exerting strict control over elected officeholders. These parties are also invariably mass membership parties: that
is, citizens can join parties for an annual fee that entitles them to participate
in party business and have a role in candidate selection (these membership
dues have also traditionally played a critical role in party financing, including
electoral campaigns). Candidate selection is also regarded as an internal party
matter, with nominees being selected by local, regional, or national party organizations. Finally, political parties in modern democracies function, for the
most part, in multiparty parliamentary systems with several parties represented in the national parliament (largely due to proportional electoral systems that award parties seats roughly according to their national share of the
vote), and where multiparty coalitions rather than single-party government
is the norm (Lijphart 1999).

When we look at the American parties, however, many of the characteristic features of political parties in other democracies are largely absent. American parties have traditionally not emphasized ideology. They have always
been highly decentralized, with state and local party units enjoying a great
deal of autonomy from the national party. In terms of organization, the
American party at all levels can exert relatively little discipline over its elected
officeholders in a separated governmental system. A large part of the reason
for this is that American parties do not select the candidates who bear the
party label, this function being given over to a broader public in another
peculiarly American political institution—the primary election. To "join"
American political parties (and participate in party primaries) American citizens are not obliged to pay dues and complete a formal membership appli-
cation, but instead simply register (or not) with one or other of the major
political parties when they register to vote.

This chapter argues that the singular nature of American parties is due to
specifically American features, such as: the separation of powers, the plurality
electoral system, and differences in American political development that sti-
fled the growth of socialism (a key element in the evolution of political parties
in European democracies) as a mass political movement in the United States.
In the forthcoming sections all of this will be discussed in more detail, and a
further argument will be made that American parties have recently become
somewhat less peculiar, as: (1) ideology has come to play a much greater role
than hitherto in American politics; and (2) parties in other advanced democ-

racies have become far less influenced by the socialist "mass party" model and have developed some more typically "American" features.

A Short History of US Parties

The framers of the US constitution had little time for "parties" a term they used synonymously with "factions"—in today's parlance, "interest groups" or "special interests" (Madison 1961). Yet they accepted such factions as inevitable in a free republic and sought to guard against their malign influence by creating a national government based on separately elected institutions with shared legislative powers. Despite the restricted franchise of the first decades of the republic, fundamental differences of opinion among the founding elite regarding the mercantilist economic policies of Treasury Secretary Alexander Hamilton, and the 1795 "Jay Treaty" with Great Britain became manifest in bitter debates in the US House (Chambers 1963). These differences led to the formation of political organizations seeking to control the government in the name of a set of commonly agreed principles rather than narrow self-interest. The Democratic-Republican or "Jeffersonian" Party—led by Thomas Jefferson and James Madison—advocated states' rights and a pro-French foreign policy, while the opposing Federalist Party—led by John Adams and Alexander Hamilton—favored a strong national government more aligned internationally with Great Britain than revolutionary France. In 1796, Jefferson lost the presidency by one electoral college vote to John Adams, but he won a convincing victory in 1800 due to the unpopularity of the Adams administration and divisions within the Federalist Party leadership (Chambers 1963; Wilentz 2005).

The first American political parties did not have much staying power, however. After 1800 the Federalists rapidly degenerated into a regional (New England) bloc, and the dominance of the Jeffersonians was so great that the party's congressional caucus (dubbed "King Caucus") dominated Congress and effectively selected Jefferson's presidential successors (Wilentz 2005). Genuine party competition thus disappeared, in essence, during the so-called "Era of Good Feelings" (1800–1825).

America's first parties had formed around tensions and disputes leading up to a presidential contest, and it was another such contest in 1824 that led to the creation of the first substantive and durable American political parties.

One major factor underlying the change was the democratization of American society and the creation of a mass electorate as most adult white males became enfranchised by the early 1820s (Wilentz 2005). The electoral potential of this immense new constituency began to be realized in the strong support of lower status voters for the presidential candidacy of Andrew Jackson in the 1824 presidential contest. Yet because Jackson's popular support was insufficiently organized to be translated into electoral college votes, Jackson ended up controversially losing the presidency in a multicandidate context to an alliance of two of his opponents, John Quincy Adams and Henry Clay, that secured the presidency for Adams.

Four years later Jackson's lieutenant, Martin Van Buren, created a national organization to mobilize Jackson's mass following behind slates of electors in the individual states committed to support Jackson in the electoral college. This organization was also programmatic, since the Jackson candidacy represented an updating of Jeffersonian principles: a curbing of the power of the federal government (and particularly the Second Bank of the United States) vis-à-vis the states, suspicion of eastern economic and political elites, and lower tariffs. The result was an overwhelming victory for Jackson, and by the time of his reelection in 1832 the Jacksonian organization had been christened the "Democratic Party." It is interesting to note that Van Buren knew exactly what he was doing in creating America's first true political party (and now the oldest among Western democracies), since his published writings reveal an eloquent (and in the American context, rare) defense of parties as essential intermediary political organizations in mass democracies (Cesar 1979). After a third triumph for the Democrats in the election of Van Buren himself to the presidency in 1836, the opponents of Jacksonian Democracy finally got their act together and created the Whig party, which, by contrast with the Jacksonian Democrats, offered a platform based on a program of internal improvements and external tariffs to protect American industry promoted by an energetic federal government.

Many features of the major American parties and the party system have persisted from the Jacksonian Era to the present day. The use of national conventions of delegates from the state parties to make presidential nominations was introduced by the Jacksonians in 1832, but the national party had virtually no existence between the quadrennial national conventions. Most party political activity was concentrated at the state and local level, where the political decisions most relevant to the most voters were made most of the time during the nineteenth century (Silbey 1994). The major political parties of the Jacksonian Era were not perhaps "ideological" in the modern sense of the term, but, as outlined above, there were clear policy differences between them (Gerring 1998). It should be noted that America had developed a mass electorate and an organized and robust national party system prior to the industrialization of American society, an important factor—as we shall see in the next section—in the failure of the European "mass party" model to take root in the United States.

The development of the Jacksonian party system in effect nullified the electoral college as an independent political institution, since the presidential electors were now composed of slates of party faithful elected in "winner-take-all" statewide popular elections by plurality vote. Except for rare occasions of deadlock, the electoral college in future would simply ratify the presidential choices made by the voters in the various states. The logic of the plurality voting system used here and in elections to Congress and state legislatures also entrenched the two-party system in the United States, since (in accordance with the famous "law" of the French political scientist, Maurice Duverger) minor parties were inevitably squeezed out of existence over the long term by the "wasted vote" argument (Duverger 1964). This factor also helps account for the extraordinary stability of the American major parties. Since the 1830s only once has one of the two major American political parties been replaced by another party: the Whig party disintegrated and was replaced by the Republicans as the slavery issue unraveled the Jacksonian party alignment in the 1850s.

The latter part of the nineteenth century was the age of party machines. In an age before secret election ballots and where all government appointments were in the gift of the winning political party right down to the very lowest levels, party organizations used their control over such appointments and the favors of government to build formidable mass and elite political constituencies—particularly in urban areas (Silbey 1994). In exchange for votes and/or financial support the machine dispensed jobs and basic welfare to the needy, favors to powerful private interests in their domain, and electoral support to their party's state and national candidates, who were also willing to trade favors for the machines' support. The onset of mass immigration from Europe during the nineteenth century provided a ready source of political capital to the urban machines in the shape of destitute and desperate immigrants who would gladly support the machine in exchange for paying jobs and poor relief. As the immigrant communities evolved politically, the ranks of the machine become a key source of political and social advancement. Even beyond the urban machines there were powerful incentives for voters to align strongly with political parties during this period. Political parties commanded all the resources of politics: money, voters, and information. Elections were exercises in political mobilization between two powerful political organizations and, as parties controlled the government, voters had powerful incentives to be mobilized by the parties (Silbey 1994). The torchlight parades, massive election rallies, and exceptionally high rates of voter participation of the late-nineteenth century may seem rather quaint to the modern observer, but to the ordinary nineteenth-century American, enthusiastic support for their political party was an essential route to a decent living and perhaps political power, if they served the organization faithfully and effectively.

The side effects of the age of the party machines were not so healthy however. Moisei Ostrogorski (1982), in his extensive study of late-nineteenth-century American parties, deplored the inefficiency and corruption of the machines and what he regarded as their degradation of liberal democratic principles. There were also significant and growing sections of American society that strove for a greater degree of professionalism in government, a merit-based civil service, significant social reform in the cities to deal more effectively with the root causes and effects of poverty, and a reduction in the influence of powerful private business interests that had regularly "captured" control of government at all levels through their support for party machines. Among these groups were the scions of the northern WASP patrician class such as Theodore Roosevelt and Henry Cabot Lodge, who felt that they had been excluded from their birthright—political power and influence—by the alliance of machine bosses and the *nouveau riche* capitalists and industrial magnates of the Gilded Age; the increasing number of highly educated and professionally trained voters who believed that their skills should be put to greater and more effective use by government; the women's suffrage movement; farmers in thrall economically to railroad corporations and their machine allies; and those who believed in social reform and empowerment of the disadvantaged. Under the umbrella of the Progressive Movement this broad alliance would launch a major assault on the party machines and begin a process of long-term party reform that would transform the organizational structure of American politics (Hofstadter 1955).

The most significant party reforms pioneered by the Progressives in the first decades of the twentieth century were the introduction of the secret ballot, the establishment of preregistration to get access to the electoral roll, and the direct primary election for choosing party candidates (Burnham 1981). The secret, government-provided ballot not only precluded much of the intimidation and electoral fraud practiced by the machines but also allowed voters to select candidates from different parties for different offices in contrast to the long-established, party-provided ballots that made "ticket splitting" very difficult. The major argument for preregistration was to rule out electoral fraud through the provision of a more accurate electoral roll. On the other hand, preregistration imposed new costs in terms of time and paperwork for voters to get onto the election register, and thus might also be interpreted as exclusionary in intent—particularly with regard to poorer, less educated voters. The direct primary was an effort to reduce the influence of machine bosses and special interests over party nominations by giving this power to a broader electorate of voters who had indicated a preference for a particular party on registering to vote (in some states all registered voters could vote in the party primary of their choice on election day). In the one-party Democratic South of the early-twentieth century, the primary was used explicitly to exclude almost all black voters and many poorer whites from political participation, and in the northern states its introduction coincided with a marked drop in election turnout by comparison with the late-nineteenth century (Burnham 1981). Ironically, while weakening the parties structurally, the regulation of parties introduced by the Progressives actually further entrenched the dominance of the Republican and Democratic party labels since preregistration and the extent of regulation of party procedures made it very hard for third and minor parties to maintain ballot access and organize nationally for the longer term.

The Progressive reforms had their greatest impact on the Western states (particularly California), that had been more recently settled and where the machines had not yet put down deep roots among the electorate. Existing machines in the urbanized northeast simply organized their forces for primary elections and continued to dominate. In presidential politics the reforms had very little immediate impact, as national party conventions and presidential nominations continued to be dominated by powerful state and local party leaders. During the course of the twentieth century, however, the changing environment of American politics undermined traditional state and locally based party organizations (Silbey 1994). Increasing levels of education and affluence made voters less economically dependent on political parties. The number of government jobs available declined due to the spread of the merit-based civil service, and the attractiveness of lower-level government jobs to an increasingly middle-class electorate also diminished. Increasing suburbaniza-tion eroded the ethnic neighborhoods of the inner city, where the machines thrived, and created a much more individualistic and nonpartisan political en-vironment (Ladd and Hadley 1978). Changes in printing technology and ris-ing literacy levels led to the development of the mass news media through the nonpartisan press in the early twentieth century, and further technological developments led to the advent of first radio and then television. These new mass media gradually supplanted the parties in their role as the primary pro-viders of political information.

The New Deal presidency of Franklin Roosevelt (1933–1945) temporarily revived the Democratic Party as a national political force, but had deleterious long-term consequences for the traditional party organizations. Roosevelt ac-tually became more and more exasperated with the congressional Demo-cratic Party (a bizarre coalition of northern progressives and reactionary segregationist southern Democrats), and increasingly preferred to govern through extensions of the power of the presidential office (Milkis 1993). Roo-sevelt also found the new medium of radio to be more effective than tradi-tional Democratic Party organizations in reaching and mobilizing voters. The New Deal's expansion of the national government moved the primary focus of politics to the national level as opposed to the state and local level, where party organizations had hitherto prevailed. The introduction of fed-erally provided welfare benefits during the 1930s also deprived the party ma-chines of yet another traditional role. All of these trends were reinforced in the postwar decades. By the 1960s the party machines were all but gone. Their influence had lasted longest in presidential politics, but after the New Deal it became apparent that candidate selection was gradually moving out of the convention hall, and this was confirmed by the post-1968 reforms in the Democratic presidential nominating process that officially relocated the arena of presidential candidate selection to state primary elections with the national conventions serving only to ratify the outcome of the primaries (Shafer 1988).

By the 1970s it appeared that the American parties had reached their nadir, with the traditional organizations now moribund and nothing having arisen to take their place in an increasingly candidate-centered politics, where the influences of interest groups and the new mass media counted for more than party officials, even elected officials. By comparison with the mass party organizations of most other established democracies, the American parties in their apparently weakened state looked increasingly out of place.

Why So Different?

The early classic works on political parties in liberal democracies were written by European scholars based on the European political experience and, as such, generally dismissed the American parties as aberrant. The Russian liberal Ostrogorski (1982) saw the late-nineteenth century American parties as characterized by corruption and self-interest, and as such, they constituted a major threat to Democratic government. In another pessimistic early work on parties Robert Michels (1962) argued that the social parties of the early-twentieth century could not practice democracy within their own ranks since they needed to be vertically organized and highly disciplined to defeat the bourgeois parties. From this Michels put forward his "Iron Law of Oligarchy": any political association with a highly developed organizational structure is likely to become oligarchical.

The most influential comparative work on political parties was Maurice Duverger's *Political Parties,* first published in 1949. In addition to his aforementioned "Law" on the relationship between party systems and electoral systems, Duverger argued that political parties basically fell into two broad types (Duverger 1964). The first and increasingly dominant type was the "mass party," originating in the socialist (and later social democratic and communist) parties that developed in late-nineteenth century Europe and were characterized by a dues-paying mass membership, a heavily ideological (generally Marxist) focus, and (following Michels) a highly disciplined and centralized organization. These parties emerged as European societies experienced the highly explosive combination of rapid industrialization, urbanization, and democratization simultaneously, and became electorally successful due to their mobilization of the new urban industrial working class. In what Duverger (1964) described as "contagion from the left" the socialists' bourgeois, aristocratic, or nationalist opponents could only compete by organizing their own mass parties around an alternative ideology such as nationalist conservatism, fascism, or (after the defeat of fascism in World War II) Christian democracy.

Duverger's second type, the "cadre party," was a much more loosely organized, informal association at the elite level, characteristic of preindustrial societies with a limited franchise, such as early-nineteenth-century Britain and France. These parties were generally legislatively based and had no formal membership, although the influential aristocrats and other notables who formed the party leadership could usually rally a local base of support when needed. Ideology was very loose, leadership highly personalized, and party lines amorphous and fluid. The earliest American parties—the Federalists and Jeffersonians—seemed to be a perfect fit for this type. Duverger's central argument, however, was that the mass party was the modern and prevalent party form, and cadre parties, where they survived, were vestiges of the preindustrial, predemocratic, era. In fact, for Duverger the organizational differences between mass parties in postwar European democracies and the totalitarian Communist Party of the Soviet Union (and pre–World War II fascist parties) were differences of degree rather than kind. The Federalists and Jeffersonians aside, American parties since the 1830s did not seem to fit either of Duverger's types and he did not quite know what to make of them. The US parties were clearly not mass parties on the European model, but they were hardly mere cadre parties either. Having accepted the mass party as *the* modern political party form, Duverger could only write off the American parties as hopelessly backward and trust that mass party organizations would ultimately come to prevail in the United States.

Duverger's view was also the mainstream view of American political scientists regarding the parties at the time his book was published. Despite the electoral successes of FDR, many parties' scholars seemed to be frustrated that the New Deal had only been partially implemented, thanks to the alliance between conservative southern Democrats and Republicans in Congress (Schattschneider 1942). Indeed these scholars generally agreed that the apparently ramshackle and ideologically incoherent Democratic Party was a relic from a bygone age and a very poor analogue to the social democratic parties of western Europe—particularly the British Labor Party (Butler 1955; Epstein 1980). The leading parties' scholars of the time—E. E. Schattschneider (1942) and V. O. Key Jr. (1949)—pointed out that effective major parties performing their critical intermediary role were essential to the full functioning of American democracy, and only through competition between strong and ideologically coherent parties could the lower orders of society find representation in government. Key's magnum opus, *Southern Politics* (1949), was a magisterial state-by-state study of the segregated, one-party Democratic, Solid South of the New Deal era. Most of the region's problems were attributed by Key to the lack of party competition, and only the latter, he argued, held the potential of lifting the South out of racism and economic backwardness.

The inadequacy of the parties was the major theme of the American Political Science Association's (APSA) 1950 report, *Toward a More Responsible Two-Party System* (Committee on Political Parties 1950). The report, written by a committee chaired by E. E. Schattschneider, saw the state of the major parties as the foremost problem in the American political system (White and Mileur 2002). According to its pages the parties did not offer genuine and meaningful choices to voters and thus were not performing their essential intermediary and "vote-structuring" functions. The authors of the report were heavily influenced by the concept of "responsible party government" (RPG) which they saw as prevalent in parliamentary systems such as the UK (Ranney 1962). The concept of RPG was basically that two parties competed for votes, offering alternative policies to the electorate, and the winning party could then claim a mandate to implement those policies when in control of the government. If the electorate turned against these policies or found the government incompetent, then the governing party could be held to account in the next election. The American parties of the mid-twentieth century: decentralized, undisciplined, and composed of regional and ethnic coalitions that reflected the party divisions of a bygone era, did not provide clear policy choices and were thus hardly well placed to be vehicles for RPG. In addressing the problem, the report had a series of proposals to encourage the parties to become more clearly defined ideologically (Committee on Political Parties 1950). While none of these came to fruition, the 1950 APSA report reflected the mainstream consensus of American scholars regarding the parties: they believed that European-style mass parties were desirable in the United States, but had no real idea how to bring them about in the context of a separated political system and a political culture highly alien to large concentrations of political power.

As mentioned in the preceding section, the erosion of the traditional American political party continued apace in the wake of the APSA report. Scholars such as Key (1955), Walter Dean Burnham (1970) and James Sundquist (1973) had proffered a theory of "realignment" or "critical elections" that related changes in party alignments, as indicated by several "critical elections" (1828, 1860, 1896, 1932), to broader changes in the direction of public policy in the United States. Realignment theory had enormous influence over the study of elections and American political history, but by the late 1960s some of its proponents were asking whether the American parties still had sufficient viability to serve as intermediary vehicles for realignment. Walter Dean Burnham (1981), in particular, traced the decline of the parties to the progressive reforms, and perceived the Progressives' introduction of pre-registration as having been instrumental in reducing electoral participation in the United States. *The American Voter* study (Campbell et al. 1960) had found that the most significant determinant of electoral choice for Americans in the 1950s was an inherited party identification, and that only a small minority of Americans (and generally the least engaged voters) lacked such an identity. By the early 1970s, however, party identities were eroding and the numbers of voters voting split tickets had increased significantly (Nie et al. 1979). Most American parties' scholars still advocated "stronger" and more ideologically coherent parties but many seemed to believe that the parties had become irredeemably weak in a "postalignment" universe, with dire consequences for governmental accountability and the distribution of political power (Burnham 1981; Ranney 1978).

One major work stood out against the trend of regarding American Parties as outliers from the European "mass party" norm. Leon Epstein's (1967) *Political Parties in Western Democracies* argued that American parties were not necessarily aberrant or retarded—just American. In addition to the obvious barriers to mass party organization constituted by the separation of powers and federalism, American parties had developed in a political context very different from the environment that spawned the mass party in Europe. There the democratization of society tended to coincide with industrialization, so that the basic human rights of the newly enfranchised proletariat were tied up with the franchise. In Europe these rights were also bitterly resisted by an entrenched aristocracy, which heightened class consciousness and the appeal of socialism. In the American context, adult male enfranchisement preceded industrialization, and basic rights were guaranteed to all US citizens by the Constitution rather than having to be extracted from a reluctant aristocracy in a bitter and prolonged political struggle. This greatly lessened the appeal of socialism in an American context. Epstein joined Louis Hartz (1955) and Seymour Martin Lipset (1967) in arguing that since America was a "new nation" lacking an established aristocracy, middle-class political mores tended to predominate, with liberal individualism at the fore. In short, the absence of feudalism and its attendant class consciousness also explained the weakness of socialism and its attendant mass party organizations (Epstein 1967; Lipset and Marks 2000).

Epstein saw the American parties as essential to democracy but also understood that what many observers interpreted as "weakness" and "party decline" was merely adaptation to a changing American political universe. Moreover, he did not follow Duverger in assuming that the European "mass party" was destined to endure as the predominant party form in democracies. The mass party's appeal was tied to socialism and class politics. Should European society evolve in such a manner that traditional class divisions were no longer so predominant, then the mass parties might find themselves losing popular support and being challenged by new parties and new styles of party organization. Indeed Otto Kirchheimer (1966) had already developed the concept of the "catch-all" party—mass parties that explicitly de-emphasized ideology to appeal to more centrist voters while retaining a mass party organizational structure—based on the postwar West German experience. In short, to Epstein it was possible that political parties in other advanced democracies might eventually become more like American parties rather than vice versa.

The consensus that American parties were trapped in inexorable decline in the 1970s needs to be qualified somewhat. While it was accurate to state that party allegiances eroded between the 1950s and the 1970s, party allegiance remained the primary determinant of electoral choice (Green Palmquist, and Schickler 2004). Moreover, while third and fourth parties had come and gone throughout the century, the Republican/Democratic duopoly had persisted through progressivism, the New Deal, two world wars, and the Cold War. In Congress, parties and party leaders may have looked weak, but, as Cox and McCubbins (1993) have argued, party remained the central organizing principle in both houses, and congressional power structures were developed to entrench the dominance of the majority party. From the New Deal to the 1990s, the internally heterogeneous Democratic Party helped preserve its majority by keeping the party leadership weak and devolving power to committees and committee chairs. By so doing the Democrats maintained majorities in both houses of Congress for all but four years between 1930 and 1980. Finally, what parties' scholars in the 1970s perceived as symptoms of inexorable party decline might instead have been indications of a transition from an obsolete party model and party system toward a new and more relevant (to most voters) configuration. This will be explored further in the next section.

Party Revival and Polarization

From the perspective of today it appears that, to paraphrase Mark Twain, the death of American political parties has been greatly exaggerated. As we enter the second decade of the twenty-first century it is evident that the major political parties are stronger in several aspects than they were at the height of the party decline era in the 1970s.

Since the early 1980s, rates of party unity and polarization in both houses of Congress have risen to levels unseen since the Progressive Era (Sinclair 2006). Party leaderships have been empowered and now fully control the floor agendas in each House (Aldrich and Rohde 2000). The seniority rule has been considerably relaxed and the autonomy of committee chairs circumscribed. Chairs that deviate from the party line have been disciplined and occasionally removed by party caucuses. In large part this partisanship has been sustained because partisan control of each chamber has been at issue in almost every election since the Republicans gained control of the House for the first time in forty years in 1994. By contrast with the period of comfortable Democratic majorities and bipartisan coalitions, margins of control for each party have been tenuous. Measures of ideology in Congress also indicate a far greater degree of ideological homogeneity among the congressional parties than at midcentury (McCarty et al. 2006). At that time many of the southern, segregationist Democrats were more conservative ideologically than most of the congressional GOP (Grand Old Party, the Republican Party nickname), but for deep-seated historical reasons preferred to caucus in the same party with northern, urban, liberal Democrats. Similarly the congressional Republicans included many genuine Progressives within their ranks. Nowadays conservative Democrats and liberal Republicans have become an extinct species, and an ideologically homogeneous conservative Republican Party and an ideologically homogeneous liberal Democratic Party face off against each other on Capitol Hill (Stonecash et al. 2003).

Another sign of party revival is that national party organizations have become far more vital and significant bodies than in the era of machine politics, when they did little more than organize the national party conventions and run the party's presidential campaign. This revival has had two dimensions: (1) the assertion of national committee authority over the state parties, and (2) the national committees' enhanced role in candidate recruitment and in campaigns at the state and federal level (Cotter and Bibby 1980). The first became evident in the early 1970s when the Democratic National Committee (DNC) sought to enforce the new national convention delegate-selection rules drafted by the McGovern-Fraser commission in response to the bitter intraparty divisions over the 1968 presidential nomination (Shafer 1983). Several state parties openly defied the new rules and the DNC eventually took them to court, prevailing in the Supreme Court case of *Cousins vs. Wigoda* in 1975. While the GOP has been more hesitant in acknowledging the supremacy of the national party over the states, the Republican National Committee (RNC) has also become more assertive in encouraging state Republican parties to include more women and minorities in the decision-making process (Bibby 1980).

The RNC, under a succession of national chairmen in the 1965–1980 period—but principally, Ray Bliss (1965–69) and William Brock (1977–81)—developed an increasingly strong role for itself in small-donor fund-raising, candidate and campaign management recruitment and training, and polling (Bibby 1980). Chairman Brock, in particular, was ingenious in finding ways for the party to raise and spend money while still conforming to the quite strict new campaign finance regulations introduced in the 1974 Federal Elections Campaign Act (FECA). In coordination with the House and Senate campaign committees, the RNC became a major player in congressional and state legislative elections by providing services to candidates. By the end of the 1980s the Democratic Party, which took much longer than the RNC to develop a mass small-donor fund-raising base, had fully caught up, and both sets of national party committees were now fully involved in providing services to candidates and campaigns. This marked the birth of what political scientist, John Aldrich (1995) has described as the "party in service": an increasingly important role for American political parties and (as we shall see) for political parties in general in advanced democracies.

What are the underlying causes of the recent party revival in American politics? Certainly the long-term political fallout of the 1960s civil rights revolution, which was not yet apparent to the party-decline scholars of the 1970s, has played a major role. The presence of segregationist, generally hyperconservative southern whites in the party of FDR, Harry Truman, and John F. Kennedy reflected civil war allegiances and made American parties ideologically unintelligible to the foreign observer and American political scientists. It was the single biggest obstacle to the kind of ideologically defined parties sought by the 1950 APSA report, and keeping the South inside the Democratic fold necessitated a weak congressional party leadership and a highly decentralized and generally conservative Congress (Cox and McCubbins 1993). After the 1965 *Voting Rights Act*, however, southern Democrats had to court black voters to keep their seats, and they also faced a growing challenge from a rapidly emerging business- and migrant-based southern Republican Party. The overall effect of this was to bring the southern congressional Democrats more in line with the national Democratic Party's generally liberal issue positions, and to move the congressional Republican Party to the right as southern conservative Republicans became a larger and larger portion of the House and Senate Republican conference (Rohde 1991).

At the presidential level, the electoral realignment of the South was largely accomplished in the 1964–1980 period, and the Republicans have dominated presidential elections in the region ever since. At the congressional level, the realignment took another fifteen years to fully complete, but now the Republican dominance in southern congressional races is almost as great as their presidential dominance. At the same time, the Democrats have become stronger in formerly progressive Republican bastions in the Northeast and Pacific Coast states. The overall effect of these regional realignments has been to create a more consistently liberal Democratic Party and a more consistently conservative Republican Party (Stonecash et al. 2003). This happened first at the elite level, but it has now filtered increasingly down to the mass level as voters "self-sort" themselves ideologically into one or the other party (Hetherington 2001; Abramowitz 2010).

This process has also led to the rise of new presidential elites in each party. In the old-style American political party, the elite was composed of machine bosses trading blocs of delegates on the convention floor (Shafer 1988). In contemporary American politics the presidential elite is composed of ideologically allied interests strongly associated with the respective national parties (Cohen et al. 2008). In the Democratic Party these are labor unions, teachers, environmentalists, feminists, gay rights organizations, trial lawyers, and groups representing racial and ethnic minorities. On the Republican side they are business groups, conservative religious organizations, gun-control advocates, and antitax groups. These elites convey their imprimatur on certain candidates through endorsements, or, less explicitly, through financial and activist support in the so-called "invisible primary" period prior to the actual presidential primary season. In general they look for the most ideologically "pure" presidential candidate that they judge to be electable (Cohen et al. 2008). Behind the scenes they are the new kingmakers of presidential politics.

The last half century has also witnessed the development of new political media that lend themselves far more easily to polarized ideological partisan combat. The 1980s repeal of the old "fairness doctrine" that required television and radio stations to give equal time to different points of view, led first to the advent of right-wing talk radio, which rapidly acquired a mass following, with some hosts, such as Rush Limbaugh, becoming powerful figures among the conservative grassroots. The advent of cable and satellite television also allowed for niche news channels that could thrive on a dedicated audience of liberal or conservative viewers, such as the Fox News Cable Channel with its clearly conservative, Republican bent, and its more recent liberal counterpart MSNBC. The Internet and the associated new social media have taken this niche marketing one step further. It is now quite easy for ideological activists to inhabit a cocoon of ideological news and commentary Websites and online communities, where they hardly ever interact with those of opposing opinions and where their existing ideological predispositions are reinforced (Prior 2007; Stroud 2011; Sunstein 2007). These new media also provide a means to reach and mobilize a large number of like-minded individuals in a very short space of time, as witnessed by the advent of the 2004 Howard Dean campaign, the anti-Iraq war movement, the 2008 Obama campaign, and the emergence of the "Tea Party" in 2009–2010 (Rasmussen and Schoen 2010).

For the new media to reinforce polarization, a preexisting receptive mass audience is required, however, and there is some evidence that new cleavages have emerged in American politics that divide the country in more fundamental ways than previously. These cleavages are based on the intensity of religious adherence and differing "lifestyles" of large segments of the population. Stronger religious adherents (across all faiths) with more traditional views tend to support the GOP, while more secular, highly educated voters have become increasingly Democratic (Layman 2001). There also seems to be strong evidence that citizens not only want to associate only with the like-minded online but increasingly want to physically live in the same communities as well (Oppenheimer 2005; Bishop 2008).

Whatever the reasons underlying the increasing polarization of American politics, it is clear that for the first time in its history, America today has parties that are ideological in the right/left sense familiar to voters in most other democracies. To that extent the hopes of the 1950 APSA committee have been fulfilled.

Conclusion

From the above it is clear that US parties have become somewhat less atypical than they used to be. The decades-long process of "ideological sorting" at both the elite and mass levels since the civil rights revolution of the mid-1960s has resulted in two increasingly polarized parties with distinctive ideologies: "liberal" and "conservative." This was clearly not the case when the authors of the 1950s APSA report were deliberating on the parties, and was not completely apparent when the "party decline" school was prevailing among US parties' scholars in the early 1970s. American parties are also much more national than they were in 1950, in large part due to the increasingly national focus of politics and government in the United States, but also due to a much more assertive role in national campaigns by national party committees—particularly in terms of providing services to candidates. And while national party committees cannot so easily bring state and local parties to heel, as in the traditionally vertical European party structures, they have become much more forceful vis-à-vis the state parties.

The diminishing oddness of the American parties is not only due to American parties moving closer to the international norm in several aspects but also is a reflection of a degree of "Americanization" of political parties in other advanced democracies over the past half century. As American politics has become somewhat more polarized and ideological, many comparable democracies have witnessed a decline in class politics and in the public resonance of long-established ideologies. At the same time there has been a dramatic erosion in electoral support for the traditional mass parties—the social democratic/labor parties and their Christian democrat/conservative rivals—in favor of new parties and social movements. Rising levels of affluence and education and the relative decline of industrial society in most of the older democracies had led to what has been widely termed as a "postmaterialist" politics with a greater focus on environmental, cultural, and lifestyle issues than the old class politics and its concomitant mass parties (Inglehart 1997). Concerns over cultural liberalization and mass immigration from the Islamic world have also led to flash protest movements and parties from the right of the political spectrum scrambling traditional class electoral alignments.

Major political parties in other advanced democracies are also beginning to more closely resemble American political parties in their operations and organization, and the development of the "party in service" has become an international, not just an American, phenomenon (Panebianco 1988; Katz and Mair 1995). Memberships in mass parties have fallen dramatically entailing that reliance on membership dues is no longer sufficient to finance major political parties, as even socialist/labor parties have been compelled to diversify their funding sources. Mass parties are also less reliant on the traditional legwork of their supporters, as polling, television advertizing, and new social media have become increasingly important in election campaigns.

So while American parties today definitely appear less alien to observers from other democracies, we should not exaggerate the degree of convergence. In general, parties of the left, right, and center in other advanced democracies still have more in common with each other structurally than they do with American parties, which remain highly decentralized and undisciplined. American parties still lack a clearly defined "membership" and party officials exercise no control over party nominations except, perhaps, informally through the influence of major "policy demanding" interests, and even these find primary electorates unpredictable and impossible to control. As long as American parties do not control the nominations of those who bear the party label while major (and minor) political parties in other advanced democracies do, they will remain highly distinctive when placed in comparative context. Moreover, the separation of powers and federalism places limits on the degree of party centralization in the United States. In short, while the US system of government remains almost unique among contemporary democracies, America's major political parties are likely to remain outliers comparatively, although perhaps not to the same degree as they have been for most of the past century.

References

Abramowitz, Alan I. 2010. *The Disappearing Center: Engaged Citizens, Polarization and American Democracy*. New Haven, CT: Yale University Press.

Aldrich, John H. 1995. *Why Parties: The Origin and Transformation of Political Parties in America*. Chicago, IL: University of Chicago Press.

Aldrich, John H., and David W. Rohde. 2000. "The Consequences of Party Organization in the House: The Role of the Majority and Minority Parties in Conditional Party Government." In *Polarized Politics: Congress and the President in a Partisan Era*, edited by Jon R. Bond and Richard Fleisher, 31–72. Washington, DC: CQ Press.

Bibby, John F. 1980. "Party Renewal in the Republican Party." In *Party Renewal in America: Theory and Practice*, edited by Gerald M. Pomper, 102–115. New York: Praeger.

Bishop, Bill. 2008. *The Big Sort: Why the Clustering of Like-Minded America Is Tearing Us Apart*. Boston, MA: Houghton-Mifflin.

Burnham, Walter D. 1970. *Critical Elections and the Mainsprings of American Politics*. New York: Norton.

_____. 1981. *The Current Crisis in American Politics*. New York: Oxford University Press.

Butler, David. 1955. "American Myths about British Parties." *Virginia Quarterly Review* 31: 46–56.

Campbell, Angus, Philip E. Converse, Warren E. Miller, and Donald E. Stokes. 1960. *The American Voter*. New York: John Wiley.

Ceaser, James W. 1979. *Presidential Selection: Theory and Development*. Princeton, NJ: Princeton University Press.

Chambers, William Nisbet. 1963. *Political Parties in a New Nation: The American Experience, 1886–1809*. New York: Oxford University Press.

Cohen, Marty, David Karol, Hans Noel, and John R. Zaller. 2008. *The Party Decides: Presidential Nominations Before and After Reform*. Chicago, IL: University of Chicago Press.

Committee on Political Parties. 1950. *Toward a More Responsible Two-Party System*. New York: Rinehart and Company.

Cotter, Cornelius P., and John F. Bibby. 1980. "Institutional Development and the Thesis of Party Decline." *Political Science Quarterly* 95: 1–27.

Cox, Gary W., and Matthew Daniel McCubbins. 1993. *Legislative Leviathan: Party Government in the House*. Berkeley, CA: University of California Press.

Duverger, Maurice. 1964. *Political Parties: Their Origin and Activity in the Modern State*. London: Methuen.

Epstein, Leon D. 1967. *Political Parties in Western Democracies*. New York: Praeger.

_____. 1980 "Whatever Happened to the British Party Model?" *American Political Science Review* 74: 9–22.

Gerring, John. 1998. *Party Ideologies in America: 1828–1996*. New York: Cambridge University Press.

Green, Donald P., Bradley Palmquist, and Eric Schickler. 2004. *Partisan Hearts and Minds: Political Parties and the Social Identities of Voters*. New Haven: Yale University Press.

Hartz, Louis. 1955. *The Liberal Tradition in America: An Interpretation of American Political Thought Since the Revolution*. New York: Harcourt, Brace.

Hetherington, Marc J. 2001. "Resurgent Mass Partisanship: The Role of Elite Polarization." *American Political Science Review* 95: 619–631.

Hofstadter, Richard A. 1955. *The Age of Reform: From Bryan to FDR*. New York: Knopf.

Inglehart, Ronald. 1997. *Modernization and Postmaterialism: Cultural, Economic, and Political Change in 43 Societies*. Princeton, NJ: Princeton University Press.

Katz, Richard S., and Peter Mair. 1995. "Party Organization, Party Democracy, and the Emergence of the Cartel Party." *Party Politics* 1: 5–28.

Key, V. O., Jr. 1949. *Southern Politics in State and Nation*. New York: Knopf.

_____. 1955. "A Theory of Critical Elections." *Journal of Politics* 17: 3–18.

Kirchheimer, Otto. 1966. "The Transformation of West European Party Systems." In *Political Parties and Political Development,* edited by Joseph LaPalombara and Myron Weiner. Princeton, NJ: Princeton University Press.

Ladd, Everett C., and Charles D. Hadley. 1978. *Transformations of the American Party System: Political Coalitions from the New Deal to the 1970s*. 2nd ed. New York: Norton.

Layman, Geoffrey. 2001. *The Great Divide: Religious and Cultural Conflict in American Party Politics*. New York: Columbia University Press.

Lijphart, Arend. 1999. *Patterns of Democracy: Government Forms and Performance in Thirty-Six Countries*. New York: Oxford University Press.

Lipset, Seymour M. 1967. *The First New Nation: The United States in Historical & Comparative Perspective*. New York: Doubleday.

Lipset, Seymour M., and Gary Marks. 2000. *It Didn't Happen Here: Why Socialism Failed in the United States*. New York: Norton.

Madison, James. 1961. "Federalist Paper No. 10." In *The Federalist Papers,* edited by Clinton Rossiter, 77–84. New York: New American Library.

McCarty, Nolan, Keith T. Poole, and Howard Rosenthal. 2006. *Polarized America: The Dance of Ideology and Unequal Riches*. Cambridge, MA: MIT Press.

Michels, Robert. 1962. *Political Parties: A Sociological Study of the Oligarchical Tendencies of Modern Democracy*. New York: Free Press.

Milkis, Sidney M. 1993. *The President and the Parties: The Transformation of the American Party System Since the New Deal*. New York: Oxford University Press.

Nie, Norman S., Sidney Verba, and John R. Petrocik. 1979. *The Changing American Voter*. 2nd ed. Cambridge, MA: Harvard University Press.

Oppenheimer, Bruce I. 2005. "Deep Red and Blue Congressional Districts: The Causes and Consequences of Declining Party Competitiveness." In *Congress Reconsidered,* edited by Lawrence C. Dodd and Bruce I. Oppenheimer, 135–157. 8th ed. Washington, DC: CQ Press.

Ostrogorski, Moisei. 1982. *Democracy and the Organization of Political Parties, Volume II: The United States*. New Brunswick, NJ: Transaction Books.

Panebianco, Angelo. 1988. *Political Parties Organization and Power*. Cambridge: Cambridge University Press.

Prior, Markus. 2007. *Post-Broadcast Democracy*. New York: Cambridge University Press.

Ranney, Austin. 1962. *The Doctrine of Responsible Party Government: Its Origins and Present State*. Urbana, IL: University of Illinois Press.

———. 1978. "The Political Parties: Reform and Decline." In *The New American Political System*, edited by Anthony King, 213–247. Washington, DC: American Enterprise Institute.

Rasmussen, Scott, and Douglas Schoen. 2010. *Mad As Hell: How the Tea Party Movement Is Fundamentally Remaking Our Two-Party System*. New York: HarperCollins.

Rohde, David W. 1991. *Parties and Leaders in the US House*. Chicago, IL: University of Chicago Press.

Schattschneider, E. E. 1942. *Party Government: American Government in Action*. New York: Farrar and Rinehart.

Shafer, Byron E. 1983. *Quiet Revolution: The Struggle for the Democratic Party and the Shaping of Post-Reform Politics*. New York: Russell Sage Foundation.

———. 1988. *Bifurcated Politics: Evolution and Reform in the National Party Convention*. Cambridge: Harvard University Press.

Silbey, Joel. 1994. *The American Political Nation: 1838–1893*. Stanford, CA: Stanford University Press.

Sinclair, Barbara. 2006. *Party Wars: Polarization and the Politics of National Policy Making*. Norman, OK: University of Oklahoma Press.

Stonecash, Jeffrey M., Mark D. Brewer, and Mack D. Mariani. 2003. *Diverging Parties: Social Change, Realignment and Party Polarization*. Boulder, CO: Westview.

Stroud, Natalie Jomini. 2011. *Niche News: The Politics of News Choice*. New York: Oxford University Press.

Sundquist, James L. 1973. *Dynamics of the Party System: Alignments and Realignment of Political Parties in the United States*. Washington, DC: Brookings Institution.

Sunstein, Cass R. 2007. *Republic.com 2.0*. Princeton, NJ: Princeton University Press.

White, John K., and Jerome M. Mileur. 2002. "In the Spirit of Their Times: 'Toward a More Responsible Two-Party System' and Party Politics." In *Responsible Partisanship: The Evolution of American Political Parties Since 1950*, edited by John C. Green and Paul S. Herrnson, 13–35. Lawrence, KS: University Press of Kansas.

Wilentz, Sean. 2005. *The Rise of American Democracy: Jefferson to Lincoln*. New York: Norton.

3

Attempting to Build a Winner

Parties and the Crafting of Electoral Coalitions

MARK D. BREWER
University of Maine

Introduction

At the federal level, American party politics takes place at a table for two. Dictated largely by the rules of the game, the reality of a two-party system virtually ensures that the two parties in question—the Democratic and Republican Parties in the case of the United States—will be at least somewhat internally heterogeneous, a situation that is only exacerbated by the exceptionally diverse nature of American society. In short, American political parties—at least the two major ones—are almost guaranteed to be multifactional creatures.

Groups are at the heart of these factions that compose American parties. As they approach each election cycle, the leaders of the Democratic and Republican parties survey the American populace with an eye toward determining which social and demographic groups they might be able to successfully draw into their respective ranks. It is worth remembering that while parties and their candidates are after the votes of *individuals*, they most often pursue

47

these individual votes with messages and appeals directed toward specific *groups*. The fact that American political parties are coalitions of various groups present in society accounts for their internal diversity.

While intraparty diversity has been constant, the groups that make up the parties' variegated coalitions have not. The electoral coalitions of both the Republican and Democratic Parties have changed a good deal over time. Part of this coalitional evolution is due to the social change that has been a constant feature of American society. Immigration, changes in residential patterns, alterations in socioeconomic status, policy changes that contract or (in most cases) expand the electorate, shifts in family structure—the list could go on and on—are all examples of instances where social change creates at least the possibility of party coalition change. Change in a party's mix of group support can also come about due to specific events and occurrences that take place. Events of unusually high importance or magnitude—such as the Great Depression or the civil rights movement of the 1960s—are especially likely to create an opportunity for the alteration of partisan coalitions. The rise of new issues in the American public dialogue also opens the door for shifts in the parties' coalitions, especially if the new issues become highly salient. Another source of coalition change lies within the parties themselves; any time a party decides to support and pursue a particular policy goal, it creates at least the possibility of a change in the existing patterns of group support as groups do not evaluate and react to individual policies in a similar fashion. In many instances these opportunities for change work in combination, thereby increasing the likelihood that change in the parties' electoral coalitions will actually occur.

Looked at in this fashion, it is clear that stability in partisan coalitions is often not in the cards; indeed, the deck appears to be heavily stacked in favor of change. The nature of change at any particular time, however, is highly uncertain, especially to the parties themselves. Party leaders spend inordinate amounts of time speculating on what change will look like, trying to determine its source(s), timing, magnitude, and duration, among other characteristics. But the reality is that the high levels of uncertainty present make nailing down the specifics of change—at least before it happens—extremely difficult, even for those party leaders whose very success or failure depends on their ability to do just that. Indeed, it seems as though the best calculations of even the most perceptive party leaders are just as likely to be wildly off the mark as they are spot on. American party history is littered with the wreckage of what seemed to be perfectly reasonable (at the time) plans for electoral success that instead resulted in failure on election day.

It is the uncertain nature of change in American electoral politics that, at least in part, makes the subject so interesting. The Democratic and Republican parties are constantly taking the measure of American society, trying to determine how—given the broad, programmatic goals of the party—they can best appeal to voters and gain control of government through victory on election day. A key component of this process involves deliberation among party leaders as to what is the most feasible way to construct a winning electoral coalition. Correct answers are not easy to come by. It is rare that there is widespread agreement among the various leaders and factions present within a particular party, and competition and disagreement among supporters of various plans of attack often become quite intense. Such a situation is more likely to be seen in the party that is out of power at a particular point in time, but can manifest itself within the party that currently holds power as well. The bottom line is that even under the best of circumstances a party can never be certain that its plan for constructing a winning electoral coalition will be successful. In American politics, opportunities for both the Democrats and Republicans to cobble together successful coalitions are always present (even when things might seem darkest for a party), but these opportunities always come with a certain amount of risk involved. Clearly more risk is present in some situations than in others, but risk is always there. Parties can never know for sure how voters will react to a particular policy stand or candidate; they can never be certain how an appeal to one group in society will play with other groups that the party may also want to attract; they can never know for sure how social change has altered the electorate, how a new issue will affect voters, or what events might occur that have the potential to alter the electoral playing field. In addition to all of these unknowns, there is also the fact that the opposing party is involved in the exact same process, and its decisions also have the potential to change the equation. Uncertainty abounds, and it is this uncertainty that makes the American party system so fluid and dynamic (Brewer and Stonecash 2009).

This chapter examines the electoral coalitions of both the Republican and Democratic parties. A heavy emphasis will be placed on mapping partisan change from the 1960s to the present, explaining how and why change took place, and examining the meaning and implications of change. Finally, the chapter will close with a discussion of where the parties are now in terms of their coalitions, and some speculation on where they might be headed in the future.

The Long Shadow of the New Deal

To a certain degree the origins of contemporary American party coalitions lie in the politics of the 1930s, when Franklin Roosevelt gained control of the Democratic Party and over time assembled what came to be known as the New Deal coalition. Indeed, more than sixty years after his death, both parties continue to be shaped by FDR's actions and his opponents' responses to these actions. It is with good reason that one regularly hears references to the New Deal in analysis of the current political environment in the United States; the electoral and policy changes produced by the New Deal represented a monumental alteration of American politics and its impact was broad, deep, and durable. The continued influence of the New Deal on today's politics reminds us of an important lesson regarding party alignments and coalitions; existing partisan arrangements rarely, if ever, disappear completely. Even when party relationships and coalitions change, the old patterns often remain discernable in the new arrangements, intermingling to a certain extent with the newly established order (Schattschneider 1960; Sundquist 1983).

The conclusion of the 1936 election cycle crystallized the contours of the New Deal coalition—white southerners, the less affluent, organized labor, Catholics, Jews, urban dwellers, and blacks living outside of the South (Axelrod 1972; Leuchtenburg 1963; Lubell 1956; Schlesinger 1960; Sundquist 1983). FDR and the Democrats did not assemble this coalition out of whole cloth. Each of these groups gravitated to the Democratic Party for a reason, and the manner in which they were brought into the Democratic fold is indicative of how parties try to craft their coalitions. Heading into the 1932 and then 1936 election cycles, Roosevelt and the Democratic Party surveyed the electorate in hopes of determining which groups they might be able to bring into their coalition, and also thought about how best to attract the members of these groups. Southern whites' support of the Democrats stretched back to the Civil War, and as long as they were left to handle internal race relations as they saw fit—which FDR was careful to do—their allegiance to the party was secure. For the have-not portion of the New Deal coalition—which to a certain degree encompassed all of the groups in the coalition—Roosevelt and the Democrats delivered specific public policy programs that benefitted the groups in question and locked in their support. The various alphabet soup programs of the First New Deal, combined with prominent Second New Deal policies like the establishment of Social Security, the guaranteeing of labor's right to organize and bargain collectively, and the huge tax increase on the most affluent provided tangible benefits to the less fortunate groups within the Democratic coalition, and also sent a clear message to these groups that the Democrats were the party looking out for their interests. Republican indifference to have-nots in American society during the 1920s combined with the Great Depression to provide the opportunity for the Democrats to craft a new majority coalition in 1932, but this opportunity was realized and the coalition cemented only when the Democrats used their control of government to enact policies that benefitted these groups (Milkis 1993; Plotke 1996; Ware 2006). In becoming the majority party in the 1930s, the Democrats saw their opportunities and took advantage.

The 1960s: Disruption of the Status Quo

With FDR winning four presidential elections in a row from 1932 to 1944, and the Democrats maintaining control of Congress by healthy margins in both chambers, it is clear that the Republican coalition of the New Deal era was smaller than the one possessed by the Democrats. But the GOP's situation in the 1940s was not as dire as it appeared at first glance. Not all groups became New Deal Democrats. Even at the height of Roosevelt's and the Democrats' popularity and success, Republicans enjoyed strong support from more affluent Americans, those working in professional or managerial occupations, rural dwellers (outside of the South), and nonsouthern white Protestants. By the mid-1940s Republicans were highly competitive with the Democrats everywhere other than the South, and in 1946 they were able to retake control of Congress. While they remained the minority party, it was clear that GOP fortunes were improving.

Republicans were presented with an opportunity to further grow their coalition in the late 1940s. By that time it was evident that the Democratic Party outside of the South had become a relatively liberal party, increasingly primed for government action on a variety of fronts (Sundquist 1983). One of the primary areas of interest for these liberals was the issue of race, particularly increasing equality for African Americans. When the Democratic Party inserted a strong (for the time) civil rights plank in its 1948 platform, the door was opened for the Republicans to make inroads in the South.

The GOP was undeniably intrigued by the possibility of increasing its support in the South, but internal factionalization prevented the party from wholeheartedly embracing a full-blown appeal for southern votes until 1964. Indeed, the 1950s saw very little change to the Republican coalition, even as the party captured both presidential elections in that decade with Dwight Eisenhower as its candidate. A good deal of Republican success in the presidential contests of the 1950s can be attributed to the personal popularity of Eisenhower, rather than to any programmatic goals or policy agendas offered by the GOP. The Republican Party of the late 1940s and 1950s—at least the wing that supported presidential candidates like Thomas Dewey and Eisenhower—was a moderate party, one that was purposely not proposing radical new policy directions nor attempting to remake its electoral coalition in any meaningful way. The Republican Party of the 1950s is often described as an "us too" party, one that presented itself to voters as largely accepting of the Democrats' New Deal policy changes but as being able to direct these changes more efficiently. Such descriptions are for the most part accurate and, despite the GOP control of the presidency in the 1950s, it was clear that the Democrats were still the majority party and that the New Deal coalition remained largely intact (Milkis 1993; Plotke 1996).

This began to change in the 1960s. Emboldened by their increasing presence within the party, liberals pushed the Democratic Party further and further left on a variety of issues as the decade progressed (Mackenzie and Weisbrot 2008). At the same time a number of changes were taking place that were radically altering the traditional makeup of American society. The African American civil rights movement often justifiably gets the most attention here, but social change was unfolding on many other fronts as well. Religion was removed from public schools by the federal courts, while at the same time sex education was being introduced into the classroom. Traditional family arrangements were changing as an increasing number of women were leaving the home and entering the paid workforce as the so-called second wave of the feminist movement gathered steam. Births to unmarried women skyrocketed, especially among teenagers. The number of divorces began to rise as well. By the end of the 1960s the sexual revolution was in full force, the counterculture was firmly ensconced among young people on college campuses across the nation, and the first stirrings of a homosexual rights movement had manifested themselves. Together these issues would come to be collectively referred to as social or cultural issues, and over time their emergence would have a large impact on American politics (Hunter 1991; Leege et al. 2002; Scammon and Wattenberg 1970). But this development would take time, and to discuss it here would be getting ahead of ourselves. For now it is enough to note that much change took place in a short period of time, resulting in an incredibly unsettled environment (Brewer and Stonecash 2007).

The unsettled nature of 1960s America eventually moved into the political realm as well. As the Democratic Party became increasingly liberal, a growing number of voices within the Republican Party argued that the way for the GOP to regain the majority status it had last possessed in the 1920s was for the party to remake itself as a clearly conservative alternative to the Democrats. These conservative voices claimed that a growing number of Americans were unhappy with the Democrats' increasingly liberal direction, opposed to a large and activist federal government, and uncomfortable with many of the social changes that were occurring. If the Republicans presented themselves as a clearly conservative party, it was argued, they would be able to attract the support of those who were disenchanted. These Republicans got their wish in 1964 when they gained control of the party and nominated conservative Barry Goldwater for president. Goldwater was not Thomas Dewey or Dwight Eisenhower; he was a conservative across the board, as was made clear in his 1960 statement of principles *The Conscience of a Conservative*. Goldwater's opposition to the 1964 Civil Rights Act marked him (and by extension the Republican Party) as conservative on race issues, and it is clear that this shift by the GOP was crucial in ratcheting up the process of bringing white southerners into the party (Carmines and Stimson 1989; Carter 1996; Leuchtenburg 2005; Pomper 1972; Rae 1989). But Goldwater was also conservative on other issues such as taxes and government spending, the proper size and scope of the federal government, and defense and foreign policy. He was also the first Republican presidential candidate to present himself as a conservative on cultural issues of any variety (Leege et al. 2002). Goldwater of course suffered one of the worst defeats in American presidential election history. But in so doing he set the stage for partisan change to come. By the end of the 1960s the new issues that emerged in that decade had disrupted the existing partisan alignment (Nie et al. 1976; Petrocik 1981). The way in which these

1960s disruptions ultimately played out proved crucial to future American politics, and continue to have relevance today (Aldrich 1995, 1999).

Parties in the 1970s and 1980s:
Confusion Followed by Clarity

There is no doubt that issues surrounding the question of race disturbed the partisan alignment that had grown out of the New Deal (Carmines and Stimson 1989; Huckfeldt and Kohfeld 1989; Jackman and Jackman 1983). It is also undeniable that the newly emerging cultural issues of the 1960s served to further destabilize the political environment, a situation that was exacerbated when the Supreme Court legalized abortion in 1973 with its decision in *Roe v. Wade* (Layman 2001; Leege et al. 2002). But in a classic example of the uncertainty discussed at the outset of this chapter, neither party was quite sure what to do in the face of changed social and political realities. The clear differentiation between the parties offered in the 1964 presidential contest between the Republican Goldwater and Democrat Lyndon Johnson was largely gone by the time the 1968 contest rolled around. In that election campaign, Alabama governor and independent presidential candidate George Wallace regularly claimed that there was not a "dime's worth of difference" between Republican candidate Richard Nixon and Democratic candidate Hubert Humphrey. Clearly Wallace's statement was not entirely accurate; there were some meaningful differences between Nixon and Humphrey (and by extension their political parties) in 1968, and the differences between the parties' presidential candidates were extended in the 1972 contest between Nixon and Democratic nominee George Mc-Govern. However, Nixon did not campaign as a thorough conservative, as Goldwater had done, nor did he consistently govern as one. The Democrats reacted to the defeat of the liberal McGovern in 1972 by nominating southern born-again Christian Jimmy Carter in 1976. While Carter is clearly seen as a liberal today, he was not perceived as one nor did he run as one in 1976. Indeed, it was difficult to see large-scale meaningful differences between Carter and his Republican opponent in 1976, Gerald Ford. In some ways Wallace's difficulty in distinguishing between the Democrats and Republicans in 1968 could be seen as extending throughout the 1970s as well. Despite rhetoric to the contrary, the Republican Party continued to essentially go along with the taxing and spending patterns established by the Democrats during the New Deal era. The Democratic Party did the same. Neither party seemed to know where it stood on increasingly controversial cultural issues, except to agree that neither wanted to get caught on the wrong side of this set of issues. There was greater difference on racial issues, but even here the racial conservatism of the Republican Party fronted by Nixon and Ford was not as clear as it had been in the Goldwater GOP.

Voters noticed this lack of difference between the parties in the 1970s. During that decade split-ticket voting went up and party identification went down, especially in the category of self-proclaimed "strong" partisans. Many scholars examining the electoral politics of that time argued that the electorate had become "dealigned," and that voters were increasingly detached from and uninterested in political parties (Beck 1977, 1979). Elections, it was claimed, were now "candidate-centered," meaning that voters ignored partisan labels and determined their vote choice based on the personal characteristics and issue positions of the individual candidates for office (Wattenberg 1987, 1998). Parties, it was often argued at the time, had lost their meaning to voters, and were well on their way to becoming irrelevant.

As James Campbell (2006) recently noted, the benefit of hindsight allows us to see that claims of dealignment and the fading away of partisanship were overblown and off-course. Partisanship is resurgent in American politics, with its effect on shaping election outcomes currently at a level not seen for decades (Bartels 2000; Hetherington 2001; Stonecash 2006). It is the case, however, that Americans relied less on partisan cues to structure their vote choice in the 1970s, and it is likely that a good deal of this decline had to do with the perceived lack of meaningful difference between the parties. This all changed in the 1980s. Just as they had in 1964, the Republicans nominated a clear conservative for president in 1980, former actor and California governor Ronald Reagan. Reagan had long been a favorite of the conservative wing of the Republican Party, first rising to national attention (at least for his politics) with an impassioned televised speech in support of Goldwater in the waning days of the 1964 campaign. Doing as Goldwater had done in 1964, Reagan campaigned as a staunch conservative, and the Republican Party provided Reagan with a platform to match. In 1980, voters had a clear choice when they went to the polls on election day.

For all of their similarities, there was of course one crucial difference between Goldwater in 1964 and Reagan in 1980: Reagan won. With Reagan's victory in 1980 and landslide reelection in 1984, conservatives' control of the

Republican Party was solidified. In addition, Reagan governed in such a way that made the conservative nature of the GOP difficult to miss, even for the most inattentive voters. On fiscal policy, he successfully enacted what was at the time the largest tax cut in American history, and desperately (although not terribly successfully) tried to cut government spending in areas other than defense. He railed against a big federal government, famously saying in his 1981 inaugural address, "government is not the solution to our problem; government is the problem." On racial issues Reagan was adamantly opposed to affirmative action and was perceived by African Americans as at best indifferent and at worst hostile to their interests. On cultural issues, Reagan's opposition to the Equal Rights Amendment, his support of a constitutional amendment banning abortion, and his desire to return prayer to public schools all served to identify him, and his party, as conservative. By the time he left office in January 1989 it was clear that the Republicans were the conservative party, and that the Democrats were the liberal option (Milkis 1993; Rae 1992). This clarity was reflected in the two parties' coalitions at the end of the Reagan era, and indeed remains evident in the coalitions of today. In the same way that Franklin Roosevelt shaped the partisan divisions of his era and beyond, Ronald Reagan's influence on America's party politics is still present more than two decades after he left office.

Current Partisan Coalitions

In the wake of Reagan's two presidential wins, conservatives were finally able to declare victory over moderates within the GOP after a four-decade fight for control of the party. From the mid-1980s forward, there was no more ambiguity about where the Republicans stood on the ideological spectrum, or for the most part on the most salient issues of the day. Democrats, too, did their part in making party divisions clearer to voters. Already widely seen as a liberal party in the early 1980s, the Democrats strengthened this image by nominating two very liberal candidates for president in 1984 and 1988— Walter Mondale and Michael Dukakis respectively. Bill Clinton tried and to a certain extent succeeded in moderating the Democrats' image in the 1990s, but if anything the ideological distinction between the parties grew in that decade as the Newt Gingrich–led Republican Revolution of 1994 both further cemented conservatives' control of the GOP and allowed the Republicans to take over control of Congress for the first time since the 83rd Congress of 1953–1955. The clashes between Clinton and Gingrich provided Americans with a clear picture of partisan difference. Images and partisan distinction sharpened still more in the first years of the twenty-first century as conservative President George W. Bush and his fellow Republican conservatives in Congress governed in a highly partisan and ideological manner, drawing the ire of a Democratic Party that remained firmly liberal. Ideological distinctions between the parties have been further enhanced and inflamed by the 2008 election of Barack Obama as president, the actions of the Democratically controlled 111th Congress (including but not limited to the passage of the federal stimulus package, health-care reform, and the repeal of the Don't Ask, Don't Tell policy regarding homosexuals serving in the US military), and the Republican recapture of the House in the 2010 election cycle largely due to energy and support from the highly conservative Tea Party movement. Voters did not miss these developments. They recognized that the ideological divide between the parties had grown significantly from the 1980s forward, and these same voters increasingly sorted themselves on the basis of these ideological divisions. The impact of individuals' ideology on their party identification and vote choice has increased substantially in recent years (Abramowitz 2010; Abramowitz and Saunders 1998; Saunders and Abramowitz 2004).

The ideological difference between the parties was not limited to only one or even a few issues; rather it extended pretty much across the board, in many ways covering the broad spectrum of issues present in the American polity. By the 1990s the clear economic differences and conflict between the parties that had existed at least since the New Deal had been joined by equally clear differences and conflict between Republicans and Democrats over issues surrounding race and cultural/social concerns. Voters recognized these differences and over time racial and cultural concerns joined economic ones as significant factors in determining Americans' vote choice and partisanship (Brewer 2005; Layman and Carsey 2002a, 2002b).

This extension of partisan conflict can be seen in the evolution of the parties' coalitions. Table 3.1 illustrates this evolution for the Democratic Party's coalition by focusing on twelve social and demographic groups that have been critical to the party's success for at least some portion of the years 1952–2008. Table 3.1 presents the percentage of each group that voted for the Democratic

TABLE 3.1 Group Components of the Democratic Presidential Coalition, 1952–2008

Year	Bottom Income Third	Southern White[1]	Union Households	Roman Catholics	Jews	Urban Dwellers[2]	African Americans	Women	Low Religious Salience	Northeast Residents[3]	Latinos	Not Married or Widowed
1952	44 (29)	50 (16)	55 (36)	52 (29)	72 (7)	49 (39)	80 (8)	41 (47)	44 (41)	41 (27)		
1956	43 (32)	51 (22)	52 (37)	46 (27)	77 (8)	45 (28)	64 (6)	37 (48)	42 (38)	32 (23)		44 (10)
1960	47 (25)	52 (20)	63 (33)	82 (38)	91 (7)	63 (29)	74 (7)	47 (49)	55 (38)	49 (30)		46 (8)
1964	73 (34)	58 (14)	83 (32)	79 (29)	89 (4)	73 (31)	100 (13)	69 (56)	69 (36)	74 (27)		70 (11)
1968	42 (31)	26 (11)	48 (29)	56 (31)	84 (6)	53 (33)	97 (20)	43 (58)	38 (38)	46 (28)		47 (17)
1972	41 (28)	20 (10)	42 (31)	39 (28)	69 (4)	50 (35)	86 (21)	38 (60)	40 (51)	40 (27)		52 (27)
1976	60 (31)	46 (16)	64 (31)	57 (29)	70 (3)	55 (30)	94 (15)	51 (56)	51 (43)	54 (24)		56 (22)
1980	52 (34)	35 (20)	50 (33)	41 (23)	48 (4)	56 (39)	92 (26)	42 (59)	38 (45)	38 (19)		44 (27)
1984	56 (31)	31 (13)	56 (31)	46 (30)	69 (4)	59 (32)	87 (21)	45 (61)	43 (46)	39 (18)	53 (6)	48 (32)
1988	57 (26)	32 (12)	58 (26)	52 (29)	73 (3)	62 (32)	90 (20)	50 (59)	47 (44)	45 (18)	70 (9)	54 (34)
1992	60 (32)	38 (14)	54 (29)	50 (26)	76 (4)	63 (33)	91 (22)	52 (58)	53 (50)	54 (22)	64 (6)	59 (37)
1996	68 (30)	41 (17)	67 (25)	55 (27)	92 (4)	61 (31)	96 (18)	59 (60)	60 (47)	61 (19)	75 (8)	61 (33)
2000	59 (34)	35 (17)	60 (18)	50 (27)	89 (5)	69 (20)	91 (18)	56 (61)	56 (46)	55 (19)	56 (5)	59 (39)
2004	57 (33)	33 (14)	64 (24)	50 (25)	76 (5)		87 (26)	52 (57)	54 (51)	51 (18)	57 (7)	55 (44)
2008	67 (32)	30 (17)	59 (14)	57 (21)	85 (3)		99 (23)	56 (60)	61 (55)	63 (16)	76 (10)	65 (37)

Source: ANES Cumulative Datafile, 1948–2008.

Note: First figure represents the percentage of a particular group voting Democratic for president, while the figure in parentheses represents the percentage of all Democratic presidential voters who possessed the group characteristic in question. Low religious salience is those who attend religious services seldom, never, or did not have a religious preference (1952–1968) and those who attend religious services only a few times a year, never, or those who did not have a religious preference (1972–2008). Jews are marked by small N's, and thus readers are urged to use caution when examining the results for this group.

presidential candidate in each year (the first figure in each cell) and the percentage of all Democratic presidential voters who possessed the group characteristic in question (the figure in parentheses).[5] The groups in the first seven columns are those that formed the core of the Democrats' New Deal coalition, while those in the last five are groups that have become more important components of the party over time.

Unfortunately the American National Election Study (ANES) did not begin in full until 1952 (there was a very small pilot study in 1948), therefore we cannot begin our empirical examination at the height of the New Deal coalition. But even with the immense personal popularity of Republican Dwight Eisenhower cutting into the traditional support groups, the outline of the New Deal coalition crafted by FDR is still visible in the 1950s, as indicated in Table 3.1. Those in the bottom third of the income distribution, southern whites, individuals residing in union households, Roman Catholics, and urban dwellers were all relatively large components of the party's coalition even as they drifted toward Eisenhower, while Jews and African Americans (mostly outside of the South because the overwhelming majority of blacks in that region could not vote until after the civil rights movement and legislation of the 1960s) were smaller but highly supportive groups within the party. Indeed in 1960—the election that may reasonably be seen as the last where the entire New Deal coalition was intact—these groups all remained key components of the Democrats' base (southern whites less so and Roman Catholics more so in that particular election due to Kennedy's Catholicism).

We see the Democratic Party's coalition slowly begin to change in the 1960s. Part of this change involved the gradual decay of the New Deal coalition (Stanley et al. 1986; Stanley and Niemi 1991, 2001). The most glaring element of this decay was the rapid decline in Democratic support among southern whites, as both their support of the party's presidential candidates and their percentages of total Democratic voters dropped precipitously (Black and Black 2002; Lublin 2004; Shafer and Johnston 2006). The same was true, although to a much lesser extent, for voters in union households and Roman Catholics. Among the other traditional New Deal coalition groups, support among those in the bottom income third, Jews, and urban dwellers remained relatively stable during this period, while African Americans became a much larger component of the party's base, a development that reflected both the increased clarity of differences between the parties on racial issues and the growth in the ability of blacks in the South to actually vote. It was also during these years that women first began their move into the Democratic coalition, a trend that would become increasingly evident in future years (Box-Steffensmeier et al. 2004; Sanbonmatsu 2002; Wolbrecht 2000).

Table 3.1 starkly demonstrates the strong impact of the Reagan era on partisan coalitions—in this case for the Democratic Party. Reagan's—and by extension the Republican Party's—strong preference to rely on free markets to determine economic outcomes and equally strong opposition to most social welfare programs reenergized Democratic support among those in the lower third of the family income distribution. The same is true among union household voters and urban dwellers, and to a lesser extent for Catholics as well. Blacks and Jews remained important parts of the Democratic coalition, and support for the party among women continued to slowly increase as well. All of these groups had good policy-related reasons for siding with the Democrats and against the increasingly conservative GOP, again highlighting the important place of public policy in partisan change.

The groups that were important to the Democratic coalition in the 1980s remain central elements of the party's base today. Less affluent Americans, voters from union households, Jews, those who reside in urban areas, African Americans, and women are all highly supportive of Democratic presidential candidates, and each of these groups (with the exception of Jews) also represents a sizeable percentage of all Democratic presidential voters. Democratic support is not as high among Roman Catholics as it once was, but this group does still account for a relatively large percentage of Democratic voters. We also see that the partisan and ideological clarity discussed earlier in this chapter has brought some new groups into the Democratic fold. Those Americans with low levels of religious salience—both attracted by the Democrats' liberalism on social issues and repelled by the GOP conservatism on this same front—have increased their Democratic support (Layman 2001), as have residents of the Northeast, a region of the United States where social liberalism is more likely to be warmly received (Speel 1998). Latinos—a rapidly growing segment of the American electorate—have shown themselves to be relatively Democratic, attracted by the party's stand on economic issues and its image as more sympathetic to the concerns and issues of immigrants (De la Garza 2004). Finally, Table 3.1 presents the Democratic presidential vote for one additional group—voters who are not married or widowed. These individuals do not make up a group in the same way as the others considered here, but, given the growth in partisan conflict over cultural issues and all of the discussion between the parties over "family values," their inclusion here is justified and the results presented verify this. Since 1988 both the Democratic support and size percentages for this group have increased. This is likely due to Democrats' acceptance of multiple types of legitimate family arrangements and the party's lack of emphasis on the necessity for and propriety of the state enforcing traditional morality.

Following the model of Table 3.1, Table 3.2 presents the Republican presidential vote (first figure) and total percentage of all GOP presidential voters (figure in parentheses) for eleven groups that have been important elements of the Republican Party's coalition for at least some period of time since 1952. The groups in the first four columns—voters in the upper third of the income distribution, nonsouthern white Protestants, rural dwellers, and those with professional or managerial occupations—were the GOP's counter of the Democrats' New Deal coalition, as evidenced by both the support and size percentages for these groups from 1952 to 1960. As was the case for the Democrats, the Republicans have also seen changes to this coalition over time. Two of these core groups—more affluent individuals and nonsouthern white Protestants—have remained quite supportive of the GOP over time. More affluent voters did reduce their support of Republican presidential candidates in the 1990s, but they returned to the Republican fold in 2004 and 2008. The haves in American society remain critical components of the Republican coalition (Bartels 2008; Stonecash 2000). Nonsouthern white Protestants followed almost the same pattern, but it is important to note that the percentage of all Republican presidential voters accounted for by this group has declined dramatically over time, reaching a low point for the years included in this study in 2008. Those who work in managerial or professional occupations were for years highly supportive of the Republican presidential candidate. This changed in 1992, and to this point has stayed changed, although the group does still account for a relatively large percentage of all Republican voters. Rural voters follow essentially the same pattern as the managers and professionals, although their percentage of all GOP voters has shrunk over time, likely due at least in part to the decrease in the percentage of Americans living in rural areas.

While these elements of continuity are certainly important, for the Republican Party perhaps more interesting components of the GOP coalition lie in the groups that have been added over time. Remember, the Republicans were the minority party in the New Deal party system, and thus they were under the

TABLE 3.2 Group Components of the Republican Presidential Coalition, 1952–2008

Year	Top Income Third	Non-Southern White Protestants	Rural Dwellers	Professional and Managerial[6]	Southern Whites	White Men	High Religious Salience	White Evangelical Protestants[7]	Roman Catholics	Suburban Dwellers	Married or Widowed
1952	61 (47)	71 (60)	62 (38)	68 (20)	50 (11)	59 (45)	59 (40)		48 (19)	62 (33)	
1956	62 (36)	71 (60)	59 (47)	66 (21)	47 (14)	57 (45)	59 (45)		54 (21)	64 (30)	60 (91)
1960	52 (46)	71 (71)	54 (55)	58 (21)	45 (17)	48 (43)	50 (47)	60 (22)	18 (8)	54 (29)	50 (90)
1964	41 (50)	43 (61)	32 (39)	46 (29)	42 (20)	36 (48)	33 (45)	35 (19)	21 (16)	38 (37)	32 (90)
1968	50 (38)	65(63)	51 (46)	54 (26)	43 (16)	51 (43)	50 (44)	50 (22)	37 (18)	50 (33)	47 (86)
1972	68 (40)	74 (51)	69 (45)	65 (24)	80 (22)	71 (45)	71 (33)	80 (23)	59 (24)	68 (36)	67 (86)
1976	57 (47)	61 (53)	51 (39)	58 (31)	53 (18)	53 (42)	51 (32)	54 (22)	41 (21)	50 (37)	50 (83)
1980	56 (35)	61 (43)	57 (38)	53 (31)	60 (27)	60 (46)	58 (32)	59 (21)	50 (22)	58 (44)	54 (80)
1984	69 (42)	72 (45)	61 (35)	61 (30)	69 (20)	67 (43)	60 (30)	74 (23)	54 (25)	65 (49)	61 (75)
1988	61 (43)	66 (46)	56 (33)	54 (34)	68 (22)	62 (43)	54 (32)	72 (25)	47 (23)	58 (50)	56 (75)
1992	39 (45)	44 (42)	37 (33)	34 (32)	46 (23)	38 (44)	46 (40)	43 (37)	30 (22)	37 (48)	39 (80)
1996	48 (42)	49 (38)	38 (31)	43 (45)	51 (29)	49 (50)	51 (40)	43 (33)	37 (26)	43 (47)	41 (77)
2000	51 (35)	53 (29)	51 (18)	45 (42)	61 (34)	54 (42)	58 (38)	64 (27)	49 (30)	48 (24)	51 (74)
2004	57 (36)	64 (35)		43 (31)	67 (27)	60 (41)	59 (29)	77 (34)	48 (24)		55 (67)
2008	58 (41)	53 (27)			67 (47)	58 (42)	61 (36)	74 (42)	43 (19)		50 (78)

Source: ANES Cumulative Datafile, 1948–2008.

Note: First figure represents the percentage of a particular group voting Republican for president, while the figure in parentheses represents the percentage of all Republican presidential voters who possessed the group characteristic in question. High religious salience is those who attend religious services every week. See endnote 7 for the categorization of evangelical Protestants.

most pressure to alter and expand their coalition. The fact that the GOP has won seven of eleven presidential elections since 1968 shows that the party was able to accomplish these tasks. One of the most important groups that Republicans have added to their coalition is Southern whites (Mellow 2008). In some ways the GOP's addition of white southerners began with Eisenhower in the 1950s, but, as Black and Black (2002) make clear, it was Reagan who finally locked these voters into the party's coalition. Indeed, only white southerner Bill Clinton was able to prevent the Republican candidate from receiving at least 60 percent of the vote among this group since 1980. The size of white southerners in the overall Republican coalition has grown as well. In a group with a fair amount of overlap with southern whites, white evangelical Protestants have also become increasingly important elements of the Republican coalition. When this development is combined with the increased GOP support by voters for whom religion is highly salient, we can see how the increased cultural conservatism of the Republicans enabled them to increase the size of their electoral coalition (Layman 2001; Leege et al. 2002). Cultural issues also likely account for at least some of the growth in Republican support among Catholics, although the increasing affluence of this group is relevant as well. We also see that white men have been quite supportive of Republican candidates since 1972 (with the exception of 1992), although their overall contribution to the Republican coalition does not match that of women to the Democratic coalition (Edsall 2006; Kaufmann and Petrocik 1999). Suburban voters—always relatively supportive of Republican candidates—increased their total contribution to the party's base from the 1960s through the 1990s (Lassiter 2006; McGirr 2001). Suburbanites' vote percentages, however, declined in the 1990s and have yet to rebound to previous levels, as best we can tell given the limitations of the data. Finally, Table 3.2 presents the Republican presidential vote figures for individuals who are either married or widowed. There is no clear pattern here.

While informative, the results presented in Tables 3.1 and 3.2 are bivariate in nature, and thus there is the possibility they could be misleading. This is particularly true due to the high degree of overlap between some of the group characteristics included here, such as African American and urban residence, or southern whites and white evangelical Protestants. In order to obtain a truer understanding of the place of these groups in the parties' respective coalitions multivariate analyses are necessary. Tables 3.3 (Democratic presidential vote) and 3.4 (Republican presidential vote) present the results of these analyses.

TABLE 3.3 Logistic Regression Coefficients for Group Components of the Democratic Presidential Coalition, by Decade, 1950s–2000s

Decade	Bottom Income Third	Southern White	Union Households	Roman Catholics	Jews	Urban Dwellers	African Americans	Women	Low Religious Salience	Northeast Residents	Latinos	Not Married or Widowed
1950s	.26 (.10)	.86 (.12)	.79 (.10)	.82 (.11)	2.16 (.26)	.05 (.10)	1.61 (.24)	-.19 (.09)	.17 (.09)	-.51 (.11)		.13 (.20)
1960s	.26 (.09)	.19 (.11)	.70 (.10)	1.49 (.11)	2.62 (.32)	.08 (.10)	3.10 (.29)	.03 (.08)	.28 (.09)	-.30 (.10)		-.11 (.13)
1970s	.38 (.10)	-.03 (.11)	.61 (.09)	.50 (.10)	1.49 (.28)	.19 (.10)	2.67 (.22)	.23 (.08)	.31 (.08)	.04 (.10)		.35 (.11)
1980s	.53 (.09)	-.01 (.10)	.80 (.09)	.46 (.09)	1.26 (.23)	.41 (.09)	2.61 (.19)	.31 (.08)	.22 (.08)	-.27 (.10)	.72 (.18)	.05 (.09)
1990s	.53 (.10)	.07 (.11)	.61 (.11)	.41 (.10)	1.76 (.34)	.31 (.10)	2.91 (.24)	.46 (.09)	.67 (.09)	.21 (.12)	.98 (.20)	.23 (.10)
2000s	.44 (.09)	-.56 (.11)	.47 (.11)	.24 (.09)	1.82 (.32)	.67 (.19)	3.45 (.22)	.44 (.08)	.69 (.08)	-.01 (.12)	1.02 (.14)	.18 (.09)

Source: ANES Cumulative Datafile, 1948–2008.

Note: All variables are coded in the same fashion as for Tables 3.1 and 3.2. Figures presented are unstandardized logistic regression coefficients with standard errors in parentheses. Coefficients significant at the .05 level or better are in bold. Urban Dwellers contains only 2000 data.

TABLE 3.4 Logistic Regression Coefficients for Group Components of the Republican Presidential Coalition, by Decade, 1950s–2000s

Decade	Top Income Third	Non-Southern White Protestants	Rural Dwellers	Professional and Managerial	Southern Whites	White Men	High Religious Salience	White Evangelical Protestants	Roman Catholics	Suburban Dwellers	Married or Widowed
1950s	.11 (.09)	**1.71 (.16)**	.09 (.11)	**.57 (.12)**	**.66 (.18)**	**-.26 (.09)**	**.20 (.09)**		**.80 (.17)**	**.24 (.12)**	.08 (.12)
1960s	**.23 (.09)**	**2.20 (.15)**	.06 (.11)	**.47 (.11)**	**1.55 (.17)**	.08 (.08)	**.30 (.08)**	-.14 (.11)	**.50 (.16)**	**.27 (.11)**	-.20 (.13)
1970s	**.36 (.09)**	**1.54 (.12)**	**.22 (.11)**	.14 (.10)	**1.41 (.15)**	**.21 (.08)**	**.26 (.09)**	.07 (.12)	**.68 (.13)**	**.30 (.10)**	**.30 (.10)**
1980s	**.49 (.08)**	**1.36 (.10)**	**.50 (.10)**	.05 (.08)	**1.19 (.13)**	**.39 (.08)**	**.22 (.08)**	**.22 (.11)**	**.65 (.11)**	**.64 (.09)**	.08 (.08)
1990s	**.32 (.09)**	**1.11 (.12)**	.13 (.12)	.09 (.09)	**1.14 (.13)**	**.32 (.09)**	**.65 (.09)**	**.30 (.10)**	**.51 (.13)**	**.27 (.11)**	**.35 (.10)**
2000s	**.61 (.10)**	**1.43 (.15)**	-.19 (.19)	-.08 (.12)	**1.76 (.15)**	**.42 (.10)**	**.44 (.10)**	**.94 (.14)**	**1.12 (.12)**	-.11 (.16)	**.24 (.10)**

Source: ANES Cumulative Datafile, 1948–2008.

Note: All variables are coded in the same fashion as for Tables 3.1 and 3.2. Figures presented are unstandardized logistic regression coefficients with standard errors in parentheses. Coefficients significant at the .05 level or better are in bold. Rural and Suburban Dwellers contain only 2000 data, and Professional and Managerial contains only 2000 and 2004 data.

In each case, presidential vote is coded as a dichotomy of a vote for the party in question or some other presidential vote, and all of the independent variables are coded as present or absent dichotomies. This allows the unstandardized logistic regression coefficients presented in the tables to be compared with each other and over time *within* a party but not *between* parties. Data are pooled and results presented by decade in order to get a clearer picture of change over time.

Looking first at the Democratic coalition, the multivariate results for the most part confirm those presented earlier from the bivariate analyses. African Americans and Jews are strongly supportive of Democratic presidential candidates throughout the entire period under examination here, and the same is true to a lesser extent among those residing in union households. Those in the bottom third of the family income distribution have consistently been important to the Democrats, and this support has grown over time. The same pattern is present, but in reverse, for Roman Catholics. Urban dwellers, women, and those with low levels of religious salience have increased their support of the party since the 1960s, while southern whites have moved from being a significant component of the Democrats' coalition to be significantly opposed to the party's presidential candidates. Latinos were strong supporters of the party in the 1980s and 1990s, and increased their support in the 2000s due mainly to strong support for Obama in 2008, while the coefficients for Northeast residents and those neither married nor widowed do not show much of a pattern.

The results for Republican presidential vote in Table 3.4 also for the most part support the earlier results. The importance of southern whites to the party has grown significantly over time, as has that of those with high levels of religious salience, white evangelicals, and Catholics. The support of those in the top income third has been relatively steady, and although nonsouthern white Protestants have declined in their tendency to support the GOP on election day, they remain a sizeable element of the party's coalition. Those in professional and managerial occupations were significant sources of party support in the 1950s and 1960s, but not since. Suburban dwellers were consistently supportive of Republican presidential candidates until the 2000 candidacy of George W. Bush, and ANES data prevents us from saying anything regarding their behavior post-2000. If there are any surprises in Table 3.4 they can be found in the results presented for rural residents and white men. The coefficients for white men are significant, but relatively small for the 1970s to 2000s. Rural dwellers fail to show much of a pattern at all. But for the most part, the multivariate results support the pictures of the Democratic and Republican coalitions described in this chapter.

Conclusion

The Republican and Democratic Parties of the early twenty-first century are very different from each other, offering Americans relatively clear policy choices across the board. These differences exist, to a certain extent, because the two parties have very different electoral coalitions. A Democratic Party whose electoral success is rooted in the support of the less affluent, union households, urbanites, women, blacks, Latinos, and those with low levels of religious salience will—if it wants to maintain the support of these groups— possess very different issue positions and champion very different public policy options than a Republican Party whose success on Election Day comes in large part from more affluent voters, southern whites, men, white Protestants (especially evangelicals), individuals for whom religion is highly salient, and rural and suburban dwellers. A properly functioning representative democracy requires the representation of diverse interests, and at least in the American context it is political parties that fulfill this representative function. Indeed, as Schattschneider (1942, 1) famously noted, American democracy would be "unthinkable" without parties.

Because of the dynamic nature of American society, political parties cannot be static and still adequately perform their representative responsibilities. They must adapt and evolve as society changes, otherwise relevant interests and groups will be left out and important issues will not be addressed in the public dialogue. Fortunately parties are highly concerned with these processes of adaptation and evolution; their ability to win elections and exercise governmental power rests on their success in properly interpreting and responding to change. As noted at the outset of this chapter, this is not an easy process, and parties and their leaders are never certain as to what they should do. Opportunities for partisan success are always there, but so, too, are risks. The results of the 2008 and 2010 election cycles are a perfect example of this dynamic. Democratic candidate Obama won the presidency in 2008 by a comfortable margin, and the Democrats added to their majorities in both the House and the Senate. Some Democrats believed that the 2008 results represented a mandate for a renewed era of liberalism and activist government, and in many ways the party delivered on this mandate in 2009–2010. The result was the birth of the Tea Party movement and disastrous Democratic losses at the polls in 2010. Given these developments it is not surprising that the Democrats are at least somewhat uncertain where the party should go next. The Republican Party faces a similar situation. The GOP was soundly thrashed at the polls in 2008, only to witness a strong resurgence in its popularity in 2010. But were voters really endorsing the policies and positions of an increasingly conservative Republican Party, or were they merely registering their unhappiness with a deep and seemingly relentless economic downturn? The GOP simply cannot be sure, and neither can the rest of us. Parties constantly evaluate election returns, examine their opportunities, and evaluate the risks as best they can, and eventually they act. Sometimes their moves pay off and sometimes they don't, but when taken together these partisan successes and failures combine to produce representation and political change in the United States.

A good deal of this political change lies in alteration of the parties' electoral coalitions (Petrocik 1981). In most instances this change unfolds slowly over time, more closely resembling Key's theory of secular realignment (1959) rather than his perhaps more famous concept of critical realignment (1955).[8] New groups rise in American society, new issues enter the public debate, the parties present new policy options—all of these phenomena come together to produce a dynamic for change. As new groups and issues arise, parties and their politicians slowly and cautiously respond to them. The masses then assess these partisan responses, and eventually they respond as well. The end result is a feedback loop where both the elites and masses each create and respond to political change (Aldrich 2003; Brewer and Stonecash 2009). The process is often messy and for many people it moves far too slowly, but in the end the American political system almost always responds to calls for change, at least in part due to the search of political parties for a winning electoral coalition.

As to what the future might hold for the two major parties in terms of their respective coalitions, the fluidity of American politics combined with the difficulty in accurately anticipating political and electoral change makes any form of prognostication at best a foolhardy endeavor. Nonetheless, there are a few things we can say about the near-term partisan coalitions with at least some degree of confidence. Looking first at the Democratic Party, it appears likely that in addition to maintaining its strong support among the less affluent in American society, the party will also increasingly rely on racial and ethnic minorities, particularly African Americans and Latinos, to win elections. Stronger Democratic support among women, city dwellers, and those with low levels of religious salience are all also likely to continue. As for the Republicans, they, too, will likely maintain the class-based element of their coalition, in their case more affluent Americans. The overlapping groups of southern whites, white men, white evangelical Protestants, and those for whom religion is highly salient will in all likelihood continue to be core elements of the GOP coalition. Two groups that provided key support to the 2000s will be interesting to watch going forward: nonsouthern white Protestants and Roman Catholics. Future Republican success could very well hinge on the behavior of these two groups. Whatever happens, both parties will undoubtedly continue their never-ending quests to build a winner.

References

Abramowitz, Alan I. 2010. *The Disappearing Center*. New Haven, CT: Yale University Press.

Abramowitz, Alan I., and Kyle L. Saunders. 1998. "Ideological Realignment in the US Electorate." *Journal of Politics* 60 (August): 634–652.

Aldrich, John H. 1995. *Why Parties? The Origin and Transformation of Political Parties in America*. Chicago, IL: University of Chicago Press.

_____.1999. "Political Parties in a Critical Era." *American Politics Quarterly* 27 (January): 9–32.

_____. 2003. "Electoral Democracy During Politics as Usual—and Unusual." In *Electoral Democracy*, edited by Michael B. MacKuen and George Rabinowitz, 270–310. Ann Arbor, MI: University of Michigan Press.

American National Election Studies. 2005. *The 1948–2004 ANES Cumulative Data File*. Stanford, CA: Stanford University and Ann Arbor, MI: University of Michigan.

Axelrod, Robert. 1972. "Where the Votes Come From: An Analysis of Electoral Coalitions, 1952–1968." *American Political Science Review* 66 (March): 11–20.

Bartels, Larry M. 2000. "Partisanship and Voting Behavior, 1952–1996." *American Journal of Political Science* 44 (January): 35–50.

_____. 2008. *Unequal Democracy*. New York: Russell Sage Foundation and Princeton, NJ: Princeton University Press.

Beck, Paul Allen. 1977. "Partisan Dealignment in the Postwar South." *American Political Science Review* 71 (June): 477–496.

_____. 1979. "The Electoral Cycle and Patterns of American Politics." *British Journal of Political Science* 9 (April): 129–156.

Black, Earl, and Merle Black. 2002. *The Rise of Southern Republicans*. Cambridge, MA: Harvard University Press.

Box-Steffensmeier, Janet M., Suzanna De Boef, and Tse-Min Lin. 2004. "The Dynamics of the Partisan Gender Gap." *American Political Science Review* 98 (August): 515–528.

Brewer, Mark D. 2005. "The Rise of Partisanship and the Expansion of Partisan Conflict within the American Electorate." *Political Research Quarterly* 58 (June): 219–229.

Brewer, Mark D., and Jeffrey M. Stonecash. 2007. *Split: Class and Cultural Divides in American Politics*. Washington, DC: CQ Press.

_____. 2009. *Dynamics of American Political Parties*. New York: Cambridge University Press.

Campbell, James E. 2006. "Party Systems and Realignments in the United States, 1868–2004." *Social Science History* 30 (fall): 359–386.

Carmines, Edward G., and James A. Stimson. 1989. *Issue Evolution: Race and the Transformation of American Politics*. Princeton, NJ: Princeton University Press.

Carter, Dan T. 1996. *From George Wallace to Newt Gingrich: Race in the Conservative Counterrevolution*. Baton Rouge, LA: Louisiana State University Press.

De la Garza, Rodolfo O. 2004. "Latino Politics." *Annual Review of Political Science* 7: 91–123.

Edsall, Thomas B. 2006. *Building Red America: The New Conservative Coalition and the Drive for Permanent Power*. New York: Basic Books.

Goldwater, Barry. 1960. *The Conscience of a Conservative*. New York: Hillman Books.

Guth, James L., and John C. Green. 1993. "Salience: The Core Concept?" In *Rediscovering the Religious Factor in American Politics*, edited by David C. Leege and Lyman A. Kellstedt, 157–174. Armonk, NY: M. E. Sharpe.

Hetherington, Marc J. 2001. "Resurgent Mass Partisanship: The Role of Elite Polarization." *American Political Science Review* 95 (September): 619–631.

Huckfeldt, Robert, and Carol Weitzel Kohfeld. 1989. *Race and the Decline of Class in American Politics*. Urbana, IL: University of Illinois Press.

Hunter, James Davison. 1991. *Culture Wars: The Struggle to Define America*. New York: Basic Books.

Jackman, Mary R., and Robert W. Jackman. 1983. *Class Awareness in the United States*. Berkeley, CA: University of California Press.

Kaufmann, Karen M., and John R. Petrocik. 1999. "The Changing Politics of American Men: Understanding the Sources of the Gender Gap." *American Journal of Political Science* 43 (July): 864–887.

Key, V. O., Jr. 1955. "A Theory of Critical Elections." *Journal of Politics* 17 (February): 3–18.

_____.1959. "Secular Realignment and the Party System." *Journal of Politics* 21 (May): 198–210.

Lassiter, Matthew D. 2006. *The Silent Majority: Suburban Politics in the Sunbelt South*. Princeton, NJ: Princeton University Press.

Layman, Geoffrey C. 2001. *The Great Divide: Religious and Cultural Conflict in American Party Politics*. New York: Columbia University Press.

Layman, Geoffrey C., and Thomas M. Carsey. 2002a. "Party Polarization and Party Structuring of Policy Attitudes: A Comparison of Three NES Panel Studies." *Political Behavior* 24 (September): 199–236.

_____. 2002b. "Party Polarization and 'Conflict Extension' in the American Electorate." *American Journal of Political Science* 46 (October): 786–802.

Leege, David C., Kenneth D. Wald, Brian S. Krueger, and Paul D. Mueller. 2002. *The Politics of Cultural Differences: Social Change and Voter Mobilization Strategies in the Post-New Deal Period*. Princeton, NJ: Princeton University Press.

Leuchtenburg, William E. 1963. *Franklin D. Roosevelt and the New Deal, 1932–1940*. New York: Harper and Row.

_____. 2005. *The White South Looks South: Franklin D. Roosevelt, Harry S. Truman, and Lyndon B. Johnson*. Baton Rouge, LA: Louisiana State University Press.

Lubell, Samuel. 1956. *The Future of American Politics*. Rev. ed. Garden City, NY: Doubleday Anchor Books.

Lublin, David. 2004. *The Republican South: Democratization and Partisan Change.* Princeton, NJ: Princeton University Press.

Mackenzie, G. Calvin, and Robert Weisbrot. 2008. *The Liberal Hour: Washington and the Politics of Change in the 1960s.* New York: Penguin Press.

McGirr, Lisa. 2001. *Suburban Warriors: The Origins of the New American Right.* Princeton, NJ: Princeton University Press.

Mellow, Nicole. 2008. *The State of Disunion: Regional Sources of American Partisanship.* Baltimore, MD: The Johns Hopkins University Press.

Milkis, Sydney M. 1993. *The President and the Parties: The Transformation of the American Party System Since the New Deal.* New York: Oxford University Press.

Nie, Norman H., Sidney Verba, and John R. Petrocik. 1976. *The Changing American Voter.* Cambridge, MA: Harvard University Press.

Petrocik, John R. 1981. *Party Coalitions: Realignments and the Decline of the New Deal Party System.* Chicago, IL: University of Chicago Press.

Plotke, David. 1996. *Building a Democratic Political Order: Reshaping American Liberalism in the 1930s and 1940s.* New York: Cambridge University Press.

Pomper, Gerald M. 1972. "From Confusion to Clarity: Issues and American Voters, 1956–1968." *American Political Science Review* 66 (June): 425–428.

Rae, Nicol C. 1989. *The Decline and Fall of the Liberal Republicans from 1952 to the Present.* New York: Oxford University Press.

_____. 1992. "Class and Culture: American Political Cleavages in the Twentieth Century." *Western Political Quarterly* 45 (September): 629–650.

Rosenof, Theodore. 2003. *Realignment: The Theory That Changed the Way We Think About American Politics.* Lanham, MD: Rowman and Littlefield.

Sanbonmatsu, Kira. 2002. *Democrats, Republicans, and the Politics of Women's Place.* Ann Arbor, MI: University of Michigan Press.

Saunders, Kyle L., and Alan I. Abramowitz. 2004. "Ideological Realignment and Active Partisans in the American Electorate." *American Politics Research* 32 (May): 285–309.

Scammon, Richard M., and Ben J. Wattenberg. 1970. *The Real Majority.* New York: Conrad McCann.

Schattschneider, E. E. 1942. *Party Government.* New York: Holt, Rinehart, and Winston.

_____. 1960. *The Semi-Sovereign People.* New York: Holt, Rinehart, and Winston.

Schlesinger, Arthur, Jr. 1960. *The Politics of Upheaval.* Boston: Houghton Mifflin.

Shafer, Byron E., and Richard Johnston. 2006. *The End of Southern Exceptionalism: Class, Race, and Partisan Change in the Postwar South.* Cambridge, MA: Harvard University Press.

Speel, Robert W. 1998. *Changing Patterns of Voting in the Northern United States: Electoral Realignment, 1952–1996.* University Park, PA: Pennsylvania State University Press.

Stanley, Harold W., William T. Bianco, and Richard G. Niemi. 1986. "Partisanship and Group Support Over Time: A Multivariate Analysis." *American Political Science Review* 80 (September): 969–976.

Stanley, Harold W., and Richard G. Niemi. 1991. "Partisanship and Group Support, 1952–1988." *American Politics Quarterly* 19 (April): 189–210.

_____. 2001. "Party Coalitions in Transition: Partisanship and Group Support, 1952–1996." In *Controversies in Voting Behavior,* edited by Richard G. Niemi and Herbert F. Weisberg, 387–404. 4th ed. Washington, DC: CQ Press.

Steensland, Brian, Jerry Z. Park, Mark D. Regnerus, Lynn D. Robinson, W. Bradford Wilcox, and Robert D. Woodberry. 2000. "The Measure of American Religion: Toward Improving the State of the Art." *Social Forces* 79: 291–324.

Stonecash, Jeffrey M. 2000. *Class and Party in American Politics*. Boulder, CO: Westview Press.

_____. 2006. *Political Parties Matter: Realignment and the Return of Partisan Voting*. Boulder, CO: Lynne Rienner.

Sundquist, James L. 1983. *Dynamics of the Party System*. Rev. ed. Washington, DC: The Brookings Institution.

Wald, Kenneth D., and Corwin E. Smidt. 1993. "Measurement Strategies in the Study of Religion and Politics." In *Rediscovering the Religious Factor in American Politics*, edited by David C. Leege and Lyman A. Kellstedt, 26–49. Armonk, NY: M. E. Sharpe.

Ware, Alan. 2006. *The Democratic Party Heads North, 1877–1962*. New York: Cambridge University Press.

Wattenberg, Martin P. 1987. "The Hollow Realignment: Partisan Change in a Candidate-Centered Era." *Public Opinion Quarterly* 51 (Spring): 58–74.

_____. 1998. *The Decline of American Political Parties, 1952–1996*. Cambridge, MA: Harvard University Press.

Woodberry, Robert D., and Christian S. Smith. 1998. "Fundamentalism et al.: Conservative Protestants in America." *Annual Review of Sociology* 24: 25056.

Wolbrecht, Christina. 2000. *The Politics of Women's Rights: Parties, Positions, and Change*. Princeton, NJ: Princeton University Press.

Endnotes

1. South is defined as the eleven states of the Confederacy.

2. Respondent type of community is not available for 2004 or 2008.

3. Northeast is defined as CT, ME, MA, NH, NJ, NY, PA, RI, and VT.

4. Certainly it would be desirable to have an indicator of religious salience that encompasses more that just church attendance, as Wald and Smidt (1993) and Guth and Green (1993) point out. However, church attendance is the only measure of religious salience available in the ANES for all of the years under examination in this study.

5. A case can be made that party identification would have been the more appropriate dependent variable here, as the primary focus of this analysis is on the coalitions of the Democratic and Republican Parties as wholes. This is the approach taken by Stanley and Niemi (1991, 2001) in their examination of partisan coalitions. Presidential vote is used here instead primarily for two reasons. First, what ultimately matters in determining election outcomes and control of government power is vote choice, not party identification. Second, changes in presidential voting patterns among groups often manifest themselves well before changes in group partisanship. The recent shifts in the South are an example of this.

6. Occupation type is not available for 2008, although the ANES indicates that this may change in future versions of the Cumulative File.

7. From 1960 to 1988 white evangelical Protestant religious tradition is determined using vcf0128a in combination with the variable for race of the respondent in the NES Cumulative Datafile. This classification scheme is not without problems. The most significant has to do with the classification of Baptists. Prior to 1972 the NES survey instrument did not differentiate among Baptists, meaning that during this period some Baptists are misclassified in the division of Protestants into mainline and evangelical traditions. There is simply no satisfactory way to deal with this problem. From 1990 to 1996, the revised classification scheme represented by vcf0128b is utilized. Beginning in 1998, NES officials stopped dividing Protes-

tants into "mainline" and "evangelical" categories as they began a review and reevaluation of the construction of the religious tradition variable. This review apparently has yet to be completed, and thus the last four versions of the NES Cumulative File offer no variable differentiating Protestants by religious tradition after 1996. In an attempt to provide at least some differentiation among Protestants for 2000 and 2004, white Protestants were identified as evangelical by denomination **only**. None of the other characteristics that the NES used to create its categories from 1990 to 1996, such as charismatic or fundamentalist identification, born-again status, or frequency of church attendance have been included here. The reasons for this decision are as follows. Charismatic or fundamentalist identification was not asked in 2000–2008; born-again status was not asked in 2004–2008; and classifying a respondent as "evangelical" or "mainline" based on frequency of attendance at worship services requires assumptions that are not warranted. For a useful discussion of classifying the religious tradition of Protestants based solely on denominational identification, see Steensland et al. (2000). For 2000 and 2004 denominations were classified as "evangelical" or "mainline" following the guidelines used by the NES from 1990 to 1996, with two exceptions. Those identifying themselves as members of the American Baptist Churches USA or Jehovah's Witnesses were removed from the evangelical category. Classifying by denomination only obviously results in undifferentiated Protestants and Christians being excluded from these analyses. This resulted in 89 respondents being removed in 2000, 77 in 2004, and 125 in 2008. This is particularly problematic given the recent growth in the number of nondenominational Protestants in the US. As Steensland et al. (2000) and Woodberry and Smith (1998) point out, this group is one of the fastest growing religious groups in America, and individuals in this group tend to exhibit beliefs that are different from those Protestants who identify themselves as having "no denomination" (as opposed to "nondenominational"). The religious beliefs of nondenominational Protestants resemble those held by evangelicals much more than those possessed by mainliners. However, without information on these beliefs in a dataset it is unwise to classify nondenominational Protestants into either Protestant tradition. Steensland et al. (2000) do classify some nondenominational Protestants into the evangelical tradition solely on the basis of church attendance, with those who attend services once a month or more being classified as evangelicals and those who attend less than once a month being omitted from further analysis. I am reluctant to follow this example because, as noted above, this requires making assumptions that are not clearly warranted or justified. In future versions of the NES survey, researchers can hope that sufficient belief and identification questions will be asked so that this important and growing component of the American religious landscape can be more fully analyzed. Full classification schemes are available from the author upon request.

8. For an excellent examination of realignment theory, see Rosenof (2003).

4

Party Activists, Ideological Extremism, and Party Polarization

MARJORIE RANDON HERSHEY,
NATHANIEL BIRKHEAD, AND BETH C. EASTER
Indiana University

*Signs at 2011 Tea Party protests in Madison, Wisconsin: "Obama
Is the Anti-Christ," and "Stop Socializing America."
And, across the street: "Tea Parties Are for Mad Hatters."*

Most Americans care very little about politics. Their participation is usually limited to voting, which conveys very little information to government beyond a "yes" to some candidates and a "no" to others. Even during hard-fought elections, wrote the respected political scientist V. O. Key Jr., the public "does not express its policy preferences with precision. The voice of the people may be loud, but the enunciation is indistinct" (Key 1961, 487).

Some public voices, however, are both loud and clear. Consider the protest signs quoted above. They were displayed at rallies of the Tea Party, a loosely organized set of groups fervently opposed to President Obama and his policies. Participants in these rallies were among the minority of Americans termed *political activists*: people who take active part in election campaigns, party events, political discussions, and who contribute to political groups.

Political parties could not survive without these activists. They perform the vital functions of calling attention to important issues, registering others to vote, canvassing door-to-door to inform people about the good and bad qualities of candidates, and urging citizens to come to the polls. Yet in recent decades, activists have been widely blamed for causing greater partisan and ideological division in American politics. Conventional wisdom suggests that activists have become more extreme in their views on big issues—Democratic activists have moved further left in comparison with most other Democrats and Republican activists are even more intensely conservative—and that they have pushed elected officials to take more extreme positions as well (e.g., see Aldrich 2011, chapter 6; Miller and Schofield 2008; Layman et al. 2010). As a result, it is claimed, activists are responsible for the fact that Republicans and Democrats in Congress are more deeply divided now on major issues, and that the members of each congressional party are more likely to vote in lockstep with their elected leadership, than has been seen in a century (Brewer and Stonecash 2009, 28–32; Hershey 2013, chapter 13; Roberts and Smith 2003).

This process of greater partisan and ideological division, and the bitter debate and gridlock that have accompanied it, is called *political polarization.* Its effects could be clearly seen in 2011 in the intense disputes that took place over the national debt and federal budget cuts. On one side, Tea Party activists demanded that Republican leaders slash federal spending to the bone. On the other side, liberal activists denounced any spending cuts agreed to by Democratic leaders, claiming that they had sold out to the Republicans. Activists on both sides saw "compromise" as a dirty word.

This increase in polarization has had profound effects, ranging from more combative election campaigns and frequent congressional paralysis (Abramowitz 2010) to higher voter turnout, as well as to increased party leadership power in Congress (Aldrich and Rohde 2009). If political activists are the culprits in this polarization, then activists are playing powerful roles in American democracy. Yet we have little evidence to guide us, beyond data showing that some types of political activists hold more extreme policy views than other voters and candidates do.

Activists might cause elected officials to become more polarized for three reasons: *resources, contact,* and *participation in nominations.* The first reason is that candidates and parties need the resources that activists can provide. Activists are among the most likely contributors to candidates and parties.

They can offer financial donations, help in contacting voters, and other outlays of time and effort. Candidates and parties need these resources. So if activists hold extreme views, then potential candidates may take more extreme stands on issues in order to get activists' support and resources. Alternatively, activists might try to recruit people with extreme views to run for office (see Aldrich 2011, 195–200; Masket 2009).

Second, because they take part in party and campaign events, activists have more frequent contact with candidates and public officials than other citizens do. Because of this contact, candidates are more likely to hear activists' views (Moon 2004) and receive the information activists offer (Abramowitz 2010, 5). Findings in other contexts (Kuklinski and Stanga 1979) suggest that the simple availability of information can affect elected officials' behavior, just as the "Your Speed Is . . . " signs can affect drivers' behavior even when no police officers are nearby. These repeated contacts can help activists learn how to communicate more effectively to candidates over time. So these more extreme activists "have the potential to distort the process of representation toward their interests, away from the preferences and interests of ordinary citizens" (Stone and Pietryka 2010, 337; see also Bafumi and Herron 2010).

Third, reforms of the presidential nominating process since the 1970s, offering more opportunities for public involvement, have also opened the door to greater activist influence over who gets to run for office (Cohen, et al. 2008). Because party and policy activists are a large proportion of the voters in primaries, and especially of caucus participants, they have a bigger say than other voters do in the selection of their party's candidates. To win nomination, then, candidates might take noncentrist stands in order to attract activists' support. Although primary voters in general have not been found to hold more extreme views than other voters (Norrander 2010, 63), candidates may nonetheless calculate that activists are the most likely participants in nominating events and thus may move toward the ideological poles where activists are thought to be found. When turnout is low, activists may dominate the vote. Activists are also more likely than other party identifiers to select delegates to party conventions and to serve as delegates themselves, which gives them the chance to affect party platforms (Nexon 1971, 716).

In addition, data support the idea of a link between activism and extremist views. Researchers have found that passionate views on policies can motivate people to become politically active (Verba, Schlozman, and Brady 1995, 399), as those who have watched political rallies can readily see. Many studies have also confirmed that activists are usually more extreme in their self-described ideology and in their attitudes on issues than are other party identifiers (see Stone and Pietryka 2010, 339–341; Abramowitz and Saunders 2005, 6–8), though the size of the "extremism gap" between activists and other partisans has varied across time (Miller and Jennings 1986; Saunders and Abramowitz 2005).

Yet we lack the answers to a number of important questions, including the direction of the influence.[1] Do extremist activists recruit and support more extreme candidates? Or do extremist candidates cause more polarized citizens to become active in politics? Some researchers suggest that candidates and elected officials drive the process. Carmines and Stimson (1989, chapter 6), for instance, show that the first groups to sort themselves by party on the issue of civil rights during the 1960s were members of Congress. The change in these elected officials' stands on race seems to have triggered a partisan sorting among activists and other members of the public, in which conservative southern Democrats slowly moved to the Republican Party and northeastern Republicans who were liberals on race switched to the Democrats.

We also know that different types of candidates and elected officials tend to appeal to, and thus to mobilize, different populations of activists. When Ronald Reagan ran for president in 1980 and 1984, he encouraged a lot of conservative Christians who had previously avoided politics to become active Republicans. Many then served as his convention delegates (Bruzios 1990, 589). Similarly in 2011 and 2012, Republicans who became active because of their zealous support for former U.S. House Speaker Newt Gingrich or libertarian Ron Paul often held different priorities from Republicans who came into the race to campaign for businessman Mitt Romney. The activists thus mobilized may then push the eventual nominee to accept their views.

The few studies that have tested the relationship between activists' and candidates' polarization have produced conflicting results. Research by Geoffrey Layman et al. (2010, 342–343) suggests that it is the party activists who have driven the polarization of American politics in recent years and have pushed elected officials to take more extreme issue stands. In contrast, Larry Bartels (2010, 12–14) finds that the patterns of presidential candidates' (perceived) issue stands do not conform to those we would expect to see if extremist activists were causing the polarization.

One reason for these conflicting results is that, as Bartels (2010, 2) points out, "We know surprisingly little about who [activists] are and how they matter." Various researchers have defined "party activists" in different ways, and there is no single, widely accepted *theoretical* definition of the term. It could include many different groups of people: those who give money to candidates or political groups, attend political conventions, go door-to-door for political causes, join the College Democrats or College Republicans, and even those who give campaign advice or think about running for office. Yet research suggesting that activists are a major source of polarization often assumes that they are an easily identified and undifferentiated group.

Who Is a "Party Activist"?

Most researchers define "activists," at least for the purposes of their research, as comprising one of two types of groups: (1) delegates to the two parties' presidential conventions, and (2) respondents to national surveys who report that they have been politically active, especially beyond voting. The many studies of presidential convention delegates (e.g., McClosky et al. 1960; Miller and Jennings 1986; Jackson and Green 2010; Layman et al. 2010), find that the two parties' delegates are much more divided on issues such as government spending, abortion, and foreign policy than other party identifiers are, with Republican delegates usually more unified than Democrats.

These studies also show that convention delegates are more polarized now than they were in earlier decades (e.g., Abramowitz 2010, 47; Jackson and Green 2010). But the increase in polarization has not been steady. For instance, the growing conservatism of Republican delegates on issues such as the provision of government services and government aid to minorities in 1992 and 1996 stopped and even reversed in 2000 (Jackson, Bigelow, and Green 2003, 61, 63)—perhaps because the nominee in 2000, George W. Bush, stressed his commitment to a more moderate-sounding "compassionate conservatism."

But presidential convention delegates, who include members of Congress and other elected officials, may not represent the whole population of party activists. Even the argument that the delegates should be defined as activists because they constitute a "presidential elite" (Jackson and Green 2010, 56) is undercut by the fact that the real choice of presidential candidate is now made by those who vote in the party's primaries and caucuses, not in the national convention. In some states (such as Indiana), delegates to *state* party conventions choose some candidates and make other important decisions. But only a few studies have surveyed these state delegates (Rapoport, Abramowitz, and McGlennon 1986; Nesbit, 1988) or people who have attended party caucuses (see Redlawsk, Tolbert, and Donovan 2011). Voters in primaries also play a central role in candidate selection. As mentioned, however, recent studies have not confirmed earlier findings that primary voters are more ideologically extreme and more intensely committed to their views than are other party voters.

The other main approach is to examine poll respondents who say that they are politically active in some way (e.g., Nexon 1971; Bruzios 1990; Carmines and Woods 2002). Most of these studies rely on the American National Election Studies (ANES 2005) questions asking respondents whether they have taken part in any of eight activities: voting; working for a party or a candidate; trying to influence others' votes; attending political meetings or speeches; displaying a button, sticker, or political sign; or giving money to a candidate, party, or other political group. Some researchers classify as "campaign activists" those who report taking part in at least three of six activities. Others require only one or two activities beyond voting, or even one or more activities of any kind.

Finally, some researchers focus on more specific types of participation, including people who report trying to influence others' votes (Baumer and Gold 2010) or those who give money to campaigns. Koger, Masket, and Noel (2009, 640–641) show that those who contributed money during the 2004 campaign were less moderate in their political views than other respondents, but not markedly so. In contrast, others find a bigger increase in polarization among presidential campaign donors from 1972 to 2004 than among other types of campaign activists, at least in their self-reported ideology (Aldrich 2011, 194; Francia et al. 2003, 60–63).

Why We Should Distinguish Among Types of Activism

Much of the research on political activists, then, treats the various individual forms of political participation as essentially interchangeable. An activist is defined as a respondent who engages in one or more of these activities; it doesn't matter which ones. However, researchers have also demonstrated that different types of participation differ in many ways: in the types of resources needed to engage in them, the amount of conflict involved in various activities, the information they convey to their target audience, and whether they take place in a social or isolated context. Being active in a campaign, for instance, involves exposure to conflict (Verba and Nie 1972, 91–93); perhaps for that reason, campaign activists might be more likely than the average citizen to be strong partisans and to take relatively extreme positions on issues. In contrast, voting is a less conflictual activity; we cast a secret ballot, whose contents we reveal only if we choose. And perhaps as a result of these differences, some kinds of activities attract a lot more participants than others do. The ANES reports that 78 percent of respondents in 2008 said they voted, 45 percent tried to influence others, 18 percent displayed a campaign button or sign, 13 percent gave money to a party or candidate, and 9 percent attended a meeting or speech, but only 4 percent worked for a party or campaign.

If different types of political activities are not interchangeable—if they attract different types of participants and convey different messages to public officials—then they may differ in their levels of polarization. Those who take part in some types of activities may hold more extreme views than others. Then, polarization among, say, campaign activists could affect candidates differently from polarization among financial contributors.

Research Questions/Hypotheses

We start by asking whether the people who engage in these different forms of participation are similar to one another in their socioeconomic characteristics and their political views. In short, is it justifiable to generalize about "political activists"? Second, do subsets of these activities cluster together to create *types* of activists? If so, do these types of activities differ according to the amount of personal contact their activity requires (e.g., trying to influence others' votes versus clicking on PayPal), or by the types of resources needed for those activities (e.g., time or money)? And are there significant differences among these clusters in the extremism of their political views? Finally, we will develop and begin to test a theory-based explanation of the impact of political activists on candidates and elected officials.

To answer these questions, we use a subset—those who report participating in some form of political activity[2]—of the ANES cumulative file analyzing the years 1984–2008. The analysis here will focus on percentage and statistical differences; readers who would like more sophisticated analyses can consult the Online Appendix for this chapter (at http://mypage.iu.edu/~nbirkhea/activists_appendix.html).

Findings: Are Different Types of Activities Interchangeable?

We begin by looking at the differences among participants in the various activities according to their income and educational levels, their partisan affiliation,[3] and their gender and race[4] (see Table 4.1).

TABLE 4.1 Types of Political Activity by Demographics

	Vote	Influence	Rally	Work	Button	Pty Ctrb	Cnd Ctrb	Other Ctrb
Lower Income	81	50	34	14	66	18	17	5
Middle Income	87	56	37	17	57	25	27	10
Higher Income	94	62	37	18	50	38	41	16
Democrats	89	57	39	18	58	27	30	12
Independents	76	44	33	13	56	13	19	8
Republicans	89	57	32	17	51	35	34	12
HS Diploma	84	54	33	16	60	24	24	8
Bachelor's Degree	96	63	40	18	46	40	45	18
Nonblacks	89	57	35	17	53	31	33	13
Blacks	85	52	37	16	68	17	21	4
Men	88	61	37	17	53	32	32	13
Women	88	52	34	17	57	27	30	10

Note: All values are percentages.

The table gives us three types of information. First, the results confirm that some types of political activities are much more common than others. For example, you'll notice that a large proportion of respondents report voting[5] or wearing a campaign button, whereas only a small percentage say that they have worked for a party or campaign or made a political contribution.

Second, the table shows how the frequency of participation changes within a given group of activists according to their social and demographic characteristics. For example, while only 18 percent of lower income respondents say they gave money to a political party ("Pty Ctrb"), more than twice as many, 38 percent, of higher income respondents report having done so. On the other hand, lower income respondents are almost as likely to work for a party or campaign ("Work") as are middle or higher income respondents. In fact, party and campaign workers are not distinctive at all in terms of their partisanship, educational levels, race, or gender.

Finally, using this information, we can compare the profiles of participants in the various activities. We find that there are several similarities in these profiles. Most notably, although the specific percentages differ from one type of activity to another, higher income people are more likely to engage in most political activities than lower income people are. The same is true of education levels: people holding at least a college degree are more likely to participate than are those with only a high school diploma. And in the case of partisanship, those who identify as either Democrats or Republicans are clearly more likely than Independents to vote, try to influence the votes of others, and give money to various groups. These are not surprising results; income and education provide the knowledge and resources for people to become politically active, and partisanship provides the motivation.

But there are some interesting differences among the various activities as well. Blacks are significantly less likely to report contributing money to a candidate, party, or other political organization than are nonblacks; this is true *even when income and education are held constant.* Second, women are significantly less likely than men to report trying to influence someone else's vote choice or to attend a political rally or speech, and they are less likely to report contributing to a party or other political group, again when other characteristics are held constant.[6] In short, these two demographic groups that have been underrepresented in politics for so long are less inclined to donate money to political actors than are whites and males, even at similar levels of socioeconomic status—a tendency that is not likely to increase their political clout. And finally, although those with more education and income are generally more likely to be politically active, they are *less* likely to display a button, sign, or bumper sticker—an unexpected finding.

The similarities that we see in the social-demographic profiles of different forms of activism are not due to extensive overlap among the participants in different activities. Table 4.2 shows the degree to which people who take part in, say, voting (the coefficient at the upper left of the table, just under the number 1), also report trying to influence other people's votes. Most of these correlations are lower than 0.10,[7] which shows relatively little overlap among activities. Only a few relationships are positive and statistically significant. Most notably, those who try to influence other people's votes are also somewhat more likely to engage in nearly every other form of participation. There is also some evidence of a cluster of financial activities: those who donate money are likely to donate to multiple organizations.

TABLE 4.2 Correlations Among Forms of Activism

	Vote	Influence	Rally	Work	Button	Pty Ctrb	Cnd Ctrb	Other Ctrb
Vote	1							
Influence	0.16*	1						
Rally	0.05*	0.13*	1					
Work	0.06*	0.17*	0.20*	1				
Button	0.02	0.12*	−0.13*	0.04*	1			
Pty Ctrb	0.08*	0.05*	−0.09*	0.01	−0.28*	1		
Cnd Ctrb	0.11*	0.11*	0.03	0.12*	−0.17*	0.31*	1	
Other Ctrb	0.07*	0.10*	0.03	0.06*	−0.03*	0.11*	0.17*	1

* $p < 0.05$

The outlier among these forms of participation is displaying a button, sign, or bumper sticker. As the negative signs of the coefficients show, individuals who display political buttons or signs are significantly *less likely* to attend a rally or meeting and to make all three types of monetary contributions. The social-demographic profile of these "displayers" shows them to be lower in income and less educated than other activists and more likely to be African American. There could be several reasons for this unexpected finding. Displaying a political button or sign is probably the least costly way of participating in politics. The decision to display a sign is not made by the activist alone; it also reflects the decisions made by campaigns and parties as to where to distribute their signs and buttons. And the fact that campaigns and parties try to place yard signs at homes along main streets, where home values might be lower than those in quieter parts of a neighborhood, might help to explain why these participants are not as high income as are those who take part in other activities. Note, however, that this is one of the most common forms of political participation; almost one in five respondents reports displaying a button, bumper sticker, or sign. So we should not be tempted to exclude these people from our examination of political activists simply due to the differences between their social-demographic profile and that of other types of activities.

To get a more complete picture of the effects of two especially interesting characteristics—education and race—on the likelihood of engaging in any of these activities, Figure 4.1 shows the predicted probabilities of participating in these activities when the respondents' education levels are taken into account. When the white dot (representing respondents with only a high school diploma) and the black dot (those with at least a college degree) for an activity are level with one another (for example, in the case of working in a campaign or for a party), this indicates that people with higher education and those with less education are equally likely to take part in that activity.

As you can see from the fact that the black dots are almost always at higher probability levels than are the white dots, people with higher levels of education are more likely to participate in almost all of these activities. In fact, even when partisanship and income are controlled, those with a bachelor's degree are almost twice as likely to report donating money to a candidate (probability = 0.38) as are individuals with only a high school diploma (probability = 0.20). The sole exception, again, is those who report displaying a political button or sign, where respondents with only a high school education are more likely to be active than are those with at least a college degree.

Figure 4.2 shows the probability of blacks engaging in the various forms of activism compared with nonblacks. The two groups are very similar in their likelihood of voting, trying to influence others' votes, attending a rally or speech, or working on a campaign; the point estimates and the 95 percent confidence intervals clearly overlap. In contrast, however, blacks are significantly more likely than nonblacks to wear campaign buttons and display yard signs or use bumper stickers, and far less likely to donate money to any of the three types of political groups, even when controlling for income and education. Others who have reported similar findings suggest that this may reflect the continuing legacy of the civil rights movement of the mid-1900s, when the political participation of blacks, who were (and are) predominantly lower income, focused on mass mobilizations and protests rather than financial donations (Verba, Schlozman, and Brady 1995, 255).

To sum up the social and demographic profiles of those who take part in various political activities, we can see a number of similarities across the activities and some intriguing differences. The activities seem to fall naturally

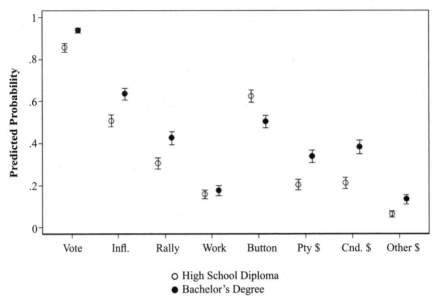

○ High School Diploma
● Bachelor's Degree

Note: The dots represent the probabilities that those with different levels of education will engage in each activity. The lines above and below each dot are the 95 percent confidence intervals; if there is any overlap between the lines of the two dots for an activity, then the difference between high school– and college-educated participants is not worth noting. If there is no overlap, then the difference between the two groups is significant. Probabilities are calculated in Stata 12.0 using "prvalue" in Scott Long's *spost* suite of commands, while holding all other variables at their means (Long and Freese 2005).

FIGURE 4.1 **Relationship Between Education and Types of Political Activity**

into three different groupings. The profiles of those who donate money to candidates, to parties, and to other political groups look fairly similar to one another. There are also similarities among the profiles of influencers, those who attend rallies or speeches, and those who work for a party or campaign. But those who display buttons or signs look like no other group of participants. To this degree, different types of activism attract somewhat different types of people.

Differences Among Types of Activists in Issue Attitudes

Do these types of activism differ in terms of participants' ideologies and issue attitudes? To test this, we created a four-point Extremism Scale in which indi-

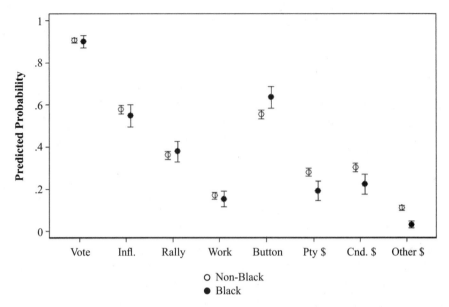

FIGURE 4.2 Relationship Between Race and Types of Political Activity

viduals calling themselves moderates are the baseline category (scored 1), those who rate themselves as somewhat liberal *or* somewhat conservative are scored 2, those who call themselves liberal/conservative get a score of 3, and extremely liberal/conservative respondents are scored 4.[8] We also looked at differences in participants' attitudes toward some specific issues prominent on the political agenda: measures of respondents' attitudes toward government spending on social services, preferences for greater or less defense spending, views on when abortion should be permitted, and "feeling thermometer" ratings of Christian fundamentalists. These findings are reported in Table 4.3.

Using the Extremism Scale (the first section of Table 4.3), we find that most types of activism are significantly and positively related to greater ideological extremism; this is true of voting, working for a party or candidate, and contributing to a party, candidate, or other political group, and it is particularly true of those who report trying to influence other people's votes. But there is no clear relationship between ideological extremism and attending political rallies or meetings or displaying a political button or sign.

TABLE 4.3 Types of Political Activity by Ideology

	Vote	Influence	Rally	Work	Button	Pty Ctrb	Cnd Ctrb	Other Ctrb
Moderate	86	48	36	14	54	25	26	8
Weak Lib/Con	89	57	39	17	51	30	33	12
Lib/Con	93	64	35	20	53	36	38	16
Extreme Lib/Con	93	78	37	20	64	33	37	16
Abortion: Always Legal	87	55	38	17	51	32	34	15
Abortion Moderate	83	53	34	17	56	28	29	9
Abortion: Never Legal	88	56	32	15	65	19	21	7
Defense: Spend Less	89	62	31	15	57	27	30	10
Defense: Spend Same	90	55	35	16	53	31	32	11
Defense: Spend More	89	58	37	17	54	29	31	12
Christ Fund: Low Rating	95	68	37	18	56	31	40	16
Christ Fund: Med Rating	91	61	33	16	58	30	33	12
Christ Fund: Hi Rating	88	62	28	16	66	28	27	9
Gov't: Spend Less	91	63	39	20	53	35	38	16
Gov't: Spend Same	89	55	35	16	52	31	31	10
Gov't: Spend More	89	57	37	17	54	30	31	12

As we have done with social-demographic differences, Figure 4.3 compares the predicted probability of participation of those who identify as "moderates" with individuals who identify as extreme liberals or conservatives. Those who identify as "extremists" are significantly more likely to vote. (This relationship was evident in 2010 in the degree to which supporters of the Tea Party, who tended to be more extreme conservatives than non–Tea Party Republicans, were more likely to vote in the midterm election; see Pew 2011.) Extremists are also more likely than moderates to try to influence others' votes, to work for a party or campaign, and to donate money to a party, candidate, or other political group. There are no activities in which moderates are more likely to participate than extremists. But moderates are just as likely as extremists to attend political rallies and meetings and to display political buttons or signs. These findings confirm that in the case of *most* forms of political activism—but not all—activists are more likely to come from the segment of respondents *willing to describe themselves* as extreme liberals or conservatives.

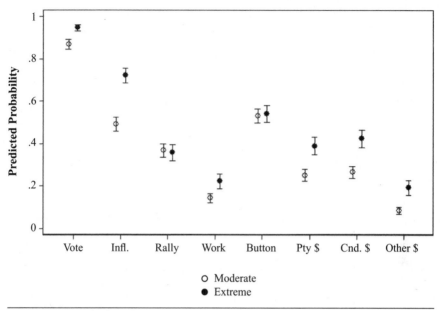

FIGURE 4.3 Relationship Between Self-Reported Ideology and Types
of Activities

When we look at specific issues, however, the pattern becomes more complicated. Instead of consistent findings that those who are more politically
active are more likely to take extreme stands; the results vary from one issue
to another. Figure 4.4 presents the predicted probability of participation by
one's views on abortion. Moderates on abortion—those who feel that abor-
tions should be permitted in some cases—are just as likely as those with extreme views (that abortion should never be permitted or should always be
permitted) to take part in most political activities. Donors to parties, candidates, or other political groups differ from this pattern, but not because they
are more likely to be extremists. Instead, these financial donors are more
likely to be pro-choice; it is the pro-lifers, not the moderates, who are the
least likely to donate. So at least in this case, extremists—those who hold extreme views on both ends of the abortion scale—are not necessarily more
likely to participate politically than moderates are.

In the case of defense spending as well, activists are not necessarily more
likely to hold extreme attitudes. The relationships are generally weak. As you

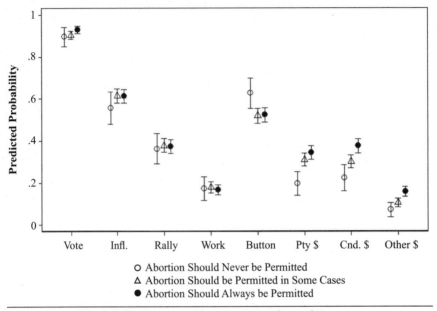

FIGURE 4.4 **Relationship Between Abortion Attitudes and Types
of Activities**

can see in Table 4.3, extremists on defense spending are more likely to try to influence others' votes than moderates are. But the reverse is true of those who give money to parties; here, moderates are slightly more likely to participate. And in the case of those who attend rallies, the relationship is directional rather than polarized: people are more likely to go to political rallies or meetings if they want to greatly increase defense spending and less likely to attend if they favor a big cut in defense spending.

Regarding activists' attitudes toward Christian fundamentalists and government spending on social services, the data in Table 4.3 also show no clear relationship between extremism and participation. There are a few instances where activists are more likely to hold extreme views: those who want either much more *or* much less government spending on social services are somewhat more likely to try to influence others, attend rallies, and donate to other political groups.

But in even more types of activities, only those who hold extreme attitudes on *one* side of the issue are more inclined to be active. For example, people who hold negative attitudes toward Christian fundamentalists ("Low rating") are more likely than other respondents to engage in most of these activities. And people who want big cuts in government spending on social services ("Gov't. spend less") are usually more likely to participate than are either those who hold more moderate attitudes or who favor much greater spending. Others have reported similar findings; comparing voters with nonvoters, Leighley and Nagler (2011, 23) show that in attitudes toward economic and social welfare issues, "In each year since 1972, voters are more conservative than are nonvoters in their beliefs regarding how much the government should do to provide jobs, health insurance and services." Thus, liberals on this question—those who want much more government spending on social services—and those who strongly approve of fundamentalists are not as likely to get their voices heard through these activities. And again we find that those who display political buttons or signs are the outliers: they are more likely to hold pro-life views and positive attitudes toward fundamentalists than are almost any of the other groups.

In short, although activists are often more likely to *describe themselves* as extremists, we do not necessarily see this pattern when looking at their views on specific issues. As Table 4.4 demonstrates, different types of activities attract somewhat different types of participants, both in their social-demographic characteristics and the extent to which they hold extreme attitudes on policy issues.

Findings: Are There Activist "Clusters"?

Next, to determine whether all these forms of participation are most appropriately combined into a single group or treated as two distinct types of activism, we used a different technique—an exploratory factor analysis[9]—with the ANES data. Our analysis suggests that the types of participation are best understood as falling into two distinct groupings (see Figure 4.5). The first includes those who attend political rallies or meetings, those who work for a party or on a campaign, and those who try to influence others' votes. The second consists of those who contribute money to candidates, parties, or other political groups. Voting is closely associated with both groupings, and those who display political buttons or signs are not closely associated with either one!

TABLE 4.4 **Distinctive Characteristics of Different Types of Activists**

Activity	Social, Demographic Characteristics	Ideological Self-Description, Issue Attitudes
Voting	Higher income, more educated, partisan	Describes self as extremist, negative toward fundamentalists, wants less gov't social spending
Influences others' votes	Partisan, men, more educated	Describes self as extremist, polarized toward fundamentalists, wants less defense spending
Attends rallies, meetings	More educated, men	Negative toward fundamentalists, wants less defense spending, polarized on gov't spending
Works for party/ campaigns	No distinctive characteristics	Describes self as extremist
Displays buttons/signs	Lower income, less educated, black	Never allow abortion, wants more gov't social spending, positive toward fundamentalists
Donates to party	Higher income, more educated, partisan, nonblack	Describes self as extremist, abortion should always be legal, wants less gov't social spending
Donates to candidate	Higher income, more educated, nonblack	Describes self as extremist, abortion should always be legal, negative toward fundamentalists, wants less gov't spending
Donates to other political groups	Higher income, more educated, nonblack	Describes self as extremist, abortion should always be legal, negative toward fundamentalists, wants less gov't spending

Note: Characteristics included are those whose relationships with types of political activity are statistically significant (see Tables A1 and A2 in the online appendix).

How can we best characterize these two different types of activism? The second grouping is easy to describe: it requires giving money. The activities outside this grouping do not; people do not need disposable cash in order to influence others, attend a rally, or make calls or go door-to-door for a candidate. Instead, they need free time. Another way to distinguish these two types of activities is that at least in many cases, giving money is a private activity while attending a meeting or talking with others is a social activity. Yet because most of the surveys we examine were conducted prior to the use

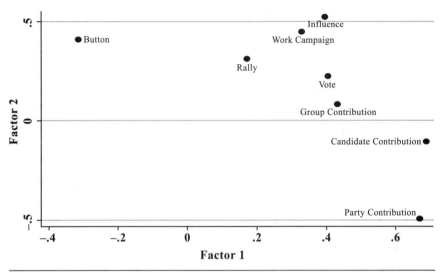

FIGURE 4.5 The Two Types of Political Activism

of the Internet for political fund-raising, some contributors to a candidate, party, or other political group may have been solicited at a social event or directly by a friend or acquaintance. So it makes the most sense to divide these activists into those who make financial contributions and those who contribute their time.

Are There Differences in Polarization Among the Activist Clusters?

In order to test whether people who participated in time-based political activities were more polarized, or less polarized, than were those who made financial contributions to political groups, we employed two types of analyses. In the first analysis, we looked at the relationship between the two types of activism and individuals' scores on the self-reported Extremism Scale, while controlling for party, race, gender, education, and income. The first column of Table 4.5 shows these relationships (using a technique known as ordered logistic regression). Changes in the predicted probabilities are shown in the table as well, to indicate the marginal effect on ideology of increasing an individual's financial or time-based activism.

The data show that when holding all else constant, people who rate themselves as more extreme in their ideology are more likely to participate in both
types of activities. In statistical terms, increasing one's financial activism
score from the minimum to the maximum almost doubles his or her likelihood of identifying as an ideological extremist, and decreases the individual's
likelihood of identifying as a moderate by about one-third. This relationship
is even more dramatic in the case of time-based forms of participation. When
time-based activism increases from the minimum to the maximum, the likelihood of identifying as an extremist is more than doubled, while the likelihood of identifying as a moderate drops by one-half.

In short, in both financial and time-based types of participation, highly
active respondents are nearly *twice* as likely to report holding extreme attitudes than are inactive respondents. But those involved in time-based political activities are more likely to report ideological extremism than are those
who donate money. In both cases the overall likelihood of identifying as an

TABLE 4.5 The Impact of Activism Types, Education, and
            Income on Ideological Position

Independent[1] Variables	Ordered Logit Estimates	Change in Predicted Probabilities			
		Moderate	Slightly Liberal/ Conservative	Liberal/ Conservative	Extremely Liberal/ Conservative
Financial Activism	0.18* (0.05)	−9%	−4%	+9%	+4%
Time-Based Activism	0.37* (0.06)	−18%	−6%	+17%	+7%
Education	0.19* (0.05)	−11%	−3%	+10%	+4%
Income	−0.12* (0.04)	+9%	+3%	−8%	−4%
Republican	1.32* (.18)	−23%	−9%	+21%	+11%
Democrat	.94* (.18)	−17%	−5%	+16%	+7%

N = 2694
$F_{(8,2189)}$ = 21.32

Standard errors in parentheses
*p < 0.05
[1]The coefficients and predicted probabilities for race and gender were estimated, though omitted
from the table.

extremist is still relatively low, but the difference between the two types of activists is clear.

Do we get the same findings if we look at attitudes toward specific issue domains? Following earlier analyses (Bartels 2010), we examine respondents' attitudes on issues relating to social welfare, moral conservatism, and antigovernment attitudes. We construct factor scores from each of the three issue domains, and again fold them so that increasing values correspond to increasing levels of extremism.[10] We estimate each of these factor scores as a function of the same independent variables as in the analysis above.

The results, which can be found in Table A8 in the online appendix, show that the two types of activism behave similarly. Financial activists and time-based activists are both more ideologically extreme with regard to moral conservatism and attitudes toward social welfare. (There is no relationship with antigovernment attitudes.) But the relationship is weak in substantive terms. Again, this suggests that the tendency for activists to hold more extreme political views on specific sets of issues is much less dramatic than many researchers have suggested.

Republicans are more likely than Democrats and Independents to adopt extreme positions on moral conservatism and social welfare. And in comparing data from 1984–1988 with those from 2004–2008 (data not shown), we found that there has been an interesting change in the relationship between antigovernment views and political activism. In the earlier period, those with relatively moderate attitudes toward government were more likely to be politically active; those who were the most antigovernment and especially those who were the least antigovernment were less active. In the 2000s, this relationship flattened, with the exception that those with the most extreme antigovernment views were more likely to be active.

Findings: A Theory-Based Analysis of Activism

We conclude by returning to the set of arguments cited early in this chapter: that activists' role in the current political polarization could result from the resources they have to offer prospective candidates, from their contact with candidates (which gives them the chance to convey information), and/or from their central role in nominating candidates. We can begin to distinguish among these pathways by examining the level of polarization of the individuals who populate them. Because the ANES data set did not have enough measures of two of these pathways in election surveys since the 1980s, we used the data from the 2008 Cooperative Congressional Election Study (see Ansolabehere 2011) to create indices of each of these possible pathways.[11]

We then estimated the relationship between each pathway of activism and respondents' levels of extremism, using the folded Extremism Scale[12] and controlling for partisanship, education, income, race, and gender. Given our findings above, we expect that those offering resources (the resource pathway) or information (the contact pathway) to candidates will see themselves as more ideologically extreme. Following Abramowitz (2008) and Norrander (2010), we do not expect to find primary voters (the nomination pathway) to be any more extreme than nonprimary voters.

The results, as well as changes in probabilities,[13] are presented in Table 4.6. We find modest support for our expectations. The coefficients for the resources and contact pathways are positive and significant, indicating that those who offer more resources to a candidate or have greater contact with a candidate are more likely to rate themselves as ideologically extreme.

With respect to the resources pathway, increasing an individual's score from the minimum to the maximum almost doubles his or her likelihood of identifying as an extreme liberal or conservative and decreases his or her likelihood of identifying as a moderate by about half. We see a similar trend in the contact pathway. Increasing an individual's contact score from the minimum to the maximum slightly increases his or her likelihood of identifying as an extremist (by about 25 percent) and decreases his or her likelihood of identifying as a moderate by nearly the same margin. And confirming Abramowitz (2008) and Norrander (2010), we find that respondents who took part in the nomination pathway, by voting in a primary, do not differ ideologically from those who don't take part.

The control variables generally behave as we should expect: compared with Independents, party identifiers rate themselves as more ideologically extreme, and among the partisans, Republicans are more likely to identify as extremists than Democrats are. Increasing income has a modest moderating effect on individuals' ideology. Blacks are more likely to call themselves moderates than whites are, all else equal. And individuals' education and gender do not have a discernable impact.

In short, in examining the ways in which activists' views can influence candidates, we find that as the cost (in either time or money) of a particular po-

TABLE 4.6 **The Impact of Activism Pathways on Ideological Position**

Independent Variables	Ordered Logit Estimates	Change in Predicted Probabilities		
		Moderate	Liberal/ Conservative	Extremely Liberal/ Conservative
Resources pathway	0.91* (−0.13)	−13%	−3%	+15%
Contact pathway	0.34* (−0.07)	−6%	No change	+7%
Nomination pathway	0.01 (−0.06)	No change	No change	No change
Education	−0.01 (−0.02)	No change	No change	No change
Income	−0.03* (−0.01)	+8%	+1%	−9%
Republican	1.54* (−0.07)	−26%	−6%	+32%
Democrat	0.74* (−0.07)	−14%	No change	+14%
Female	−0.05 (−0.05)	+1%	No change	−1%
Black	−0.91* (−0.11)	+20%	-6%	−14%

N = 8582
F(9,8573) = 91.63
Standard errors in parentheses
*p < 0.05

litical activity increases, so does the likelihood that participants will rate themselves as ideologically extreme. Voting in a primary carries a relatively small cost in time and information gathering. Contacting an elected official or attending a meeting is more costly in time and other personal resources, and donating to a political campaign costs even more. The next step is to find out more about the issue preferences of those who take part in these different types of political activities and the ways in which these preferences are articulated to candidates. How do the types of participants in these pathways differ from one another? Which of the pathways have the greatest effects on candidates and elected officials? And finally, to what extent does the polarization we see so vividly in American politics stem from activists influencing candidates, and to what extent does it arise because of the nature of the candidates themselves?

Conclusion

This chapter has presented evidence for several conclusions about political activists. First, although the profiles of people who engage in various types of political activities are similar in many ways, there are also some important differences among them. For instance, blacks and women are less likely to contribute money to candidates and other political groups than whites and males are, even when income and educational levels are held constant. Women are significantly less likely than men to try to persuade other people how to vote and to attend political rallies. And one type of political activism differs from all the others. People who report wearing a political button or displaying a political sign—one of the most common types of participation—tend not to engage in other forms of activism. They also break the pattern that political activists generally are more educated and have higher incomes than inactive citizens do; people with only a high school diploma are more likely to display buttons and signs than are people with college degrees. As a result, treating all forms of participation as if they are interchangeable hides some interesting and potentially important differences.

We find that people who are politically active cluster into two types of participation: those that involve giving money and those that involve donating time. People who engage in either type of participation are more likely to see themselves as extreme, in an ideological sense, than are those who participate less. This is especially true of those who take part in time-based forms of participation. But with respect to respondents' attitudes toward specific issues, we do not see a clear-cut pattern of greater extremism. In some cases, activists are more extreme. On other issue domains, it is those who hold extreme attitudes on *one* side of the issue who are more likely to be active. For instance, donors to all three types of political groups are more likely to be strongly pro-choice and to want big cuts in government social spending than they are to hold moderate attitudes toward these issues or to be intensely pro-life and pro-spending. On the whole, we can more successfully predict activism on the basis of respondents' general ideological self-description and social-demographic characteristics than on the basis of their attitudes toward specific issues.

Our findings, then, offer some support to the common notion that political activists are more extreme in their views than other citizens are, at least in the extent to which they characterize themselves as extreme liberals or conservatives. But the relationship between activism and extremism is not as marked or as consistent as it is often portrayed. It is worth noting that the strongest relationships between activism and extremism have been reported in surveys of national convention delegates, a population that might not be highly representative of the larger population of political activists, and in studies that examine "core partisans" (Bartels 2010) or the "engaged public" (Abramowitz 2010, chapter 2)—those who not only take part in political activities but who also report political knowledge and interest, concern about election outcomes, and a much higher level of enthusiasm for their own party than for the other party.

To go beyond these findings and to learn more about activists' roles in political polarization, we need to develop clearer expectations as to how activists' attitudes and behavior affect elected officials. Could activists with extreme attitudes on a few highly publicized issues push candidates to adopt extremely liberal or conservative stands? Or would the activists have to present a consistent pattern of increasing extremism across a wide range of public concerns? Or is it that there are now fewer cross-cutting cleavages among activists that would otherwise temper their views of the other party, with the result that activists of the two parties are less likely to talk with one another and to understand and respect one another's views?[14] Alternatively, it might be that activists are not the main culprits after all—that candidates and elected officials have led the polarization process and try to attract like-minded activists who have the resources needed for victory. Or it might be that we are seeing different patterns of extremism, and of the relationship between activists and candidates, in the Republican Party than we do among Democrats.

And even as we continue to learn about the nature and views of political activists, activism might be changing. Greater use of the Internet and social networking to attract small donors could change the profile of monetary contributors and their differences from other types of participants. If the Obama campaign's effort to get donors to become canvassers and campaign volunteers is imitated by other candidates, then the distinctions we have identified between those who donate money and those who donate time might fade. The importance of activists to candidates and elections, however, is sure to continue.

References

Abramowitz, Alan I. 2008. "Don't Blame Primary Voters for Polarization." *The Forum* 5. www.bepress.com/forum/vol5/iss4/art4.

_____. 2010. *The Disappearing Center: Engaged Citizens, Polarization and American Democracy.* New Haven, CT: Yale University Press.

Abramowitz, Alan, and Kyle Saunders. 2005. "Why Can't We All Just Get Along? The Reality of a Polarized America." *The Forum* 3. www.bepress.com/forum/vol3/iss2/art1.

Aldrich, John H. 2011. *Why Parties? A Second Look.* Chicago: University of Chicago Press.

Aldrich, John H., and David W. Rohde. 2009. "Congressional Committees in a Continuing Partisan Era." In *Congress Reconsidered,* edited by Lawrence C. Dodd and Bruce I Oppenheimer, 217–239. 9th ed. Washington, DC: CQ Press.

ANES (American National Election Studies). 2005. *The 1948–2004 ANES Cumulative Data File.* Stanford, CA: Stanford University and Ann Arbor, MI: University of Michigan.

Ansolabehere, Stephen. 2011. "CCES Common Content, 2008," April 13. *hdl.handle.net /1902.1/14003,* Version 4.

Bafumi, Joseph, and Michael C. Herron. 2010. "Leapfrog Representation and Extremism: A Study of American Voters and Their Members in Congress." *American Political Science Review* 104: 519–542.

Bartels, Larry M. 2010. "Base Appeal: The Political Attitudes and Priorities of Core Partisans." Paper presented at the Annual Meeting of the American Political Science Association, Washington, DC.

Baumer, Donald C., and Howard J. Gold. 2010. *Parties, Polarization, and Democracy in the United States.* Boulder, CO: Paradigm Publishers.

Beckel, Michael. 2011. "Political Donors' Gender Disparity." Center for Responsive Politics, OpenSecrets Blog, August 26. *www.opensecrets.org/news/2011/08/political-donors-gender -disparity.html#.Tlh3VybUtrQ.facebook.*

Brewer, Mark D., and Jeffrey M. Stonecash. 2009. *The Dynamics of American Political Parties.* New York: Cambridge University Press.

Bruzios, Christopher. 1990. "Democratic and Republican Party Activists and Followers: Inter- and Intra-Party Differences." *Polity* 22: 581–601.

Carmines, Edward G., and James A. Stimson. 1989. *Issue Evolution: Race and the Transformation of American Politics.* Princeton, NJ: Princeton University Press.

Carmines, Edward G., and James Woods. 2002. "The Role of Party Activists in the Evolution of the Abortion Issue." *Political Behavior* 24: 361–377.

Cohen, Marty, David Karol, Hans Noel, and John Zaller. 2008. *The Party Decides: Presidential Nominations Before and After Reform.* Chicago: University of Chicago Press.

Francia, Peter L., John C. Green, Paul S. Herrnson, Lynda W. Powell, and Clyde Wilcox. 2003. *The Financiers of Congressional Elections.* New York: Columbia University Press.

Hershey, Marjorie Randon. 2013. *Party Politics in America.* 15th ed. New York: Pearson Longman.

Jackson, John S., and John C. Green. 2010. "The State of Party Elites: National Convention Delegates, 1992–2008." In *The State of the Parties* edited by John C. Green and Daniel J. Coffey. 6th ed., 55–77. Lanham, MD: Rowman and Littlefield.

Jackson, John S., Nathan S. Bigelow, and John C. Green. 2003. "The State of Party Elites: National Convention Delegates, 1992–2000." In *The State of the Parties* edited by John C. Green and Rick Farmer. 4th ed., 54–78. Lanham, MD: Rowman and Littlefield.

Key, V. O., Jr. 1961. "Public Opinion and the Decay of Democracy." *Virginia Quarterly Review* 37: 481–494.

Koger, Gregory, Seth Masket, and Hans Noel. 2009. "Partisan Webs: Information Exchange and Party Networks." *British Journal of Political Science* 39: 633–653.

Kuklinski, James H., and John E. Stanga. 1979. "Political Participation and Governmental Responsiveness." *American Political Science Review* 73: 1090–1099.

Layman, Geoffrey C., Thomas M. Carsey, John C. Green, Richard Herrera, and Rosalyn Cooperman. 2010. "Activists and Conflict Extension in American Party Politics." *American Political Science Review* 104: 324–346.

Leighley, Jan E., and Jonathan Nagler. 2011. "Who Votes Now? Alienation, Indifference and Inequality." Paper presented at the annual meeting of the American Political Science Association, Seattle, WA.

Long, Scott J., and Jeremy Freese. 2005. *Regression Models for Categorical Outcomes Using Stata*. 2nd ed. College Station, TX: Stata Press.

Masket, Seth E. 2009. *No Middle Ground: How Informal Party Organizations Control Nominations and Polarize Legislatures*. Ann Arbor, MI: University of Michigan Press.

McClosky, Herbert, Paul Hoffman, and Rosemary O'Hara. 1960. "Issue Conflict and Consensus among Party Leaders and Followers." *American Political Science Review* 54: 406–427.

Miller, Gary, and Norman Schofield. 2008. "The Transformation of the Republican and Democratic Party Coalitions in the US." *Perspectives on Politics* 6: 433–450.

Miller, Warren E., and M. Kent Jennings. 1986. *Parties in Transition*. New York: Russell Sage Foundation.

Moon, Woojin. 2004. "Party Activists, Campaign Resources and Candidate Position Taking." *British Journal of Political Science* 34: 611–633.

Nesbit, Dorothy Davidson. 1988. "Changing Partisanship Among Southern Party Activists." *Journal of Politics* 50: 322–334.

Nexon, David. 1971. "Asymmetry in the Political System: Occasional Activists in the Republican and Democratic Parties." *American Political Science Review* 65: 716–730.

Norrander, Barbara. 2010. *The Imperfect Primary*. New York: Routledge.

Pew 2011. Pew Research Center for the People & the Press. "The Tea Party and Religion." February 23. *www.pewforum.org/Politics-and-Elections/Tea-Party-and-Religion.aspx*.

Rapoport, Ronald B., Alan I. Abramowitz, and John McGlennon. 1986. *The Life of the Parties*. Lexington, KT: University Press of Kentucky.

Redlawsk, David P., Caroline J. Tolbert, and Todd Donovan. 2011. *Why Iowa?* Chicago, IL: University of Chicago Press.

Roberts, Jason M., and Steven S. Smith. 2003. "Procedural Contexts, Party Strategy, and Conditional Party Voting in the U.S. House of Representatives, 1971–2000." *American Journal of Political Science* 47: 305–317.

Saunders, Kyle L., and Alan I. Abramowitz. 2004. "Ideological Realignment and Active Partisans in the American Electorate." *American Politics Research* 32: 285–309.

Stone, Walter J., and Matthew T. Pietryka. 2010. "Party, Constituency, and Representation in Congress." In John C. Green and Daniel J. Coffey, eds., *The State of the Parties*. 6th ed., 333–347. Lanham, MD: Rowman and Littlefield.

Verba, Sidney, and Norman H. Nie. 1972. *Participation in America*. Chicago: University of Chicago Press.

Verba, Sidney, Kay Lehman Schlozman, and Henry E. Brady. 1995. *Voice and Equality*. Cambridge, MA: Harvard University Press.

Endnotes

1. Layman et al. 2010 is the main exception in addressing this question.

2. The subset comprises respondents who report engaging in at least one of the following activities: trying to influence someone else's vote choice, working on a campaign or for a

party, attending a rally or political meeting, wearing a button or displaying a yard sign, donating money to a political party, a candidate, or another political organization. In the analysis we also compare the profiles of each of these types of participation with the profiles of those in the subset who report having voted.

3. Partisan leaners are coded as partisans. "Pure" Independents are omitted as the reference category.

4. Coded as black/nonblack.

5. The percentages reporting having voted are unusually high, in part because these estimates are inflated by survey respondents, but also because we are looking only at the percentage of voters among respondents who report that they engage in more active forms of participation (see note 2).

6. Note that the Center for Responsive Politics reports that "during the 2010 election cycle, female donors accounted for only about a quarter of all money raised by candidates, parties, and political action committees. The same is true so far during the 2012 election cycle." See Beckel (2011).

7. This is not very surprising, however, given the low rates of participation in some categories.

8. The assumption in this folded measure is that extremists are likely to behave similarly regardless of whether one is an extreme liberal or an extreme conservative. Alternative analyses that do not use the folded measure, and thus do not make this assumption, yield similar results.

9. The online appendix provides further details on the factor analysis.

10. When we used a separate model for liberal extremism than for conservative extremism, rather than using a single model for both types of extremism, we found similar results for the coefficients of interest.

11. Using voting in the primary as the sole indicator of nomination activity has limits. Casting a primary vote carries only limited power over nominations. A better test would be to identify respondents who were involved in the actual recruitment of candidates (see Cohen et al. 2008). But such data are very difficult to obtain. The respondent's report of casting or failing to cast a primary vote does at least provide us with a broad measure of participation in candidate selection.

12. Note that the CCES asks respondents to identify themselves on a 5-point, rather than 7-point ideological scale. The "somewhat liberal/conservative" option is omitted. The substantive conclusions are the same.

13. Moving from the minimum to maximum value of the independent variable, while holding all other variables at their mean.

14. We are grateful to Bruce Oppenheimer for suggesting this point.

5

Local Party Viability, Goals, and Objectives in the Information Age

DANIEL M. SHEA
Allegheny College

J. CHERIE STRACHAN
Central Michigan University

MICHAEL WOLF
Indiana University–Purdue University Fort Wayne

Building on a sea change that began in the 1960s, the means of political engagement have continued to evolve at a rapid pace over the past decade. New methods of mobilization were wielded by inventive, ambitious candidates—as deftly illustrated by President Barack Obama's efforts to reach young voters via his "net-roots" campaign—but also by a myriad of new organizations flush with cash in the wake of eroding campaign finance regulations (Shea 2010; Johnson 2011; Thurber and Nelson 2010). The ability to narrowcast carefully targeted voter messages, once a resource-, labor-, and time-intensive endeavor, has come to fruition with the ease of new technologies. Now, voters are just (if not more) apt to receive a text message, e-mail or tweet directly from a candidate or an advocacy group than they are to answer a knock on the door or receive a phone call from a party activist. As candidate-centered—or as Shea

(1996) has termed them, consultant-driven—campaigns take even deeper root in the American electoral process, and the array of well-heeled advocacy groups attempting to influence electoral outcomes continues to multiply, one might question what, if any, distinct functions are left for local party organizations in a process that they once dominated. Local parties, at the front lines of voter mobilization for nearly two centuries, once again face a dramatically shifting context that appears to further challenge their political relevance.

Yet political parties have proved their resilience in the past, responding to the first wave of candidate-centered campaigns by reinvigorating their organizational infrastructure both up and down the federalism ladder (Bibby 1990). Avoiding dire predictions of waning influence, national, state, and even local party committees transformed themselves into "service parties," capable of delivering professional services and truckloads of cash to their primary-anointed nominees (Herrnson 1990, among many others). Since Cotter et al.'s (1984) nationwide assessment of state and local committees, studies have continued to document the transformation, adaptability and viability of local party organizations (Freindreis et al. 1994; Steed et al. 1998; Freindreis and Gitelson 1999; Crowder-Meyer 2011).

This chapter, based on a summer 2011 survey of 481 local party leaders, contributes to this literature by exploring whether local party committees in the United States have continued to respond to the challenges of the twenty-first century with similar vitality, or whether predictions of atrophy first aired in the 1980s simply took longer than anticipated to materialize. Did the initial emergence of service parties represent a last-ditch, but inevitably futile, effort to remain relevant? Findings from our survey indicate that the opposite is true. Across the board, local party organizations have not only maintained the institutional resources they fought to establish three decades ago but have kept abreast of new communication technology and fund-raising strategies—further cementing the role of resource provider in a candidate-centered political process.

Perhaps a more engaging question, above and beyond this descriptive account, is what impact this transformation has had on core party functions that led party scholars to equate political parties with stable democracy. Has the drive to remain electorally relevant led local party chairs to become even more "rational," focused on winning elections at all cost? Have they jettisoned the functions of a "responsible" party that earned parties such revered status among democratic theorists? And if so, at what cost to American democracy?

Schlesinger (1985) believed that the parties' new organizational strength would finally produce the ideological and policy uniformity of responsible parties, thus making it easier for voters to hold elected officials accountable. Yet, critics of service parties questioned whether organizational prowess alone was evidence of vitality. Shea (1999) and Coleman (1994), among others, claimed that the parties' rational emphasis on helping candidates over mobilizing voters would undermine the classic democratic functions of linking citizens to leaders and aggregating the voices of the people—activities that had historically differentiated political parties from narrow special interests.

Blurring the distinctions between rational and responsible parties, our findings support the accuracy of both these scholars' predictions. No longer Tweedle Dee and Tweedle Dum, today's local party organizations offer the electorate distinct, coherent choices, but also often fail to effectively engage new groups of voters, including young adults and new immigrants, or to build a broad base among the electorate.

These findings lead us to conclude that the stark differences drawn between rational and responsible parties reflect the unique historical circumstances of 1950s America, as well as the distinct scholarly traditions informing each model. In short, these ideal types are largely theoretical models, not an empirically grounded typology. As White and Shea (2004) have argued, the foremost problem with using the election/policy dimension to define the essence of parties is that these typologies are static and cannot account for the diversity of party structures and functions in the United States. The activities, structure, and goals of local parties continually evolve as new conditions arise. A close reading of American history suggests that local party goals and activities change based on a host of contextual factors (White and Shea 2004; Shea and Harris 2006a, 2006b). Rather than strain the models by trying to determine whether today's parties more closely resemble a rational or a responsible party, we propose using these insights from classic political science literature to identify the party functions that are normatively most desirable in a democratic system, followed by an empirical assessment of when these functions are apt to be performed by rational political actors. While national politics can paint these trends in broad strokes, the diversity of circumstances and structures at the local party level offers the potential for more detailed, nuanced insights.

Normative Ideals of Party Functions

Inheriting their political philosophy from earlier thinkers, nineteenth century scholars were hostile toward the parties and paid them little attention (Epstein 1986, 13). Even if they acknowledged that parties inevitably emerged in democratic systems, writers in this period were more likely to highlight the shortcomings of party activities than to note any potential benefit (see, for example, Bryce 1919). Scholarly advocates did not emerge until the turn of the century, precisely when government officials were moving to curb the excessiveness of party machines. Echoing the claims of many party leaders at the time, academics began to recognize political parties as instruments of genuine popular sovereignty. This shift in thinking reflected contemporary concerns, as burgeoning urban centers made town-meeting-style democracy impractical, and the growing plight of inner-city residents highlighted the need for effective intermediaries. Michels ([1911] 1962), often cited as attacking political parties, more accurately implies that given the "iron law of oligarchy," political parties are the best option available in a democracy.

Explicit party advocacy, however, did not reach its full form by the 1940s, with Herring (1940), Schattschneider (1942), and Key (1947) leading the way. The celebration of American-style democracy following World War II led scholars to search for the true underpinnings of our democratic system; parties were identified as the key ingredient—a view that gained further legitimacy with the report of the Committee on Political Parties of the American Political Science Association in 1950.

Not long after parties gained full acceptance in academia, two strains of thought emerged regarding core party functions and how those activities complement democracy. These two approaches, the rational party model and the responsible party model, are often described as ideal types, reflecting opposite ends of a continuum of all the potential ways to organize and prioritize party activities. As suggested above, however, the models are not mutually exclusive, as parties often simultaneously engage in rational and responsible behavior. Perhaps this overlap occurs because the two models emerged separately, from distinct scholarly traditions with different normative underpinnings and agendas.

Reflecting this country's Madisonian tradition, those holding a pluralist, procedural view of democracy thought parties were comparable to interest groups—one of a variety of competing organizations that people might use to pursue their political interests (Schattschneider 1942; Downs 1957; Wilson 1962; Epstein 1967, among many others). These scholars applied an economic or market analogy to political parties, emphasizing a competitive struggle with party leaders as profit-maximizing entrepreneurs. Their singular goal is the capture of political office for material gain. Labeled as the "minimalists," "rational-choice," "economic," or "rational-efficient" model, this approach acknowledges that parties can provide both systemic and individual level benefits—but that these are merely the by-product of concerted office-seeking activity.

The inherent, although perhaps not explicit, version of democracy underpinning this approach is that those with intense political interests will successfully find their way into various intermediary organizations, and that public policy will emerge as disparate groups blunt one another's agendas— a process that simultaneously provides access to the system and promotes stability by softening excessive public demands. The need to mobilize the electorate and to garner broad public support is downplayed. Even though majoritarian politics might make government more efficient and accountable, it would also empower "the masses." In the philosophical underpinnings of the rational-efficient party model, fear of a tyrannical majority trumps concern for majoritarianism.

The scholars who articulated this approach were largely satisfied with the performance of American democracy. Their goal was not prescription, but prediction. By framing political parties as rational actors, motivated to win office in order to achieve material gain, rational party scholars hoped to gain the ability to understand and anticipate partisan political choices. Of course the outcomes of rational acts lead to a more stable system, as Madison so skillfully tells us in *Federalist* No. 10.

The second, and in many ways diametric, view of parties reflects America's Jeffersonian influence. Unlike Madison, Jefferson feared that the system of government devised in our Constitution placed too many stumbling blocks in the path of average citizens who would struggle to make a distant and unresponsive government heed their concerns. Such obstacles also have the potential to destabilize democracy, as those who feel ignored lose faith in their government and may even engage in increasingly aggressive protest politics to vent their frustration. Advocates of the responsible party approach, also labeled the "normative" or "party-democracy" model, saw political parties as the solution to this dilemma. They believed that political parties should not only attempt to win elections but facilitate citizens' political participation by mobilizing voters—especially new groups of voters such as young people and new immigrants. Further, political parties should aggregate their supporters' interests, and clearly articulate their resulting demands. Clear policy positions would not only make it easier to cast an informed ballot but also to hold elected officials accountable. The ends, in this model, are the implementation of clearly defined policies; winning elections serves only as a means to this end (Schattschneider 1942; Duverger 1954; Neumann 1956, among many others).

Unlike rational party scholars, advocates of the responsible party model were unhappy with American democracy, which they believed focused on the agendas of narrow special interests at the expense of a broader common good. Hence their agenda was largely normative and prescriptive rather than predictive.

Beyond core motivations, the two models suggest a number of important differences relating to structure, organization, and activities—as outlined in Table 5.1. Keep in mind, however, that the characteristics associated with the rational-efficient party model are based on the assumptions of a single-minded party leader's preferences, in the context of the American political system circa 1950. Similarly, the criteria associated with the responsible party-democracy model were those that scholars deemed essential to enact their preferred version of democratic governance in the same era.

A few points are worth brief mention. The organizational structure of rational-efficient parties consists of a cadre of political entrepreneurs. Party organizations are centralized, with no formal party membership. The organizational style is professional where workers, leaders, and candidates are often recruited from outside the organization or are self-recruited. Efficiency is stressed above all else. There is little, if any, organizational continuity after the election.

Responsible (party-democratic) parties, on the other hand, maintain a highly integrated structure. Formal membership is critical and grassroots committees play an important role in recruiting new members. Volunteers rise through the ranks as loyal, hardworking activists. Candidates who receive support from the party organization are recruited from within its ranks to ensure policy and ideological purity.

TABLE 5.1 **Contrasting Attributes of Rational-Efficient and Party-Democracy Models of Party**

	Rational-Efficient	*Party-Democracy*
View of democracy:	Pluralist view Conflict avoided	Party goal definers Conflict part of change
Functions:	Election activities	Linkage Aggregation Articulation Participation Community service
Objectives:	Win elections/ Control office Efficiency	Policy Ideological unity
Structure:	Cadre/Professional Granted autonomy	Mass membership Amateur
Role in government:	None: Members granted autonomy	Interdependence between member and party organization
View of intraparty democracy:	Hinders efficiency	Essential
Incentives for participation:	Material	Mix of purposive, social, and material

Note: Adapted from Shea 1995, 61.

In the responsible party model, a candidate's ability to win is subordinate to ideological and policy considerations. The models are at odds regarding their role in government, as we might expect. In the rational-efficient model, elected officials are allowed to do as they wish once elected, as long as their activities help win the next election. In fact, we might expect rational-efficient party leaders to promote compromise solutions, as they might attract middle-of-the-road voters in the next election. Such pragmatism is not the case with the responsible party model. Here, with a high degree of interdependence between the party and elected officials, voters must make judgments as to what the party stands for. Elected officials are expected to vote according to the party agenda, developed after a robust, intrademocratic process. Little dissention from the platform is tolerated and compromise would be rejected.

Given their alternative orientations, it should not be surprising that scholars from each perspective waged a sustained, often aggressive, debate over which side was more accurate. Indeed, party scholars usually operate within the assumptions of one model or the other—whether they are explicit about their underlying orientation or not. For some time, scholars debated whether American political parties were becoming more rational or more responsible, often turning to party unity scores in Congress and state legislatures to bolster their case. Historically, for example, American parties have seemed quite rational, tolerating ideological diversity and rarely producing party-line votes. In recent years, however, party unity scores have jumped, leading some to suggest important changes are underway (Pomper 2003). Yet scholars still cannot agree on which model is a better fit for American political parties, and after fifty years, the intensity of this debate has faded.

Yet in combination, these models provide a powerful approach for assessing the vitality of political parties. The argument that party leaders will approach campaigns with an eye toward rationality is persuasive, because even those whose motivations extend beyond material gain cannot enact policies without first winning elections. Yet many political observers, including the three coauthors of this chapter, believe that American democracy functions best when parties fulfill the normative functions identified in the responsible party model. Under the right circumstances, the two goals of rationality and responsibility are not mutually exclusive. Politicians' choices can be structured in such a way that the by-products of their rational choices enhance democratic outcomes. Taking note of the impact of varying circumstances enables political scientists and political leaders to engage in an ongoing American tradition of statecraft—that is, purposefully shaping institutions and laws so that playing the game of politics will inevitably produce democratic outcomes, regardless of the players' intentions. This idea, dubbed "new institutionalism" by scholars, suggests that desired outcomes can be shaped by particular structures.

Rational Actions and Responsible Outcomes

Even a cursory review of party history in the United States reveals that rationality can reinforce responsibility, albeit in unanticipated ways. The very invention of the modern party structure, for example, reflected pragmatic politicians' responses to the collective action dilemma of an expanding American electorate (Aldrich 1995). As communication was primarily restricted to face-to-face interactions, politicians also focused on campaign messages with broad appeal, and they staffed their state and local committees with party workers to canvass constituents (McGerr 1986). These efforts to mobilize wide swathes of the electorate were not undertaken as an altruistic endeavor to enhance democracy. Quite simply, shrewd politicians (like Martin Van Buren and Mark Hanna who devised and funded early modern party organizations) undertook these actions because they knew their candidates would be more likely to win elections (Schier 2000).

The normative by-products of such ambitions, nevertheless, were numerous, including high electoral turnout and the mobilization of even the least likely voters, such as new immigrants, the lower classes, and the less educated (Kleppner 1982). Because they needed to gain widespread support and could not send tailored messages to different groups within their coalitions, the parties and their candidates were forced to focus on highly salient issues that affected many people (Shefter 1994). Even though the party system in this era was far from perfect, riddled with corruption and graft, it fulfilled a number of normative, or responsible, party functions. Most notable of these were the linkage and aggregation functions, as average citizens were sought out, pulled into the political process, and their shared concerns amplified. Imagine the potential challenges to government stability if the concerns of large waves of incoming immigrants had not been channeled into legitimate intermediary organizations with the ability to influence legislative agendas. The melting pot may well have boiled over!

Given the size and diversity of their coalitions, as well as the incentive structure of a two-party system, party leaders' stands on less-salient issues often overlapped, especially in more mundane political times in between critical, realigning elections. These tendencies, which make perfect sense to rational partisan activists, undermined the normative goal of distinct and well-publicized party agendas—making it more difficult for voters to hold elected officials accountable for their decisions after gaining office. The cumbersome coalition of conservative, southern Democrats and progressive, northeastern Democrats in the 1950s and 1960s would be a clear example.

Skipping ahead to more recent history, the latter half of the twentieth century saw changes in the political landscape that discouraged rational politicians from performing any of these normative functions. Public attitudes about political parties had grown especially sour in the wake of the turbulent 1960s. The number of Americans willing to claim affiliation with either party took a nosedive and it seemed that we were headed toward a partyless age. Broder's *The Party's Over* (1971) seemed to capture the mood of the times.

On top of—and perhaps partly fueling—this change, many candidates came to realize that parties were no longer necessary or even desirable. Historically, party workers were needed to bring the candidate's message to the voter, but by the 1960s television, radio, and direct mail could reach more voters in one single day than party operatives could contact in weeks. Party assistance also came with a price tag: dictates from the party boss and the perception that the candidate was a pawn of the party leaders. Mass communication technology, combined with campaign finance reform and the shift to primary elections, encouraged candidates to "run their own show" and to be seen as "independent minded." New-style campaign consultants burst on the presidential election scene in the 1960s, and were making inroads into even the most local level by the 1990s (Strachan 2003). While perhaps part of a broad network of affiliated party units (Herrnson 2009), campaign operatives could be hired and their allegiance would be solely to the candidate.

As candidates pitched themselves as independent, voters saw little reason to hold to any notion of partisanship. Party organizations lost even more sway and as more citizens became "independent," the parties' abilities to articulate distinct policy preferences diminished, voting cues were lost, and turnout in elections dropped. Once in office elected officials saw little reason to stick to the caucus, leading to less policy coherence and a less efficient legislative process. Moreover, because of these changes, divided government has become the norm since 1968 rather than the exception. This era saw a decline in responsible party functions, as clearly articulated and distinct party platforms no longer helped ambitious politicians win office. Hence the electorate's ability to make informed choices during elections and to hold public officials accountable was substantially diminished. This, of course, pushed voters to question the value of partisan labels, adding more fuel to the cycle.

Perhaps even more troubling, the same era discouraged political parties from expending resources to bring new voters into the political fold. Innovations in both communication technology and means of voter research continued to evolve, allowing candidates to move from broadcasting to narrowcasting their messages. Technology enabled them to reach smaller and smaller groups, and eventually individual voters, with messages carefully tailored to their specific concerns. Rather than attempting to pull the largest number of people possible into the electoral process and identify the political concerns they have in common—fulfilling the normative functions of linkage and aggregation—the most successful candidates now focus their campaign resources on selectively targeting *only* those citizens who are both likely to vote and likely to support their agendas. As noted by Schier, "Political parties . . . strive to prevail in elections and policy-making by motivating carefully targeted segments of the public to vote or press demands upon elected officials" (2000, 1).

Political party operatives quickly realized that these new technologies were making them irrelevant. Yet instead of sharpening their relationship with the voters, the parties chose to expand the very types of services that allowed candidates to ignore large portions of the electorate. National party operatives, at first mostly at the Republican National Committee, became service oriented, meaning that they chose to broaden activities to include a host of high-technology services to candidates. They developed, for example, computerized direct mail operations, in-house television and radio production studios, and sophisticated polling operations. This effort also meant hiring new professionals—their own new-style campaign consultants—and greatly expanding their facilities.

There have been significant ramifications of this change. For one, while parties seemed back on their feet, sophisticated services require ever more resources, and in an effort to get around campaign finance laws new loopholes were being discovered each year, leading to cynicism among voters. Notably, this money was spent to further refine the ability to engage in the selective mobilization of the electorate. This process, now labeled microtargeting, is entrenched, and the technology needed to profile and "activate" individual voters improves with every election (Johnson 2011; Thurber and Nelson 2010). At least until 2008, these tactics were primarily used to mobilize, "the educated, the wealthy and the powerful" and voting levels, especially among the lower classes, declined as a result (Rosenstone and Hansen 1993, 239–241.)

Specifically, the parties have spent little of their new largesse to draw new (and from a rational perspective, unreliable) voters into the political process. Despite the disproportionate size of the millennial generation, the first demographic group to challenge the sheer demographic weight of the baby boomers, most party chairs fail to see young voters as an important source of future support. Party organizations and candidates have done little to facilitate their participation (Shea and Green 2007).

Similarly, the parties' efforts to incorporate recent waves of immigrants from Asia and Latin America pale in comparison to efforts in America's past. After conducting an in-depth study of this issue, Wong (2006, 198) concludes:

> Immigrants arriving in America today encounter an institutional landscape that differs fundamentally from that encountered by European immigrants of the past. Political parties no longer have a strong presence at the neighborhood level, nor do they work hand in hand with community organizations to mobilize immigrants.

Wong worries that the sporadic efforts of other civil society organizations and community groups cannot counteract the lack of an "intense, consistent, and committed" local effort to guide new immigrants into the American political process (Wong 2006, 198). Tight races in 2000 and 2004 led candidates to take a risk and target both young people and new immigrants, especially Hispanics, in the 2008 election. But Wong warns that such efforts rely on the microtargeting tactics described above. They are symbolic and selective, not true mass mobilization endeavors. Thus, the parties' responses to a host of changes have reduced the responsible by-products of their choices.

On the other hand, throughout the exact same time frame, the parties have become more ideologically distinct—offering voters increasingly divergent choices at the polls. When service parties first emerged, elected officials were indeed loathe to advertise their partisanship to voters, who characterized themselves as increasingly independent. Elected officials within the parties, characterized by "Rockefeller Republicans" in the Northeast and conservative "Boll Weevil" Democrats in the South, were far from ideologically coherent. Since that time, however, a dramatic process of party sorting has occurred—with conservatives finding their way back to the Republican Party and liberals seeking out a more comfortable home with the Democrats. State and local elected officials were the final refuge of the old parties' control during this rolling realignment from Democratic to Republican control in the South and from Republican to Democratic control in the Northeast (see Black and Black 2002; Reiter and Stonecash 2011). Now moderates anywhere in either party likely face more ideological challengers in primary elections. To some observers, this purification of the two parties includes a geographic sorting, where people have shifted views or physically have moved to locations where their neighbors were likely to share not only their incomes, lifestyles, and values—but also their ideological and partisan orientations (Bishop 2008; Abramowitz 2010). The national party polarization process may create an ideological party atmosphere that could trickle down to local parties, especially if those localities are now apt to be neatly divided into partisan camps.

This sweeping account of party history suggests that parties respond to changing circumstances in order to maintain their leverage in the electoral process. Sometimes these changes produce responsible by-products for our democracy, but sometimes these healthy by-products are undermined. The sheer number and diverse circumstances facing the local party should add a more detailed layer to these insights. Hence this chapter focuses on the changing circumstances and behavior of local party organizations.

Study Design

This chapter relies on a survey conducted in the summer of 2011. A randomly selected list of 4,000 local party committees was compiled (roughly 2,000 from each party) and each was sent a survey via e-mail Survey Monkey in late June. After three prompts, some 481 party leaders returned the survey—yielding a margin of error of plus or minus 4.5 percent. Fifty-eight percent of the respondents were Democrats; 42 percent were Republicans. A vast majority of these party leaders had held their post for more than five years, and (95 percent) of respondents were party chairs. Some 42 percent of the Democratic respondents and 25 percent of the GOP respondents were women. The distribution of chair between urban, rural, and suburban counties closely matches national demographics.

For comparative purposes, we make reference to a similar data set collected by one of the authors (Shea) about a decade ago. Here a telephone survey of 805 local party leaders was conducted between October 1 and November 10, 2003. Each interview lasted roughly thirty minutes, and the questions dealt with a host of issues. Rather than a random sample from the entire population of counties, a list of the Democratic and Republican local party chairs in the 1,000 most populated counties in the United States was compiled. From this list of 2,000 potential respondents, 403 Democratic and 402 Republican local party chairs were randomly selected and interviewed. Findings from this survey were reported in Shea and Green (2007) and elsewhere.

Findings

Party Viability

Our first issue to assess is local party viability. That is, how are parties doing in light of campaign finance changes and the blossoming of the new media age? Are they adapting to these changes or struggling to keep up? Do they have sufficient staff and resources, and are they vibrant community-based organizations? Relatedly, how do local party leaders perceive the future of local party organizations in America?

We begin our analysis with perceptions of the role of local party committees in the twenty-first century. Respondents were first asked to select a term that "best fits" their party organization. The results of this query are found in Figure 5.1. The overwhelming perception by party leaders is that their party committees are doing better than in the past. That a robust 40 percent would indicate they are doing "much better" and, conversely, just 6 percent would suggest they are doing somewhat or much worse, clearly indicates wide optimism. They were then asked to use a ten-point scale to describe the condition of their party committee during the past decade. Figure 5.2 notes the results of this question. Here again, it would seem that party leaders are quite optimistic—especially Republican leaders. As for controls beyond party affiliation, little variation was found, with the notable exception of location. That is, party chairs located in rural areas are modestly less optimistic than are party chairs in urban and suburban areas.

A second area focuses on the specific resources available to party committees. For example, do they have a full slate of committee volunteers and do they boast a party headquarters? These sorts of indicators—specific measures of resources—lay at the heart of many studies of party viability. Table 5.2 explores several oft-used institutional measures drawn from prior work. Along with the 2011 data, the table relies on findings from the Shea and Green survey in 2003. It is interesting to note that the percentage of committees boasting a headquarters, either year-round or during campaign periods, declined rather significantly in the eight-year period. At the same time, the number of committees with a Website increased from 59 percent in 2003 to 76 percent in 2011.

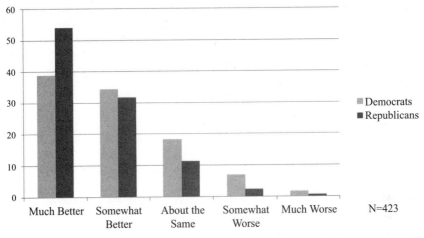

Thinking about the past decade, which of the following statements best describes the general condition of our local party committee?

FIGURE 5.1 Party Leaders' Evaluation of Local Party Committees' Condition: General

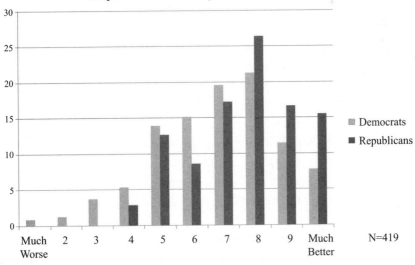

How would you describe the condition of your party committee compared to most other points in the last decade?

FIGURE 5.2 Party Leaders' Evaluation of Local Party Committees' Condition: Comparative

TABLE 5.2 Measures of Local Party Viability in 2003 and 2011

Does Your Party Maintain a Year-Round Headquarters?	
- yes in 2003	36 %
- yes in 2011	21 %
Does Your Party Have a HQ During Campaign Periods?	
- yes in 2003	62 %
- yes in 2011	41 %
Does Your Party Committee Have a Website?	
- yes in 2003	59 %
- yes in 2011	76 %
Does Your Committee Have a Full Time Staffer?	
- yes in 2003	7 %
- yes in 2011	7 %
Average Annual Budget	
- 2003	$34,000 ($.1 min, $220k max)
- 2011	82% < $20K , 90% < $50K

Note: N = 803 in 2003, N = 475 in 2011.

Local political parties allocate their time and energy among a variety of election activities, including voter registration drives, get-out-the-vote (GOTV) efforts, campaign events, campaign services, and noncampaign events. Table 5.3 notes the importance placed on different forms of activities, controlled by party. Here respondents were asked to use a ten-point scale, with 10 being very important. Clearly, chairs from both parties are focused on voter registration efforts, particularly GOTV initiatives. With the modest exception of voter registration drives, there is very little variance between parties. Surprisingly, noncampaign efforts were perceived to be somewhat more important than general campaign services. Perhaps this emphasis, along with willingness to engage in voter registration drives, is a responsible by-product of the tightness of recent elections and anticipation of a highly contested presidential race again in 2012.

Local Parties and New Technologies

Numerous instruments of communication aid local party committees' efforts to mobilize local voters or build party attachments. Viable parties blend all sorts of these, as well as mobilizing members to participate in party meetings,

TABLE 5.3 Percentage of Activities Considered Significant to
Local Party Committees

	Percentage Rating "7" or Higher on 10-Point Scale	
	Democrats	*Republicans*
Voter Registration Drives	60.2 %	51.1 %
GOTV Efforts	79.1 %	72.2 %
Fund-raising	73.8 %	78.8 %
Campaign Events	67.3 %	72.2 %
Campaign Services	45.6 %	50.8 %
Noncampaigning Efforts	55.4 %	60.7 %

Note: N = 481. Respondents were asked to use a scale of 1 to 10 to "rate the significance of the following activities to your party committee."

campaign events, and fund-raising. Table 5.4 provides a breakdown of the many means of communicating with voters as well as the typical attendance at different types of party meetings. Republicans have a slight edge with technology—particularly reaching more party members via Twitter and to some extent YouTube or LinkedIn, though some commented that they use "plain old e-mail" or other twentieth century mechanisms of communication like the phone or mail. Mostly party leaders heavily use mainstream contemporary technologies such as their Website, Facebook, or Twitter to connect with party followers.

Also of interest are the conditions that drive up face-to-face meetings with party members. There are differences between the parties here, too. Republicans get higher turnout at general meetings and fund-raisers, though, as one would expect given the nature of service parties, both parties' attendance at fund-raisers trumps the level of attendance at general meetings or campaign work projects despite this being a relatively conservative measure.[1] This finding fits with the parties' reported viability efforts reported in Table 5.3.

Goals and Functions

A series of questions were asked to measure the party leader's attitudes regarding his or her party committee's goals and objectives. While not referring specifically to the rational/responsible theoretical models, these questions nevertheless tap into what scholars traditionally view as key distinctions. For

TABLE 5.4 **Party Committee Outreach Communication Tools and Regular Event Attendance**

Website	
- Democrats	78 %
- Republicans	77 %
Facebook	
- Democrats	65 %
- Republicans	62 %
LinkedIn	
- Democrats	2 %
- Republicans	6 %
Twitter	
- Democrats	12 %
- Republicans	22 %
YouTube	
- Democrats	4 %
- Republicans	7 %
E-mail	
- Democrats	13 %
- Republicans	15 %
Mass e-mail program/other program/database	
- Democrats	5 %
- Republicans	1 %
Telephone/US Mail/Newsletter	
- Democrats	2 % for each tool
- Republicans	2 % for each tool
How many members regularly attend Regular Meetings	
- Democrats	31 (min = 0, max = 250)
- Republicans	41 (min = 0, max = 500)
How many members regularly attend Campaign Work Projects	
- Democrats	31 (min = 0, max = 350)
- Republicans	29 (min = 0, max = 175)
How many members regularly attend Fund-raisers	
- Democrats	94 (min = 0, max = 800)
- Republicans	131 (min = 0, max=1500)

Note: Democratic N = 267, Republican N = 193. E-mail, Mass e-mail program/other program/database, and Telephone/US Mail/Newsletter calculated by authors from open-ended response. In addition, one Republican mentioned using newspapers. One Democratic party leader connected via cable TV, another a weekly host radio show, and a third canvassing. Two Democratic leaders reported connecting with the rank-and-file through a blog or through the newspaper.

example, each respondent was asked whether it is more important to support candidates who have broad electoral appeal or those who support the party's official policy positions. That is, does the party leader place winning elections (rational) ahead of the promotion of a policy agenda (responsible). In 2003, some 38 percent of party leaders suggested "broad appeal," and 58 percent suggested supporting candidates with consistent policy positions as more important. Things tightened in the 2011 poll, with some 44 percent noted "broad appeal" and 42 percent noted "consistent policy position."

We asked if it was more important for the party committee to help candidates win elections or to help voters develop a long-term attachment to the party. In 2003, 61 percent thought helping their candidate win was more important, and 37 percent suggested connecting with voters more central. By 2011 this pattern had shifted, 53 percent suggested helping candidates was more important, and 35 percent connecting with voters.

We also asked a question that taps into perceptions of the proper conduct of party affairs: whether local party committees are best run by professional operatives or by rank-and-file party members. In 2003, 43 percent suggested the professional approach and 53 percent noted the amateur model. In 2011 it was 30 percent for the former, and 56 percent for the latter.

Table 5.5 notes partisan differences on these three questions. There is a rather dramatic increase in the number of Democratic chairs who believed their party should back candidates with broad appeal; a 28 percent increase from 2003 to 2011. Conversely, there was a big jump in the number of GOP chairs who believe their parties should back candidates with consistent policy positions. Some 62 percent held this position in 2003, but in 2011 it had jumped to 75 percent. One explanation for this shift might be the strategic position of each party. That is, in 2003 the Democrats seemed to be in the ascendance, winning elections and gaining favor with voters, so it might make sense that they would tout the virtues of their policy agenda. Conversely, given that the GOP was struggling during this period, it would make sense that they would presume a more election-centered approach. But of course the opposite seems to be true in recent years; the fortunes for Republican candidates in 2011 seemed bright, thus party leaders would feel better pushing their agenda.

We then introduced what we believe to be an important control. Chairs were asked to assess the partisan context of their county; whether voters

TABLE 5.5 Perceptions of Party Goals and Objectives, 2003 and 2011

	2003		2011		Change 2003–2011	
	Dem	Rep	Dem	Rep	Dem	Rep
Help candidates or	59 %	66 %	59 %	63 %	+ 0	3
Help voters	41 %	34 %	41 %	37 %	+ 0	+ 3
Broad appeals or	42 %	38 %	70 %	25 %	+ 28	– 13
Consistent policy positions	58 %	62 %	30 %	75 %	– 28	+ 13
Professional model or	42 %	47 %	35 %	32 %	– 7	– 15
Amateur model	57 %	52 %	65 %	68 %	+ 8	+ 15

Note: 2003 N = 806; 2011 N = 475.

tend to be strong partisans or mostly independent ("up for grabs"). An identical number of Democratic and Republican chairs (78 percent) reported, "Voters in our area tend to be strongly partisan and stick to party lines." But when we merge this finding with perceptions of party goals, a rather stark difference emerges. Of the Democrats who see voters in their area as mostly partisan (again, 78 percent), 69 percent believe that their committee should support candidates with broad appeal (rather than candidates with consistent policy positions). For Republicans, who see their electorate as highly partisan, just 22 percent wish to back candidates with broad appeal.

Willingness to Compromise

Questions on willingness to compromise suggest the broader party polarization in America has reached down to local party committees. Only 2.5 percent of the party leaders in our survey think that their local area has become less polarized than in the past, and only 1.5 percent think the United States is less polarized. In contrast, 83 percent of Democrats and 71 percent of Republicans believe the United States has become more polarized, and 72 percent of Democrats and 58 percent of Republicans think their local area has polarized. One hallmark of the responsible party model is the loyalty to one's own party and opposition toward the opposing party. As the previous section demonstrated, the vibrancy of partisan beliefs of a local area affect the two parties' leaders differently concerning the type of electoral appeals they believe should be made.

Party leaders have very different beliefs about what important political values are, and the tools of contemporary campaigns either fit, or perhaps

TABLE 5.6 What Party Organization Priorities Should Be by Nature of Voters in Area

What should be the priority of local party organization?

	Help candidates win elections	Help voters develop long-term attachments	N	Support candidates with broad electoral appeal	Support candidates with consistent issue positions	N
Voters tend to be strong partisans who stick to party line						
- Democrats	55 %	45 %	158	69 %	31 %	159
- Republicans	58 %	42 %	113	22 %	78 %	112
Voters are mostly independent and are up for grabs in each election						
- Democrats	66 %	34 %	80	74 %	26 %	77
- Republicans	73 %	27 %	55	31 %	69 %	54

drive, these beliefs into differing directions based on party. First, Republican Party leaders think it is much more important to have politicians who stand firm on principles than to be able to compromise (88 percent to 12 percent), whereas the opposite holds for Democratic committee leaders (78 percent to 22 percent). This is a stunning difference; rarely have scholars uncovered such a stark contrast between the views of local party leaders.

The culture of local campaign management stirs these distinctions even further, as illustrated in Table 5.7. Where campaign hired guns are the norm, Democratic party leaders are less apt to believe that politicians should compromise to get things done, while the influence of a professional consultant increases Republican party leaders' willingness to compromise, though the distinctions between the parties remain enormous. In turn, the volunteer-run campaign culture makes Republican local leaders want less compromise, while the opposite is true for Democrats.

Even more interesting is the subtle but noticeable shift in Democratic committee leaders' belief that compromise is important for politicians where campaigns are not ugly compared to where they are nasty—which is already very high. Republican leaders tend to favor principled stands from politicians where the campaigns are more civil while preferring slightly more compromise (if 15 percent of party leaders can be considered even slight) where campaigns are hard hitting.

Clearly these patterns show that professionalized campaigns at the local level—while still less frequent than the volunteer model—are not being adopted as a result of party leaders who are willing to sell out in preference for ideologically bland candidates. The two parties have dissimilar values; the adoption of one campaign style over another does not diminish these differences and may actually exacerbate them.

As noted above, one of the measures that might be used to define important differences between party leader goals and objectives is a willingness to find compromise solutions. In brief, responsible party leaders might be less willing to "cut deals" than might rational operatives.

Attracting New Voters

An important aspect of local party work centers on the role that these organizations play in drawing new voters into the political process and into the party rubric. From a rational vantage, new recruits are sought in order to secure an electoral advantage, and from the responsible model, they are essential for main-

TABLE 5.7 Influence of Nature of Campaigns in Party Committee's Area and Campaign Professionalization on Party Leaders' Views of Compromise

	Which is more important in a politician?		
	Ability to compromise to get things done	*Willingness to stand firm in support of principles*	*N*
Campaigns Hire Consultants to Run Campaigns			
- Democrats	82 %	18 %	61
- Republicans	32 %	68 %	25
Campaigns Usually Run by Volunteers			
- Democrats	91 %	9 %	172
- Republicans	20 %	80 %	140
Campaigns often hard-hitting, negative, and ugly			
- Democrats	85 %	15 %	117
- Republicans	26 %	74 %	47
Campaigns stay upbeat, positive, rarely ugly			
- Democrats	92 %	8 %	115
- Republicans	20 %	80 %	116

taining intraparty democracy. As noted in the 1950 APSA report, "Widespread political participation thus foster responsibility as well as democratic control in the conduct of party affairs and the pursuit of party policies" (1950, 65).

The issue of youth disengagement from politics has been widely discussed (Wattenberg 2012). Perhaps, as noted by Shea and Green, "There has been a decline in the scope, size, and effectiveness of mobilizing institutions" (2007, 24). Campaigns are now run by candidate organizations that use modern technology to reach voters directly. If these campaigns are aided by "rational" political parties—units designed to provide services to candidates—the net result may be the absence of broad-based institutions concerned with young voter mobilization. It is costly to mobilize nonvoters, especially juxtaposed with persuading existing uncommitted voters. Simply stated, following the logic discussed in the previous section, we would expect responsible parties to be more interested in youth engagement activities than would rational parties.

We asked the party leaders if they had developed programs specifically designed to attract voters between the ages of eighteen and twenty-five. A nearly identical number of Democratic (58 percent) and Republican (59 percent) respondents answered that they had. We then introduced a key measure of party outlook/goals (whether it is more important to back candidates with broad appeal or to back with consistent policy positions), and a similar picture emerges, as noted in Table 5.8. We also explored any difference regarding perceptions of how successful these programs have been, noted in Table 5.9, but here again there seems to be little difference between parties or between parties with different core goals/objectives. Simply stated, it would seem that when it comes to attracting new voters, a local committee's overall goals seem to have little bearing.

TABLE 5.8 Party Priorities: Programs to Attract Young Voters

| | Party developed specific programs to attract young voters 18–25? | | |
What should be priority of local party organization?	Yes	No	N
Support candidates with broad electoral appeal			
Democrats	54 %	46 %	164
Republicans	67 %	33 %	42
Support candidates with consistent issue positions			
Democrats	63 %	37 %	71
Republicans	55 %	45 %	124

TABLE 5.9 View of Party Role by Success of Young Programs

| | How successful have the programs directed at young people been in your area? | | | |
What should be priority of local party organization?	Very Successful	Somewhat Successful	Not at All Successful	N
Support candidates with broad electoral appeal				
Democrats	9 %	70 %	21 %	91
Republicans	0 %	86 %	14 %	18
Support candidates with consistent issue positions				
Democrats	16 %	71 %	13 %	45
Republicans	13 %	72 %	15 %	68

Discussion

The good news here, for those who believe the vitality of local party organizations is important, is that the parties continue to keep pace with dramatic changes in the electoral landscape. Their role as service providers has not been superseded, and they continue to provide valuable campaign services to their nominees. Yet determining precisely what these changes mean for the health of American democracy is a more difficult task.

At first glance, the claim that the parties are still relevant is bolstered by the fact that political parties have resumed at least some of the important functions outlined by responsible party scholars in the 1950s. Many local party chairs prefer candidates to stake out distinct claims during elections and to hold firm to these convictions once in office. Our data show a very strong disinclination by many party leaders, particularly GOP chairs, to support candidates who favor compromise solutions. We might consider this shift a principled stance, a clear responsible move. Voters in these districts cannot complain that the two major parties are indistinguishable, and these same voters can readily hold the parties accountable if they fail to perform as promised.

On the other hand, responsibility may be an inadequate explanation of local party conditions. Granted, our measures of viability and technology tell one story of local Democratic and Republican parties pursuing similar ends, but we cannot make any similar general statement about local party *goals* because the two parties' goals differ diametrically. Democratic local committee leaders want politicians to compromise while Republicans want politicians to stand firm on principle. Democratic Party leaders' preferences have shifted dramatically toward wanting candidates who make broad appeals, while Republican leaders' preferences have shifted in exactly the opposite direction, all in the span of eight years and almost without regard to how partisan the local electorate is. So as party scholars have debated whether local parties are becoming more rational or responsible, we have missed the dynamics of local Republican Party and Democratic Party goals shifting right under our noses.

Further, it is unlikely that these distinctions sprouted organically from the local parties, but likely result from grafting stark national party divisions onto local party politics. We cannot conclude how much polarization has resulted from the bottom up or is the result of national partisan polarization creeping down, but the former would be much more responsible and democratically healthy. Clarity on cultural issues of national importance, for example, may not help voters distinguish candidates' positions on property taxes, economic development, or infrastructure spending.

In other words, this intriguing finding of Republican leaders preferring candidates with consistent policy positions and eschewing compromise with the other side may look like responsibility, but ideological extremity alone does not sufficiently approximate responsibility. What if a majority of voters, perhaps a majority in each party, favors middle-of-the-road solutions? We believe it entirely likely that the rejection of compromise reflects a desire to build support from a particular wing of each party, not an assessment of the will of the rank and file. When politics is guided by the acts and motivations of the "political class," the entire nature of representation is distorted (Fiorina 2009). Clearly, the notion of "responsible" party behavior is also twisted.

Consequently, we hesitate to claim that these are the types of choices envisioned by the original advocates of the responsible party model—because the things that both Democratic and Republican local party leaders are still quite focused on is providing professional campaign services. These services do not include the linkage and aggregation functions at the normative core of this approach. Recall that the Jeffersonian underpinnings of this model, unlike pluralism, stress the importance of empowering average citizens. Party coherence should not be celebrated if it comes at the expense of important segments of the electorate from the two major parties' coalitions. Achieving party coherence through a process of selective mobilization might make the party platforms easier to summarize. It does not, we would argue, make the parties truly responsible.

As Schlesinger (1985) predicted years ago, party organizations' institutional support has played a role in facilitating the development of today's narrow, but coherent party agendas. Yet when local parties facilitate microtargeting and selective mobilization, they help to prevent the disruption of existing coalitions by avoiding the mobilization of new voters. Historically, parties have always been reluctant to disrupt their winning coalitions. Eras that precede realigning elections, for example, are often characterized by the parties' efforts to straddle a new critical issue with the potential to fracture their base (Sundquist 1973). Yet new means of voter targeting exacerbate this tendency, allowing parties to pay exclusive attention to old issues that their supporters care about, while avoiding a principled stand on new issues of concern to the broader electorate. Imagine, for example, how different the agendas of the two major parties might look if they reflected the policy concerns of young people and new immigrants. "In a healthy democracy, the parties bear responsibility for providing representation in government for all people . . . rather than for only society's most advantaged groups" (Wong 2006, 199). From this perspective, local party performance disappoints.

On a more positive note, we doubt that mobilization of this scale could be successfully undertaken by any organization save the local party committees; sustaining their viability is important for this reason alone. Further, given the shifting political tides over the past several decades, it is possible that local party leaders could decide to turn their institutional resources and financial largesse toward this task. We have found that local parties fit the "parties-in-service" model described by John Aldrich (1995). Their activities are aimed at the here and now, winning particular elections and helping specific candidates. Yet under the right circumstances, such as the need to substantially increase the size of the party's base to win office, broader mobilization efforts could be seen as an effective way to help specific candidates. For example, mobilization becomes essential when the size of one's base is no longer adequate.

Hence this chapter is a preliminary step in understanding not only *what* local parties do, but *why* they do it. The data provided here is largely descriptive, but still provides hints at the mix of circumstances that encourage parties to undertake activities with responsible by-products. Moreover, the local variation described above, combined with the sheer number of local party organizations, offer the opportunity to systematically tease out these important influences. This knowledge could be used to identify local parties engaged in best practices, and in-depth case studies of these could, in turn, help us more to precisely understand *how* these normative benefits for democracy are produced. Hence our future research agenda has both scholarly and normative ends, as we hope to develop empirically grounded insights into how best to restore local parties' performance of the linkage function at the heart of the responsible party model.

References

Abramowitz, Alan. 2010. *The Disappearing Center: Engaged Citizens, Polarization, and American Democracy.* New Haven, CT: Yale University Press.

Aldrich, J. 1995. *Why Parties? The Origin and Transformation of Political Parties in America.* Chicago, IL: University of Chicago Press.

American Political Science Association. 1950. Committee on Political Parties. "Toward a More Responsible Two-Party System." *American Political Science Review* 44: Supplement.

Bibby, John F. 1990. Party organization at the state level. In *The Parties Respond*, edited by L. Sandy Maisel, 21–40. Boulder, CO: Westview.

Bishop, Bill. 2008. *The Big Sort: Why the Clustering of Like-Minded Americans Is Tearing Us Apart*. Boston, MA: Houghton-Mifflin.

Black, Earl, and Merle Black. 2002. *The Rise of the Southern Republicans*. Cambridge, MA: Belknap Press.

Broder, David. 1971. *The Party's Over: The Failure of Politics in America*. New York: Harper and Row.

Bryce, J. 1919. *The American Commonwealth*. New York: The MacMillan Company.

Coleman, John J. (1994). "The Resurgence of Party Organization? A Dissent from the New Orthodoxy." In *The State of the Parties: The Changing Role of Contemporary American Parties*, edited by Daniel M. Shea and John C. Green. Lanham, MD: Rowman and Littlefield.

Cotter, Cornelius P., James L. Gibson, John F. Bibby, and Robert J. Huckshorn. 1984. *Party Organizations in American Politics*. New York: Praeger Publishers.

Crowder-Meyer, Melanie. 2011. "The Party's Still Going: Local Party Strength and Activity in 2008." In *The State of the Parties: The Changing Role of Contemporary American Parties*, edited by John C. Green and Daniel J. Coffee. 6th ed. Lanham, MD: Rowman and Littlefield.

Downs, Anthony. 1957. *An Economic Theory of Democracy*. New York: Harper and Row.

Duverger, Maurice. 1954. *Political Parties*. New York: Wiley.

Epstein, Leon D. 1980. "Whatever Happened to the British Party Model?" *American Political Science Review* 54: 406–27.

_____. 1986. *Political Parties in the American Mold*. Madison, WI: University of Wisconsin Press.

_____. 1967. *Political Parties in Western Democracies*. New York: Praeger.

Fiorina, M. 2009. *Disconnect: The Breakdown of Representation in American Politics*. Norman, OK: University of Oklahoma Press.

Freindreis, John, and Alan R. Gitelson. 1999. "Local Parties in the 1990s: Spokes in the Candidate-Centered Wheel." In *The State of the Parties,* edited by John C. Green and Daniel M. Shea. 3rd ed. Lanham, MD: Rowman and Littlefield.

Freindreis, John, Allan Gitelson, Gregory Flemming, and Anne Layzell. 1994. "Local Political Parties and Legislative Races in 1992." In *The State of the Parties,* edited by Daniel M. Shea and John C. Green. Lanham, MD: Rowman and Littlefield.

Herring, E. Pendleton. 1940. *The Politics of Democracy: American Parties in Action*. New York: Norton.

Herrnson, Paul. 1990. "Reemergent National Party Organizations." In *The Parties Respond: Changes in the American Party System,* edited by L. Sandy Maisel, 41–66. Boulder, CO: Westview Press.

_____. 2009. "The Roles of Party Organizations, Party-Connected Committees, and Party Allies in Elections." *Journal of Politics* 71: 1207–1224.

Johnson, Jason. 2011. *Political Consultants and Campaigns: One Day to Sell*. Boulder, CO: Westview.

Key, V. O., Jr. 1947. *Politics, Parties, and Pressure Groups*. New York: Thomas Y. Crowell Company.

Kleppner, P. 1982. *Who Voted? The Dynamics of Electoral Turnout, 1870–1980*. New York: Praeger.

McGerr, M. E. 1986. *The Decline of Popular Politics: The American North 1865–1928.* New York: Oxford University Press.

Michels, Robert. 1962 [1911]. *Political Parties: A Sociological Study of the Oligarchical Tendencies of Modern Democracy.* New York: Collier Books.

Neumann, Sigmund. 1956. "Toward a Comparative Study of Political Parties." In *Modern Political Parties,* edited by Sigmund Newmann. Chicago, IL: University of Chicago Press.

Pomper, Gerald M. 2003. "Parliamentary Government in the United States: A New Regime for a New Century?" In *The State of the Parties: The Changing Role of Contemporary American Parties,* edited by John C. Green and Rick Farmer. 6th ed. Lanham, MD: Rowman and Littlefield.

Reiter, Howard L., and Jeffrey M. Stonecash. 2011. *Counter Realignment: Political Change in the Northeastern United States.* New York: Cambridge University Press.

Rosenstone, S. J., and J. M. Hansen. 1993. *Mobilization, Participation and Democracy in America.* New York: Macmillan.

Schattschneider, E. E. 1942. *Party Government.* New York: Rinehart.

Schier, S. 2000. *By Invitation Only: The Rise of Excusive Politics in the United States.* Pittsburgh, PA: University of Pittsburgh Press.

Schlesinger, Joseph A. 1985. "The New American Political Party." *American Political Science Review* 79: 1152–1169.

Shea, Daniel M. 1995. *Transforming Democracy: State Legislative Campaign Committees and Political Parties.* Albany, NY: State University of New York Press.

_____. 1999. "The Passing of Critical Realignment and the Advent of the "Base-Less" Party System." *American Politics Quarterly* 27, 1: 33–57. A special edition on the changes in the American party system.

_____. 1996. *Campaign Craft: The Strategies Tactics and Art of Political Campaign Management.* 1996. New York: Praeger.

_____. 2010. "The Obama Net-Roots Campaign, Young Voters and the Future of Local Party Organizations." In *The State of the Parties,* edited by John C. Green and Daniel J. Coffee. 6th ed. Lanham, MD: Rowman and Littlefield.

Shea, Daniel M., and John C. Green. 2007. *The Fountain of Youth: Strategies and Tactics for Mobilizing America's Young Americans.* Lanham, MD: Rowman and Littlefield.

Shea, Daniel M., and Rebecca Harris. 2006a. "Gender and Local Party Leadership in America." *Journal of Women, Politics and Policy* 28: 61–85.

_____. 2006b. "Rural Party Politics in America." In *Government in the Countryside: Politics and Policies in Rural America,* edited by Gary Aguiar. Dubuque, IA: Kendell/Hunt.

Shefter, M. 1994. *Political Parties and the State: The American Historical Experience.* Princeton, NJ: Princeton University Press

Steed, Robert, John Clark, Lewis Bowman, and Charles Hadley, eds. 1998. *Party Organizations and Activism in the American South.* Tuscaloosa, AL: University of Alabama Press.

Strachan, J. Cherie. 2003. *High-Tech Grassroots: The Professionalization of Local Elections.* Boulder, CO: Rowman and Littlefield.

Sundquist, James L. 1973. *Dynamics of the Party System.* Washington, DC: Brookings Institution.

Thurber, J. A., and C. J. Nelson. 2010. *Campaigns and Elections American Style.* 3rd ed. Boulder, CO: Westview.

Wattenberg, Martin P. 2012. *Is Voting for Young People?* Upper Saddle River, NJ: Pearson.

White, John K., and Daniel M. Shea. 2004. *New Party Politics: From Hamilton and Jefferson to the Information Age.* 2nd ed. New York: Bedford/St. Martin's Press.

Wilson, James Q. 1962. *The Amateur Democrat: Club Politics in Three Cities—New York, Chicago, Los Angeles.* Chicago, IL: University of Chicago Press.

Wong, Janelle S. 2006. *Democracy's Promise, Immigrants and American Civic Institutions.* Ann Arbor, MI: University of Michigan Press.

Endnotes

1. Some party leaders provided two different numbers when explaining the number of people attending. For example, sometimes a "big name" would bring in more people for a fund-raiser. To rectify this, we put the number as the midpoint between the two numbers provided. While not ideal and data are lost, it is at least a very conservative way to produce measurable numbers.

6

National Parties in the Twenty-First Century

PAUL S. HERRNSON
University of Maryland

Once characterized as poor, unstable, and powerless, national parties in the United States have adapted to the candidate-centered, money-driven, "high-tech" style of contemporary campaign politics. Party organizations—the Democratic and Republican national, congressional, and senatorial campaign committees—entered the twenty-first century as financially secure, institutionally stable, and highly influential in national politics. In this chapter, I examine the national parties' development and their evolving relations with state and local party committees, interest groups, political consultants, and others who participate in contemporary elections. One of the major themes I develop is that, because the national parties are centrally located in networks of organizations and individuals that participate in politics, they can be best understood as enduring multilayered coalitions.

Party Formation and Development

American political parties are principally electoral institutions. They were created to help meet the needs of candidates for public office (Aldrich 1995), and they continue to focus more on elections and less on initiating policy change than do parties in other western democracies (Epstein 1986). National party development has been influenced by the broader political environment and pressures emanating from within the parties themselves. The Democratic National Committee (DNC) was formed during the 1848 Democratic National Convention for the purposes of organizing and directing the presidential campaign and tending to the details associated with planning future conventions (e.g., Cotter and Hennessy 1964). The Republican National Committee (RNC) was created in 1856 to formally bring the Republican Party into existence and conduct election-related activities similar to those performed by its Democratic counterpart.

The congressional and senatorial campaign committees were created in response to heightened electoral insecurities resulting from major political upheavals. The National Republican Congressional Committee (NRCC) was formed in 1866 by Radical Republican members of the House who believed they could not rely on President Andrew Johnson or the RNC for assistance with their elections. Following the Republican example, the Democrats formed the Democratic Congressional Campaign Committee (DCCC). The Democratic Senatorial Campaign Committee (DSCC) and the National Republican Senatorial Committee (NRSC) were organized in 1916 to help incumbent senators campaign after the Seventeenth Amendment transformed the Senate into a popularly elected body.

The six national party organizations have not possessed abundant power during most of their existence. Even during the height of the parties' influence (circa the late-nineteenth and early-twentieth centuries), power was concentrated at the local level, usually in countywide political machines that possessed a virtual monopoly over the tools needed to run a successful campaign. Power mainly flowed up from county organizations to state party committees and conventions, and then to the national convention. The national, congressional, and senatorial campaign committees had little, if any, power over state and local party leaders.

Nevertheless, party campaigning was a cooperative endeavor. Individual branches of the party organization were primarily concerned with electing candidates within their immediate jurisdictions, but their leaders worked together because they recognized that ballot structures and voter partisanship linked the electoral prospects of their candidates (e.g., Schattschneider 1942). They also understood that electing candidates to federal, state, and local governments would enable them to maximize the patronage and other benefits they could extract for themselves and supporters. The national party organizations, and especially the national committees, provided the financial, administrative, and communications resources necessary to coordinate and set the tone of a nationwide campaign (e.g., Bruce 1927). Local party committees used their proximity to voters to collect electoral information, conduct voter registration and get-out-the-vote drives, and organize other grassroots activities (e.g., Merriam 1923). State party committees used their relatively modest resources to channel electoral information up to the national party organizations and arranged for candidates and other prominent party leaders to speak at local rallies and events (e.g., Sait 1927).

Party Decline

The transition from a party-dominated system of campaign politics to a candidate-centered system was brought about by legal, demographic, and technological changes in American society and reforms instituted by the parties themselves. The direct primary and civil service regulations instituted during the Progressive Era deprived party bosses of their ability to handpick nominees and reward party workers with government jobs and contracts (e.g., Key 1958; Roseboom 1970). They weakened the bosses' hold over candidates and political activists and encouraged candidates to build their own campaign organizations.

Demographic and cultural changes reinforced this pattern. Increased education and social mobility, declining immigration, and a growing national identity contributed to the erosion of the close-knit, traditional ethnic neighborhoods that formed the core of the old-fashioned political machine's constituency. Growing preferences for movies, radio, and televised entertainment reduced the popularity of rallies, barbecues, and other types of interpersonal communication at which the machines excelled. Voters began to turn toward nationally focused mass media and away from local party committees for their political information. These developments were accompanied by a general decline in the parties' ability to structure political choice (Carmines, Renten, and Stimson 1984), to furnish symbolic referents and decision-making cues for voters (Nie, Verba, and Petrocik 1979), and to foster party unity among elected officials (Deckard 1976). These trends, weakened the parties' ties with voters and rendered some of their campaign techniques obsolete.

Candidates' adaptation of technological innovations from the public relations field to the electoral arena further eroded their dependence on parties. Advancements in survey research, data processing, and mass media advertising provided candidates with new tools for gathering information from and communicating messages to voters. The emergence of political consultants allowed some candidates to hire nonparty professionals to run their campaigns (e.g., Sabato 1981). These developments helped transform election campaigns from party-focused, party-conducted affairs to events that revolved around individual candidates and their campaign organizations.

Two sets of reforms initially appeared to weaken party organizations and reinforce the candidate-centered nature of US elections, but as noted later they can be best understood as transforming the organizations' roles in party and electoral politics. The reforms introduced by the Democrats' McGovern-Fraser Commission to make the presidential nominating process, and Democratic Party politics in general, more open and representative had the unintended consequences of increasing the influence of issue and candidate activists (frequently labeled "purists" or "amateurs") at the expense of longtime party "regulars." The rise of the purists led to tensions over fundamental issues such as whether winning elections or advancing particular policies should have priority (Wilson 1962; Polsby and Wildavsky 1984). This made coalition building and electioneering more difficult. It also contributed significantly toward making candidate-centered campaign organizations the major actors in presidential elections. The reforms were debilitating to both parties, but they were more harmful to the Democratic Party that introduced them (Ranney 1975; Polsby and Wildavsky 1984).

The Federal Election Campaign Act of 1974 and its amendments (FECA) also had some negative effects on the parties. Among its most important provisions were those requiring that all money spent in federal elections (sometimes referred to as "hard money") originate as contributions voluntarily given by individuals to candidates, party committees, or political action committees (PACs); be raised and contributed within a set of mandatory limits; and be publicly disclosed. The law also created a new agency, the Federal Election Commission (FEC), to administer the law. The FECA hampered national party fund-raising and campaign activities and made it difficult for state and local party organizations to participate in federal elections (e.g., Price 1984). The result was a decreased role for parties in presidential and congressional elections. The FECA also set the stage for interest groups to assume a more prominent role in the financing of these contests. The number of interest group PACs skyrocketed from 608 in 1974, to more than 5,400 in 2010. Moreover, spending by PACs and other interest group entities exceeded $700 million in the 2010 congressional elections—more than three times the total spent by both major parties (Herrnson 2012).

Changes in the parties' environment and internal governance fostered the emergence of a candidate-centered election system. Under this system, most candidates assembled their own campaign organization to compete for their party's nomination and then to contest the general election. In the case of presidential elections, a candidate who secured the party's nomination also won control of the national committee. In congressional elections, most campaign activities were carried out by the candidate's own organization both before and after the primary. At first, the parties' seeming inability to adapt to the new high-tech, money-driven style of campaign politics resulted in their being pushed to the periphery of the elections process.

The Strengthening of National Parties

Although party decline was a gradual process that took its greatest toll on party organizations at the local level, party renewal occurred over a relatively short period and was focused primarily in Washington, DC. As was the case in earlier periods, national party change was shaped by the needs of candidates. Many candidates did not have the skills or funds needed to meet the demands of the new style of campaigning. Some turned to political consultants and interest groups for help. Candidates' need for greater access to technical expertise, political research, and money created an opportunity for national party organizations to become the repositories of these resources (Schlesinger 1985). Party leaders responded to these demands after electoral crises that heightened officeholders' anxieties furnished them with the opportunities and incentives to augment the parties' organizational apparatuses (Herrnson 1993).

The Watergate scandal and the trouncing Republican candidates experienced in the 1974 and 1976 elections provided a crisis of competition that was the catalyst for change at the Republican national party organizations. The GOP lost forty-nine seats in the House in 1974, had an incumbent president defeated two years later, and controlled only twelve governorships and four state legislatures by 1977. Moreover, voter identification with the Republican Party dropped precipitously, especially among voters under thirty-five. In response, the Republican national, congressional, and senatorial campaign committee leaders initiated programs to help elect GOP candidates and strengthen state and local party committees. This was an important step in transforming the committees' missions and placing them on a path that would strengthen them organizationally.

The institutionalization of the Democratic national party organizations occurred in two phases. The tumultuous 1968 Democratic National Convention created a factional crisis between liberal reform-minded purists and party regulars. The crisis and the party's defeat in November created an opportunity for the McGovern-Fraser Commission to restructure the party's presidential nomination process. By design, the reforms made the process more participatory and increased the size and demographic representativeness of the DNC and the national convention. Two unanticipated results were the proliferation of presidential primaries and the front-loading of the nomination calendar. By empowering the DNC to oversee state party compliance with national party rules, the reforms boosted the national committees influence in both party and presidential politics.

The second phase of Democratic national party institutionalization followed the party's massive losses in the 1980 election. The defeat of incumbent President Jimmy Carter, the loss of thirty-four House seats (half of the party's margin), and loss of control of the Senate constituted a crisis of competition that created an opportunity for change at the Democratic national party organizations. Unlike party reform, Democratic Party renewal was preceded by widespread agreement among Democrats that the DNC, DCCC, and DSCC should increase the party's electoral competitiveness by emulating the GOP's party building and campaign service programs.

Both the Democrats' and the Republicans' national party organizations entered a new phase of development in response to the weakening of federal regulations governing campaign finance and the enactment of legislation to shore up those regulations. A series of Supreme Court rulings and FEC decisions allowed parties and interest groups to spend funds not subject to federal regulations (so-called "soft money") on broadcast "issue advocacy" advertisements as long as those ads did *not expressly* advocate the election or defeat of a federal candidate. Soft money originates from sources—mostly corporate, trade association, or labor union general treasuries and in amounts that are prohibited under the FECA. Because soft money is much easier to collect than hard money, both parties made considerable efforts to raise it. By the 2000 election cycle, the Democratic national party organizations raised $245.2 million in soft money, and the Republicans collected $249.9 million, accounting for 53 and 41 percent of their total respective receipts. Moreover, party and interest-group soft-money expenditures on issue-advocacy ads and other forms of voter contact equaled, and even exceeded, the amounts spent by the candidates in a few competitive congressional races (e.g., Magleby 2003). Some political observers and practitioners considered soft money a revitalizing force for the political parties.

The major goals of the Bipartisan Campaign Reform Act of 2002 (BCRA) were to ban political parties from raising or spending soft money to influence federal elections and to prohibit interest groups from broadcasting soft-money-funded issue-advocacy ads thirty days before a primary or caucus and sixty days before the general election.[1] Although some anticipated the BCRA would greatly weaken national party organizations, the parties managed to adapt to it. First, they reinvigorated their efforts to raise hard money and managed to raise substantial funds in ensuing elections. Second, they compensated for their inability to broadcast issue advocacy ads by increasing their spending on hard-money-funded independent expenditures, which can *expressly* advocate the election or defeat of federal candidates but must be made without the knowledge or consent of a candidate, member of the candidate's campaign organization, or someone advising that organization. Third, they put greater effort into influencing the contributions, independent expenditures, and issue-advocacy spending of their interest group allies. Fourth, several party leaders and operatives, predominantly those associated with the GOP, created organizations that were legally outside of their national party's formal apparatus but designed to advance party goals by conducting independent mass media campaigns and coordinated grassroots campaigns (Herrnson 2012). The most recognizable of these outside spending groups are the pro-Republican American Crossroads and Crossroads GPS. Founded by Karl Rove, Mike Duncan, and Ed Gillespie, each of whom had served as a White House adviser or RNC chairman under President George W. Bush, these organizations spent almost $40 million to help elect Republicans to Congress in 2010.

Institutionalized National Parties

The institutionalization of the national party organizations refers to their becoming fiscally solvent, organizationally stable, larger and more diversified in
their staffing, and adopting professional-bureaucratic decision-making procedures. These changes were necessary for the national parties to develop
their election-related and party-building functions. They also helped the national parties increase their influence with others that participate in elections.

National party fund-raising improved greatly from the 1970s through
2010. During this period, the national parties set several fund-raising records
using a variety of approaches to raise money from a diverse group of contributors. The increased competitiveness over control of the federal government following the Republican takeover of Congress in 1995 helped fuel the
growth of both parties' fund-raising efforts (Figure 6.1). The availability of
soft money following the 1990 election made it relatively easy for the national
parties to respond to the increased pressure resulting from this heightened
competition—that is, until the BCRA went into effect following the 2002
election cycle. Republican committees raised more money than their Democratic rivals throughout most of this period. However, the Democrats managed to shrink the Republicans' fund-raising advantage from 6.7 to 1 in the
1982 election cycle to 1.3 to 1 in the 2006 election cycle. Following their taking control of the presidency, the House, and the Senate in 2008, the Democrats were poised to overtake the Republicans in fund-raising. Indeed during
the 2010 elections, national Democratic party organizations raised $518.3
million to the GOP's $444.7 million. Party competition and control of the na-
tion's political institutions are likely to have a major impact on both parties'
future fund-raising successes.

The national parties raise most of their contributions from individuals,
and roughly 62 percent of these consist of contributions of less than $200. In-
dividual contributions are mainly collected using direct mail, e-mail, and
telemarketing techniques that reach out to individuals who are motivated by
salient issues or ideological causes. Websites first proved to be potent fund-
raising tools in the 2004 presidential election, and social media had a notable
impact in 2008. However, these new methods are more effective for raising
money for prominent candidates than party committees. Fund-raising din-
ners, receptions, and personal solicitations are effective for raising contributions of all sizes from individuals who enjoy the social aspects of politics, and

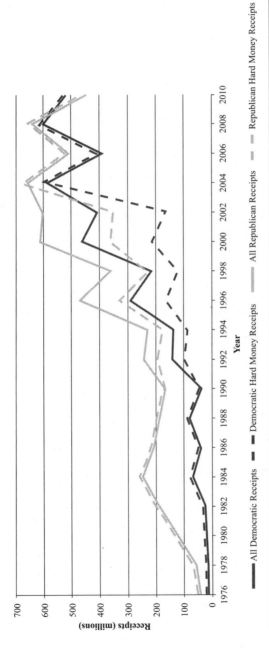

Source: Compiled from Federal Election Commission press releases and Center for Responsive Politics data.

Notes: Hard money receipts consist of federally regulated funds raised by the parties' national, congressional, and senatorial campaign committees. All receipts consist of all federally regulated and unregulated funds raised by the aforementioned committees.

FIGURE 6.1 National Party Receipts, 1976–2010

are essential to raising large donations (Brown, Powell, and Wilcox 1995; Francia et al. 2003).

Success in fund-raising has enabled the national parties to invest in the development of their organizational infrastructures. Prior to their institutionalization, the national party organizations had no permanent headquarters. Their transience created security problems, made it difficult for the parties to conduct routine business, and did little to bolster their standing in Washington (Cotter and Hennessy 1964). All six national party organizations are now housed in party-owned headquarters located only a few blocks from the Capitol. The buildings provide convenient locations to carry out research, host fund-raising events, and hold meetings with candidates, interest group leaders, political journalists, and campaign consultants. They also provide a secure environment for the committees' computers, records, and staffs (see e.g., Herrnson 1988, 2012).

Each national party organization has a two-tiered structure consisting of members and professional staff. The members of the Republican and Democratic national committees are selected by state parties and the members of the parties' congressional and senatorial campaign committees are selected by their colleagues in Congress. National committee staffs typically number in the hundreds. During the 2010 election season, the two congressional campaign committees employed about eighty full-time staff and the two senatorial campaign committees each employed roughly sixty full-time staff. Committee staffs are divided along functional lines; different divisions are responsible for administration, fund-raising, research, communications, and campaign activities. The staffs have a great deal of autonomy in running the committees' day-to-day operations and are extremely influential in formulating their campaign strategies (Herrnson 2012).

The institutionalization of the national parties has had a significant impact on their relationships with other party organizations. DNC and RNC programs to provide state and local parties with modern office equipment and introduce innovations in fund-raising, research, communications, voter targeting and mobilization, and campaign strategy in general have increased their clout within the party hierarchy. National, congressional, and senatorial campaign committee transfers to state and local parties have had a similar impact. In combination with the DNC's and RNC's rule-making and enforcement functions, the national parties' abilities to distribute or withhold resources have altered the flow of power within the parties. Traditionally it radiated upward from state and local party organizations to the national committees, now it also courses downward from the national, congressional, and senatorial campaign committees to the state and local parties.

National party institutionalization also has had an impact on the behavior of members of Congress and other politicians. Most have come to recognize these organizations as critical to their party's overall performance in elections. Both parties' congressional leaders, most of their senior members, and virtually all others who wish to maintain or someday occupy positions of power in the House or Senate have made substantial investments of time and money in their party's congressional or senatorial campaign committee. During the 2010 election, substantial numbers served as committee members, assisted with fund-raising, or participated in candidate services programs. Most also made a substantial contribution from their leadership PAC, personal campaign committee, or both. In 2010, the DCCC and NRCC collected $30.8 million and $28.7 million, respectively, from these sources. The DSCC and NRSC collected $10.3 and $4.5 million (Herrnson 2012).

The relationships between political parties, interest groups, and political consultants also have been affected by the institutionalization of the national parties. At first, many political observers believed that the proliferation of PACs and the rise of political consultants would hasten the decline of parties (e.g., Sabato 1981, 1985). However, it is now widely recognized that individuals and groups in the interest group and political consulting communities and the national parties cooperate with each other to advance their common goals.

Political Parties as Enduring Multilayered Coalitions

The institutionalization of the national parties resulted in their occupying core positions in the networks of organizations and individuals who participate in politics. Contemporary political parties are best conceptualized as enduring multilayered coalitions comprising formal party organizations and leaders, party members and party-connected organizations, party allies consisting of a variety of individuals and groups that participate in politics, and the party identifiers that provide each party's broad base of support (Herrnson 2009). Party coalitions are held together by overlapping goals. The individuals and groups that belong to the inner three layers maintain ongoing relationships, share information, coordinate strategies and tactics, and occasionally support each other financially.

The roles and contributions of each coalition member are shaped by their specific goals, resources, and the regulations governing their activities. Rather than carry out all of the activities once associated with a political party, formal party leaders and their organizations conduct some of these efforts on their own and guide many of the endeavors of others in their coalition. The most important members of a party's coalition are its formal leaders. These consist of individuals who are elected or appointed to positions in government or in extragovernmental party committees. They possess the most power within the party and exhibit the greatest loyalty and commit the most resources to it. They are responsible for party governance; define the party's specific goals, strategies, and tactics; control most of its resources; and are most able to mobilize the efforts of other coalition members. At the federal level, they include the president, the parties' congressional leaders and caucuses, and the officers and members of the parties' national, congressional, and senatorial campaign committees.

The next layer of the party consists of party members and the organizations they create to pursue partisan and individual objectives. Party members are loyal to their party, commit significant resources to it, are involved in party governance and decision making, and coordinate their efforts with those of formal party leaders and organizations. However, they possess less authority and influence within the party and place less emphasis on the attainment of party goals than do formal party leaders. Part of the explanation for these differences is that the success of party leaders is intertwined with the advancement of their party's objectives, which are the result of compromises reached among party members, whereas the successes of party members involve the advancement of their policy and career goals, some of which are distinct from their party's overall objectives. Party members in the national government include members of Congress, cabinet officers, judges who weigh partisan considerations in their decision making, and the political and other aides who assist these officeholders with their duties. Outside of the government, party members consist of candidates, elected officials, and their personal campaign committees and leadership PACs—referred to as party-connected committees.

The third layer of the party consists of party allies. These include lobbyists, other interest group leaders, political consultants, media elites, political activists, and other individuals who overwhelmingly support just one party. Party allies also include lobbying, public relations, and law firms, think tanks, partisan media outlets, PACs, super PACs, 527 committees, and 501(c) organizations, and other groups that also provide most of their backing to one party. Party allies routinely work with party leaders and members to advance their party's objectives. However, party allies possess less loyalty, less influence over party governance and decision making, and less commitment to achieving party goals than party leaders and members. Party allies also coordinate fewer of their efforts with these more centrally located elements of their party's coalition. This is in large part due to their location outside of the formal party apparatus and their interest in promoting goals other than those advanced by formal party leaders. Interest group leaders, PACs, and other interest group entities that participate in federal elections, for example, are overwhelmingly supportive of one party most of the time, but their first set of loyalties is to the organized interest (or interests) they represent. When the goals of these interests clash with the party goals of party leaders or members, party allies put the goals of those they represent first.

The final layer of the party consists of its electoral coalition. Sometimes referred to as the party's electoral base or identifiers, these individuals are much less actively engaged in politics than the individuals and groups in the other layers of the party. Indeed, they are often the targets of the mobilization efforts spearheaded by party leaders, members, or allies. Located outside of both parties' coalitions are nonaligned individuals and groups, including independent voters, donors, journalists, and interest groups whose support the parties seek to win in elections and the policy-making process.

National Party Campaigning

The institutionalization of the national parties has provided them the wherewithal to play a larger role in elections, and national party campaign activity has increased tremendously since the 1970s. Still, the electoral activities of the national parties, and party organizations in general, remain constrained by election law, established custom, and limited resources.

Candidate Recruitment

Candidate recruitment is one of the areas where party influence is limited. Most candidates for elective office in the United States are self-recruited and conduct their own nominating campaigns. The DNC and the RNC have a hand in establishing the basic guidelines under which presidential nominations are contested, but neither expresses a preference for candidates for its party's presidential nomination. National party organizations, however, may get involved in nominating contests for House, Senate, and state level offices. They actively recruit some candidates to enter primary contests and just as actively discourage others. Most candidate recruitment efforts are concentrated in competitive districts, where a party seeks to nominate the best qualified candidate for the upcoming election. However, national party officials also encourage candidates to run in other districts in order to strengthen local party committees and deepen their candidate pools. Party recruitment efforts have enabled the parties to expand the number of races that are competitive, particularly in nationalized election cycles. When participating in candidate recruitment, national party staff in Washington, DC, and regional coordinators in the field meet with state and local party leaders to identify potential candidates. Armed with polls, the promise of party campaign money and services, and the persuasive talents of members of Congress and even presidents, party leaders and staff seek to influence the decisions of potential candidates. Both parties have had success in encouraging what are typically referred to as quality candidates—those with prior political experience, high name recognition, reputations as problems solvers among local voters, and the ability to fund a campaign—to run for Congress, governor, and other offices (Canon 1990; Stone and Maisel 2003). Of course, presidential candidates rarely need any encouragement from party committees.

National party candidate recruitment and primary activities are not intended to do away with the dominant pattern of self-selected candidates assembling their own campaign organizations to compete for their party's nomination; nor are these activities designed to restore the turn-of-the-century pattern of local party leaders selecting the parties' nominees. Rather, most national party activity is geared toward encouraging, or in a few cases discouraging, the candidacies of a select group of politicians who are considering running in competitive districts. Less focused recruitment efforts attempt to arouse the interests of a broader group of party activists (e.g., Herrnson 1988, 2012).

National Conventions

The national conventions are technically a part of the nomination process. After the 1968 reforms were instituted, however, the conventions lost control of their nominating function and became more of a public relations event than a decision-making one. Conventions still have platform writing and rule-making responsibilities, but these are overshadowed by speeches and other events designed to attract the support of voters.

Contemporary national conventions are notable for their choreography. Featuring impressive backdrops, staging, and video presentations tailor-made for television, they are intended to convey messages of unity, energy, and the inevitability of victory in the general election. Disputes among convention delegates over party rules or platforms are relegated to meeting rooms where they attract relatively little media attention. Protestors are directed to special "protest sites" away from the convention halls to minimize their press coverage.

The substitution of public relations for decision making at national conventions has not come without costs. Many television networks have responded to what they perceive to be a lack of newsworthiness by providing only limited television coverage. In contrast to the gavel-to-gavel coverage that many twentieth century conventions safely assumed they would get and actually received, the organizers of the 2008 Democratic National Convention had to be careful to schedule their convention around the Olympics and the organizers of the 2008 Republican convention were concerned that their nominee's acceptance speech would have to compete with a Thursday-night football game between the defending Super Bowl champion New York Giants and the Washington Redskins.

Other convention activities include policy seminars, fund-raising, and planning for the general election campaign and future party events. Meetings are arranged for major donors to meet with party leaders and other luminaries to socialize, discuss policy, and find ways to put their resources to best use in the upcoming general election. Nonpresidential candidates are given access to television and radio taping and satellite up-link facilities. "Meet and greet" sessions are used to introduce competitive challengers and open-seat candidates to PAC managers, other interest group leaders, individual big contributors, party leaders, and the media. The atrophy of the national conventions' nominating function has been partially offset by an increase in its general election-related activities. Once considered a decision-making forum, a national convention is now viewed as a major networking and public relations event.

The General Election

Candidate recruitment and nominations reinforce the candidate-centered nature of US elections. Rules requiring candidates for the nomination to compete in primaries and caucuses guarantee that successful candidates enter the general election with their own sources of technical expertise, in-depth research, and connections with other political elites. These reforms combined with the federal campaign finance law to limit national party activity and influence in elections. For example, presidential general election candidates who accept public funding are restricted from accepting contributions from any other sources, including the political parties. With the exception of the Democrats' 2008 presidential nominee, Barack Obama, every major-party presidential candidate has accepted public general election funding since 1976, when it first became available. Given that most presidential candidates can raise substantially more money than they can receive from the presidential election campaign fund, it is unlikely that future candidates will accept public funding, and its limits, in the future.

Nevertheless, the national parties do assume important roles in contemporary presidential elections. They furnish presidential campaigns with staff, legal and strategic advice, and public relations assistance. National committee opposition research and archives serve as important sources of political information. National committee coordinated expenditures can boost the total resources partially under the candidates' control by more than 20 percent. Joint fund-raising committees reduce the costs of soliciting contributions and enable candidates and party committees to increase the funds each is able to raise. National party transfer to state parties for voter-mobilization drives and party-building activities improve the prospects of presidential candidates. The same is true of the unlimited independent expenditures the national parties are allowed to make to *explicitly* exhort a candidate's election or defeat (without the knowledge or consent of candidates, candidates' campaigns, and those assisting the campaigns). Hybrid campaign ads, first introduced by the GOP in 2004, enable a party committee and a candidate to share the costs of an advertisement that features both the candidate and a generic party message. These ads' major advantage is that they enable a candidate to appear in twice as many advertisements per dollar than would have been the case if the ads were purchased solely by the candidate's campaign; their major disadvantage is that because they must refer to more than just the candidate, they produce a muddled message (Corrado 2011).

Combined, these forms of party spending can be impressive. In 2008, the DNC made $6.4 million in coordinated expenditures on behalf of Obama and $1.1 million in independent expenditures criticizing Republican nominee Senator John McCain. Democratic joint fund-raising committees raised almost $203.7 million, most of which was transferred to Obama's campaign committee and the DNC. The DNC also transferred $45.6 million to Democratic state and local parties. The DNC probably could have played a larger direct role in the 2008 presidential election, but because Obama's fund-raising prowess gave him a huge financial advantage over McCain the DNC focused on other priorities (Corrado 2011).

The RNC assumed an even larger role in McCain's bid for the White House. It made $18.9 million in coordinated expenditures on behalf of McCain and $53.5 million in independent expenditures attacking Obama. Republican joint fund-raising committees raised $172 million, most of which was transferred to the RNC, which, in turn, transferred $77.7 million to state and local Republican organizations. The RNC and the McCain campaign jointly produced $57.9 million in hybrid ads (Corrado 2011). These were helpful in raising McCain's visibility, but the requirement that they discuss more than the candidate resulted in unfocused content. National party spending was especially important to McCain because his acceptance of federal funds largely limited his campaign's general election expenditures to $84.1 million.[2]

National party organizations also play a big role in congressional elections. They contribute money and campaign services directly to congressional candidates and provide transactional assistance that helps candidates attract other resources from other politicians, political consultants, and PACs. They also make independent expenditures to win voter support for their candidates. Most national party assistance is distributed by the congressional and senatorial campaign committees to candidates competing in close elections, especially to nonincumbents. This reflects the committees' goal of maximizing the number of congressional seats under their control (Jacobson 1985–1986; Herrnson 2012).

As is the case with presidential elections, federal law limits party activity in congressional races. National party organizations are allowed to contribute a total of $15,000 to House candidates. The parties' national and senatorial campaign committees are allowed to give a combined total of $35,000 to Senate candidates. State party organizations can give $5,000 each to House and Senate candidates. National party organizations and state party committees also are allowed to make coordinated expenditures on behalf of their candidates, giving both the party and the candidate a measure of control over how the money is spent. Originally set at $10,000 per committee, the limits for coordinated expenditures on behalf of House candidates were adjusted for inflation and reached $43,500 in the 2010 election cycle.[3] The limits for coordinated expenditures in Senate elections vary by the size of a state's population and are also indexed to inflation. They ranged from $87,000 per committee in the smallest states to almost $2.4 million per committee in California during the 2010 election.

Democratic party organizations spent about $8 million on contributions and coordinated expenditures in House elections and $15.9 million in Senate elections in 2010. The Republicans spent roughly $9.6 million and $19.4 million in these elections. This spending followed well-established patterns. More funds were distributed as coordinated expenditures than as contributions because the latter are subjected to higher ceilings. Most party support originated at the appropriate congressional or senatorial campaign committee. Other party organizations that become involved in House or Senate elections typically follow a congressional or senatorial campaign committee's strategy. State party committees that were short on money were assisted financially by a national party organization so that the parties could concentrate resources in the races they considered priorities.

The national parties usually target competitive campaigns for their largest contributions and coordinated expenditures, and the 2010 elections were no exception. Both parties distributed more than 90 percent of their House contributions to candidates for seats that were competitive in at least one point during the election season (see Figure 6.2).[4] The Democrats committed 78 percent of their funds to incumbents in close races, 4 percent to challengers who either won or were in a reasonably close contest, and 9 percent to open-

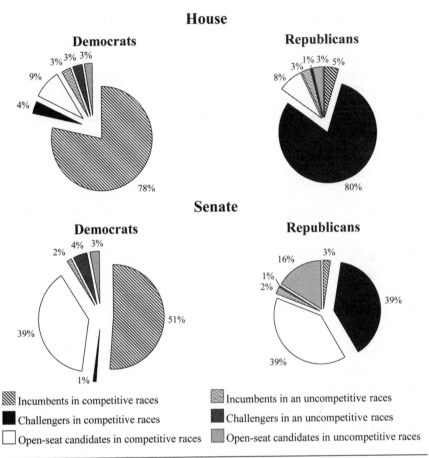

FIGURE 6.2 The Allocation of Party Contributions and Coordinated Expenditures in the 2010 Congressional Elections

Source: Herrnson, Paul S. 2012. *Congressional Elections: Campaigning at Home and in Washington.* 6th ed. Washington, DC: CQ Press. 2012, p, 108.

Notes: Figures include contributions and coordinated expenditures by all party committees to major-party general election candidates in contested races. N = 812 for the House N = 72 for the Senate.

seat candidates in closely contested elections. The Republicans resource allocation in House races was almost the mirror image of the Democrats' spending, as the GOP committed 80 percent of its funding for House candidates to challengers, for example. Although the distributions of party contributions and coordinated expenditures in Senate contests do not mirror each other as closely, they also show that Democratic party committees invested substantially more in supporting incumbents, Republican party committees devoted more to promoting challengers, and both parties committed substantial funds to winning open seats.[5] The distributions of party funds in 2010 were strongly influenced by the political environment, as is usually the case. Voter anger over the nation's stalled economy, high unemployment rate, a large number of housing foreclosures, public dissatisfaction with the federal government, and Democrats' control of the White House and congressional majorities forced the Democrats into a defensive posture that focused on incumbent protection. These same conditions encouraged the Republicans to aggressively support the candidacies of their party's challengers.

In addition to providing financial support, parties furnish competitive congressional candidates with campaign services, ranging from candidate training to fund-raising to voter targeting. The national parties hold training seminars for candidates and campaign managers, broker relationships between candidates and political consultants, help congressional campaigns file reports with the FEC, and perform other administrative and legal tasks. National party staffs in Washington and field coordinators also help candidates formulate strategy and tactics.

The parties' congressional and senatorial campaign committees help candidates raise money from individuals and PACs in Washington, DC, in their districts and states, and around the nation. They provide candidates with direct fund-raising assistance, including raising money on their behalf at events, through the mail, and on the Internet, and advising them on how to solicit large contributions from individuals and PACs. They also provide indirect fund-raising assistance when they publicly prioritize some candidates over others and disseminate information to channel the flow of resources to their priority candidates. These efforts have a significant impact on the contribution decisions of party members, party allies, and other donors. The House Democrats' Red to Blue Program and the House Republicans' Young Guns Program have been especially effective in helping priority challengers and open-seat contestants raise money (Herrnson 2012). Unfortunately for candidates who do not qualify for such programs, their lack of party backing usually makes fund-raising more difficult because it gives potential donors a reason to turn down a solicitation.

The national parties also assist congressional candidates with issue and opposition research, gauging public opinion, campaign communications, and other election activities. As is the case with campaign contributions and expenditures and fund-raising assistance, the parties' congressional and senatorial campaign committees distribute the vast majority of this support to candidates on their priority lists, who are involved in competitive contests (Herrnson 2012).

National party campaign activity also includes campaign assistance that is not provided directly to any single candidate. Referred to as outside campaigns because they are conducted largely outside of candidate campaign organizations, they consist of coordinated grassroots efforts and independent media communications. Coordinated grassroots campaigns involve voter targeting, registration, and turnout efforts. They are largely financed and coordinated by national party organizations in Washington, DC, and rely heavily on state and local party committees for their implementation. The national parties are also responsible for the introduction of many innovations in this area, including precinct-based geodemographic targeting, microtargeting, and programs to encourage early and absentee ballot voting. In 2010, party grassroots campaigns involved tens of millions of dollars.

The national parties' independent media campaigns involve independent expenditures that *expressly* exhort voters to vote for or against a candidate or call for a candidate's election or defeat. Following the BCRA's ban on party soft money, the national parties greatly increased their independent expenditures. Most of these ads are either negative or comparative in tone. One explanation for this involves voters. Simply put, negative ads are more likely than positive ads to be remembered and to motivate voters to go to the polls (Goldstein and Freedman 2002; Brooks 2006; Brooks and Geer 2007). Another explanation is strategic: when parties do most of the dirty work associated with attack politics, their candidates can take the high road and air mainly positive ads. This *de facto* division of labor enables the candidates to state truthfully that they are unable to influence negative ads that are aired by party committees, interest groups, or others.

In 2010, the Democrats made roughly $65.3 million in independent expenditures to influence the outcomes of the House elections and another $39.4 million to influence the Senate contests. The Republicans spent almost $46.1 million and $25.9 million for these same purposes. As is typical, these expenditures were overwhelming devoted to attacking the opposing party's candidates. They also were more tightly focused on close contests than were party contributions or coordinated expenditures. Fewer than 2 percent of them were spent on races with victory margins of more than 20 percent (Herrnson 2012).

"Party-connected" contributions, made by personal campaign committees and leadership PACs of current members of Congress and the federal accounts of other politicians, have become a significant source of resources for congressional candidates. Leadership PAC contributions, like other PAC contributions, are limited to $5,000 in each stage of the campaign (primary, general election, and runoff). Contributions from one member of Congress's (or retiree's) campaign account to another candidate's campaign account are limited to $2,000. During the 2010 elections, Democrats contributed $19.7 million in party-connected contributions to House candidates in major-party contested races and $5.6 million to Senate candidates in contested races; Republicans spent $16.4 million and $5.9 million in these elections. Total party-connected spending in House contests reached $16.8 million, more than twice as much as formal party committees distributed in contributions and coordinated expenditures. Senate candidates raised $11.5 million in party-connected contributions, about one-third the amount they raised in party contributions and coordinated expenditures. The comparatively generous ceilings for party coordinated expenditures in Senate races and the small number of senators and senator-sponsored leadership PACs largely account for the differences between House and Senate elections (Herrnson 2012).

The distribution of party-connected funds to House and Senate candidates shadowed the distribution of party contributions and coordinated expenditures. The major differences in the spending patterns are that party-connected committees distributed more of their funds in House races to incumbents, including those in one-sided contests, and somewhat less to challengers. The patterns for Senate races show a greater concentration of contributions given by members of both parties to candidates in open seats and incumbents with a relatively easy path to reelection. The differences in the spending patterns for party committees and party-connected committees are informed by differences in their goals. The parties' seat maximization goals encourage them to target close contests, regardless of candidates' office-holding status. The sponsors of party-connected committees are interested in seat maximization, but they also want to collect postelection payoffs, such as support in their bids for leadership posts, committee assignments, and preferred policies (Wilcox 1989; Currinder 2003; Brewer and Deering 2005; Heberlig, Hetherington, and Larson 2006). The latter objective encourages them to support candidates who are likely to serve in the next Congress, mainly incumbents (who collectively enjoy a better-than-90-percent election rate in most election years), and candidates for open-seat contests (who as a group have a 50 percent chance of winning).

Party contributions and coordinated expenditures accounted for roughly 3 percent of the resources collected by House candidates in competitive elections, and 7 percent of the funds collected by competitive Senate contestants (Herrnson 2012). Even though individuals and PACs still furnish candidates with most of their campaign funds, political parties are the largest single source of campaign money for most candidates. Party money comes from one, or at most a few, organizations that are primarily concerned with one goal—the election of their candidates. Individual and PAC contributions, by contrast, come from a multitude of sources that are motivated by a variety of concerns. The inclusion of party-connected money, which is given by a relatively small number of organizations, boosts the level of party support to 9 percent for both House and Senate candidates. Of course, party and party-connected money comprise a much larger portion of some candidates' resources than others. The 2010 campaign run by successful Republican challenger Steven Southerland in Florida's 2nd congressional district is typical of those of challengers who are poised to knock off an incumbent in that it raised 16 percent of its funds from party and party-connected committees. The 2010 Senate race between Senate Majority Leader Harry Reid and Republican challenger Sharron Angle is also typical of a hotly contested Senate race in the amounts of financial assistance the candidates secured from party and party-connected sources. Despite both candidates raising record funds from a variety of sources in their Nevada Senate race, Reid collected 18 percent and Angle about 7 percent of their respective resources from party and party-connected committees.[6]

Data have yet to be compiled for the distribution of party-allied money in the 2010 election. Nevertheless, insights can be gained from analyzing the contributions of labor union PACs, which constitute one of the Democratic Party's staunchest allies. Labor PACs contributed $57.7 million to House and Senate candidates in major-party contested elections in 2010. They made more than 95 percent of these contributions to Democrats, an amount that easily meets the threshold for an organized interest to qualify as a party ally. Labor PACs made roughly 80 percent of their House and 50 percent of their Senate contributions to Democratic incumbents, which is similar to the contribution patterns for party organizations and party-connected committees. Where labor PAC contributions differed from those made by these more central layers of the Democratic coalition is in the incumbents targeted.

Labor PACs delivered 40 percent of their contributions to Democratic House members and senators in safe seats. Democratic party organizations and party-connected committees, on the other hand, delivered the overwhelming majority of their incumbent contributions to incumbents whose electoral fortunes were uncertain. Some labor PACs also differed from these other party coalition members in that they failed to support Democratic incumbents who faced strong primary competition. Indeed, organized labor provided substantially more support to Lt. Governor William Halter than incumbent Senator Blanche Lincoln in Arkansas's 2010 Democratic Senate primary (Herrnson 2012).

The efforts of labor PACs in 2010 are consistent with those of all of the allied PACs that participated in the 2006 House elections. Each allied PAC directed at least 90 percent of its contributions, independent expenditures, and internal communications to candidates associated with just one party. Despite this high level of partisanship, allied PACs distributed their money differently than party committees and the personal campaign committees and leadership PACs that distribute party-connected funds. Specifically, allied PACs showed a greater propensity to help primary challengers and support House incumbents in safe seats. This behavior is consistent with many allied PACs' emphasis on securing political access to advance the interests of their sponsors. It is important to stress that even though allied PACs are less inclined to embrace the election-oriented objectives of the individuals and groups belonging to the more central layers of the party, they are, by definition, substantially more supportive of candidates belonging to their preferred party than are PACs allied with the opposing party or neither party (Herrnson 2009).

The same is true of individual donors who are allied with one party. Most individuals who make significant contributions to congressional candidates ($200 or more) make few contributions and are heavily influenced by partisanship when deciding which candidates to support. Despite their overwhelming support for candidates of their preferred party, the contributions of these individual allies do not always comport with their national party's election-oriented goals. In fact, individual significant donors have a propensity to contribute to candidates in their state regardless of the competitiveness of those candidates' elections (Francia et al. 2003).

Of course, contributions represent only a portion of the election-related activities of allied interest groups and individuals. Democratic interest group allies, including labor unions and environmental groups, for example, routinely provide their preferred candidates with an array of campaign services, including polls, issue research, and volunteers. Groups allied with the GOP distribute similar support to Republican candidates. Some allied groups conduct grassroots campaigns and independent media campaigns similar to those carried out by party committees. Opinion leaders, political consultants, party activists, and think tanks that are allied with a party also undertake efforts to assist that party's candidates. As is the case with allied PACs and individual donors, when these allies' preferences differ from those of their national party they do not follow the party's lead when choosing candidates for support.

The Impact of National Party Campaigning

Given the substantial efforts the national parties put forth in congressional elections, it seems reasonable to ask whether they make a difference. When asked, candidates competing in close elections, who receive the bulk of national party assistance, say the answer is yes. Not surprisingly, party assistance has a greater impact on the campaigns waged by challengers and open-seat candidates, who generally have less campaign experience and fewer advantages in fund-raising, than on the campaigns of incumbents (Herrnson 1988, 2012).

Although not as active in state and local elections as they are in presidential or congressional contests, national parties provide support to some candidates for lower level offices. The DNC, the RNC, and affiliated organizations, such as the Democratic Legislative Campaign Committee and GOPAC, work with state party leaders to recruit candidates, formulate strategy, and distribute campaign money and services. The national committees hold workshops to help state and local candidates learn the ins and outs of modern campaigning. The committees also recommend professional consultants and disseminate strategic and technical information through party magazines and briefing papers. It is important to note that national party strategy for distributing campaign money and services to state and local party organizations and candidates is influenced by considerations related to House, Senate, and presidential races. For example, national party leaders and members invested heavily in the elections held in Virginia in 2009. Concerns over party control of the state house for the post-2010 redistricting process encouraged national Democratic party organizations and party-connected committees to contribute $2.6 million to Democratic state and local party committees. These same concerns led their GOP counterparts to distribute roughly $4.6 million to the state's Republican organizations.[7]

Conclusion

American political parties are principally electoral institutions, and they developed in response to changes in their environment and the changing needs of their candidates. National party organizational change that occurs rapidly is associated with electoral instability, factional infighting, or political unrest. Gradual change is made in response to technological advances and modest alterations in the regulatory environment in which the parties operate. The institutionalization of the national parties has made them stronger, more stable, and more influential in their relations with state and local party committees, political consultants, and interest groups. More important, this development has enabled the national parties to play important roles in contemporary elections. They make campaign contributions and coordinated expenditures to assist their presidential and competitive congressional candidates. They provide services in areas of campaigning requiring technical expertise, in-depth research, and connections with other individuals and groups who possess some of the resources needed to conduct a viable campaign. They carry out independent media campaigns to improve the prospects of candidates in competitive races and coordinated grassroots campaigns designed to turn out voters in support of party candidates for all levels of office.

Perhaps just as important, the national parties influence the decision making of others in their coalitions. This includes party members who make party-connected contributions from their personal campaign accounts and leadership PACs. It includes party allies comprising organized interests that sponsor PACs, super PACs, 527 committees, or 501(c) organizations; political consultants that provide campaign services; and individuals that contribute to campaigns, work for partisan think tanks or media outlets, or otherwise participate in politics. It also comprises the voters who make up a party's electoral base and the voters that lean toward a party or its candidates in a given election. The national parties emergence as the central players in the enduring multilayered coalitions that structure politics is one of the most significant developments in US politics.

References

Aldrich, John H. 1995. *Why Parties? The Organization and Transformation of Parties in America.* Chicago, IL: University of Chicago Press.

Brewer, Paul R., and Christopher J. Deering. 2005. "Interest Groups, Campaign Fundraising, and Committee Chair Selection: House Republicans Play 'Musical Chairs.'" In *The Interest Group Connection*, edited by Paul S. Herrnson, Ronald G. Shaiko, and Clyde Wilcox. Washington, DC: CQ Press.

Brooks, Deborah Jordan. 2006. "The Resilient Voter: Moving Toward Closure in the Debate Over Negative Campaigning and Turnout." *Journal of Politics* 68: 684–696.

Brooks, Deborah Jordan, and John G. Geer. 2007. "Beyond Negativity." *American Journal of Political Science* 51: 1–16.

Brown, Clifford W., Lynda W. Powell, and Clyde Wilcox. 1995. *Serious Money*. New York: Cambridge University Press.

Bruce, Harold R. 1927. *American Parties and Politics*. New York: Henry Holt.

Canon, David T. 1990. *Actors, Athletes, and Astronauts: Political Amateurs in the United States Congress*. Chicago, IL: University of Chicago Press.

Carmines, Edward G., Steven H. Renten, and James A. Stimson. 1984. "Events and Alignments: The Party Image Link." In *Controversies in American Voting Behavior*, edited by Richard G. Niemi and Herbert F. Weisberg. Washington, DC: Congressional Quarterly.

Corrado, Anthony. 2011. "Financing the 2008 Presidential General Election." In *Financing the 2008 Election*, edited by David B. Magleby and Anthony Corrado. Washington, DC: Brookings Institution Press.

Cotter, Cornelius P., and Bernard C. Hennessy. 1964. *Politics Without Power: The National Party Committees*. New York: Atherton Press.

Currinder, Marian L. 2003. "Leadership PAC Contribution Strategies and House Member Ambitions." *Legislative Studies Quarterly* 28: 551–577.

Deckard, Barbara Sinclair. 1976. "Political Upheaval and Congressional Voting." *Journal of Politics* 38: 326–345.

Epstein, Leon D. 1986. *Political Parties in the American Mold*. Madison, WI: University of Wisconsin Press.

Federal Election Commission. 2008. "FEC Summarizes Party Financial Activity." http://www.fec.gov/press/press2008/20081029party/20081029party.shtml.

Francia, Peter L., John C. Green, Paul S. Herrnson, Lynda W. Powell, and Clyde Wilcox. 2003. *The Financiers of Congressional Elections*. New York: Columbia University Press.

Goldstein, Ken, and Paul Freedman. 2002. "Campaign Advertising and Voter Turnout." *Journal of Politics* 46: 721–740.

Heberlig, Eric, Mark Hetherington, and Bruce Larson. 2006. "The Price of Leadership: Campaign Money and the Polarization of Congressional Parties." *Journal of Politics* 68: 992–1005.

Herrnson, Paul S. 2012. *Congressional Elections: Campaigning at Home and in Washington*. 6th ed. Washington, DC: CQ Press.

———. 2009. "The Roles of Party Organizations, Party-Connected Committees, and Party Allies in Elections." *Journal of Politics* 71: 1207–1224.

———. 1993. "Political Leadership and Organizational Change at the National Committees." In *Politics, Professionalism, and Power*, edited by John Green. Lanham, MD: University Press of America.

———. 1988. *Party Campaigning in the 1980s*. Cambridge, MA: Harvard University Press.

Jacobson, Gary C. 1985–1986. "Party Organization and Campaign Resources in 1982." *Political Science Quarterly* 100: 604–625.

Key, V.O. 1958. *Politics, Parties, and Pressure Groups*. New York: Thomas Y. Crowell Company.

Magleby, David B. 2003. *The Other Campaign: Soft Money and Issue Advocacy in the 2000 Congressional Elections*. Lanham, MD: Rowman and Littlefield.

Merriam, Charles E. 1923. *The American Party System.* New York: Macmillan.
Nie, Norman H., Sidney Verba, and John R. Petrocik. 1979. *The Changing American Voter.* Cambridge, MA: Harvard University Press.
Polsby, Nelson W., and Aaron Wildavsky. 1984. *Presidential Elections.* New York: Charles Scribner's Sons.
Price, David E. 1984. *Bringing Back the Parties.* Washington, DC: Congressional Quarterly.
Ranney, Austin. 1975. *Curing the Mischiefs of Faction.* Berkeley, CA: University of California Press.
Roseboom, Eugene H. 1970. *A History of Presidential Elections.* New York: Macmillan.
Sabato, Larry J. 1981. *The Rise of the Political Consultants.* New York: Basis Books.
_____. 1985. *PAC Power.* Toronto, ON: Penguin Books.
Sait, Edward M. 1927. *American Political Parties and Elections.* New York: Century Company.
Schattschneider, E. E. 1942. *Party Government.* New York: Holt, Rhinehart, and Winston.
Schlesinger, Joseph. 1985. "The New American Political Party." *American Political Science Review* 79: 1151–1169.
Stone, Walter J., and L. Sandy Maisel. 2003. "The Not-so-Simple Calculus of Winning: Potential US House Candidates' Nomination and General Election Prospects." *Journal of Politics* 65: 951–977.
Wilcox, Clyde. 1989. "Share the Wealth: Contributions by Congressional Incumbents to the Campaigns of Other Candidates." *American Politics Quarterly* 17: 368–408.
Wilson, James Q. 1962. *The Amateur Democrat.* Chicago, IL: University of Chicago Press.

Endnotes

1. The BCRA actually created new classification of political advertising referred to as electioneering communications, which for practical purposes are issue-advocacy ads broadcast during the restricted period.

2. McCain also was able to raise and spend additional funds on general election and legal compliance. He raised $46.4 million for this purpose.

3. Coordinated expenditure limits for states with only one House member were set at $87,000 per committee in 2010.

4. Elections decided by 20 percent of the vote or less or in which a challenger defeated an incumbent by a larger margin are categorized as competitive; all others are categorized as uncompetitive. The races categorized as competitive with the lists of competitive races compiled by political journalists who handicap elections (see Herrnson 2012).

5. Most of the Republicans' heavy spending in uncompetitive open seats took place in the contests in Alaska and Florida, where the party's nominees had to compete against a Democrat and a defeated Republican primary candidate to win a GOP-held seat.

6. Figures compiled from Federal Election Commission and Center for Responsive Politics data (FEC 2008).

7. Figures compiled from Federal Election Commission and Center for Responsive Politics data (FEC 2008).

Parties and the Presidential Nominating Contests
The Battles to Control the Nominating Calendar

BARBARA NORRANDER
University of Arizona

The presidential nomination calendar extends from the Iowa caucuses and New Hampshire primary, typically held in February, to several clusters of states on "Super Tuesdays" in March, and finally, to a few states holding out with traditional primary dates in the first weeks of June. The order of the states along this calendar is not structured in any rational manner. States adopt dates to their pleasing, with the national political parties trying to impose some restrictions. Yet each election cycle introduces another example of the conflict between the national parties, state parties, and candidates in trying to mold the presidential nomination calendar to satisfy their own individual goals.

The 2008 campaign demonstrates the full extent of these conflicts. According to the national Democratic Party's plan, Iowa was scheduled to hold its caucuses on January 14 with the New Hampshire primary set for January 22. The Nevada caucuses and South Carolina primary were added to the January schedule to expand the demographic characteristics of voters in the early contests. All other states could select dates from February to June. Florida and Michigan, however, were unhappy with this structure and fought to be included among the early contests. Michigan adopted January 15 for its primary, and Florida set its primary for January 29. Iowa moved its caucuses up to January 3, leaving candidates in the quandary of whether and how to campaign during the December holiday period. New Hampshire defended its first-in-the-nation primary status by moving to January 8. Michigan maneuvered its way into being third, the Nevada caucuses occurred on January 19, followed by South Carolina's primary on January 26. Florida elbowed ahead of the rest of the states with its January 29 primary. Meanwhile, twenty-one states, Washington DC, American Samoa, and Democrats Abroad opted for the first "legal" date of February 5.[1] The traditional title of "Super Tuesday" for a multistate primary date did not seem to fit the gigantic February 5 event, so Super Duper Tuesday and Tsunami Tuesday were suggested as more appropriate metaphors.

With half of the states holding primaries or caucuses by February 5, many commentators speculated the presidential nomination season would come to a close by early February. Indeed, John McCain had the Republican contest nearly wrapped up after Super Duper Tuesday, amassing 57 percent of the delegate total needed for victory. More important, Fred Thompson, Rudy Giuliani, and Mitt Romney exited the race, leaving only Mike Huckabee and Ron Paul as contenders. McCain officially controlled the needed 50 percent of Republican convention delegates on March 4 after winning nine of the next ten post–Super Tuesday primaries. Only a close protracted race between two equally strong candidates on the Democratic side produced a nomination battle that for the first time in twenty-four years extended to the end of the primary and caucus calendar.

The 2008 nomination calendar continued the trend of front-loading, as more and more states scheduled their primary or caucuses at the front of the line. The perils of such a compact calendar have been well argued by political scientists and political commentators. William Mayer and Andrew Busch (2004a) in their book on the front-loading problem list a number of these concerns. With one or more super Tuesdays scheduled on the heels of Iowa and New Hampshire, voters have little time to become fully aware of the candidates, their issue positions, or leadership qualities. Candidates spend exorbitant time campaigning in Iowa and New Hampshire but then mount superficial campaigns of quick stopovers and heavy television advertising in advance of the next phase's multistate primary dates. Candidates who win early quickly become front-runners, gaining the most media coverage and new campaign dollars, thus making it more difficult for other qualified candidates to catch up. Indeed, many candidates concede the race after only a few primaries have been held. Thus, the nomination contests in recent decades concluded by mid-March, leaving some American voters with no say as their states' primaries were scheduled after all but one of the serious candidates had left the race. With a quick conclusion to the nomination race, the fall general election contest between the two parties crept into the late spring months, perpetuating the notion of an endless campaign interfering with the ability of elected officials to govern during election years (Wayne 2000). Thus, in recent decades the front-loaded nomination calendar posed the potential for a rush to judgment in the nomination phase, where some voters had more influence than others, followed by a prolonged interparty battle that interfered with effective governing. The next sections of this chapter will discuss how the conflicting goals of the national parties, the state parties, and the presidential contenders produced the hodgepodge of primary and caucus dates.

Timeliness of Convention Delegate Selection: The Goals of the 1970 Reforms

Through the first half of the twentieth century, most delegates to the two national party conventions represented their state parties and not presidential candidate preferences. Most national convention delegates were selected from local party representatives who gathered together at state conventions. Even in those states that used presidential primaries to select convention delegates, a common format was for the ballot to list only those individuals seeking to become delegates and not to list the presidential candidates' names. Since delegates represented the states, the timing of the selection of these delegates did not matter. However, the nationalization of politics, the weakening of local and state parties, the growth of national media sources, and the rising education and wealth levels of Americans gradually changed the nature of the national conventions. By the late 1950s, the conventions were increasingly populated by delegates who represented presidential candidates (Shafer 1988). When this change occurred, when and how convention delegates were selected started to matter.

The disjuncture between traditional delegate selection procedures and the new call for delegates committed to particular presidential candidates boiled over at the 1968 Democratic convention. In that year, incumbent president Lyndon Johnson was challenged first by Minnesota Senator Eugene McCarthy and then by New York Senator Robert Kennedy. In March, after a narrow victory over McCarthy in the New Hampshire primary, President Johnson withdrew from the nomination contest. His vice president, Hubert Humphrey, stepped in as the candidate of the party's traditional base. Humphrey played the rules of the "insider" candidate and did not enter any of the presidential primaries. McCarthy and Kennedy played the "outsider" game of contesting primaries to win delegates and to convince other delegates of their electability. McCarthy won an important primary victory over Kennedy in the May 28 Oregon primary. Kennedy countered with a victory over McCarthy in the June 4 California contest before being assassinated. Yet only 49 percent of the convention delegates were selected through the primaries and winning delegate support in other states proved difficult (Stanley and Niemi 2000).

In 1968, twenty-four states began some part of the delegate selection process before the election year—before Johnson withdrew and McCarthy and Kennedy became candidates. For example, in Michigan, the national convention delegates were selected by the Michigan state convention, whose delegates were drawn from county-level conventions. The delegates to these county conventions were selected two years earlier in the 1966 primary elections. Twenty-six states used some variant of a state convention to select convention delegates, though most of these allowed for rank-and-file party members to participate at some level. In ten states party or elected officials (i.e., the governor) selected at least part of the convention delegation (Democratic National Committee 1970). Only sixteen states and Washington, DC, held presidential primaries in 1968. Even winning a primary did not guarantee gaining delegates. McCarthy won 76 percent of the popular vote in the Pennsylvania primary, but separately elected delegates on the primary ballot and delegates awarded by the state party committee resulted in 84 percent of the convention delegates committed to Hubert Humphrey instead (Chester, Hodgson, and Page 1969).

The 1968 Democratic convention held in Chicago saw antiwar protesters clash with police outside the convention halls and heated arguments between convention delegates inside. Humphrey secured the nomination, but McCarthy and Kennedy delegates felt slighted. Before the close of the convention, a resolution was adopted to appoint a committee to develop fairer guidelines for the selection of delegates to the 1972 convention. This lead to the Commission on Party Structure and Delegate Selection, chaired first by Senator George S. McGovern (1969–71) and then by Representative Donald M. Fraser (1971–72). The commission is most commonly referred to as the McGovern-Fraser Commission. This commission developed eighteen guidelines, accepted by the Democratic National Committee for the 1972 convention. The adoption of these guidelines established the principle that national party rules should have superiority over state party rules and state laws (Ranney 1975), a principle supported by Supreme Court rulings such as *Democratic Party of the United States v. La Follette* (1981). The McGovern-Frazer guidelines also cemented the connection between delegate selection and candidate choices. As for the nomination calendar, the McGovern-Fraser guidelines included a provision for the timeliness of delegate selection. All Democratic delegates would need to be selected in procedures that started after January 1 of the election year. Additional provisions focused on opening up the delegate selection procedures to all Democratic voters.

The 1970s Democratic Party reforms had unintended consequences. One of these was the proliferation of presidential primaries. The authors of the McGovern-Fraser guidelines wanted to make all of the available delegate selection procedures more fair and open. Yet many states found switching to a primary the easiest way to comply with the new rules. There were other reasons states switched to primaries, including the extensive media coverage given to primary elections and a desire in some states to separate presidential politics from other party activities. As a result, the number of Democratic primaries increased from seventeen in 1968, to thirty in 1976, and thirty-nine in 2008 (Stanley and Niemi 2000, 62).[2] Even though the Republican Party was not part of the 1970s reforms, when states adopted primaries for the Democratic Party they usually did so for the Republican Party as well.[3]

A second unintended consequence of the 1970s Democratic Party reforms was that increasingly these presidential primaries were being clustered at the start of the primary calendar, in a process that has come to be known as front-loading. The incentives for states to move their presidential primary dates forward developed as candidates adapted their strategies to the new format of numerous state primaries. Jimmy Carter in 1976 showed that by early victories in the Iowa caucuses and the New Hampshire primary he gained momentum—an advantage in subsequent fund-raising, media attention, and perceived electability. Most candidates adopted the early-is-better strategy, spending extraordinary amounts of time and money campaigning in the early primary states, hoping to win early and capture momentum. Those candidates who did not do well in the early contests soon learned that it made more sense to quit the race than to try to continue a campaign with limited resources and little hope of catching up to the front-runner. Thus, voters in the early primary states appeared to be having the most influence on the parties' nominations. Their choices influenced the subsequent standing of the candidates and winnowed a number of contenders from the field. The front-loading of candidate strategies gave states an incentive to adopt early primary dates, front-loading the election calendar as well.

National Party Attempts to
Control the Nomination Calendar

Since 1980 for the Democrats and 2000 for the Republicans, the national parties have created "windows" of allowable dates for delegate selection. Between 1980 and 2000 the Democratic window spanned from the second Tuesday in March until the first or second Tuesday in June. The first Republican Party's window in 2000 allowed for February primary dates. Except for the February 1 New Hampshire primary, the Republican Party had the rest of February 2000 calendar to itself.[4] Several states held Republican primaries in February and Democratic caucuses later in the election year. For example, in Arizona the state-sponsored primary was set for February 22, a date favored by the Republican Party in the state. Since Arizona Democrats could not use this date, they held a party-sponsored primary on March 11 and allowed for Internet voting in the prior four days (Solop 2001). National Democratic Party leaders became frustrated that the Republicans in 2000 had the media's focus to themselves for their February primaries. This led the Democrats in 2004 to expand their window to include February primaries. Thus, in 2004 and 2008, Democrats and Republicans had the same calendar for primaries and caucuses from February to June. For 2012, the two parties have moved back the start of the window to the first Tuesday in March.

The Iowa caucuses and New Hampshire primary typically fall outside of the parties' "window" of allowable primary dates. These two states adopted their early dates when early was not necessarily viewed as better. New Hampshire enacted its presidential primary in 1913 and soon scheduled it for the second Tuesday in March to coincide with their town meetings. Not much attention was given to New Hampshire and its early primary date until the 1950s, when it added a nonbinding candidate preference poll to its delegate-selection primary format.[5] Being able to declare winning and losing candidates in the New Hampshire primary led to increasing media coverage and candidate attention. The Iowa caucuses moved forward in 1972 to accommodate the multiple intermediate-level meetings (county conventions, congressional district conventions, and state convention) within a state rule requiring thirty days between events and an unusually early Democratic National Convention scheduled for July 9 (Norrander 2010). As being early gained greater importance, these two states fiercely held onto their "first-in-the-nation" status. The Democratic Party often granted these two states exemptions to the calendar rules, but the Republican Party traditionally did not. In 2008, the Democratic Party, in an attempt for a more representative group of early states, added South Carolina (primary) and Nevada (caucus) to the first round. These two states were selected to provide a greater voice for minority voters in the early Democratic selection process. For 2012, both parties have sanctioned these four early contests. However, by the fall of 2011 the plan for these first four events to be held in February followed by the remaining contests beginning in March had fallen apart. Florida moved its primary to January 31, forcing the first four states to scramble to position their dates before Florida's. Arizona and Michigan adopted primary dates in February. Once again, the nomination calendar appeared to be out of the control of the national parties.

The two parties have adopted a carrot-and-stick approach in their attempts to control the primary and caucus calendar. As a carrot, the two parties have offered additional delegates to states that hold later primaries. Thus, in 2000 the Republican Party offered bonus delegates to states scheduling primaries on March 15 or later; and the Democrats' 2008 plan provided bonus delegates to primaries held after March 31. Neither party's bonus delegates proved successful in convincing states to hold back their primary dates. The number of additional delegates was too small and the probability that the nomination contest would be over before a late primary was held was too great. For 2012, the Republican Party is trying a different carrot. States that schedule their primary elections on or after April 1 may use any delegate distribution rule, including winner-take-all. States that adopt earlier primary dates must use proportional representation rules to divide the state's delegation on the basis of the primary results. This is the first time that the national Republican Party is dictating delegate distribution rules to the states. It is hoping that the clout a state could gain by being able to award all of its delegates to one candidate will be a sufficient carrot to convince states to hold later primaries. This type of carrot is not available for the Democratic Party, which has required that all primaries and caucuses use proportional representation rules since 1992.

The stick approach to controlling the nomination calendar involves reducing the number of delegates for states that schedule their primaries before the allowable window. Thus, in 2008 the Republican Party removed half of the delegates from five states (New Hampshire, Michigan, South Carolina, Florida, and Wyoming) that held early primaries or caucuses (Wyoming) before February 1.[6] This penalty had little effect on the race, as Republican candidates continued to campaign heavily in these states. John McCain's victories in New Hampshire, South Carolina, and Florida were crucial to his early lead and caused the withdrawals of Fred Thompson and Rudy Giuliani. The Democratic Party attempted to put more teeth into their penalty by taking away all of the offending states' delegates and persuading candidates not to campaign in these states. Thus, initially the Democratic Party punished Michigan and Florida by removing all of their delegates and the candidates did cease their campaigns in these states. As well, Barack Obama and three other candidates withdrew their names from the Michigan ballot, though Clinton and two other candidates' names remained. All of the candidates' names remained on the Florida ballot. When the extended battle between Barack Obama and Hillary Clinton made every last delegate vital to deciding who would win the nomination, the Democratic National Committee on May 31 tempered its view, restoring half of Michigan's and Florida's delegate count and awarding Clinton eighty-seven delegates and Obama sixty-eight delegates (Norrander 2010, 77–78).

Throughout much of the 1990s and the first decade of the twenty-first century, the two parties at the national level have tried to thwart the forward march of presidential primary dates. Many of their efforts have had little effect. The national parties simply do not control the actual selection of primary and caucus dates. These are the purviews of the state legislatures and state parties. The "carrots" that the national parties can offer are not enticing enough for states to adopt later primary dates, and the "sticks" have been inconsistently applied and insufficiently strong to dissuade states from jumping to the front of the line. In addition, the national parties have not been of one voice in trying to stem front-loading. Some party officials have even pointed to advantages from front-loading. An early close to the nomination battle allows the party to coalesce behind the presumptive nominee, heal any lingering animosity among the supporters of the losing candidates, and concentrate on the general election battle with the opposing party's candidate (Busch 2008). Still, more often than not, the two national parties have been frustrated in their attempts to control the presidential nomination calendar and convince state parties and legislatures to conform to national party rules.

State Parties and State Legislatures and the Presidential Nomination Calendar

Most of the focus on state parties and state legislatures is how their actions have contributed to front-loading. Thus, researchers explore factors that lead states to move their primary date forward (Carman and Barker 2005; Mayer and Busch 2004a) or switch from caucuses to primaries (Rice and Kenney 1984; Walz and Comer 1999). A main reason for states to move their primaries forward is to insure that their presidential primary is held before the nomination race is effectively over. With candidates withdrawing from the contest when they began to lag behind, unofficial nominees are often apparent before the last half of the scheduled primaries. Only in the early primary states do voters choose among all the candidates. Politicians in moralistic states may be particularly in tune with the need to hold an early primary in order to guarantee their citizens an electoral choice among the full slate of candidates (Carman and Barker 2005). The political culture in these moralistic states emphasizes the role of citizens coming together to participate in politics. Moralistic political culture states are found mainly along the northern tier of the United States.

Voters in the early primary states also receive more attention from the candidates. Because early contests are crucial to the nomination outcome, candidates spend many days campaigning in these states. Prior to the 2004 Iowa caucuses, Howard Dean spent seventy-six days campaigning in the state while Kerry racked up seventy-three days (Hull 2008). John McCain held 114 town meetings in New Hampshire in front of its 2000 primary (Norrander 2010). Further, the outcomes of Iowa and New Hampshire change the level of media coverage that candidates receive, helping or hindering their chances in subsequent primaries (Hunsaker 2011). Even the American public tends to know which candidates won in Iowa or New

Hampshire (Redlawsk, Tolbert, and Donovan 2011). Thus voters in Iowa and New Hampshire, and other early primaries, appear to have more influence on the nominations than voters in other states.

Early primary states accrue economic benefits. Campaigns spend considerable money in these states, setting up local headquarters, airing television and radio advertisements, and paying for frequent visits by the candidates. Media organizations, likewise, spend money as their reporters follow the candidates to these states. One estimate is that in 2000 the New Hampshire primary brought $264 million into the state (Mayer and Busch 2004a). Meanwhile, California governor Arnold Schwarzenegger expressed his frustrations that candidates would come to California to raise funds and then turn around and spend them in Iowa and New Hampshire (MacAskill 2007). As candidates campaign in the early states they also pay attention to issues of concern to their voters, such as ethanol subsidies in Iowa. Holding an early primary or caucus may even improve a state's chances of receiving federal grant money (Mixon and Hobson 2011).

All of the above reasons have given states the incentive to move their primary dates forward. As a result, the presidential nominating calendar has become increasingly front-loaded. Mayer and Busch (2004a) have demonstrated this front-loading by listing the number of primaries held in each week of the nomination calendar and the cumulative percentage of delegates chosen. For example, on the fourth week of the 1988 nomination season, fifteen states held their primaries on Super Tuesday. In 1972, no primary was held in the fourth week and only three primaries were held earlier than that. In 2000, 68 percent of the delegates had been chosen by the seventh week, while this figure was not reached until the thirteenth week in 1980. Yet the movement of primaries is more than a steady march forward. Some states move the dates of their primaries backward, some have experimented between holding caucuses and primaries, and some have stayed put, keeping their original primary dates.

States can have a variety of reasons for moving the date of their presidential primaries backward on the nomination calendar. An early presidential primary date usually means that a state must separate the primary for its congressional and state-level offices from the presidential primary. Thus, state coffers must pay for two primaries rather than one. In some instances, states leaders may believe the extra cost is worth it to gain more clout. Also, some states hold their congressional primaries in late summer or early fall, and as such, would have to hold their presidential primary separately. California is the most recent example of a state deciding that two primaries are too expensive. After moving to the front of the line with a February 5 primary in 2008, for 2012 the state is returning to its traditional June congressional primary date. The move will save the state and local governments approximately $100 million. In previous years, other states have moved their primaries backward to consolidate them with congressional primaries or canceled their presidential primary altogether to return to party-sponsored caucuses. Some states consolidated the two types of primaries by moving both forward on the election calendar but found that state legislators did not like the early start date for their reelection campaigns. These states, too, subsequently moved their primary dates backward. Thus, states that have experimented with early presidential primary dates may have found them to be too expensive, not to increase voter participation, and to have placed them in a crowded schedule filled with other state primaries such that they did not gain in candidate or media attention. As a result, presidential primaries are moved backward on the calendar or canceled.

Most of the states' activities in selecting primary dates are uncoordinated. Each state acts alone in trying to maximize its goals. Yet, a few times states have come together in efforts to group their primaries in the regional primary format. The most successful of these efforts produced the southern regional primary on Super Tuesday of March 8, 1988. This effort was mainly the objective of Democratic Party leaders in the region, who felt that previous Democratic nominees had been too liberal. Southern Republicans, however, did not object, reasoning that the primaries might draw more voters into the Republican camp. The Southern Legislative Conference, along with other regional groups, helped to coordinate the activities across the various state legislatures. The result was simultaneous primaries for fifteen southern states, which coincided with the date chosen by six other states for their primaries or caucuses. Expectations were that a southern regional primary would garner more attention from the candidates for the region and its issues, would spark the interest of the national media in covering southern politics, and would lead to an increased level of political participation by southern voters. While these goals were met in some states, other party leaders felt that their state did not receive as much attention as promised and the costs of holding the primaries were too high (Norrander 1992). The southern regional primary was not replicated in subsequent years, as one by one southern states left the first Tuesday in March date. Other efforts for regional primaries have occurred in the New England and Rocky Mountain states.

The Influence of
Candidates and Their Supporters

Some states adopted primaries or advanced the date of their primaries to help out home-state candidates. Prior to the 1976 primaries, Texas adopted a primary in hopes of providing its senator Lloyd Bentsen with an easy primary victory. Likewise, North Carolina moved to the primary format to assist its former governor Terry Sanford, while Georgia made the switch to advance the cause of its recent governor Jimmy Carter (Norrander 1992). Missouri adopted a primary in 1988 in order to help Democratic Representative Dick Gephardt in his quest for the presidency (Cain and Mullin 2002). Such strategies, however, do not always work out. Only Jimmy Carter's candidacy proved successful.

Sometimes supporters of rival candidates confront each other in trying to manipulate a state's primary date. In advance of Ronald Reagan's 1980 bid for the Republican nomination, his supporters in South Carolina favored a date for their state's primary that would be earlier than other southern primaries to give Reagan an initial southern victory against a potentially strong showing by former Texas governor John Connally in the rest of the South. Connally's supporters opposed the new date for the South Carolina primary but lost out on the rule change. Connally also lost the South Carolina primary to Reagan, ending his presidential bid (Kamarck 2009).

Presidents have the most influence over nomination rules. Before his 1980 bid for renomination, Jimmy Carter convinced Alabama, Florida, and Georgia to hold early primaries to counter any advantages his rival Ted Kennedy would have in the early New Hampshire and Massachusetts primaries. Carter also maneuvered the Democratic reform commission of that year to adopt a window of allowable dates that would concentrate more states at the beginning of March, a concentration thought to advantage him as the front-runner (Kamarck 2009; Norrander 1992). Walter Mondale as a former vice president had more mixed results in trying to shape the 1984 nomination to his favor. His supporters in Rhode Island and Massachusetts moved their primaries forward, but he was unable to convince his home state of Minnesota to adopt a primary or get New Jersey to move its primary forward. Even a successful quest for a favorable calendar, however, can be thwarted as anticipated rivals fade and unanticipated new ones arise. The Mondale organization wanted more Eastern and Midwestern events to counter the presumed southern support for the more conservative Ohio senator John Glenn, but the more liberal Colorado senator Gary Hart became his main rival instead (Kamarck 2009).

The Moving Parts of the Presidential Nomination Calendar: 1968–2008

The presidential nomination calendar has been influenced by the actions of the national parties, state parties and legislatures, and candidates and their supporters. As a result, the nomination calendar has a new look with each passing election cycle. Table 7.1 shows the movement in presidential primary dates, along with the Iowa caucuses, between 1968 and 2008. States are listed by the week in each month in which they held their primary, with weeks defined as beginning on Tuesday and ending on Monday. In a few instances, a month had a fifth week, but these are combined with the fourth week totals. States that moved a primary at least two weeks earlier on the election calendar are highlighted by a bold print and a single underline. States adopting a new primary are indicated by a single underline. This movement is generally the result of switching from a caucus to a primary. Some states did this more than once and are designated as "new" primaries if more than one election season passed between the first and second primary. Backward movement, by more than one week, is designated by parentheses. States without any of these designations have approximately the same dates as their primaries in the previous year.

A few patterns can be discerned from Table 7.1. First, only four states have remained with the caucus format throughout the 1968–2008 nomination cycles: Iowa, Alaska, Hawaii, and Wyoming. Iowa, obviously, benefits from being the first in the nation event, even if it is a caucus. The other three are states with small populations and remote locations that probably would not be able to attract candidate attention even if they switched to a primary. Eight states (CO, KS, ME, MN, MO, NV, ND, VA) had traditional caucus formats, experimented with a primary, and—with one exception (Virginia)—eventually returned to the caucus format. Most experimented with the primary format in the 1980s or 1990s. Another eight states (ID, IN, MT, NE, NM, PA, VT, WV)

TABLE 7.1 Primaries (and Iowa Caucuses) Held in Each Calendar Week, 1968–2008

Week	1968	1972	1976	1980	1984	1988	1992	1996	2000	2004	2008
Jan 1											IA
Jan 2										IA **DC**	**NH**
Jan 3			IA						**IA**		**MI**
Jan 4										NH	SC **FL**
Feb 1						IA	IA	IA	**NH** DE[D]	**AZ** DE **MO OK SC** MI	**AL** AZ **AR CA CT** DE **GA IL MA** MO **NJ NM[D] NY** OK TN **UT LA**
Feb 2									DE[R]	**TN VA**	(DC) **MD** VA
Feb 3				**PR[R]**	(IA)	NH	NH	NH DE	SC	**WI**	WI WA
Feb 4			NH	NH	NH	**SD**	SD	AZ[R] **ND** SD SC PR	AZ[R] **MI VA WA**	UT	
Mar 1	NH	NH	**MA VT**	MA VT SC	VT	VT SC	**CO** GA MD SC	CO **CT** GA ME MD MA RI VT **NY** AZ[D]	**CA** CT GA ME MD MA MO NY **OH** RI VT CO UT AZ[D]	CA CT GA MD MA NY OH RI VT	OH RI TX VT
Mar 2		**FL**	FL	**AL** FL **GA** PR[D]	AL FL GA MA **RI** PR	AL **AR** FL GA **KY LA** MD MA **MS** MO **NC** OK RI **TN** TX VA	FL LA MA MS OK RI TN TX	FL LA MS OK **OR** TN TX	FL LA MS OK TN TX	FL LA MS TX	MS

Week	1968	1972	1976	1980	1984	1988	1992	1996	2000	2004	2008
Mar 3		**IL**	IL	IL	IL	IL PR	IL MI	IL MI **OH WI**	IL	IL	
Mar 4			NC	CT NY	CT	CT	CT	**CA NV WA**			
Apr 1	WI	WI	NY WI	KS WI LA	NY WI	WI	KS MN NY WI		**PA** (WI)		
Apr 2					PA						
Apr 3						(NY)					
Apr 4	MA PA	MA PA	PA TX	PA TX		PA	PA	PA		PA	PA
May 1	AL DC IN OH	AL DC IN OH TN NC	AL DC GA IN	DC IN (NC) TN	DC TN (LA) TX	DC IN OH	DC IN NC	DC IN NC	DC IN NC	IN	IN NC
May 2	NE WV	NE WV	NE VW	MD NE	IN MD NC OH	NE WV	NE WV	NE WV	NE WV	NE WV	NE WV
May 3		MD MI	ND MI	MI OR	NE OR ID	OR	OR WA	AR	(OR)	AR KY OR	KY OR
May 4	FL OR	OR RI	AR ID KY NV OR (TN)	AR ID KY NV		ID	(AR) ID (KY)	ID KY	AR ID KY	ID	PR ID
Jun 1	CA NJ SD	CA NJ NM SD	MT RI SD	CA NM NJ MT OH RI SD (WV) MS	CA MT NY NM SD WV	CA MT NJ NM	(AL) CA MT NJ NM (OH)	AL MT NJ NM	AL MT NJ NM (SD)	AL SD NM	MT SD NM[R]
Jun 2	IL		CA NJ (OH)		ND	ND	ND			MT NJ	
Jun 3	NY	NY									

Sources: Guide to US Elections 2005; Norrander 2009.

Notes: Bold underline = significant movement forward on calendar; Parentheses = significant movement backward on calendar
Single underline = new primary.
D or R inside brackets indicates separate primaries held by each party.

have held primaries since at least 1976, and retained essentially the same date throughout the period. With the exception of Vermont, these "stand pat" states hold late in the season primaries coupled with their congressional primaries. Most of these late primary states get overlooked in recent nomination politics, but when a more lengthy campaign does occur they can be key contests, such as Pennsylvania in 2008. Four more states (KY, NC, OR, SD) experimented by moving their primary dates forward but subsequently moved them back to where they started.

The final group of twenty-seven states has contributed to the general front-loading of the primary calendar. Three states crept forward, a little at a time. One of these is New Hampshire in its attempts to remain in front of the rest of the states. Likewise, South Carolina inches forward to retain its claim to being the first southern primary. Finally, Delaware, a late entrant to the primary calendar, has slowly moved its date forward since 2000. Nine states made a single leap forward on the nomination calendar (AZ, DC, MS, NJ, ND, OK, RI, TX, UT). Some of these states were traditional holdouts against front-loading, such as New Jersey, which only succumbed to moving to the front of the line in 2008 to match the changes by California and New York. Other states, such as Texas and Mississippi, moved forward once but not to the front of the line. Both of theses states moved to join the 1988 southern regional primary and then stayed put. Three states moved forward and backward and forward again. Arkansas and Alabama moved forward to join the 1988 southern regional primary, returned back to their traditional dates, but in 2008 succumbed to the draw of the February 5 Super Duper Tuesday. Ohio also moved backward and forward but ended up at the beginning of March. The final group of fifteen states (AR, CA, CT, FL, GA, IL, LA, MD, MA, MI, OH, NY, TN, WA, WI) are the most consistent participants in the front-loading phenomenon, moving forward at least twice in their attempts to gain more clout. California is the prime example of a state seeking more clout. In the pre-reform era, its last-of-the-season primary date was often crucial to gain momentum going into the summer conventions. California held onto its June primary through 1992, but then began the front-loading movement in earnest. It first moved to the end of March, then to the beginning of March, and finally to the beginning of February. Florida and Michigan pursued front-loading strategies to the extent that they violated both parties' rules on allow-able primary dates in 2008.

Table 7.2   Types of Calendar Movement by Election Cycle (in percents)

Year	Forward Movement	New Primary	Backward Movement	No Change	Number of Primaries
1972	9	13	0	78	23
1976	10	27	7	54	30
1980	8	16	5	70	37
1984	10	3	3	84	31
1988	26	8	0	66	38
1992	3	13	10	74	39
1996	19	9	0	72	43
2000	14	7	7	72	43
2004	21	0	0	79	39
2008	37	0	2	60	43
All years	16	10	3	71	366

Table 7.2 summarizes the types of movement by each election cycle. Over all the years, an average of 71 percent of the primary schedule remained intact from four years earlier. Thus, a core of stability always anchors the nomination calendar, a fact overlooked in the debate over front-loading. The most tranquil year was 1984, when 84 percent of the schedule replicated the 1980 calendar. The years of 1976 and 2008 showed the most changes in the schedule, but for different reasons. In 1976 most of the changes came from new adoptions of primary laws. In 2008, the cause was the highest level of front-loading movement across these ten election cycles. The front-loading effects of the regional southern primary are shown in 1988, with 2004 being the other year in which at least one out of five states moved their primary forward. Backward movement by states is the least common practice. The table does not list the number of states abandoning primaries in any given year, but seven states permanently (at least through 2008) returned to the caucus format. Also, in years of tight state budget a small number of states canceled primaries, and when an incumbent president is running for reelection, the primary of his party is canceled in some states, as well.

The past three decades have seen states jockeying for prime positions on the presidential nomination calendar. More than half of the states have participated in the front-loading movement of more and more primaries being held in the earliest months of the election year. Most of these states are seeking more clout in determining the outcome of the two parties' presidential nominations. Yet, the mostly uncoordinated efforts by these states, urged on at times by specific candidate supporters, produces an election calendar that is compact and disorderly. The calendar also is biased toward some states, while other states hold primaries that occur after the nomination race is essentially over.

Can the Nomination Calendar Be Improved?

The hodgepodge nature of the presidential primary and caucus calendar seems to call out for reform. There is no lack of ideas about alternatives. Some advocate for a single, national primary to replace the fifty separate state events. Others argue for a series of regional primaries, with the ordering of the regions rotated across election years. A third proposal (called the Delaware Plan) groups states by population sizes and schedules the smallest states first and the largest states last. Advocates for each reform make claims about greater fairness by increasing the chances for meaningful participation by voters in all states. As such, turnout in these primaries should increase, reducing the potential biases that small turnout levels can create. Candidates, too, would benefit from a more rational schedule in which to plan their campaigns. (For addition explanations and arguments of these reform plans see Mayer and Busch 2004a, chapter 5; Norrander 2010, chapter 4; Redlawsk, Tolbert, and Donovan 2011, chapter 10.)

Since the early twentieth century, numerous bills have been introduced into Congress to reform the presidential nomination process. None of these bills has progressed very far, and some scholars argue that Congress does not have the authority to adopt a national primary or the regional primary format due to the differences in language concerning presidential versus congressional elections in the Constitution (Mayer and Busch 2004b). Groups of states have attempted to form their own regional primary, but only the South succeeded to a great extent. Finally, the national Republican Party in 2000 attempted to adopt the small-state-first large-state-last plan. Such a rule change required a vote at the national convention, but the proposal was rejected by the convention's Rules Committee as supporters of presumptive nominee George W. Bush did not want controversies over format changes to disrupt the convention.

Widespread reform is unlikely to happen, given the record of recent attempts. States will continue to schedule primaries or caucuses based on their own set of goals, whether it is to gain more clout, advance the candidacy of a favorite son or daughter, or save the state treasury the costs of a separate presidential primary election. The calculus of the state parties and legislators will be shaped by the dynamics of the previous election cycle. When the prior nominations were all but decided by March, state leaders will calculate a greater need for an early primary. Following an extended nomination battle, states may be more willing to hold back on the date for their primary. States also will compete against one another, making moves and countermoves to gain their own advantage. Against these maneuverings by state party leaders, the national parties will continue to try to maintain some control over the start of the nomination calendar and encourage states to adopt a more diverse set of primary dates.

References

Busch, Andrew E. 2008. "Federalism and Front-Loading." *Publius* 38: 538–55.

Cain, Bruce E., and Megan Mullin. 2002. "Competing for Attention and Votes: The Role of State Parties in Setting Presidential Nomination Rules." In *The Parties Respond,* edited by L. Sandy Maisel. 4th ed. Boulder, CO: Westview.

Carman, Christopher J., and David C. Barker. 2005. "State Political Culture, Primary Front-Loading, and Democratic Voice in Presidential Nominations: 1972–2000." *Electoral Studies* 24: 665–87.

Chester, Lewis, Godfrey Hodgson, and Bruce Page. 1969. *An American Melodrama: The Presidential Campaign of 1968.* New York: Viking Press.

Democratic National Committee. 1970. *Mandate for Reform: A Report of the Commission on Party Structure and Delegate Selection to the Democratic National Committee.* Washington, DC: Democratic National Committee.

Guide to US Elections. 2005. 5th ed. Washington, DC: CQ Press.

Hull, Christopher C. 2008. *Grassroots Rules: How the Iowa Caucus Helps Elect American Presidents.* Stanford, CA: Stanford University Press.

Hunsaker, Rob. 2011. "Effects of Iowa and New Hampshire in US Presidential Nomination Contests 1976–2008." In *Why Iowa,* edited by David P. Redlawsk, Caroline J. Tolbert, and Todd Donovan. Chicago, IL: University of Chicago Press.

Kamarck, Elaine C. 2009. *Primary Politics: How Presidential Candidates Have Shaped the Modern Nominating System.* Washington, DC: Brookings Institution Press.

MacAskill, Ewen. 2007. "Presidential Race 2008: Slow Road from Iowa to Washington to Be Replaced by Fast-Track Selection." *Guardian* (London). April 5, 29.

Mayer, William G., and Andrew E. Busch. 2004a. *The Front-Loading Problem in Presidential Nominations.* Washington, DC: Brookings Institution Press.

———. 2004b. "Can the Federal Government Reform the Presidential Nomination Process?" *Election Law Journal* 3: 613–25.

Mixon, Franklin G., Jr., and David L. Hobson. 2001. "Intergovernmental Grants and the Positioning of Presidential Primaries and Caucuses: Empirical Evidence from the 1992, 1996, and 2000 Election Cycles." *Contemporary Economic Policy* 19: 27–38.

Norrander, Barbara. 1992. *Super Tuesday: Regional Politics and Presidential Primaries.* Lexington, KY: University Press of Kentucky.

_____. 2009. "Democratic Marathon, Republican Sprint: The 2008 Presidential Nominations." In *The American Elections of 2008*, edited by Janet M. Box-Steffensmeier and Steven E. Schier. Lanham, MD: Rowman and Littlefield.

_____. 2010. *The Imperfect Primary*. New York: Routledge.

Ranney, Austin. 1975. *Curing the Mischiefs of Faction: Party Reform in America*. Berkeley, CA: University of California Press.

Redlawsk, David P., Caroline J. Tolbert, and Todd Donovan. 2011. *Why Iowa*. Chicago, IL: University of Chicago Press.

Rice, Tom W., and Patrick Kenney. 1984. "Boosting State Economies: The Caucus-Convention vs. the Primary." *Presidential Studies Quarterly* 24: 357–60.

Shafer, Byron E. 1988. *Bifurcated Politics: Evolution and Reform in the National Party Convention*. Cambridge, MA: Harvard University Press.

Solop, Frederic I. 2001. "Digital Democracy Comes of Age: Internet Voting and the 2000 Arizona Democratic Primary Election." *PS: Political Science & Politics* 34: 289–93.

Stanley, Harold W., and Richard G. Niemi. 2000. *Vital Statistics on American Politics 1999–2000*. Washington, DC: CQ Press.

Walz, Jeffrey S., and John Comer. 1999. "State Responses to National Democratic Party Reforms." *Political Research Quarterly* 52: 189–208.

Wayne, Stephen. 2000. "A Proposal to Reform the Presidential Nomination Process." *Nominating Future Presidents: A Review of the Republican Process*. Washington, DC: Republican National Committee.

Endnotes

1. The two parties allow US territories (Puerto Rico, Guam, American Samoa, Virgin Islands) to participate in the presidential nomination process, though residents of these entities cannot vote in the fall presidential election. The Democratic Party provides a mechanism for Americans living abroad to be represented at the national convention, as well.

2. The number of Republican primaries was one fewer in 1992 and two more in 2008 than for the Democratic Party.

3. The Republican Party did have one early reform commission called Republican Committee on Delegates and Organization or "Do Committee." Appointed in 1969 by the national party chair, it proposed ten new rules that were mostly adopted by the 1972 convention (Ranney 1975, 3).

4. Democratic primaries were held in Delaware and Washington State in February but these were "beauty-contest" primaries not connected to the selection of convention delegates.

5. New Hampshire abandoned its delegate selection portion of the primary ballot in 1977.

6. Iowa and Nevada were not punished by the Republican Party for their early caucus dates because neither state chose national convention delegates in this initial round.

8

Political Parties and Campaign Finance
Challenges and Adaptations

DIANA DWYRE
California State University, Chico

The role of parties in campaign finance has changed dramatically since the rise of national party organizations in the early1800s.[1] For over 100 years, the parties were central to organizing, funding, and waging campaigns for candidates running under their labels. The parties changed and adapted to various developments and shifts in the political environment in order to retain this central role in US campaigns. Yet since the early 1900s, the parties have faced significant challenges to their role and influence in campaigns. The Progressive reformers of the early 1900s fundamentally changed the electoral landscape in which the parties operate. The move to candidate-centered politics in the 1960s and 1970s, and the recent reforms, court decisions, and regulations of the early twenty-first century have created a strategic environment in which parties must compete with many other groups that also aim to influence the outcome of elections. Yet, as they have done in the past, the parties have worked to adapt and adjust to changes and challenges in their environment. The ambitious office seekers and officeholders who created and maintain the parties "have used or abused, reformed or ignored the political party when doing so has furthered their goals and ambitions" (Aldrich 1995, 4).

Many scholars and other observers have long argued that parties play a central and important role in elections. The 1950 American Political Science Association's report, *Toward a More Responsible Two-Party System*, called for a more robust and central role for parties in all realms of politics. Morris Fiorina and many others have argued that party-centered politics are more likely to insure the political accountability of officeholders (Fiorina 1980; see also Broder 1972; Sundquist 1983; Aldrich 1995; LaRaja 2008). Parties are the only electoral actors primarily interested in building a majority coalition over the long term, and thus they are the funders most likely to spread their resources beyond the most competitive races, which in turn can make more races competitive. Indeed competitive elections are widely seen as an important if not necessary ingredient for a legitimate representative democracy (see, for example, Schmitter and Karl 1991, 82).

In this chapter, I discuss the role that political parties have played in financing elections, focusing primarily on the national parties. First, a brief review of the historical place of parties in the financing of elections shows that the parties have gone from being central actors to one of many players that raise and spend money to influence the outcome of elections. Second, I look at the reform period that began in the 1970s and examine how parties adapted to the rapidly and dramatically changing regulatory landscape. The final section of this chapter analyzes the effects of recent changes to campaign finance rules, which the parties are working to adjust and adapt to in order to continue to play a relevant and important financial role in American elections.

Early American Parties: Parties at the Helm

Ever since truly competitive elections emerged in the 1830s with the rise of the Whigs to oppose Jackson's grassroots Democratic Party, US political parties have been primarily electoral organizations, less involved in the development of policy or the activities of their elected officials in government than their counterparts in other Western democracies (Epstein 1986). Indeed, in order to achieve any other goals, such as policy goals, parties must first get their candidates elected to office (Downs 1957; Mayhew 1974). Then, as now, parties primarily organized and mobilized voters. During the nineteenth century, parties were the central organizers of campaigns, sponsoring speeches, rallies, bonfires, marches, and other party hoopla to build enthusiasm for the party's candidates (Dwyre 2010, 69–72; LaRaja 2008).

By 1848, the Democrats had created a central committee, the Democratic National Committee (DNC), with one member from each state to develop and coordinate party activities nationwide between elections (Nichols 1967, 371). The Republican National Committee (RNC) was well financed for its first real campaign in 1856. Both national parties sought to build party organizations in the states and raised funds primarily from "high-level benefit seekers," such as bankers and corporate leaders, to support state party organizations and mobilization efforts (Aldrich 1995, 112; see also Nichols 1967, 375–376). What would eventually become the powerful but corrupt political party machines that were bankrolled by big corporate interests were being developed during this pre–Civil War era.

The DNC and RNC were most concerned about the presidential contest, and they were generally inactive during the congressional midterm elections (Kolodny 1998). So, during the chaotic post–Civil War period, partisans in the House of Representatives established their own congressional campaign committees, as factional national politics led congressional incumbents to feel particularly insecure about their own reelections. The National Republican Congressional Committee (NRCC) was established in 1866, and the Democratic Congressional Campaign Committee (DCCC) soon thereafter. Senators created their own campaign committees, the National Republican Senatorial Committee (NRSC) and the Democratic Senatorial Campaign Committee (DSCC), after ratification of the Seventeenth Amendment in 1913, which required the direct election of senators. As before, political changes or crises motivated politicians to turn to and redesign their parties to help them achieve their goals (Aldrich 1995). If one arm of the party is not serving the reelection interests of some of its members, why not create another arm?

As the nation left the Civil War behind and entered an era of rapid industrialization and massive immigration, the parties became highly sectional. The Democrats controlled politics in the South, and cities in the North with Democratic Party machines such as New York's Tammany Hall. The Democrats also drew support from farmers and the working class, who had not shared in the prosperity from rapid economic expansion during the Industrial

Revolution. The Republicans received support only from blacks in the South, who were quickly disenfranchised by Jim Crow laws such as poll taxes, literacy tests, and whites-only primaries after Reconstruction. Northeastern and Midwestern industrialists also supported the GOP (Grand Old Party, the nickname adopted by the Republicans).

By the mid-1890s, the parties were on opposite sides of important national issues in the midst of an economic downturn. Republican corporations and bankers were pitted against Democratic farmers and workers, as they debated the virtues of gold versus silver as the basis for US currency. This extreme polarization provided an incentive for partisans to turn to their parties and work to respond to the new political environment (Aldrich 1995). For the GOP, this meant extensive party organizational development characterized by a great increase in GOP fund-raising capacity. The Republicans were terrified of a possible Democratic takeover and of the consequences if the "toiling masses" managed to take control of government (Sundquist 1983, 156). So the GOP mounted "a massive and crushing counterattack" led by political operative Marcus Hanna, Republican nominee William McKinley's campaign manager (Sundquist 1983, 156).

Hanna raised millions of dollars by "assessing major corporations . . . one-fourth of one percent of capital" (Sundquist 1983, 156).[2] It was the biggest spending campaign to date, with the GOP reporting that it spent $3.5 million, and other observers estimating the party's spending at many times as much (Sundquist 1983, 156). Hanna also developed a highly professional campaign operation that helped McKinley win, in part because of voter coercion. Workers were threatened by their bosses, the faithful were preached to by their pastors, and borrowers were pressured by their bankers to vote Republican (Sundquist 1983, 156–157).

The late nineteenth century saw the rise of both Democratic and Republican urban political party machines. The bosses built armies of loyal partisans who were mobilized on election day to support candidates hand-picked to serve the interests of the party machines' benefactors, the "industrial, corporate and banking interests that benefited from the policies enacted by machine-elected officials" (Dwyre 2010, 76). This method of funding the party machines with big contributions from the affluent "fat cats" and their corporations was not much different from the assessments Marc Hanna charged the GOP's corporate supporters in the 1890s (Sorauf 1992, 2). By the

1920s, both parties were raising most of their money from big contributors. For example, Louise Overacker found that in 1928, 69.7 percent of the Democratic National Committee's receipts and 68.4 percent of the Republican National Committee's receipts came from contributions of $1,000 or more (Overacker 1932, 133), enough to buy "two of Henry Ford's Model T's" (Sorauf 1992, 3).

Of Babies and Bathwater:
Throwing Out the Parties Along with the Bosses

Given the obvious and inherent corruption of the political party machines, it is not surprising that the movement to clean up politics targeted the parties. The Progressives emerged at the turn of the century and sought to root out what they saw as "excessive political expediency and increasingly sordid partisan manipulation of democratic politics" (Silbey 2002, 11). The Progressives did want to reduce the power of big business in politics, as Teddy Roosevelt so colorfully demonstrated with his crusade to *bust the trusts*. Additionally, Congress passed the Tillman Act in 1907 that banned direct contributions to presidential and congressional candidates from corporations and banks. Yet the Progressives concentrated most of their reform efforts on the political party machines and the processes they controlled: "reform required dethroning the political bosses who in alliance with the holders of concentrated economic power defended the status quo" (Sundquist 1983, 172; see also Dwyre 2010).

To break the party machines' power, the Progressives enacted measures "that attacked and ultimately destroyed several of the links between parties and voters" (Silbey 2002, 11). The Progressives worked to regulate many of the parties' functions in order to diminish their power, and thus began to transform parties from private associations into "public utilities" (Epstein 1986, chapter 6). The Australian (secret) ballot, the Seventeenth Amendment (the direct election of US senators, ratified in 1913), various direct democracy mechanisms, and the civil service system are some examples of the Progressives' efforts to take power away from the party bosses.

Other reforms, such as voter registration requirements, worked to exclude the masses from politics. Crenson and Ginsberg argue that "Progressives not only objected to the corruption that was unquestionably an aspect of party politics during this era but also opposed the growing political power of the big-city parties and their working-class and immigrant supporters as a corruption of the democracy envisioned by the founders" (Crenson and Ginsberg 2002, 56).

The introduction of the primary election was the Progressive reform that most weakened the power and influence of political parties, by taking the ability to nominate candidates for office away from party leaders and giving it directly to the voters. Indeed, the primary election has contributed significantly to the shift from party-centered to candidate-centered politics. Pomper argues that the direct primary "accomplished its intended aim, the substitution of individualist political action for that of cohesive party majorities" (Pomper 1992, 120). The United States slowly moved into a "postparty" era in which the parties adapted to serve the interests of their politicians in a significantly changed and often more hostile environment (Silbey 2002, 13–18). Yet before the big shift from party-centered to candidate-centered politics began in earnest in the 1960s, both parties rallied somewhat during the New Deal years.

The New Deal and Some Party Resurgence

An extended period of party decline following the Progressive reforms was briefly interrupted by a bit of party resurgence around the New Deal (Crenson and Ginsberg 2002; see also Andersen 1979). The election of Franklin Roosevelt reenergized the Democratic Party and motivated the GOP to mobilize in response. The Democrats realized that their "electoral success in 1932 might not survive the crisis that caused it or bring any lasting change in the distribution of political power" (Crenson and Ginsberg 2002, 59). FDR channeled New Deal resources to cities with established and loyal Democratic party organizations, including some of the remaining party machines in cities such as Pittsburgh and Chicago, and gave Democratic Party leaders some control over the distribution of those resources. Not surprisingly, unemployed working-class voters "willingly gave their political support to the party organizations that provided them with crucial jobs or emergency relief funds" (Crenson and Ginsberg 2002, 60).

FDR and congressional Democrats also helped labor strengthen its hand in dealing with business by supporting changes in the law such as the Wagner Act, which protected workers' right to organize. Thus, labor unions were highly motivated to support the Democrats. For instance, the Congress of Industrial Organization (CIO) gave approximately $2 million to help reelect FDR in 1936 (Crenson and Ginsberg 2002, 60). The newly mobilized working-class, union, immigrant, young, female, and other voters remained loyal to the Democratic Party, and the New Deal coalition enabled the Democrats to control Congress for all but two sessions between 1933 and 1981, and to occupy the White House for much of that time.

After World War II, the labor unions and urban party machines that supported the New Deal Democratic Party resurgence lost influence. Additionally, new issues that did not naturally unify voters across regions, such as civil rights, became politically salient. Yet, although the Progressive reforms had chipped away at party power and the party coalitions were shifting, campaigns remained quite party centered through the 1950s. The major parties continued to raise some money from the candidates themselves, often extracting contributions from candidates who sought the party's nomination, but the big money was still raised from the infamous fat cats. However, much of what the parties did was not very costly, for "it rested heavily on services volunteered or bartered for some party-controlled favor" (Sorauf 1992, 2). This was about to change.

Big Money, Candidate-Centered Campaigning, and the Road to Reform

Parties remained central to the campaign process into the 1960s. Soon, however, the parties' influence would be challenged by other developments. Postwar prosperity and the well-established activist government motivated the creation of a great number of interest groups. These groups were not connected to the parties but were formed to access and pressure the government directly. They were and are today independent of the parties that used to channel the demands of the public: "By the 1960s, every policy impulse had its own organization that moved readily into the legislative and administrative arenas, largely as if parties did not exist" (Silbey 2002, 14). Moreover, many of these interest groups began to engage in campaign activities traditionally performed by the parties, such as financing candidates and mobilizing voters.

Candidates themselves also began to hire independent, nonparty consultants to do polling, craft political messages, mobilize voters, and raise money for their campaigns—services previously provided by the parties (Agranoff 1972; Medvic 2001; Sabato 1981). By the 1960s, candidates at all levels were using radio to communicate directly to voters, and some began to use television. On television, candidates presented themselves not as part of the party team, but as individuals making personal rather than partisan appeals (Ranney 1983). These developments, contributed to erosion of the linkage role that parties traditionally played connecting voters to elected officials in government and enhancing the potential for holding officeholders accountable (Lawson 1980; Fiorina 1980). Indeed, party identification declined during the 1960s and 1970s, as more voters began to identify themselves as Independents and to split their tickets by, for example, voting for one party's nominee for president and another party's candidate for the US House or Senate. Party domination of the campaign arena was giving way to the candidate-centered campaigning that has characterized US elections ever since.

The move to candidate-centered campaigns also meant a move to candidate-*funded* campaigns. Candidates had to raise a lot of money themselves to pay for the services that had previously been provided by their parties for all candidates up and down the ticket. The cost of an individual campaign rose significantly, not only because direct mail, radio, and TV were costly, but also because individual candidates were now paying for what the parties used to provide for many candidates with great economies of scale. Herbert Alexander reported that all campaign spending on American campaigns went from about $200 million in 1964 to approximately $425 million by 1972, a figure well beyond the rate of inflation (Alexander 1984, 11). By 1980, spending on all campaigns had reached $1.2 billion (Alexander 1992, 1).

Not surprisingly, candidates turned to the same sources that had funded the parties for so long—the big money contributors from business, industry, banking, and labor. As Sorauf notes, "the burden of raising campaign money passed from party to candidates, and the fat cats became as important to the candidates as they had been for the parties" (Sorauf 1992, 5). Republican Richard Nixon and Democrats Robert Kennedy and Eugene McCarthy, contenders for their parties' presidential nomination in 1968, each received at least one $500,000 donation, and when John Rockefeller jumped into the Republican race, his stepmother gave him $1.5 million for his campaign (Alexander 1992, 15). These big money contributions were nothing, however, compared to the nearly $2.8 million that Combined Insurance Company chairman W. Clement Stone gave to Nixon for his nomination and general election campaigns in 1968 (Alexander 1992, 15).

Labor unions provided much of their support in the form of in-kind contributions—volunteers to register voters and get them out to vote on election day—and this support was given almost exclusively to Democrats. In 1968, unions registered 4.6 million voters, provided 100,000 volunteers to make phone calls and canvass door-to-door, and deployed nearly 95,000 union members to get out the vote on election day (Alexander 1992, 16). How much of this union support was delivered on behalf of individual candidates and how much of it for the Democratic Party in general is difficult to say, and much of the 1968 union effort was for the Democrats' presidential nominee, Hubert Humphrey. Of course, mobilizing voters in support of the top of the ticket will usually help those down the ticket as well.

In the late 1960s, the parties were still raising quite a lot of money, with most of it coming from large donations (Alexander 1992, 15, 17). For example, corporations continued to fund many of the expenses related to each party's convention. A tradition started by FDR, selling advertising in the official convention book and selling high-priced copies of the book, continued to bring in significant sums. The parties even began to produce the books in off years. For the 1966 midterm elections, the Republicans charged $10,000 and the Democrats $15,000 per advertising page for their official party books (Alexander 1992, 17).[3] Yet the parties were adjusting to the new candidate-centered politics. Campaigning itself was changing. Candidates relied on the emerging class of campaign professionals, not on their parties, to handle their advertising, polling, and organizing. Most of the big urban party machines had faded, and voters were becoming less inclined to see themselves as members of a political party.

There were *some* campaign finance rules in place prior to the 1970s, yet these rules were not terribly effective at regulating the source or amount of money in American elections, and there was little enforcement of the rules. In 1925, Congress reinforced disclosure requirements and raised the House and Senate spending limits it had added in 1911, and in 1940 contributions to candidates were limited for the first time. The ban on corporate contributions had been in place since 1907, and a ban on union contributions to candidates was added in 1947 (Sorauf 1992, 5–6). Yet there was no agency to insure these rules were followed, and enforcement was left to the Justice Department, which brought no prosecutions. Needless to say, few were following the letter of the law.

The 1970s Reforms and the Court's Response:
New Challenges for Parties

In 1971, before the Watergate scandal, the Democratic Congress enacted the Federal Election Campaign Act (FECA) and the Revenue Act of 1971, in response to the rapidly increasing costs of the new media campaigns as well as to the "gnawing fear within the Democratic party that it had lost the money chase to the Republicans . . . Democrats began to fear that their old ability to raise big money as a party—a skill based heavily on party control of public spending in the cities—would not transfer to their candidates" (Sorauf 1992, 7). The 1971 reforms limited expenditures on media advertising, enhanced disclosure of contributions and expenditures, and established the presidential public financing system, which would not take affect until the 1976 election.[4] The Revenue Act established a modest tax deduction to encourage small contributions, and it stipulated that the public funding for presidential contenders be given directly to the candidates, not to their parties, a clear sign that American politics had become firmly candidate centered.[5]

The 1972 elections featured fat cats and corporate big money as usual. For instance, Richard Nixon's Committee to Reelect the President approached large corporations and suggested each give $100,000, a strategy reminiscent of Marcus Hanna. However, thanks to the 1971 FECA, for the first time much of this campaign-finance activity was effectively publicly disclosed. So, after the bungled burglary of the Democratic National Committee headquarters in the Watergate complex in June 1972 and a range of other illegal acts by Nixon and his operatives, the newly enhanced disclosure rules helped reveal that Nixon's reelection committee also violated both fund-raising and spending laws. An infamous example is the revelation that Nixon supporters were giving paper bags full of cash to his reelection campaign. Congressional hearings and legal action also revealed the immense scale of corporate giving in violation of the law, some of it from foreign sources. Watergate special prosecutor Archibald Cox brought cases that resulted in twenty-one major US companies pleading guilty to making illegal corporate contributions, and most of the money ($842,500 of the $968,000 reported) had gone to the Nixon campaign (Alexander 1992, 18).

The Watergate break-in and the other "dirty tricks" led not only to Richard Nixon's resignation from the presidency but also to new momentum for more campaign finance reform. The 1974 amendments to the FECA solidified the presidential public funding system, and limited contributions to federal party committees and political action committees. Contributions to federal candidates were limited to $1,000 per election and no more than $25,000 for contributions to all candidates. The 1974 amendments also established spending limits for House and Senate races as well as limits on the amount a candidate could spend on his or her own race. Finally, Congress created the Federal Election Commission (FEC) in 1975 to administer and enforce the new Federal Election Campaign Act. While the FEC is often criticized as weak and ineffective, particularly since it is made up of equal numbers of Democrats and Republicans who split many votes and stall action on important decisions, the agency is a tremendous improvement on the lax enforcement that existed before it was established.

A number of FECA provisions were challenged in court and the candidate spending and self-funding limits never took effect, because they were struck down by the Supreme Court in *Buckley v. Valeo* (1976). The Court asserted that such limits were a substantial restraint on First Amendment free speech rights, and thus the *Buckley* case marked the beginning of the march toward a campaign finance system shaped by a clear preference for liberty (free expression) over fairness or equality (rules that level the playing field). The Justices, however, carved out an exception in that they allowed limits on spending if a candidate *voluntarily* accepted public funding, which allowed the presidential public funding program to be implemented.

The parties were certainly not favored in this new campaign finance regime. Indeed, the Supreme Court struck down all limits on expenditures *except* those made by political parties. Moreover, the tremendous growth of interest groups since the 1960s led to a great proliferation of the campaign finance affiliates of these groups, their political action committees (PACs), after passage of the FECA, a development that was somewhat unexpected. This sudden influx into the campaign-funding arena of hundreds of new political organizations meant that the parties were now just one of many groups raising and spending money in elections. The number of federal PACs rose significantly at first and then leveled off: there were 608 registered PACs in 1974; 4,009 by 1984; 3,933 in 1994; 4,040 in 2004; and 4,611 in January 2009 (Federal Election Commission 2009). Indeed, the explosion in the number of PACs quickly meant that the "amount of money a House or Senate candidate can collect from possibly hundreds of PACs easily eclipses the amount that parties are permitted to give to and spend on behalf of a candidate" (Farrar-Myers and Dwyre 2001, 139). As candidates searched for resources to run for office in the new candidate-centered environment, they became less dependent on their parties and looked to PACs and individual contributors to fill their campaign accounts.

Many scholars and other observers declared the parties all but dead during the solidly candidate-centered political era of the 1970s and 1980s. David Broder declared that *The Party's Over* (1972), William Crotty chronicled *American Political Parties in Decline* (1984), and Martin Wattenberg brought us into the 1990s explaining *The Decline of the American Political Parties* (1990). The parties' diminished financial role was only part of the story, as we witnessed a *dealignment* of voters as their attachment to the parties loosened, and the party coalitions that had been fairly stable since the New Deal shifted as new issues presented voters and the parties with new choices. For example, the Democratic Party lost many working-class and southern voters as issues such as civil rights, women's rights, the Vietnam War, abortion, and the environment gravitated to the top of the political agenda. The Republicans lost voters in the wake of the Watergate scandal and Nixon's resignation.

Adapting After Reform

Forced into this new environment, both parties had to regroup and retool. As they had done in the past when faced with changing circumstances and waning influence, the parties worked to adapt, to reinvent themselves. For example, Herrnson notes that in the 1980s the Republican "crisis of competition drew party leaders' attention to the weakness of the Republican national, congressional and senatorial campaign committees" (Herrnson 2002, 52). The GOP turned to a new breed of more entrepreneurial party leaders such as William Brock, who concentrated on enhancing the party's organizational capacity. Soon after, the Democrats initiated similar efforts to reinvigorate their national party committees.

Both parties emerged from this period of transition with stronger, more professional party organizations, each financially secure and more diversified in their activities: the parties "evolved from organizations that *did the work* to elect their candidates to organizations that *provided the resources* to their candidates to get *themselves* elected" (Dwyre 2010, 86). As Aldrich notes, "over time . . . the parties as organizations have adapted to the changing circumstances, and a new form of party has emerged, one that is 'in service' to its ambitious politicians but not 'in control' of them as the mass party sought to be" (Aldrich 1995, 273; see also Herrnson 1988).

Perhaps the most visible change was that both parties' national committees and congressional campaign committees began to raise significantly more money. Much of this, beginning in the 1980s, was *soft* or nonfederal money (banned since the 2002 Bipartisan Campaign Reform Act). Soft money is money raised in amounts exceeding the federal contribution limits from sources prohibited under the 1907 Tillman Act (corporations) and the 1947 Taft-Hartley Act (unions). Parties could take soft-money donations in any amount from virtually any source (individuals, labor unions, corporations, and other organizations), but they were only permitted to spend soft money on party-building activities, not on direct candidate support. Million-dollar soft money contributions from a single corporate leader or Hollywood executive were not unusual.

Soft money helped the national parties invest in their organizational infrastructure. They established permanent headquarters for all their national committees, expanded their professional staffs, acquired advanced technology for fund-raising, polling, and accounting, and engaged in systematic party-building efforts to reenergize state party organizations (Herrnson 2002). The parties interpreted the soft-money guidelines quite broadly and exploited a loophole that allowed them to raise and spend soft money under the looser campaign finance laws of many of the states (Dwyre 1996). For example, they used soft money for state-level mobilization efforts in congressional districts with close races. The DNC used soft money to run so-called "issue ads" a full year before Bill Clinton's reelection campaign in the 1996 election; money that candidate Clinton could not raise and still remain eligible for public financing. These ads avoided any express advocacy that encourages voters to vote for or vote against a particular candidate, and thus the ads were about "issues" and not technically considered campaign ads. As long as words of express advocacy were not used, ad sponsors (parties, nonparty groups, or individuals) could spend unlimited soft money to pay for such ads (see La Raja 2002, 165–170). These words of express advocacy, such as "vote for," "vote against," "support," or "oppose" became known as the "magic words." As long as such words were not used, an ad was considered an *issue ad* that was not subject to the funding limitations of express advocacy campaign ads. Yet these so-called issue ads are often indistinguishable from campaign ads that must be funded with money subject to contribution limits, and most often issue ads are more negative than ads run by candidates (Herrnson and Dwyre 1999).

Figure 8.1 shows the national party committees' receipts from 1980 to 2010 (adjusted for inflation in 2010 dollars).[6] Party income is clearly going in a positive direction, with ups and downs that follow the presidential and nonpresidential election cycles. If we focus in on the years when soft money was permitted, between 1992 and 2002 (shown in Figure 8.2), we can see that soft money was a big part of the parties' income during that decade. As Figure 8.1 shows, the decade is also when the parties began to raise more *hard* or federal money (money raised in limited increments from noncorporate and nonunion sources). In part, this increase in hard-money receipts was a function of the requirement that soft-money expenditures be matched with some portion of hard money. So, the parties needed more hard money in order to spend all of the soft money they were raising.

In their zeal to raise soft money, both parties attracted unwelcome negative attention. For example, President Bill Clinton invited major contributors to mingle with him and other federal officials at social and sporting events and to spend the night in the Lincoln Bedroom, and both parties accepted foreign soft-money contributions (La Raja 2002, 168–169). Critics charged that party soft money circumvented the prohibition against corporate and union contributions, busted the contribution limits, and generally defied the spirit of campaign finance laws intended to reduce possible undue influence of big-money contributors. The congressional reformers who banned party soft money with the Bipartisan Campaign Reform Act (BCRA) in 2002 (the McCain-Feingold Act) argued that soft-money contributions to parties presented an opportunity for undue influence and quid pro quo corruption, for such substantial sums might buy elections and sway votes in Congress (see Dwyre and Farrar-Myers 2001).

Others, however, opposed the ban on soft money in the McCain-Feingold bill. Indeed, the parties' new financial strength allowed them to transition to the institutionalized professional organizations that they are today. Ending

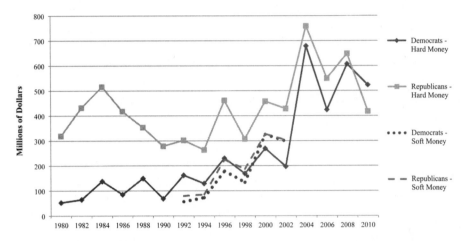

Source: Compiled by author from Federal Election Commission press releases; 2010 hard money from Center for Responsive Politics 2011d.

Note: Figures reflect funds raised from January 1 of the year preceding the election through December 31 of the election year.

FIGURE 8.1 National Party Receipts, 1980–2010

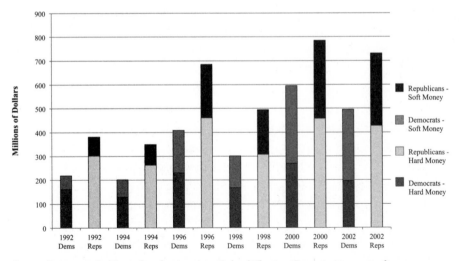

Source: Data compiled by author from various Federal Election Commission press releases.

Note: Figures reflect funds raised from January 1 of the year preceding the election through December 31 of the election year.

FIGURE 8.2 National Party Committee Hard and Soft Money Receipts, 1992–2002

this source of funding for parties, they argued, would weaken parties relative to interest groups and others who spent money in elections. This was seen as detrimental to an electoral system in which the parties are the only campaign finance participants promoting the interests of majorities (La Raja 2003; La Raja 2008, esp. Chapter 6; Milkis 2003; see also Dwyre and Farrar-Myers 2001, 157, 219). Some argued that a party soft-money ban would hit the Democrats harder than the Republicans, calling it "The Democratic Party Suicide Bill," because of the Republicans' traditional fund-raising edge over the Democrats, as can be seen in Figure 8.1 (Gitell 2003). Nevertheless, BCRA ended party soft money and regulated so-called issue ads so that any broadcast that featured the name or likeness of a federal candidate run thirty days before a primary election or sixty days before the general election was deemed an *electioneering communication* that cannot be paid for with unlimited soft money or with corporate or union funds.

Figure 8.1 shows that the parties did not suffer much after the soft money ban went into effect in 2003. To counter the loss of soft money, both parties significantly expanded their efforts to raise money from small contributors. The 2004 election cycle, a presidential election year, featured the largest party fund-raising totals since accurate records have been kept in the 1970s, and all of it was hard money. The 2004 Democratic presidential candidate Howard Dean demonstrated the potential of the Internet for raising small donations. Then, as DNC chair in 2006, Dean developed and executed a "fifty-state strategy" that raised and invested money in many states that had previously seen little support from the national party. Although criticized by many party regulars as a waste of money on lost-cause races, Dean's fifty-state strategy produced upset Democratic congressional victories in states such as Kentucky and New Hampshire. While the midterm elections of 2006 and 2010 did not reach the party fund-raising totals of the 2002 midterms, the high point of soft money fund-raising, both parties raised more *hard money* in 2006 and 2010 than they had in 2002.

The national parties also used their enhanced finances to upgrade and expand their mobilization efforts. Both parties have invested in advanced technologies to identify and target voters for mobilization. For example, data mining of data sets with different types of information about potential voters helps the parties identify voters more likely to support their candidates based on policy preferences, lifestyle, demographics, and other factors. The parties have harnessed this targeting information for what have been some of the most successful phone banking, door-to-door canvassing, and direct-mail campaigns in decades (Dwyre and Kolodny 2006).

The Democratic and Republican party committees also have a robust presence on the Internet, and they now employ information technology and networking professionals to keep up with the many quickly evolving tools and outlets. Today's e-mail, blogs, YouTube, Facebook, phone applications, and Twitter may seem antiquated in just a few years, and the parties are likely to keep up with any new technologies. However, most of the recent electronic pioneering has come from candidates rather than their parties. Barack Obama's 2008 presidential campaign demonstrated the power of mobilizing both voters and dollars through electronic media, and the parties are continuously working to adopt and update such methods for their own organizations. As we have seen before in times of significant and rapid change in their environment, the parties generally adapt to changes around them rather than act as agents of change.

The Post-Reform/Deregulation Era

Although the parties seem to have survived and, in some respects thrived after the ban on party soft money, the BCRA may have marked a turning point for parties in electoral politics. Note, for example, that the parties' fund-raising totals for the 2008 election cycle are slightly lower than their totals for the 2004 election after a general pattern of increases from one presidential election year to the next (see Figure 8.1, and note that figures are adjusted for inflation to show real change over time). Indeed, while 2008 was the most expensive election ever, with spending on all federal races topping $5 billion, most of that money was raised by candidates, particularly Democratic presidential candidate Barack Obama, who raised over $745 million (Center for Responsive Politics 2008).

The parties have not kept pace with other campaign finance actors, so that the financial influence of parties *relative to* other campaign finance actors appears to be diminishing. Indeed, there is a growing number and wide variety of outside groups that are raising and spending money to influence the outcome of elections, especially the most competitive ones. Unless the parties significantly increase their financial role in these close races, they will be but a small voice among many other noncandidate voices competing for the attention of voters. If we continue to think it is important that parties play a significant and meaningful role in American elections, such a shift in the relative influence of parties would not be a welcome development.

At least two factors are contributing to this new campaign finance environment. First, there have been a number of changes to the campaign finance rules themselves. As we have seen, when there are changes to the rules governing any of the various campaign finance actors, the overall campaign finance system also changes, and the *relative* ability of the various campaign finance actors to raise and spend money may shift as a result of changes to the rules. Over time, the various actors adjust and adapt to the new campaign finance environment, and as some take advantage of new opportunities to enhance their role, others may only partially overcome some of the disadvantages brought on by the changes. As before, the recent modifications to campaign finance rules have been particularly hard on parties and candidates by restricting their fund-raising and spending activities relative to other actors.

Second, we have seen more competition in elections for offices at all levels. Control of the US House and Senate has been truly up for grabs a number of times in the past decade. There has been more partisan turnover in state legislative and gubernatorial races, and many candidates are doing well in territory that used to belong exclusively to the other party. This increased competitiveness motivates many political actors to step up their fund-raising to take advantage of a more favorable electoral environment, and to spend more in more races to influence the outcome of elections that now may look like a good bet rather than a lost cause. Consequently, there is also now more competition for campaign dollars. Yet the parties are subject to more restrictive fund-raising rules than most other campaign finance actors, making it more difficult for them to compete effectively for those dollars.

Recent Changes in the Campaign Finance Landscape: From Reform to Deregulation

Campaign finance changes in the past decade have been particularly hard on parties and their candidates in ways that have reduced their fund-raising and spending power relative to other actors. The BCRA ban on party soft money was designed to cut off a possible avenue for quid pro quo corruption, for parties were seen as closely associated with their candidates and therefore an easy conduit for influencing them (Dwyre and Farrar-Myers 2001). Without soft money, parties now have to spend more time and energy raising funds in small increments.

Even though the law also raised the limits on hard-money contributions and indexed them to inflation, the parties are still in a very different financial situation than before. The BCRA is one of a number of reform laws that have focused on parties and left them at a disadvantage relative to other campaign actors, such as the Progressive reforms aimed at weakening the parties almost 100 years ago. The BCRA was followed by a number of court decisions that, in the name of deregulation, have further reduced the ability of parties to play a meaningful financial role in American elections.

In addition to banning soft money, the BCRA also prohibited the use of soft money by *any* organization for broadcast communications that refer to a federal candidate on the ballot thirty days before a primary election and sixty days before a general election. These *electioneering communications* mention but do not explicitly urge the viewer to vote for or against a candidate, and they must be paid for with hard money raised in limited increments from noncorporate and nonunion sources. Yet in 2007, the Supreme Court ruled in *Federal Election Commission v. Wisconsin Right to Life* that corporations and unions were allowed to use their treasury funds for such electioneering communications. The *Wisconsin* decision has given corporations and unions an advantage over parties, because they can use unlimited amounts of their profits and dues on advertising close to election day, while the parties must raise their money in limited increments.

Since the Federal Election Campaign Act and its amendments were passed in the 1970s, corporations, unions, and other groups could raise money from employees, shareholders, members, and others in limited amounts through a political action committee. Contributions to and from traditional PACs are limited, and all fund-raising and spending is disclosed to the public by reporting it to the Federal Election Commission. Corporations and unions are still prohibited from making contributions directly from their treasuries to candidates or parties, but *Wisconsin Right to Life* opened up an avenue for unlimited spending as long as that spending was not coordinated with a candidate or party.

Then, in 2010, the campaign finance rules for individuals, corporations, unions, PACs, and other groups changed dramatically. These changes, in turn, affected the overall campaign finance environment for candidates and parties as well. The most significant modifications to the system were the Supreme Court's *Citizens United v. Federal Election Commission* decision handed down in January 2010, a related decision by a lower court, *SpeechNow.org v. Federal Election Commission,* in March 2010, and some key FEC rulings related to these decisions. These changes gave individuals, corporations, unions, PACs, and other noncandidate and nonparty groups greater flexibility in how they could raise and spend money to influence elections, while leaving the limits and restrictions on party and candidate fund-raising and spending intact.

In the *Citizens United* case, the Supreme Court overturned two previous high court decisions and a hundred years of laws by rejecting the longstanding tenet that corporations should be barred from spending money directly in federal elections to avoid corruption or even the *appearance* of corruption.[7] In the five to four ruling, the Court's majority stated that "government may not suppress speech on the basis of the speaker's corporate identity," and that "independent expenditures, including those made by corporations, do not give rise to corruption or the appearance of corruption" (*Citizens United* 2010, 50, 5).[8] Independent expenditures are expenditures made by individuals, parties, groups, and now corporations and unions that expressly advocate the election or defeat of a candidate by, for example, using words such as "vote for" or "defeat," as long as they do not coordinate their activities with candidates or parties (i.e., independent expenditures are *express advocacy* ads that advocate the election or defeat of a candidate, while electioneering communications are *issue ads* that mention a candidate but do not expressly advocate for his or her election or defeat). The *Citizens United* decision presumably extends to unions, and, indeed, labor unions acted as if it did in the 2010 midterm elections.

With *Citizens United*, the Supreme Court conferred First Amendment political free speech rights on corporations, ending over 100 years of prohibitions on corporate electoral spending. There were state bans on corporate campaign contributions as far back as the 1860s, and a ban on corporate and bank contributions in connection with federal elections has existed since passage of the Tillman Act in 1907. In *Citizens United*, the Court actually recalibrated its view of corruption by narrowing the sphere of legitimate state regulation to cover only contributions to candidates and parties because of their potential for direct quid pro quo corruption. Much of the outcry against the decision relates to this assertion that big independent spending by corporations and unions does not create the potential for corruption. Indeed, in his dissent, Justice John Paul Stevens argued:

> The difference between selling a vote and selling access is a matter of degree, not kind. And selling access is not qualitatively different from giving special preference to those who spent money on one's behalf. Corruption operates along a spectrum, and the majority's apparent belief that *quid pro quo* arrangements can be neatly demarcated from other improper influences does not accord with the theory or reality of politics (*Citizens United* 2010, 57).

Corporations and unions are still prohibited from making contributions directly from their treasuries to candidates or parties, but *Wisconsin Right to Life* and *Citizens United* opened up other channels for unlimited spending as long as that spending is not coordinated with a candidate or party. The *Wisconsin* decision opened the door slightly, and then *Citizens United* pushed the door wide open. Corporations and unions can now use general treasury funds to make unlimited electioneering communications, which mention but do not urge a vote for or against a candidate, and unlimited independent expenditures, which expressly advocate for the election or defeat of a candidate, a potentially far more effective method of voter persuasion.

A few months after the *Citizens United* decision, and just a few months before the 2010 election, in March 2010 the District of Columbia Circuit Court of Appeals handed down a decision that addressed the contribution side of the campaign finance equation (the decision was later affirmed by the US Supreme Court by its refusal to hear the case to overturn the verdict). In *SpeechNow.org v. Federal Election Commission,* SpeechNow, a nonprofit association organized under section 527 of the Internal Revenue Code formed to make only independent expenditures, challenged the constitutionality of the $5,000 limit on contributions from individuals to their group as well as the political committee registration and disclosure requirements.

The DC Circuit Court held that limits on contributions made by individuals to independent expenditure groups such as SpeechNow are indeed unconstitutional in light of the Supreme Court's decision in *Citizens United,* in which the Court held that there is not a governmental anticorruption interest in limiting independent expenditures. The appeals court reasoned that since, according to *Citizens United,* independent expenditures do not cause corruption or the appearance of corruption, then neither do contributions to groups that make those independent expenditures. The nine-judge panel ruled unanimously that "contributions to groups that make only independent expenditures cannot corrupt or create the appearance of corruption" and that limits on individual contributions "violate the First Amendment by preventing plaintiffs from donating to SpeechNow in excess of the limits and by prohibiting SpeechNow from accepting donations in excess of the limits" (*SpeechNow .org* 2010, 14, 16). One might say that *SpeechNow.org* knocked the campaign finance regulation door off its hinges.

Then, in July 2010, the Federal Election Commission issued two advisory opinions to clarify the implementation of these court decisions. The first opinion confirmed that independent expenditure-only political committees are not subject to federal contribution limits as a result of the *SpeechNow.org* decision. In the second opinion, the FEC went beyond the *SpeechNow.org* decision and determined that *Citizens United* exempted independent expenditure-only committees from the prohibitions on *corporate* and *union* contributions as well as individual contributions. These FEC rulings and the recent court decisions thus made it possible for a PAC to raise unlimited amounts from individuals, corporations, other groups, and unions, and to spend unlimited amounts to make express advocacy independent-expenditure appeals close to an election as long as they do not coordinate with candidates or parties.

The *SpeechNow.org* and *Citizens United* decisions and the FEC rulings led to the development of a new type of campaign organization—the independent expenditure-only political committee or *super PAC*. Like traditional PACs, super PACs are still required to register their committees and disclose their contributions and spending to the FEC, but super PACs cannot make contributions directly to candidates or parties as traditional PACs do. These new independent expenditure-only PACs can spend all of their money on elections, and the public can follow their activities because super PACs must disclose what they raise and spend. Yet super PACs may not be as transparent as they seem. Super PACs are permitted to accept unlimited contributions from 501(c) nonprofit corporations, which do not have to disclose the source of *their* contributions. Thus, the money that was originally given to the 501(c) group is wiped clean of its original source when that money is then given by the 501(c) group to a super PAC. This is perfectly legal (for now), yet this type of fundraising by super PACs gets around the disclosure requirement.

Corporations and unions can now also make unlimited contributions to 527 committees, groups organized under section 527 of the Internal Revenue Code. If a 527 committee's primary activity is to nominate or elect one or more federal candidates and it accepts contributions or makes expenditures of over $1,000, it must register with the FEC and must disclose its donors and expenditures. As with other organizations now able to take corporate and union money, there are more federally focused 527 committees than at any time since 2004, but their spending is down as big-money contributors are likely looking for other outlets for their dollars, generally outlets where their contributions can remain anonymous (CRP 2011a; see also Dwyre 2011a).

Indeed, the campaign finance development that caused the most controversy in 2010 was the surge in the use of nonprofit, tax-exempt corporations organized under section 501(c) of the Internal Revenue Code for activities designed to influence the outcome of federal elections. A 501(c) non-profit corporation is permitted to engage in political campaign activity for candidates, provided that this is not its *primary* activity, which generally means that no more than half of the organization's budget may be spent on election-related activities. While these electorally active 501(c) groups report some of their spending, they are not required to disclose their donors. This aspect of the law is not new, but it has attracted a great deal of attention because of the increased use of 501(c) groups for electoral activity in 2010, and thus the increased level of undisclosed campaign finance activity overall (Dwyre 2011a and 2011b). Individuals, groups, and now corporations and unions that want to spend money to influence elections but do not want to publicly disclose they are doing so are legally permitted to channel now unlimited amounts through these 501(c) organizations. We can expect that much of the corporate money spent in elections will now be channeled through 501(c) groups, as businesses naturally aim to avoid activities, political or otherwise, that might alienate current or potential customers (Dwyre 2011b, 21).

After the 2007 *Wisconsin* decision and the 2010 *Citizens United* and *Speech Now.org* decisions and FEC rulings, these various nonparty groups spent record amounts, and they are expected to raise and spend even more in future elections. Figure 8.3 shows the reported spending of corporations and unions, PACs, super PACs, 527 committees, and 501(c) organizations from 2004 to 2010 (adjusted for inflation in 2010 dollars). The influx of corporate and union money after the *Wisconsin* decision in 2007 is seen in the increase in spending by 501(c) organizations in 2008, the preferred vehicle, particularly for corporations that do not want to reveal their political activities. These nonprofit corporations spent nothing in 2006, but after the *Wisconsin* decision they spent over $79 million in 2008. Such spending increased to over $134 million in 2010, even though corporations and unions could have spent the money directly themselves. The new super PACs made a strong debut in 2010, spending over $65 million, and 527 committees seem to have become a less desirable vehicle for campaign spending. Corporations spent so little directly on independent expenditures in the first year than they were permitted to after the *Citizens United* decision (only about $50,000) that this spending is not even visible on Figure 8.3.

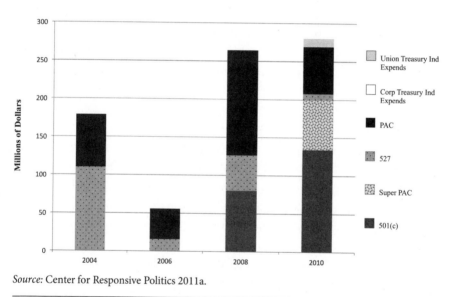

Source: Center for Responsive Politics 2011a.

FIGURE 8.3 **Reported Nonparty Outside Spending by Group Type, 2004–2010**

So how does this increased financial activity of nonparty groups compare to political party spending? Have parties kept pace with nonparty groups? Unfortunately, comparable and reliable data for outside spending by party and nonparty groups (various types of spending for issue ads, independent expenditures, electioneering communications, and communication costs) are not available for elections before 2006. However, we can examine outside spending for three recent election cycles, 2006, 2008 and 2010, a presidential and two midterm elections. Figure 8.4 shows the party and nonparty outside

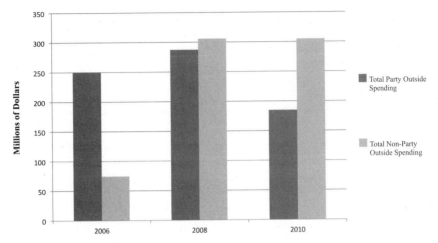

Source: Compiled by author from data from the Center for Responsive Politics 2011c.

FIGURE 8.4 **Party and Nonparty Outside Spending in Federal Elections, 2006–2010**

spending totals (in 2010 dollars), with a clear shift toward increased non-party spending and decreased party outside spending.

It is not possible to say that this change in relative spending by party and nonparty groups is a direct result of *Wisconsin Right to Life, Citizens United, SpeechNow.org,* and the FEC rulings. However, this shift in the balance of spending in federal elections supports the concern of those who argue that an influx of corporate and union money will drown out the voices of candidates and parties and shape elections to achieve the electoral and policy goals of moneyed interests rather than of voters.

Moreover, parties face an additional challenge in competing for dollars with their own presidential nominees. La Raja reports that from 1992 to 2004, the ratio of party to nominee fund-raising narrowed as candidates raised more *within* the presidential public financing system and the parties did not keep pace (La Raja 2011, 213–215). In 2004 both George Bush and John Kerry declined to accept public matching funds for their primaries, thus they were allowed to raise more money since they did not have to abide by the stricter contribution limits. Party and nominee fund-raising were nearly equal that year. Then in 2008, Democratic nominee Barack Obama became the first presidential nominee since the debut of the presidential public financing program in 1976 to decline public funds. Republican nominee John McCain still raised slightly less than the RNC, while Obama raised $746 million to the DNC's $260 million (La Raja 2011, 215). Obama was competing for contributions from many of the same donors that had given to the party in the past, and he was also able to significantly expand his donor base through extremely effective fund-raising on the Internet.

The 2012 election features many new super PACs and 501(c) corporations, as well as new ways that various fund-raisers have found to raise money. Super PACs are the choice of many. Indeed, nearly all of the candidates seeking the GOP presidential nomination and Democratic presidential incumbent Barack Obama have super PACs formed by their supporters, unions have super PACs, and even cable TV comedy show host Stephen Colbert has his own super PAC. Big money contributors are giving the maximum allowed contribution to a candidate and then sending unlimited amounts, sometimes as much as $5 million, to a super PAC supporting that candidate (Overby 2011; Zeleny and Rutenberg 2012, 1).[9] A new fund-raising tactic features a candidate at an event where money is being raised for a super PAC, but the candidate stays just inside the law by leaving the event before it is over and not actually asking for money him- or herself (Confessore 2011). Others with money to spend on elections are directing funds to 501(c) organizations, but we will never know the source of much of that money, because these nonprofit corporations do not have to disclose who contributes to them.

Of course, many of these super PACs, 501(c) groups, and 527 organizations are created by partisans focused on electing candidates from their political party, but these groups may not coordinate with candidates or their parties. So, a group's activities are sometimes inconsistent with or even contrary to the strategies pursued by the candidate and party it is trying to help. There are many examples of noncandidate groups injecting issues into a campaign that the candidate the group favors does not want raised. Moreover, outside group advertisements are generally more negative than candidate ads, and candidates are sometimes blamed for the negative tone of the campaign.

Conclusion

While the parties have certainly not been the primary funders of campaigns since the rise of candidate-centered politics in the 1960s and 1970s, the parties' diminished place in contemporary campaign finance is a development that concerns those of us who argue that parties play an important and vital role in the American representative democracy. Only parties seek to represent majorities, while all other organizations pursue narrower interests. By bringing together a multitude of narrower interests, each party attempts to represent large segments of American society. Moreover, if parties are strong in both elections and in government, that partisan connection can help link voters to officeholders and make it possible for the public to impose some measure of collective responsibility on government for its action or inaction (Fiorina 1980).

These recent campaign finance changes may not have been designed to weaken the political parties as the Progressive reforms were, but the altered campaign finance landscape is not very friendly territory for contemporary parties. Candidates, parties, and traditional PACs are now the only participants in the campaign finance system subject to fund-raising and spending limits, and parties can only coordinate with their candidates in ways that are financially limited as well. Moreover, although parties may make unlimited independent expenditures just as interest groups can, since the 2002 ban on party soft money, the parties must raise their money in limited amounts from noncorporate and nonunion sources. Yet the *Citizens United* and *SpeechNow .org* decisions now allow many groups to raise money in unlimited amounts from virtually any source. So it is no surprise that these nonparty groups are able to out-raise and out-spend the parties, as well as some candidates, particularly in the closest races (see Dwyre 2011a).

These changes are too new to know exactly how the parties will fare in this altered campaign finance landscape, but it is quite clear that the party organizations face regulatory and strategic disadvantages that others interested in influencing the outcome of elections do not. La Raja argues that "political parties adapt and survive, but the byzantine regulatory structure weakens parties relative to other groups by imposing costly regulatory burdens uniquely on parties, while providing incentives for wealthy nonparty groups to enter the fray of campaigns" (La Raja 2008, 117–118). Others include these groups as part of a broader "partisan web" (Koger, Masket, and Noel 2009; see also Herrnson 2009; and Grossmann and Dominguez 2009). For example, Herrnson argues that if parties are viewed as "enduring multilayered coalitions" that include allied partisan groups such as PACs, 527 committees, and 501(c) organizations, there is evidence "of increased party influence that is missed by narrower definitions of parties" (Herrnson 2009, 1221). Indeed, as Herrnson notes, the formation of many of these groups was driven in part by "the introduction of constraints on the activities of party organizations [and] the creation of opportunities for political action by others" (Herrnson 2009, 1221). Thus the recent increase in campaign finance activity by various nonparty groups can be seen as one way that the parties are adapting to this new environment.

American parties have always aggregated various special interests in an effort to build winning coalitions. The best example is the Democratic Party's long-term partnership with labor unions. Current campaign finance law prohibits direct coordination between parties and nonparty groups for spending on elections, making it difficult for the parties to orchestrate or synchronize their efforts with their allied groups. Perhaps, however, the assorted and somewhat independent efforts of the various parts of these multilayered partisan coalitions can be focused enough on the same goal of electing a set of candidates to actually expand the reach and influence of the parties. Certainly this may not work in the primary election period, for formal party organizations and nonparty groups do not always endorse the same candidates. Yet where they can agree on candidates in the general election, party and nonparty partisan groups do generally focus on the same races, usually the most competitive ones, and together they can direct significant resources toward the goal of electing the same candidates.

This broader view of parties can be seen as a way that the parties have adapted to changes in their environment. If the party organizations are constrained in their ability to support their candidates, then their partisans can create new organizations to do so. Indeed, many of the leaders of these newer groups were once party insiders or elected officials.[10] Yet it remains to be seen if this expanded party network can perform in a way to play the important and vital role that we expect of political parties in the American representative democracy.

References

Agranoff, Robert. 1972. "Introduction: The New Style Campaigning." In *The New Style in Election Campaigning*, edited by Robert Agranoff. Boston: Holbrook.

Aldrich, John H. 1995. *Why Parties: The Origin and Transformation of Party Politics in America*. Chicago, IL: University of Chicago Press.

Alexander, Herbert. 1992. *Financing Politics*. 4th ed. Washington, DC: CQ Press.

———. 1984. *Financing Politics*. 3rd ed. Washington, DC: CQ Press.

Andersen, Kristi. 1979. *The Creation of a Democratic Majority, 1928–1936*. Chicago, IL: University of Chicago Press.

Austin, Michigan Secretary of State, et al. v. Michigan State Chamber Of Commerce 1990. 494 US 652.

Broder, David. 1972. *The Party's Over: The Failure of Politics in America.* New York: Harper and Row.

Buckley v. Valeo. 1976. 424 US 1.

Center for Responsive Politics. 2011a. "Citizens United Decision Profoundly Affects Political Landscape." May 5, 2011. http://www.opensecrets.org/news/2011/05/citizens-united-decision -profoundly-affects-political-landscape.html.

_____. 2011b. "527s: Advocacy Group Spending." http://www.opensecrets.org/527s/index.php.

_____. 2011c. "Total Outside Spending by Election Cycle, All Groups." www.opensecrets.org /outsidespending/index.php.

_____. 2011d. "Political Parties Overview, 2010." www.opensecrets.org/partiesindex.php.

_____. 2008. "Money Wins Presidency and 9 of 10 Congressional Races in Priciest US Election Ever." Press release. November 5. http://www.opensecrets.org/news/2008/11/money -wins-white-house-and.html.

Citizens United v. Federal Election Commission. 2010. 558 US 08–205.

Confessore, Nicholas. 2011. "Lines Blur Between Candidates and PACs with Unlimited Cash." *New York Times,* August 27.

Crenson, Matthew, and Benjamin Ginsberg. 2002. *Downsizing Democracy: How America Sidelined Its Citizens and Privatized Its Politics.* Baltimore, MD: Johns Hopkins University Press.

Crotty, William. 1984. *American Political Parties in Decline.* 2nd ed. Boston, MA: Little, Brown.

Downs, Anthony. 1957. *An Economic Theory of Democracy.* New York: Harper and Row.

Dwyre, Diana. 2011a. "After *Citizens United* and *SpeechNow.org*: Considering the Consequences of New Campaign Finance Rules." Paper presented at the annual meeting of the American Political Science Association, Seattle, Washington, September 3.

_____. 2011b. "Old Games, New Tricks: Money in the 2010 Elections." *Extensions,* Summer 2011. Norman, OK: Carl Albert Congressional Research and Studies Center.

_____. 2010. "Evolution, Reinvention and Survival: Party Organizations and the Mobilization of Resources." In *New Directions in American Political Parties,* edited by Jeffrey M. Stonecash. New York: Routledge.

_____. 1996. "Spinning Straw into Gold: Soft Money and US House Elections." *Legislative Studies Quarterly* 21, 3 (August).

Dwyre, Diana, and Victoria Farrar-Myers. 2001. *Legislative Labyrinth: Congress and Campaign Finance Reform.* Washington, DC: CQ Press.

Dwyre, Diana, and Robin Kolodny. 2006. "The Parties Congressional Campaign Committees in 2004." In *The Election After Reform,* edited by Michael J. Malbin. Lanham, MD: Rowman and Littlefield.

Epstein, Leon D. 1986. *Political Parties in the American Mold.* Madison, WI: University of Wisconsin Press.

Farrar-Myers, Victoria A., and Diana Dwyre. 2001. "Parties and Campaign Finance." In *American Political Parties: Decline or Resurgence?* edited by Jeffrey E. Cohen, Richard Fleisher, and Paul Kantor. Washington, DC: CQ Press.

Federal Election Commission v. Wisconsin Right to Life. 2007. 551 US 449. Cited here as *Wisconsin Right to Life.* 2007.

Federal Election Commission. 2009. "Number of Federal PACs Increases." Press release. March 9.

Fiorina, Morris P. 1980. "The Decline of Collective Responsibility in American Politics." *Daedalus* 109, 3 (Summer): 25–45.

Gitell, Seth. 2003. "The Democratic Party Suicide Bill." *Atlantic Monthly* (July/August): 106–113.

Grossman, Matt, and Casey Dominguez. 2009. "Party Coalitions and Interest Group Networks." *American Politics Research* 37, 5 (September): 767–800.

Herrnson, Paul S. 2009. "The Role of Party Organizations, Party-Connected Committees, and Party Allies in Elections." *Journal of Politics* 71, 4 (October): 1207–1224.

_____. 2002. "National Party Organizations at the Dawn of the Twenty-First Century." In *The Parties Respond: Changes in American Parties and Campaigns,* edited by L. Sandy Maisel. Boulder, CO: Westview Press.

_____. 1988. *Party Campaigning in the 1980s.* Cambridge: Harvard University Press.

Herrnson, Paul S., and Diana Dwyre. 1999. "Party Issue Advocacy in Congressional Elections." In *The State of the Parties: The Changing Role of Contemporary American Parties,* edited by John C. Green and Daniel M. Shea. 3rd ed. Lanham, MD: Rowman and Littlefield.

Josephson, Matthew. 1938. *The Politicos, 1865–1896.* New York: Harcourt, Brace.

Koger, Gregory, Seth Masket, and Hans Noel. 2009. "Partisan Webs: Information Exchange and Party Networks." *British Journal of Political Science* 39 (April): 633–653.

Kolodny, Robin. 1998. *Pursuing Majorities: Congressional Campaign Committees in American Politics.* Norman, OK: University of Oklahoma Press.

La Raja, Raymond. 2011. "Back to the Future? Campaign-Finance Reform and the Declining Importance of the National Party Organization." In *The State of the Parties: The Changing Role of Contemporary American Parties,* edited by John Green and Daniel Coffey. Lanham, MD: Rowman and Littlefield.

_____. 2008. *Small Change: Money, Political Parties, and Campaign Finance Reform.* Ann Arbor, MI: University of Michigan Press.

_____. 2003. "Why Soft Money Has Strengthened Parties." In *Inside the Campaign Finance Battle: Court Testimony on the New Reform,* edited by Anthony Corrado, Thomas E. Mann, and Trevor Potter. Washington, DC: Brookings Institution Press.

_____. 2002. "Political Parties in the Era of Soft Money." In *The Parties Respond: Changes in American Parties and Campaigns,* edited by L. Sandy Maisel. Boulder, CO: Westview Press.

Lawson, Kay. 1980. *Political Parties and Linkage: A Comparative Perspective.* New Haven: Yale University Press.

Mayhew, David. 1974. *Congress: The Electoral Connection.* New Haven: Yale University Press.

McConnell v. Federal Election Commission. 2003. 540 US 93.

Medvic, Stephen. 2001. *Political Consultants in US Congressional Elections.* Columbus, OH: Ohio State University Press.

Milkis, Sidney M. 2003. "Parties Versus Interest Groups." In *Inside the Campaign Finance Battle: Court Testimony on the New Reform,* edited by Anthony Corrado, Thomas E. Mann, and Trevor Potter. Washington, DC: Brookings Institution Press.

Nichols, Roy F. 1967. *The Invention of the American Political Parties: A Study of Political Improvisation.* New York: The Free Press.

Overacker, Louise. 1932. *Money in Elections.* New York: Macmillan.

Overby, Peter. 2011. "Top Donors Use Super PACs to Sidestep Money Limits to Candidates." National Public Radio. October 4, 2011. http://www.npr.org/blogs/itsallpolitics/2011/10/04/141061496/top-donors-use-super-pacs-to-get-around-money-limits-to-candidates (accessed October 7, 2011).

Pomper, Gerald M. 1992. *Passions and Interests: Political Party Concepts of American Democracy.* Lawrence, KS: University Press of Kansas.

Ranney, Austin. 1983. *Channels of Power.* New York: Basic Books.

Sabato, Larry J. 1981. *The Rise of Political Consultants: New Ways of Winning Elections.* New York: Basic Books.

Schmitter, Philippe, and Terry Karl. 1991. "What Democracy Is . . . and Is Not." *Journal of Democracy*, no. 2 (Summer): 75–88.

Silbey, Joel. 2002. "From 'Essential to the Existence of Our Institutions' to 'Rapacious Enemies of Honest and Responsible Government': The Rise and Fall of American Political Parties, 1790–2000." In *The Parties Respond: Changes in American Parties and Campaigns*, edited by L. Sandy Maisel. 4th ed. Boulder, CO: Westview Press.

Sorauf, Frank. 1992. *Inside Campaign Finance: Myths and Realities.* New Haven: Yale University Press.

SpeechNow.org v. Federal Election Commission. 2010. 599 F.3d 686 (D.C. Cir.).

Sundquist, James L. 1983. *Dynamics of the Party System: Alignment and Realignment of Political Parties in the United States.* Washington, DC: Brookings Institution Press.

Wattenberg, Martin P. 1990. *The Decline of American Political Parties: 1952–1988.* Cambridge, MA: Harvard University Press.

Wisconsin Right to Life. 2007. See *Federal Election Commission v. Wisconsin Right to Life.*

Zeleny, Jeff, and Jim Rutenberg. 2012. "Gingrich Patron Could Have a Plan B: Romney." *New York Times.* February 5: 1 and 14.

Endnotes

1. This chapter draws from Dwyre 2011b. Copyright 2011, Carl Albert Congressional Research and Studies Center, University of Oklahoma, all rights reserved.

2. Sundquist notes that Standard Oil contributed $250,000, and the Beef Trust gave $400,000. He cites Josephson 1938, 699.

3. The Democrats published a special memorial to President Kennedy in 1964 that brought in an estimated $1 million in profit (Alexander 1992, 17). The GOP's 1965 book was titled "Congress: The Heartbeat of Government." The Democrats' 1966 volume was called "Toward an Age of Greatness," and the party distributed it at a movie premier fund-raiser (Alexander 1992, 17).

4. Congressional Democrats agreed to delay the debut of the presidential public financing system until 1976 in order to "neutralize Richard Nixon's opposition," for Nixon would then be out of office (Sorauf 1992, 8).

5. The tax deduction was ended with the 1986 tax reform law.

6. All six national party committees are included: the Democratic National Committee, the Democratic Senatorial Campaign Committee, the Democratic Congressional Campaign Committee, the Republican National Committee, the National Republican Senatorial Committee, and the National Republican Congressional Committee.

7. *Citizens United* overturned two previous decisions. *Austin v. Michigan Chamber of Commerce,* a 1990 ruling that upheld the ban on corporate spending for express advocacy that supports or opposes a candidate, was overruled, as was the part of the 2003 *McConnell v. Federal Election Commission* decision (the decision that upheld most of the Bipartisan Campaign Finance Reform Act of 2002) that restricted corporate and union campaign spending on broadcast, cable, or satellite transmission of electioneering communications (i.e., issue ads) that aired thirty days before a primary election and sixty days before the general election.

8. *Citizens United v. Federal Election Commission* 2010. All citations in this paper refer to the slip opinion 130 S. Ct. 876 (2010) and are hereafter cited as *Citizens United* 2010.

9. Billionaire casino executive Sheldon Adelson and his wife each gave $5 million by February 2012 to Winning Our Future, the super PAC supporting Newt Gingrich for the GOP presidential nomination. And, of course, they could give more since such contributions are not limited (Zeleny and Rutenberg 2012, 1)

10. For example, President George W. Bush's former advisor Karl Rove and former RNC chair Ed Gillespie are founders of two of the most influential new groups—the 527 group American Crossroads and its allied 501(c)(4) group Crossroads GPS.

9

Boehner's Dilemma

A Tempest in a Tea Party?

WALTER J. STONE
University of California, Davis

L. SANDY MAISEL
Colby College

TREVOR C. LOWMAN
University of California, Davis[1]

The 2010 elections to the US House of Representatives produced a Republican resurgence that more than made up for their losses in 2006 and 2008. Having lost control of Congress in the 2006 elections, the Republicans roared back in 2010, gaining 63 seats and winning a relatively comfortable majority with 242 of the 435 seats in the House (56 percent of the seats). In the process, they installed their leader, John Boehner, from Ohio's 8th district, as the 61st Speaker of the House, replacing California Democrat Nancy Pelosi, who had served in that capacity for the previous four years. Political pundits and other observers were divided in their explanations of the Republicans' impressive victory, but most agreed it resulted from some combination of the public's negative reaction to the lingering Great Recession, which began in 2008, and the Republicans' ability to capitalize on opposition to President Obama's policies, especially the mounting debt they linked to government spending and the Health Care Reform Act of 2010, dubbed "Obamacare." Some of the Republican seat gain reflected a return to partisan equilibrium after two elections in which Democrats made impressive gains.

Prominent among the factors at work in 2010 was the Tea Party movement, a loose coalition of groups, activists, and political entrepreneurs committed to a conservative ideology based on reducing the size of the federal government and lessening the impact of government on citizens' lives, reducing the national debt, and opposition to health-care reform, especially the individual mandate. Tea Party activists dominated the political discussion, especially within the Republican Party, during the summer of 2010 and into the fall campaign. In many states, candidates backed by Tea Party groups challenged traditional Republican leaders for control of local organizations and for critical nominations in hotly contested races.

The conventional wisdom on the role of political parties in the nominating processes below the presidential level holds that party organization's key role is played either in recruiting candidates for office or "derecruiting" those who seek to oppose a preferred candidate in a primary. The extent to which the party is effective in this role varies with national party effort and local party rules and norms (Maisel and Brewer 2012, chapter 6). This view follows directly from the decline in the role of parties since the advent of direct primary elections (Key 1956). Clearly, in states and localities in which Tea Party activists were most successful at dominating the nominating process, the local organization played less of a role. However, two competing theories attempt to explain the Tea Party role. One holds that the Republican Party itself was changing and that Tea Party activists reflect that change. The other holds that Tea Party activists have been within the Republican Party all along, at the far-right extreme. By this explanation, 2010 reflects their ascendancy, in part at least because of increased levels of participation.

The 2010 elections were fought against a backdrop of a longer-term pattern of polarization between the parties in Congress and in the public. Party polarization has meant that compromise between the parties is difficult or impossible. Following the elections the Republican Party was united in its opposition to many of President Obama's policies, especially on budgetary and tax issues, even at the risk of seeming to be obstructionist. Certainly the newly elected class of Republicans was seen as intransigent in its commitment to conservative principles.

In the debt ceiling and budget negotiations between Speaker Boehner and President Obama in the summer of 2011, the nascent "grand bargain" on the debt ceiling would have required Republicans in the House to accept new taxes as part of a compromise aimed at reducing the national debt by cutting spending and generating new sources of revenue. Press reports at the time indicated that Boehner and Obama reached the outlines of such a bargain that would have involved far more concessions from the Democrats on spending cuts than it did from the Republicans in the form of increased revenues. Despite a deal some saw as "too good to pass up," Boehner had to withdraw because he could not persuade Republican newcomers to the House to go along with *any* increase in revenues. On this and other issues, the newcomers elected in 2010, including but not limited to members who affiliated themselves as candidates with the Tea Party movement, held fast to their conservative positions.

The opposition of Republican newcomers to compromise with the Democratic president raises questions about the extent to which victories by Tea Party conservatives reflected the ideological views of voters in their districts or whether their unwillingness to move at all from their conservative principles would jeopardize the Republican majority in 2012. After all, the Republicans' majority status resulted from their ability to win "swing" districts, defined as districts that move from control by one party to the other, in this case districts that had been held by the Democrats before the 2010 election. Presumably these districts were more moderate than core Republican districts held by the GOP prior to the 2010 elections. Yet the Tea Party Republicans and other newcomers elected from these districts seemed to be more conservative and less willing to compromise than Speaker Boehner and many of the more senior members of their party.

Political scientists often think about questions related to polarization and representation by referring to a spatial model that places individual candidates and officeholders in a one-dimensional space or line that describes their positions from extremely liberal on the left to extremely conservative on the right. Likewise, districts or other groups of voters can be placed on the same line according to their positions. While the liberal-conservative dimension does not capture all aspects of politics in America, it does a good job of describing the major lines of conflict between the parties, among both Representatives in Congress and voters in the electorate. The concept of party polarization, then, refers to a situation in which most Democrats are liberal—with perhaps many relatively extreme in their liberalism—and most Republicans are conservative, again with many on the extreme end of the spectrum.[2] We adopt a simple spatial model in order to map the positions of candidates and districts before and after the 2010 elections. This mapping will help illustrate the dilemma Speaker Boehner faced in his negotiations with the president, and focus our attention on the sources and possible consequences of the makeup of the Republican majority in the 112th Congress.

The 2010 Congressional Election Study

A fundamental problem political scientists have had applying the spatial model to the study of congressional elections has been an inability to place both candidates on the same liberal-conservative scale. It is easy to determine the liberal-conservative positions of incumbents based on their voting records in the House, which can be scaled on a liberal conservative dimension using NOMINATE or interest-group ratings (such as ADA or ACA) to scale roll-call votes in a left-to-right order. The problem with this method is that it does not permit comparisons with challengers who have not established a comparable record of roll-call votes that can be used to determine their position. Even the few studies that have used questionnaire data on House candidates to determine the placement of incumbents and challengers on the same scale have not been able to place districts or voters within districts on the same scale. Recently, several scholars have made use of constituent survey questions that ask ordinary citizens to indicate how they would vote on roll-call issues their Representatives have voted on in the House to place House members and their constituents on the same liberal-conservative scale, but this approach leaves out challengers. As we will show, getting the full picture requires identifying the liberal-conservative placements of incumbents, challengers, and constituents on the same scale.

The approach we take to solving this problem is different. The 2010 Congressional Election Study conducted at the University of California, Davis, conducted several surveys of constituents in a national random sample of 100 US House districts. These surveys asked constituents resident in the sample districts to respond to a standard seven-point liberal-conservative question by indicating their position ranging from "very liberal" (coded –3) through "very conservative" (coded +3). In addition to collecting the survey data on these questions from constituents in the sample districts, we also asked panels of "district expert observers" in the same districts to give their best judgment of each candidate's positions on exactly the same liberal-conservative scale scored in exactly the same way. District experts were national convention delegates, state legislators, and online respondents screened for their expertise about and attentiveness to politics in their district.[3] We ended up with an average of just over 30 experts per district, whose judgments we averaged after adjusting their ratings for partisan bias.[4] These average placements, then, become our measure of where each candidate running in each of our sample districts stood on the liberal-conservative scale identical to the scale on which constituents placed themselves.[5]

An Ideological Map of the 2010 Elections

Figure 9.1 uses the district expert placements of the candidates running in their districts on a seven-point liberal-conservative scale and the constituent self-placements on the same scale to compare the positions of Democratic and Republican candidates with districts prior to the 2010 elections. Figure 9.1 makes apparent several well-known facts about the American political landscape. First, the parties as represented by their candidates for the House of Representatives are polarized, with Democrats placed clearly to the left of center and Republicans placed even more to the right of center. Because the Democrats held the majority prior to the election, the average incumbent was moderately liberal, but there is no doubt that the two parties were distinctly different in their ideological positions.[6]

Because we asked constituents their positions on the same liberal-conservative question that we asked experts to use in placing the candidates, we can directly compare the positions of districts to candidates. Note that the average House incumbent was more liberal than the average district, an indication that Congress as a whole was out of step with the nation (as indicated by the position of the average district). On this fact alone, we might expect the electorate to issue a corrective in the 2010 elections by defeating some Democrats (who were relatively liberal) and electing more Republicans (who were more conservative) so that Congress as a whole would shift in the conservative direction toward the national average.

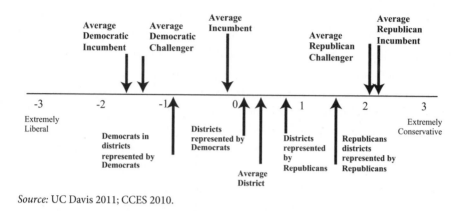

Source: UC Davis 2011; CCES 2010.

FIGURE 9.1 Ideological Map Before 2010 Elections

It is also evident in Figure 9.1 that districts represented by Democrats were to the left of districts represented by Republicans, although the degree of polarization between districts represented by each party is nowhere near as great as the polarization we observe between the two parties' candidates. If we think of the process of representation within districts as a partisan one—a not unreasonable concept given how important party identification is in explaining voters' choices between candidates in House elections—we can see that the polarization between partisan constituencies begins to approximate the polarization between candidates and between incumbents in the House. Still, Democratic incumbents were .72 units more extreme in their liberalism than Democratic constituents in their districts, while Republican House members were .57 units more extreme than GOP identifiers in their districts. This suggests that a good portion, but by no means all, of the polarization between candidates is linked to polarization found in the electorate.[7]

Despite the overall difference between the parties, Democratic challengers were somewhat more moderate than Democratic incumbents, while Republican challengers were modestly more moderate than Republican incumbents. This pattern has been observed before (Burden 2004), although some have suggested it results from a tendency of incumbents to move away from their districts. The truth is quite the opposite. Democratic challengers were more moderate because, by definition, they ran in Republican-held districts, which are more conservative than Democratic districts. Likewise, Republican challengers ran in Democratic-held districts. Once we take into account the positions of the districts in which they ran, both Democratic and Republican incumbents were more representative of their districts on average than challengers in their parties were, relative to the districts in which they ran.[8]

Figure 9.2 shows a map of the ideological changes that occurred as a result of the 2010 elections. The map is on the same liberal-conservative continuum as in Figure 9.1, rescaled to emphasize the area between –2 and +2, which is where most of the candidate and constituency groups were located. The first thing to notice is that the average incumbent in the 112th Congress after the election was moderately conservative, noticeably to the right of where the average incumbent in the House was located during the 111th Congress, before the election. This shift in a conservative direction resulted, of course, from the party turnover that occurred as a result of the election, swapping Republicans for Democrats in a number of districts.

A second thing to notice is that Democratic incumbents shifted to the left as a result of the election, as did Democratic districts. This is a direct consequence of taking out of the Democratic Party in the House the more conservative swing districts and the relatively moderate Democratic incumbents who represented them. Swing districts in 2010 are shown in Figure 9.2 and are more

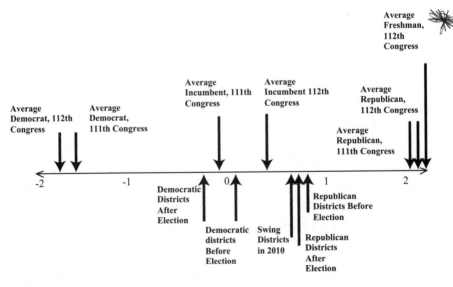

Source: UC Davis 2011; CCES 2010.

FIGURE 9.2 Ideological Change as a Result of the 2010 Elections

conservative than Democratic districts and more moderate than Republican-held districts. Switching these districts out of the Democratic Party meant that party shifted to the left as it also transitioned to minority status. Adding these districts to the Republican stock of seats meant that the GOP was nudged in a more moderate direction, since the average swing district was more moderate than the average Republican district before the election.

The results so far fit with what we would expect: core Democratic districts are relatively liberal and elect Representatives who are more extreme in their liberalism; Republican districts do likewise on the conservative side. The districts that change hands from one party to the other tend to be between the two parties' core districts. One reason these swing districts are more moderate is because they are composed of more balanced proportions of constituents from both parties, whereas core districts in each party are dominated by larger majorities of partisans in the party that holds the seat.[9] Predominantly Democratic districts are more liberal than the swing districts, while districts with strong Republican majorities are more conservative. Taking a significant number of swing districts out of the Democratic Party leaves that party more liberal while moderating the Republican Party as a whole.

The surprising result of the 2010 elections was on the Republican Party in the House. We know from Figure 9.1 that Republican challengers as a whole were slightly less conservative than Republican incumbents; however, when the winning challengers are added to the GOP in the House as a result of the elections, the Republican conference actually became more conservative. The reason, as indicated in Figure 9.2, is that the new freshman Republicans were more conservative than Republicans who were in Congress prior to the election. This is largely associated with the conservative positions of Tea Party freshmen, who were most conservative of all.

We are now in a position to appreciate "Boehner's Dilemma." If the Republicans are to retain their majority status, they cannot afford to lose too many swing districts in 2012 and beyond. It is apparent, however, that the newly elected members of the Republican conference in 2010 were not only more conservative than senior members of their party but also substantially out of line with their districts. As we noted, the reason challengers are more moderate than incumbents is because they run in districts held by the opposite party. If the pattern of relative moderation held among *winning* Republican challengers in 2010, Speaker Boehner's efforts to strike a "grand bargain" with

President Obama might not have been opposed primarily by these former challengers, now freshman, because they would have been relatively moderate rather than extreme in their conservative views. By passing on the debt compromise, Boehner and his party risk being seen as intransigent extremists out of step with the rest of the country. But it was the newly elected Republicans, selected from districts closest to being representative of the country as a whole, who most insistently opposed the deal. It would seem that Speaker Boehner's refusal to compromise puts these districts at risk of swinging back to the Democrats in 2012. Thus, his dilemma as leader of his party in the House was whether to respond to extremists in his party who opposed any compromise with President Obama and risk branding his party as too extreme for the moderate swing districts that produced the Republican majority, or to appeal to more centrist interests, accept the compromise, and risk a revolt within his own party in Congress.

The irony of relatively moderate districts electing extremists unwilling to compromise on national policy may put Boehner and the Republican majority at risk, but it also raises questions about why it occurred. How did relatively extreme Republicans, most visibly Tea Party Republicans, get elected from less conservative swing districts?

Tea Party Conservatives and the Republican Tide in 2010

Table 9.1a provides a descriptive analysis of three groups of districts in the 2010 elections: core Democratic districts that were in Democratic hands before and after the elections; swing districts that switched from Democratic to Republican as a result of the elections; and core Republican districts that were represented by Republicans before and after the elections.[10] The first row of the table shows the numerical scores of non–Tea Party and Tea Party Republican candidates on the seven-point liberal-conservative scale used by district experts to place the candidates. Recall that the most conservative possible score is 3.0. In the core Democratic and swing districts, the Republican candidates were challengers; the non–Tea Party candidates in core Republican districts were incumbents.[11] The table shows that Tea Party Republican candidates were more conservative than non–Tea Party Republicans in each of the three types of district. Note as well that Tea Party Republicans in swing

TABLE 9.1a Candidate and District Ideology in 2010

	Core Democratic Districts		Swing Districts		Core Republican Districts	
	Non-TP	*TP*	*Non-TP*	*TP*	*Non-TP*	*TP**
R Candidate Ideol.	1.82	2.06	2.17	2.31	2.13	2.55
% Obama	71.5	66.7	48.6	47.7	42.4	43.4
District Ideology	−.15	−.03	+.65	+.64	+.75	+.83
N	(27)	(18)	(6)	(13)	(31)	(1)

*Open seat held by GOP before the election.

Source: UC Davis 2011.

Note: Core Democratic Districts are districts held by the Democrats before and after the 2010 elections; Swing Districts are districts that changed from Democratic to Republican in the elections; Core Republican Districts were held by the Republicans before and after the elections.

districts, all of whom became part of the freshman class of newly elected Republicans in the 112th House (at 2.31 on the scale), were noticeably more conservative than core Republican incumbents (at 2.13 on the liberal-conservative scale). These results, of course, confirm the conventional view that the Tea Party freshmen Republicans were more extreme in their conservative ideology than Republicans who had been in the House before the elections.

The second two rows in Table 9.1a show that districts were more conservative in swing districts than in core Democratic districts, and more conservative still in core Republican than in swing districts. Support for Obama in 2008 was strong in core Democratic districts, while on average Obama failed to carry the districts that swung to the Republicans two years later in 2010. It is no surprise that the Obama vote share was lowest in core Republican districts. Likewise, using the district ideology score from the CCES survey, districts are more conservative across the three groups in the table.

Notice in Table 9.1a that there is a tendency for districts in which Tea Party Republicans ran to be somewhat more conservative than those in which non–Tea Party candidates ran. This raises the question of whether the Tea Party candidates were more conservative simply because they were from more conservative districts. The data in Table 9.1a suggest that is not the case since the most conservative group of Republican candidates were from swing districts, but the regression analysis in Table 9.2 confirms that Tea Party Republicans were more conservative than expected, based on the ideology of the districts in which they ran. The coefficient in the first row indicates that Republican candidates were responsive to their districts' ideology

TABLE 9.2   Regression of Candidate Ideology on District Ideology, Tea Party Affiliation, and District Controls

	Republican Candidate Ideology		Democratic Candidate Ideology	
	b	SE	*b*	SE
District ideology	.28***	.07	.68***	.11
Tea Party candidate	.21**	.08	−.06	.12
Democratic incumbent	−.04	.09	.20	.14
Open seat	.07	.10	.00	.15
Adjusted R-sq.	.23		.33	
N	100		95	

Source: UC Davis 2011.

Note: ** < .05; *** < .01; two-tailed tests.

in their own ideological position taking. That is, as districts in 2010 were more conservative, so also were the Republican candidates running in them. However, it is also clear that Tea Party Republicans were more conservative than expected based on their districts' ideology: on average they were about .2 units more conservative than we would anticipate from their district ideological preferences. This, too, fits with the prevailing view of Tea Party Republicans being relatively extreme in their ideology.

The Puzzle of Extreme Republican Freshmen in 2010

The fact that newly elected Republicans, most especially those who identified themselves as aligned with the Tea Party, were so conservative raises a puzzle: How did these relatively extreme conservatives get elected from the most moderate districts in the 2010 Republican coalition? Many observers of the 2010 elections commented on such Tea Party candidates as Christine O'Donnell in Delaware and Sharron Angle in Nevada, who lost elections that the Republicans might well have won if they had nominated less extreme candidates. However, none of these observers has pointed to seats in which Tea Party Republicans lost House elections that the party might otherwise have won. How is it that their fellow Tea Partiers in the House managed to win?

One possibility is that Tea Party candidates in 2010 outspent their Democratic opponents and thus were able to increase their visibility and attractiveness to voters who, on purely ideological grounds, would not have supported

TABLE 9.1b Candidate and District Ideology and Candidate Spending in 2010

	Core Democratic Districts		Swing Districts		Core Republican Districts	
	Non-TP	*TP*	*Non-TP*	*TP*	*Non-TP*	*TP**
Republican Candidate Ideology	1.82	2.06	2.17	2.31	2.13	2.55
% Obama	71.5	66.7	48.6	47.7	42.4	43.4
District Ideology	−.15	−.03	+.65	+.64	+.75	+.83
Relative Spending (median)	−$881K	−$773K	−$96K	−$612K	+$904K	−$221K
N	(27)	(18)	(6)	(13)	(31)	(1)

*Open seat held by GOP before the election.

Source: UC Davis 2011.

Note: Core Democratic Districts are districts held by the Democrats before and after the 2010 elections; Swing Districts are districts that changed from Democratic to Republican in the elections; Core Republican Districts were held by the Republicans before and after the elections. Relative spending is the Democratic candidate's spending minus the Republican candidate's spending, in $100,000.

them. This explanation would fit with a generally skeptical view of money in American elections that explicitly or implicitly assumes that money has a distorting influence. Table 9.1b, however, provides data inconsistent with this view. The last row of the table, added to the data already presented in Table 9.1a, demonstrates that spending was not the explanation for the Republicans' success. A negative relative spending score indicates that Democratic candidates outspent their Republican opponents; a positive score indicates the Republicans in that group outspent Democrats (in $100,000s). Thus, for example, Democratic candidates running in core Democratic districts outspent non–Tea Party Republicans by an average (median) of $881,000. The results show that Democrats outspent Republicans, *especially* Tea Party Republicans, in swing districts, so the fact that such conservative candidates won in these districts cannot have been due to their ability to outspend their Democratic opponents.

The final entries in Table 9.1c indicate that the victory by conservative Republicans in swing districts, even those who were affiliated with the Tea Party movement, was not because they were out of step with their districts *relative to their Democratic opponents*. The row presenting the ideological position of Democratic candidates shows that Democrats running in swing districts were substantially more moderate than Democrats running in core Democratic

TABLE 9.1c Candidate and District Ideology, Candidate Spending, and Relative Proximity of Candidates to District Ideology in 2010

	Core Democratic Districts		Swing Districts		Core Republican Districts	
	Non-TP	*TP*	*Non-TP*	*TP*	*Non-TP*	*TP**
Republican Candidate Ideology	1.82	2.06	2.17	2.31	2.13	2.55
% Obama	71.5	66.7	48.6	47.7	42.4	43.4
District Ideology	−.15	−.03	+.65	+.64	+.75	+.83
Candidate Spending (median)	−$881K	−$773K	−$96K	−$612K	+$904K	−$221K
Democratic Candidate Ideology	−1.80	−1.85	−1.30	−1.25	−1.40	−1.30
Relative Proximity to District	−.32	−.26	+.42	+.23	+.80	+.41
N	(27)	(18)	(6)	(13)	(31)	(1)

*Open seat held by GOP before the election.

Source: UC Davis 2011.

Note: Core Democratic Districts are districts held by the Democrats before and after the 2010 elections; Swing Districts are districts that changed from Democratic to Republican in the elections; Core Republican Districts were held by the Republicans before and after the elections. Relative spending is the Democratic candidate's spending minus the Republican candidate's spending in $100,000. Relative proximity to the district is based on district experts' placements of the candidates and district ideology based on the 2010 CCES survey.

districts. Moreover, they were even more moderate in an absolute sense than their Republican opponents. Democratic candidates running in swing districts against Tea Party Republicans were only 1.25 units to the left of the middle of the liberal-conservative scale (−1.25). At the same time, their Tea Party Republican opponents were over one full unit more extreme relative to the midpoint of the scale, at +2.31 (top row). The fact that Democratic candidates in these districts were relatively moderate and Republicans were relatively extreme, of course, was what gave many observers the impression that the Tea Party Republicans had managed to get elected even though they were dramatically out of line with their district preferences. A further inference might also have been that voters had chosen poorly based on factors other than their fundamental ideological interests in electing so many extreme conservatives.

The bottom row of the table, however, indicates that this story of extreme conservative Republicans being elected against the ideological interests of their districts does not fit the evidence. Because we know the ideological positions of each candidate running in the districts in our study (based on the placements provided by our panels of district experts), we can calculate the ideological proximity of candidates to their districts relative to each other *and* their districts. A simple spatial model of district voting suggests that if the Republican candidate is closer to the district's preferences than the Democratic candidate, the Republican should win. The advantage of this approach is that it compares candidate positions not to the zero point on the scale (Democratic candidates were more moderate than Republicans in the swing districts), but relative to the district in which they were running.

The last row of Table 9.1c shows that on average Democratic candidates won in districts where they were closer to their districts' ideological preferences than their Republican opponents, and that Republicans won in districts where they were closer than their Democratic opposition, *including the swing districts that elected the most conservative Republican candidates!* A negative relative proximity score indicates that the Democratic candidates were closer to their districts' ideological preferences than the Republican candidates running in the same districts; a positive score indicates the Republicans were closer to their districts than the Democrats. Notice that for non–Tea Party and Tea Party Republicans alike, the Republicans running in swing districts were closer on average to their districts than their Democratic opponents, even though it is also true that the Democratic candidates were closer to the midpoint of the liberal-conservative scale, and the Tea Party Republicans were relatively extreme. The reason for this result is that the swing districts were not at the midpoint of the liberal-conservative scale. In fact, they were fairly conservative in their ideological preferences. As a result, the moderate Democrats were not moderate enough to be closer to their districts than the Tea Party Republicans and the Tea Party Republicans were not extreme enough to be further from their districts than their moderate (in an absolute sense) Democratic opponents. In short, the swing districts in our sample voted as a group for exactly the candidates they should have based on ideological proximity, and there is no "puzzle" associated with the election of the Tea Party Republicans in 2010. Or if there is a puzzle, it is why the Democratic candidates did not moderate even further so as to be more attractive to the districts in which they ran.

It is worth noting that, whereas the 2010 results do not appear to be anomalous (the correct candidates appeared to win based on their ideological proximity to their districts), it may well be that previous elections were anomalous in this sense. For instance, the Democratic winners in 2008 or 2006, moderate as they were, may have been substantially out of line with their districts, in which case 2010 was simply a return to equilibrium rather than an outlier election as it seems often to be perceived. There are other possibilities as well, but the clear implication of the analysis so far is that the 2010 results appear to be in line with district opinion, and that the "extreme" Tea Party Republicans were not so extreme after all, at least compared with their districts and their Democratic opposition.

Tempest in a Tea Party?

The foregoing analysis suggests that the election of Tea Party Republicans and other conservatives running for the GOP in 2010 may have been a result of normal political forces at work in congressional elections. It was not due to the Tea Party Republicans outspending their opponents; it was apparently not due to a national Republican tide or the glamour of the Tea Party movement seducing voters away from their fundamental ideological preferences; and it was emphatically not because Republican conservatives pulled the wool over their own districts' eyes. If anything, it was due to *Democratic* candidates' inability to be more representative of their districts' preferences, compared with their Republican opponents, however "extreme" in an absolute sense GOP candidates were.

This analysis presented in the extended versions of Table 9.1 is based only on a rough descriptive account of a threefold classification of districts in 2010. We can conduct a more theoretically secure analysis by conducting a regression analysis designed to explain 2010 Republican candidates' vote share in the election in all districts in the sample (see Table 9.3). The analysis allows us to observe the effects of three classes of variables: the ideological and partisan makeup of districts; the resources and status of the candidates; and the relative ideological proximity of the candidates to their districts.

The fundamental conclusion from Table 9.3 is that the usual variables of interest in explaining House election results account very well for Republican vote share in 2010. District partisanship and ideology, as indicated by presidential vote share and lagged vote share from the previous midterm elections, have strong effects on Republican vote share. The more the district voted for President Obama in 2008 and the more Democratic its vote in 2006 the lower

TABLE 9.3 Regression Analysis of Republican District Vote Share, 2010

	b	SE
Partisan makeup of district		
Democratic vote share in 2006	-.07**	.03
Obama vote share, 2008	-.58***	.05
Candidate resources		
Democratic incumbent	-2.00	1.43
Republican incumbent	7.59***	1.54
Democratic candidate spending (logged)	-.38	.36
Republican candidate spending (logged)	2.21***	.50
Candidate ideology		
Relative proximity	1.58**	.62
Tea Party candidate	1.13	1.02
Adj. R-sq.	.95	
N	95	

Source: UC Davis 2011.

Note: ** < .05; *** < .01; two-tailed tests.

the Republican vote share was in 2010. Republican incumbents and Republican expenditure levels helped boost their vote share, while Democratic incumbency and spending did not have significant effects dampening Republican vote share. We interpret this as indicating the strength of the national Republican tide. It is also an indication of a 2010-specific effect, although a national tide for one or the other of the two parties is not an unusual event—2006 was a tidal election in favor of the Democrats, for instance.

Finally, the relative ideological proximity of the candidates to their districts had a significant impact on Republican vote share. As the relative ideological proximity became increasingly positive (increasingly indicated the Republican was closer to the district than the Democrat), Republican vote share increased. This effect is independent of the partisan makeup of the district and of the resource differences between the candidates. Notably, however, the presence of a Tea Party Republican running in the race had no significant effect, negative or positive, on Republican vote share. In other words, the analysis suggests that the Tea Party movement, as represented in this analysis by the presence of a candidate affiliated with the movement, had no discernable impact on the outcome.[12] This is consistent with what other scholars have found. One possibility is that a candidate's affiliation with the Tea Party or a voter's expressed support for the Tea Party is another indication of a conservative ideology. If so, the other variables in the analysis capture ideological differences both between candidates running against one another, and in the district makeup and preferences.

Party Polarization and Boehner's Dilemma

Our conclusion that the 2010 elections reflected conditions that are typical of many midterm elections raises the question of whether Boehner's Dilemma is also a normal part of the contemporary political landscape. We believe that it is. As Figure 9.1 and a great deal of other evidence shows, the contemporary American party system is polarized, with Democrats in Congress and in the electorate on the left, and Republicans on the right. In the politics of congressional elections, this means that each party has a stock of relatively secure districts—liberal districts that reliably elect Democrats to Congress, and conservative districts that routinely elect Republicans. While most House districts fall into one of these two camps, there is a relatively small set of swing districts that are ideologically situated between the two parties. These districts motivate change in the system, electing Democrats in one election (e.g., 2006), only to turn to the Republicans in a later election (e.g., 2010). This is a somewhat stylized characterization of the three types of districts—core Democratic, swing, and core Republican—but it captures a logic built into the polarized nature of American politics today.

This view of polarization between the parties explains the fundamentals of Boehner's Dilemma in the aftermath of the 2010 elections. The national tide against the Democrats rooted in dissatisfaction with the state of the economy and a mobilized opposition to President Obama's economic stimulus and health-care reform policies shifted a substantial number of relatively centrist swing districts from the Democrats to the Republicans, creating a Republican majority in the House. Boehner's Dilemma was how to govern in that context. Should he respond to the core of his party, including the conservative freshmen elected in 2010 by refusing to compromise with President Obama on budget, debt ceiling, and jobs bills when they involve any increase in revenues? If he took that position, he would solidify his support in his Conference and avoid a revolt from the right. That course, however, risked branding the GOP as intransigent, extreme in its views, out of step with the country. If that perception were sufficiently widespread, it might open the door to the Democrats to nominate moderate candidates in swing districts and, possibly, the majority. That, of course, would end Speaker Boehner's tenure.

Figure 9.3 shows that something like this situation in reverse faced the new Democratic majority and its leader, Speaker Nancy Pelosi, following the 2006 elections.[13] The Democratic Party became slightly more moderate as a result of the 2006 elections, as did the average Democratic district. This reflects the fact that the swing districts picked up in the election were relatively conservative. At the same time, of course, the average House member became more liberal, owing to the increase in seats controlled by the Democrats and the corresponding decrease in the size of the Republican conference. In 2006, there was no Democratic "Tea Party" movement, and the freshmen Democrats elected in that year were relatively moderate in their positions. Still, the underlying polarization between the parties created a situation after the 2006 elections not unlike that faced by the Republicans after they won in 2010.

By winning a sufficient number of swing districts to make them the majority party in the House, the Democrats took control of the chamber and elected Nancy Pelosi speaker. Her dilemma was the mirror image of John Boehner's problem four years later. The Democrats had languished in the minority for

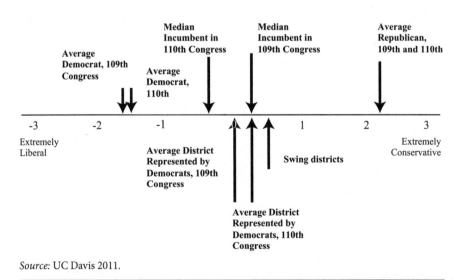

Source: UC Davis 2011.

FIGURE 9.3 Pelosi's Dilemma in 2006

twelve years, since the Republicans won control of Congress in the 1994 elections. The liberal core of the party dominated the committee and subcommittee leadership positions because of their seniority, and they had an agenda: ending the war in Iraq; confronting President Bush on a range of issues from health-care reform, to managing the economy, to the handling of prisoners at Guantanamo Bay. Speaker Pelosi had to decide whether to respond to this core of the party at the risk of branding the party as too liberal for the swing districts just captured in the election, or to tamp down the enthusiasm on the left in order to maximize the party's chances of holding the moderate swing districts.

One possible response to this dilemma—a response arguably consistent with both Speaker Pelosi's and Speaker Boehner's behavior—is to make hay while in the majority, and risk the consequences in subsequent elections. In a polarized system, this will lead to swings in national policy and/or obstruction and gridlock, depending on whether the majority party in the House controls the rest of the government. The Pelosi-Obama emphasis on health-care reform, by all counts a landmark piece of legislation passed once the Democrats held the presidency, Senate, and House following the 2008 elections, fits this model. Speaker Boehner's strident opposition to any increased revenue from tax increases or reform also fits, although of course the Republicans did not control the rest of the government following the 2010 elections.

This analysis relates to questions about the nature of the congressional party. There is a lively debate in the scholarly literature on Congress about how much the congressional party and, by extension, party leaders in Congress, affect outcomes and member behavior (e.g., Cox and McCubbins 1993; 2005; Krehbiel 1998; Rohde 1991). Our analysis relates to this debate because it focuses on the tension between preferences of the party caucus (the median member of the majority party) and the preferences of the median district, which creates and sustains the House majority.

The dilemma faced by Speaker Boehner reflects partisan pressures associated with the preferences of his rank and file alongside the imperatives of maintaining the Republican majority by appealing to swing districts. That these same districts actually shifted the median Republican in the House to the right in 2010 only sharpened Speaker Boehner's dilemma because it appeared that a significant portion of his conference, especially freshmen members elected in 2010, was open to dumping him from the speakership if he opted for a moderate course. Future work on parties, party leaders, and district representation must come to a more complete understanding of how these forces play out in congressional politics.

Conclusion

Political journalists had a field day with the Tea Party and its impact on the Republican Party. Immediately after the 2010 elections, they pointed to the United States Senate seats held by Democrats against Tea Party nominees who wrested nominations from more moderate Republican candidates in states such as Colorado, Delaware, and Nevada. The implication was that the Tea Party success in these races ended up costing the Republicans seats it would otherwise have won. These conclusions reinforced the belief that traditional party organizations had indeed lost control of the nominating process.

In the House, the Republicans did become the majority party—and Tea Party candidates were prominent among the newly elected Republican freshmen. Thus, the extent to which Tea Party activists dominated the nominating process for House elections—whether because the Republican party was changing or because Tea Party activists, already in the GOP were increasingly mobilized—did not seem to cost the Republicans seats in Congress. In fact, we can find no instance of a Tea Party insurgent beating an organization Republican candidate and then losing the general election.

Our analysis does show, however, that while Tea Party House nominees were more conservative than incumbent Republicans running for reelection, and more conservative than the average voter in their district, they were less out of line with their district's ideological preferences than their Democratic opponents. Thus, the elections of 2006 and 2008 may well have been the aberrant elections, in which case voters returned in 2010 to their ideological preferences. The conservative Tea Party candidates, who moved the Republican Conference further to the right, were more like the average voter in their district than the Democrats they replaced, thought to be moderate, but still more liberal than the district preference.

Because these freshmen ran touting their conservative ideology, particularly on issues relating to the size of the federal government and shrinking the extent to which the federal government intrudes on citizens' lives, it should be no surprise that they were not willing to compromise in ways that Speaker Boehner and other establishment Republicans were. The Speaker resolved his dilemma—of whether to give in to conservative elements in his Conference or compromise with President Obama on a deficit reduction package—by siding with those standing firm on their conservative principles. What impact will this decision have on the 2012 elections? For an answer, prognosticators should look beyond the Tea Party. The Tea Party is neither the savior of the Republican Party nor the potential cause of its demise. The key factor is whether the Democrats nominate candidates whose views are close to those of their districts. Political tides are important; how the country responds to the fiscal crisis is important; but how closely candidates' views—in this case Tea Party incumbents' and their Democratic challengers' in 2012—are to those of voters whose support they seek should not be disregarded.

References

Abramowitz, Alan I., and Kyle L. Saunders. 1998. "Ideological Realignments in the US Electorate." *Journal of Politics* 60, 3: 634–652.

———. 2008. "Is Polarization a Myth?" *Journal of Politics* 70, 2: 542–555.

Ansolabehere, Stephen, J. James M. Snyder, Charles Stewart III. 2001. "Candidate Positioning in US House Elections." *American Journal of Political Science* 45, 1: 136–159.

Bafumi, Joseph, and Michael C. Herron. 2010. "Leapfrog Representation and Extremism: A Study of American Voters and Their Members in Congress." *American Political Science Review* 104, 3: 519–542.

Bond, Jon R., Richard Fleisher, and Nathan Ilderton. 2011. "Was the Tea Party Responsible for the Republican Victory in the 2010 House Elections?" American Political Science Association annual meeting. Seattle, WA.

Burden, Barry C. 2004. "Candidate Positioning in US Congressional Elections." *British Journal of Political Science* 34, 2: 211–227.

CCES (Cooperative Congressional Election Study). 2010. http://projects.iq.harvard.edu/cces/.

Cox, Gary W., and Mathew D. McCubbins. 1993. *Legislative Leviathan: Party Government in the House*. Berkeley, CA: University of California Press.

———. 2005. *Setting the Agenda: Responsible Party Government in the US House of Representatives*. New York: Cambridge University Press.

Fiorina, Morris 2006. *Culture War? The Myth of a Polarized America*. New York: Pearson.

Fiorina, Morris P., Samuel A. Abrams, and Jeremy C. Pope. 2008. "Polarization in the American Public: Misconceptions and Misreadings." *Journal of Politics* 70, 2: 556–560.

Jacobson, Gary C. 2011. "The President, the Tea Party, and Voting Behavior in 2010: Insights from the Cooperative Congressional Election Study." American Political Science Association, annual meeting. Seattle, WA.

Jessee, Stephen A. 2009. "Spatial Voting in the 2004 Presidential Election." *American Political Science Review* 103, 1: 59–81.

Key, V. O. 1956. *American State Politics*. New York: Knopf.

Krehbiel, Keith. 1998. *Pivotal Politics: A Theory of US Lawmaking*. Chicago, IL: University of Chicago Press.

Maisel, L. Sandy, and Mark D. Brewer. 2012. *Parties and Elections in America: The Electoral Process*. 6th ed. Lanham, MD: Rowman and Littlefield.

Rohde, David W. 1991. *Parties and Leaders in the Postreform House*. Chicago, IL: University of Chicago Press.

Stonecash, Jeffrey M., Mark D. Brewer, and Mack D. Mariani. 2003. *Diverging Parties: Social Change, Realignment, and Party Polarization*. Boulder, CO: Westview Press.

Stone, Walter J., and Elizabeth N. Simas. 2010. "Candidate Valence and Ideological Positions in US House Elections." *American Journal of Political Science* 54, 2: 371–388.

UC Davis. 2011. Congressional Election Study 2006–2010. http://electionstudy.ucdavis.edu/.

Endnotes

1. We are grateful to the National Science Foundation for the support to carry out the 2010 study (SES-085237). Information about the study is available at http://electionstudy.ucdavis .edu/. Trevor Lowman was supported on a Research Experiences for Undergraduates supplemental award. Helpful comments and suggestions were made by Matt Buttice and participants at the Policy Watch seminar, UC Davis.

2. There are different conceptions and definitions of polarization in the literature, which has led to controversy about how much polarization there is in contemporary American politics. Fiorina et al. (2008) define polarization as extremism on individual issues, while Abramowitz and Saunders define polarization as consistency across issue items. Fiorina concludes that there is relatively little evidence of polarization because, on individual issue or liberal-conservative items, there has been little increase in the amount of extremism in the electorate. Abramowitz and Saunders (2008) argue there has been a noticeable increase in polarization because there has been an increased tendency for voters to take consistently liberal or conservative stands across individual issue items, and because the correlation between party identification and issue positions has increased in recent decades.

3. Information about the study, including the survey instruments used in the district-expert surveys, is available on the project Website: http://electionstudy.ucdavis.edu/.

4. The adjustment is made on individual expert ratings by regressing ratings on a party dummy variable coded +1 for experts in the same party as the candidate, –1 for experts in the opposite party, and 0 for independent experts. The coefficient on this variable indicates partisan bias. We correct for this bias by subtracting the coefficient from expert ratings, leaving the estimated ratings independent experts would have given.

5. The expert surveys were conducted in October 2010. The constituent surveys were conducted both before and after the election, although we report results from the pre-election survey in this chapter. The source for the constituent survey in this chapter is the 2010 Cooperative Congressional Election Study (CCES). For more information on this study see http://projects.iq.harvard.edu/cces/.

6. There is no overlap between the distributions (the most conservative Democrat in the study was to the left of the least conservative Republican). Likewise, within the districts in the study, all Democratic candidates were more liberal than their Republican opponents, usually by a substantial degree.

7. We estimate that about two-thirds of the polarization between candidates in each party is matched by polarization between partisans in the electorate.

8. Democratic incumbents were .35 units closer to their districts than Democratic challengers were to theirs, while Republican incumbents were closer to their districts than GOP challengers were to theirs by *exactly* the same amount.

9. According to the 2010 CCES survey, in Democratic districts before the election, Democrats had a party identification plurality advantage of 11.5 percent, whereas Republican districts had a plurality advantage in identifiers with the GOP of 7.8 percent. Swing districts that flipped from the Democratic to Republican Party in 2010 had a Republican plurality advantage of only 1.6 percent.

10. In our sample of 100 districts, no district switched from Republican to Democratic hands, although among all 435 districts three swung against the tide from the GOP to the Democratic Party.

11. The one Tea Party Republican candidate in a core Republican district ran in an open seat. We had no Tea Party candidates who were Republican challengers in core Republican districts. Our source for identifying Tea Party House candidates was the *New York Times*: http://www.nytimes.com/interactive/2010/10/15/us/politics/tea-party-graphic.html.

12. There are possible effects that would not necessarily show up in our analysis, including the mobilization effects linked to the organizational efforts of Tea Party groups in the election noted earlier in this chapter.

13. The data in Figure 9.3 are from the same sample of 100 districts used in the 2010 study. The study was begun in 2006 in these districts, with smaller panels of district experts in each district. Otherwise, the design of the study was similar to the 2010 study (Stone and Simas 2010).

10

Political Parties and the Media

The Parties Respond to Technological Innovation

DIANA OWEN

Georgetown University

Historically, the functions, operations, and status of American political parties in election campaigns have been influenced by developments in communications technology. Parties adapted to changes in the media environment in the predigital era. In the early years of the Republic, newspapers were the primary source of political information, and the messages they disseminated were controlled heavily by political parties (Pasley 2001). Television precipitated a shift in party control over media messaging, as candidates took to the airwaves independent of parties. Today political parties operate in a media system that has been in the midst of a radical transformation since the 1990s. Parties must navigate a complicated media landscape that combines elements of traditional mass media, such as print newspapers and television network news, and novel platforms for informing and engaging the public in politics made possible by new digital technologies, such as Websites, blogs, social networking sites, video-sharing platforms, and Twitter feeds.

The two major political parties initially were slow to respond to these changes in the present-day communications environment. However, they stepped up their new media game substantially following the 2008 presidential election, which showcased the successful use of social media by Democrat Barack Obama's campaign organization. While some candidate committees still outpace party organizations in terms of their digital media innovation and their ability to attract voter and press attention to their communications, parties are redefining their place in the world of new media politics. The major parties have developed strong Web-based presences that provide consistent platforms for disseminating messages, engaging citizens, and fundraising during and between elections. At the same time, minor parties and grassroots movements that have assumed some party functions have been able to capitalize on the opportunities afforded by digital media platforms to become visible players in the political process.

This chapter explores how American political party organizations have adapted to the new media environment during election campaigns. It addresses the question: How have the parties responded to technological developments in election campaign communication? The chapter begins by examining the evolution of the communication functions of political parties. Early on, parties took a personalized approach to communicating with constituents in elections, and shifted to a mass messaging approach when broadcast communication became prevalent. Today, parties employ a combination of people-intensive, broadcasting, and digital media techniques to carry out their electoral role (Norris 2005). The chapter next examines the ways in which parties manage their relationship with mainstream media, and explores how party organizations are portrayed by the press. It then discusses how the two major political party organizations are reasserting their position in the campaign hierarchy through their use of new media-based innovations. Barack Obama's presidential election operation in 2008 provided a blueprint for party organizations to follow as they adjusted their approach to campaign media. Parties in the post-2008 era are pursuing robust new media strategies in election campaigns as they seek to elect candidates to office, recruit new members, and influence media coverage. Finally, the chapter examines the media strategies of alternatives to the two major parties that are establishing a foothold in the political process and challenging the status quo. The Tea Party, which is more of a decentralized grassroots political movement than a textbook political party, has been able to use social media to mobilize citizens and attract candidates to run under its label who have been elected to office. In addition, virtual alternatives to the two major parties have proliferated online, which may mark the naissance of the next wave in political organization.

Communication Technology and Political Party Functions

Epstein defines political parties in terms of their electoral role. A political party is "any group, however loosely organized, seeking to elect governmental officeholders under a given label" (Epstein 1989, 3). The loosely organized parties in the United States can be viewed as "networks of cooperating actors" consisting of candidates, officeholders, donors, campaign workers, activists, allied interest groups, and friendly media outlets (Koger, Masket, and Noel 2009, 636). The extent to which parties behave cooperatively with other actors within this network influences their ability to achieve shared goals. Network activities require collaboration, coordination, and creating linkages among associates that are essential to parties' successfully performing their electoral functions in the new media age.

The core functions of political party organizations as they relate to elections include the recruitment of political leaders, the integration and mobilization of citizens and groups, the articulation and aggregation of interests, and the formulation of policy positions (Norris 2005). Communication is central to parties performing these functions and activating their networks. Parties' communications apparatuses provide the conduit through which citizens connect with and engage in the political process (Sartori 1976; Rommele 2003). They also provide the channels that support parties' interactions with journalists and media outlets. Political party functions have evolved along with transformations of the political media system prompted by new technologies. Technological advances also have precipitated changes in the mechanics of campaigning and related operations, such as marketing and opinion research. Recent advances in public opinion polling, consumer preference research, and audience tracking, for example, have made it possible to microtarget citizens with specifically tailored messages that can aid fundraising and voter mobilization.

Norris identifies three phases of party campaign communications based on the channels employed. Parties used people-intensive communication from the mid-nineteenth century until the 1950s. During this time, party campaign organizations were decentralized and locally focused and relied on print media. Modern broadcasting channels shaped party campaign communications from the early 1960s to the late 1980s when audiences got their news and current affairs information largely through major television networks. This period coincided with the professionalization of political campaigns and the nationalization of party election operations. Parties adopted Internet channels for communication in the 1990s (Norris 2005). The Internet phase is now more accurately described as the period of digital media channels. The parties have augmented their use of Websites with a range of additional platforms, such as Facebook pages, Twitter feeds, and YouTube channels. Parties have moved far beyond computer-based technologies, and have developed applications for cell phones and tablets like the iPad that are not Internet based. In the present phase, national party organizations not only manage communications through established national, state, and local bureaucracies, they also coordinate decentralized, grassroots campaigns through their social media networks.

Party Functions in the Print and Broadcast Media Eras

During the period when people-intensive channels of campaign communication prevailed, parties played a dominant role in electoral politics. They organized voters, drafted candidates, managed campaigns, and set the issue agenda. Their approach to politics hinged largely on developing close relationships with voters through personal interactions and their use of print media, which was later joined by radio broadcasts. Newspapers often were overtly partisan, and their messages were crafted to appeal to the parties' constituents. Parties worked through newspapers to mobilize voters, publicize their platforms, and advertise on behalf of candidates. Their methods were conducive to campaigns that were relatively short in duration, especially compared to today's endless electoral contests. Between elections, newspapers provided continuity by keeping voters and activists connected to party organizations. Newspapers facilitated linkages between parties at the local, state, and national levels as well as across geographic regions of the country. As Pasley observes, "Party newspapers thus contributed in fundamental ways to the very existence of the parties and to the creation of a sense of membership, identity, and common cause among political activists and voters" (2001, 11). In addition, precinct workers, candidates, and party officials reached out to their constituents directly. Public meetings, speeches, mass rallies, debates, and torchlight parades were organized by parties in communities on behalf of candidates, which served to enhance parties' personalized approach to campaigning (Schudson 1998).

The advent of television contributed to a shift in the importance of political parties in elections. Coinciding with the rise in broadcast communications, campaigns became professionalized. Parties moved from a personalized to a business-oriented approach to communicating with voters (Gibson and Rommele 2001). Party and candidate organizations used television to reach a mass audience. They adapted their strategies to conform to the conventions of a visual mass medium and short-form, fixed-time news broadcasts. Candidates conveyed their messages in increasingly quick sound bites that were interspersed amidst journalists' commentary. Poll results proliferated in the news, driving horse-race journalism that focused more on campaign tactics than issues and candidate qualifications (Patterson 1980). The television medium encouraged candidates to develop image-based appeals in order to create a sense of pseudointimacy with voters as campaigns moved away from people-intensive communication channels (Hart 1999). According to Patterson, the news media compromised the parties' hold over the candidate selection process as the press built momentum around certain candidates and dismissed others (Patterson 2002). Candidates could work around the party hierarchy and infrastructure by taking their messages directly to the public through television. The Republican and Democratic national nominating conventions became carefully scripted pseudoevents, rather than spontaneous expressions of partisan spirit (Kerbel 2002).

The professional, candidate-centered campaigns of the broadcast media era shifted authority away from parties to media strategists and political consultants who worked for hire (Farrell and Webb 2000; Gibson and Rommele 2001; Rommele 2003). Party organizations became irrelevant to many voters (Patterson 2002). Candidate organizations and consulting firms took on many of the functions previously relegated to parties, such as recruiting candidates, formulating campaign strategies, prioritizing issues, organizing volunteers, fund-raising, communicating to voters, and mobilizing the electorate (Patterson 1980, 1994; Rubin 1981; Ranney 1983; Owen 1991). The length of campaigns increased as candidates needed to start fund-raising early in order to afford campaign professionals and costly television advertising buys.

Party Functions in the New Media Era

Aspects of the people-intensive and broadcasting campaign approaches remain in the current period characterized by a party's aggressive use of digital media platforms. Direct personal appeals through door knocking and mass rallies still are persuasive in convincing voters to support a candidate and turn out to vote (Green and Gerber 2004). Broadcast media are important to parties as they seek to convey common messages to voters.

Digital technologies have allowed parties to reintegrate personalized approaches to communication into their campaign strategies on a more vast scale than is possible through conventional people-intensive, face-to-face methods. Parties can use e-mail, text messaging, and social media strategies to develop personal connections that complement their more depersonalized mass media tactics, such as television advertising. Political parties now employ professional media managers with digital media skills who hold important roles within the organizational hierarchy (Norris 2005).

New media allow parties to contact individuals and organizations efficiently and without the constraint of geography. National party organizations can readily become involved in local campaigns and vice versa. Obscure state level candidates can receive national press attention that is sparked by new media, a phenomenon that became evident in the 2010 midterm elections. Christine O'Donnell, a Tea Party–backed Republican candidate for Senate in Delaware, became the second most prominent newsmaker in 2010, behind only President Barack Obama, largely due to viral videos, blog posts, and Twitter feeds that fed mainstream news media (Project for Excellence in Journalism 2010). In addition, new media facilitate parties' narrowcasting and microtargeting efforts by enabling them to deliver strategically developed content tailored to particular voters no matter where they are located. Social media also can facilitate internal political party communications and resource sharing (Gibson and Rommele 2001; Gibson et al. 2003).

The two major parties' embrace of new media has reinvigorated their role in the electoral process. Following the 2008 elections, parties sought to become more directly involved in campaign management using digital technologies. Unlike large circulation newspapers and radio and television platforms with wide audience reach, it is feasible for party organizations to develop and support their own digital media. Parties can be stable hubs for maintaining, updating, and innovating with digital platforms. They can support the digital infrastructure for contesting elections across campaigns. Candidate organizations, on the other hand, take down or suspend their digital communications after elections. Parties' ability to maintain a consistent digital presence throughout and between election cycles has enhanced their organizational relevance for cooperating actors in their networks, especially candidates, voters, and media personnel.

Party organizations can use new media to perform a wide range of functions that were traditionally handled offline as well as to engage the political world in novel ways. New media offer diverse channels for disseminating information to the public and providing resources for journalists. People can choose to consume text-based, audio, or video information that ranges from serious position papers to humorous clips. Parties can engage the interactive features of digital media to promote opinion formation. They can host multiway discussions where people can share ideas and experiences, discuss issues, candidates, and events, and express their frustrations. These discussions can be regularized as ongoing conversations among the party faithful that serve to reinforce their commitment. Party platforms can provide access to platforms that facilitate the building of interactive bridges between leaders, candidates, activists, and supporters, such as social networking sites (Norris 2005). Parties can use digital techniques to recruit members and engage people who they otherwise would not reach. People lacking the inclination or the ability to take part in offline activities, like attending rallies or stumping for a candidate, can participate vigorously through digital party platforms (Rommele 2003). During elections, parties can coordinate campaign efforts, distribute materials, fund-raise, recruit volunteers, canvass voters, solidify their base supporters, and reach out to the uncommitted—and do it virtually.

Parties and the Mainstream Media Today

Mainstream media are sources that traditionally have been affiliated with professional news organizations, and are characterized by their ability to reach large audiences quickly. They are associated with a broadcast model of communication, and produce content of general societal interest that appeals widely to a mass audience. Mainstream media have the resources and the stature to regularly set the agenda for politics (Chomsky 1997; Hamilton 2004; McChesney 2004; Bennett 2005). Newspapers, television news programs, news magazines, and radio news shows are mainstream news sources. However, the lines between mainstream media and new media have become blurred in the current era. Cable television has precipitated a tremendous expansion in channels and the development of niche news offerings that attract people favoring specific partisan and ideological perspectives (Jamieson and Cappella 2008; Stroud 2011; Chalif 2011). Mainstream print and broadcast media sources have developed digital counterparts that integrate novel platforms, such as blogs, Twitter feeds, and video eyewitness reports by average citizens into their news products (Owen 2012). Further complicating matters, it has become difficult to distinguish between some traditional and new media products. Blogs, like the *Huffington Post*, have the look and feel of the online version of mainstream newspapers, although the content is substantially different and more overtly opinionated.

The two major political parties actively seek to manage mainstream print and broadcast media to effectively promote their candidates, leaders, policy prescriptions, and activities. They work especially hard to attract positive coverage by prestige sources, such as the *New York Times* and the *Washington Post*, that are influential in setting the agenda for news across a wide spectrum of sources. Parties court the mainstream media using well-worn tactics, such as issuing press releases, brokering interviews between party representatives, candidates, and journalists or talk show hosts, and holding news conferences. In the current era, party Websites, blogs, and social media have become regular sources of information for news outlets. However, to date news organizations are somewhat limited in the way that they make use of social media and Twitter feeds in their reporting of news stories, including from parties (Holcomb and Gross 2011). During the 2012 nomination campaign, the Democratic and Republican parties created election-related videos almost daily that they posted to their Websites and YouTube channels with the expectation that they will be picked up by news organizations, particularly the cable channels, which often occurred. Party operatives work the press in an effort to gain positive publicity during their major events, such as the national nominating conventions (Kerbel 2002).

As Kerbel notes, journalists' portrayals of political parties are based primarily on the people associated with them in their networks—candidates, elected officials, and party convention delegates. Stories tend to deal with the political motives that drive these actors rather than on party institutions themselves. Thus, the image of party organizations that emerges is predicated heavily on their electoral role and strategic decisions. Parties are portrayed as "highly personalized, nonideological organizations engaged in blurring rather than sharpening distinctions in an effort to present a compelling political image for television" (Kerbel 2002, 191).

Despite their best efforts at media management, mainstream press coverage of parties is substantially more negative than positive. A stock media frame has reporters lamenting the state of the Democratic and Republican parties. Journalists routinely report that party organizations are on life support and that they have lost touch with the American people. Yet evidence suggests that the media cover political parties as much in the current era as they did in the 1950s, and that the Democratic and Republican party labels remain highly relevant to voters (Jarvis 2001). Press reports also highlight bickering between members of the same party. The focus on partisan bickering can be excessively high during nominating contests, exacerbating the difficulties parties face in uniting for the general election. Another common frame is that there are no meaningful ideological or policy differences between the political parties, and so the parties offer little guidance to voters who seek to make decisions between clear alternatives. Perhaps the most prominent media frame highlights conflicts between the two major parties (Kerbel 2002). As avowed adversaries, the parties promote this perspective, which is amplified during election campaigns. This frame may appear to be somewhat at odds with the view that there are no distinctions between the parties. However, partisan conflicts are most often portrayed in terms of personal battles between candidates or prominent individuals, rather than as battles between ideologically distinct institutions. Press coverage can exaggerate partisan conflicts, which can work against bipartisan efforts to regulate the electoral environment or pass legislation (Paletz, Owen, and Cook 2011).

Parties and New Media

American political parties, as long-established, diffuse, organizationally cumbersome organizations, had been slow to adapt to the fast-changing new media environment. Parties had conventions for dealing with the media that were developed in the mainstream press age that they did not hurry to revise.

Their approach to new media initially was cautious, and reflected the media management strategy that characterized their relationship with traditional news outlets. These tactics were not effective when dealing with digital media that are fast-paced, freewheeling, and difficult to control. In addition, party elites have been divided about how vigorously to embrace new media. Some officials believe that digital media present parties with opportunities to enhance their role. They feel that keeping ahead of the new media curve is imperative for maintaining relevance and appealing to younger citizens. Other officials are concerned that an intensive focus on technology distracts parties from their fundamental responsibilities of recruiting new candidates and broadening the party's appeal through more conventional methods. They note that the number of people who engage actively in politics through digital platforms is small, especially compared to those who follow politics through television (Rhoads 2009). In fact, less than 20 percent of the public used social networking sites or Twitter in the 2010 midterm elections, compared to 66 percent of the electorate who got most of their news from television, and 33 percent who relied mostly on newspapers (Pew Research Center 2010).

Political parties' approach to innovation with new media applications has typically been more conservative than that taken by candidate organizations and interest groups, especially in the pre-2008 election era. The candidate-centric electoral process largely relegated parties to a supporting role as campaign organizations dictated media strategies. Further, candidates have been more likely to experiment with new media applications during the nominating phase of elections when they are willing to take risks as they attempt to attract uncommitted constituencies to their camp than during the general election when they are working to solidify their base using more traditional media management techniques (Owen 2011, 2012). In hotly contested nominating campaigns, parties engage in antiopposition media messaging through their press releases and Websites that often is less visible than the candidates' more aggressive, innovative strategies. For example, Republican Senate candidate Scott Brown used Twitter to launch viral attacks against his opponent, Martha Coakley, that were disseminated too quickly to refute effectively; Brown won the election (Mustafaraj and Panagiotis 2010). The conflict frame that pervades much political news coverage is accommodated by candidates' attacks on their opponents through new media.

Candidate organizations also have been innovative in their online voter outreach and volunteer recruitment efforts.

The US trend of candidate organizations breaking new ground in campaign communication ahead of political parties is in contrast to the situation in many other western democracies where campaigns are waged largely through political parties (Ward et al. 2008). Independent candidate sites are a more recent phenomenon in European nations, as evidence of the "Americanization" and globalization of campaigns has become apparent (Negrine and Papathanassopoulos 1996; Scammell 1997; Gibson et al. 2003; Rommele 2003). Currently, American parties are moving in the direction of their European counterparts and increasing their organizational presence in campaigns through digital media. The Obama campaign's digital media initiative in 2008 set the gold standard for political organizations. The Democratic and Republican parties, taking cues from Obama in 2008, have assumed a more central role in digital campaign organizing in the lead up to the 2012 election than in the recent past.

Political Party Websites

Websites form the backbone of parties' and candidates' digital media presence (Druckman, Kifer, and Parkin 2009). Websites are repositories of information and platforms hosting political discussion and engagement tools. They also provide a gateway to party organization and candidate social media, such as YouTube channels and Facebook pages.

Candidate organizations often have been ahead of parties in innovating with Internet platforms. Bill Clinton's presidential campaign committee was the first to use Internet applications for election purposes in 1992 by putting biographical information and position papers online. John McCain's campaign organization in 2000 employed innovative Web-based strategies for fund-raising and voter mobilization as he sought the Republican presidential nomination. During the 2004 presidential nominating campaign, Democratic contender Howard Dean's campaign broke new ground by using the Internet to fund-raise effectively and encourage grassroots participation through blogging and meet-ups (Bimber and Davis 2003; Foot and Schneider 2006). The centerpiece of the Obama campaign organizations' monumental digital media operation was the Obama '08 Website. The site went through several iterations as the campaign progressed, with new features introduced at each interval. The Website was a one-stop shop for voters, interest groups, and journalists, and contained a tremendous amount of information presented in text, audio, and video format. Versions of the site during the nomination campaign included a campaign time line, headquarters pages for the primary states where people could pledge themselves to the candidate, and mobile applications. Over the course of the campaign, the site hosted a great deal of user-generated content, including event videos, amateur campaign ads, and party platform drafts devised by citizens online. The Obama '08 site provided a space for personalized campaigning through My Barack Obama—or "MyBo"—which allowed people to post their own blogs that had RSS feeds that prompted reporters to regularly link to the site. Over one million individual users established accounts on MyBo (Zeigler 2008). The Obama team also created special function Websites, such as one called, "Fight the Smears" that debunked Internet rumors (Falcone 2008). Over 8.5 million people visited the Obama '08 Website over the course of the campaign (Lutz 2009). Reporter Jason Horowitz wrote of the Obama campaign Website: "The campaign has taken the Internet technology pioneered by Howard Dean in 2004, expanded on it and built what is in essence a multimedia company capable of competing with the traditional press in communicating with supporters. And that audience has, in turn, responded with hundreds of millions of dollars in campaign contributions, thousands and thousands of volunteer hours, and instant, on-demand outrage directed at media outlets whose coverage is deemed unfair to the candidate" (Horowitz 2008).

It is important to recognize that party Websites must accomplish a broader set of aims than candidate sites, which focus exclusively on getting people elected to office. The Republican and Democratic national committee Websites are integral to other party activities, such as supporting officials in office, issue organizing, and coordinating state and local party operations. As multipurpose Websites aimed at broad audiences, the DNC and RNC Websites have serviceable design features that are easy to navigate.

While they may not be as elaborate or technically advanced as the best candidate sites, the Republican and Democratic party Websites have been solid campaign resources at the state and national level (Farmer and Fender 2005). American parties first developed rudimentary Websites in the 1990s that, like candidate sites, functioned primarily as brochureware that hosted documents, press releases, speeches, and party news. They were resources for supporters seeking to galvanize their connection to the party and rein-force their political beliefs and candidate preferences. Party sites became in-creasingly sophisticated with each election campaign, incorporating novel elements that corresponded to new media trends. They offered dynamic graphics, photos, videos, ads, interactive polls, and media clips. Sites were heavily oriented toward providing information to journalists that would showcase their candidates positively and attack the opposition. They often presented candidate ads before they were played on television in an effort to gain free media coverage.

To control the flow of information in a volatile and uncertain environment, parties, like political officeholders, initially were hesitant to stimulate mean-ingful interactions with voters by taking advantage of the interactive capabil-ities of digital media. They made scant use of discussion boards or comment sections until after the 2000 election (Davis and Owen 1998; Davis 1999; Gib-son and Ward 2000). Further, early party Websites did little to attract young voters by appealing to their issue interests or propensity to engage online (Xenos and Bennett 2007). By the 2002 midterm elections, campaign Websites had begun to incorporate a variety of interactive and multimedia features that collected voter information and e-mail addresses, gauged opinion, facilitated voter registration, advertised events, recruited volunteers, and fund-raised. Parties used their Websites for personalized appeals, and reached out to spe-cific constituencies, like young people, women, and black and Latino voters, through special sections on their Websites. Like candidate sites, party organi-zations increasingly allowed citizen-generated content—blogs, videos, and eyewitness accounts of campaign events—on their Websites (Druckman, Kifer, and Parkin 2009). The sites also provide gateways to social media tools that the parties used to connect with actors in their networks.

The Republican National Committee (RNC) rolled out a new Website (www.gop.com) in October 2009 in an effort to "promote increased grass-roots participation and innovation, better communication, improved plat-form compatibility and smarter marketing and fund-raising tools." The site got off to a rocky start, but after the design and content limitations were cor-rected it marked an upgrade from its predecessor (Barr 2009). The Website has a simple, clean appearance, and is structured to accommodate Web pages focused on particular topics, some of which are specifically aimed at defeating President Barack Obama in the 2012 election. For example, "Hope

Isn't Hiring" is a page responding to Barack Obama's fund-raising tactics. These Web pages feature ads and specific fund-raising goals targeting Democratic candidates, such as former Speaker of the House Nancy Pelosi.

The Democratic National Committee (DNC) unveiled a new Website (www.democrats.org) in September 2010. The Website sported a new logo evocative of the Obama for America campaign image, and presented the tag line: "Democrats: Change That Matters." The revamped Website was part of an effort to rebrand the DNC so that it no longer appears to be an organization that "conjures up visions of old men sitting around a conference room table" (Stein 2010). The site incorporates many of the features that have been integral to the Obama campaign sites in 2008 and 2012, especially interactive and video elements. In addition to its main Website, the DNC has launched a series of specialized Websites. One site blasts changes in the voting laws in fourteen states. Another site attacks Republican House Minority Leader John Boehner for his associations with lobbyists and special interest groups. The Website is presented in the style of a game, and the color pallet is shades of orange in order to mock Boehner's perpetual tan.

Party and Candidate Website Traffic

Party Websites through the 2008 election cycle attracted far fewer people than major news platforms and candidate Websites. Much of the information available on party Websites was redundant, reproducing content already appearing on candidate sites or repurposed from other online sources, such as news sites. Candidate organization sites offered office seekers direct, unfiltered access to voters, and were more candid reflections of candidates' principles and views than party sites (Bimber and Davis 2003). In addition, candidates do a better job of publicizing their Websites than parties. Table 10.1 depicts the percentage of people using particular Websites to gain information about the 2008 presidential election. Four percent of the public went to a political party or interest group Website compared to 13 percent who visited a presidential candidate's site. CNN's Website drew the largest audience for campaign information, with just over one-quarter of online information seekers consulting the site. Other news organization sites and news portals, such as Yahoo, Google, and AOL, had far fewer visitors than CNN. The size of the audiences for conservative (4 percent) and liberal blogs (2 percent) was similar to that of political parties.

TABLE 10.1 Websites Used to Get Information About the 2008 Presidential Campaign (Percentage of people who went online for campaign information)

Website	Percentage of Online Information Seekers
CNN	27%
Yahoo	17%
Presidential Candidate Websites	**13%**
MSNBC/NBC	13%
FOX	11%
MSN/Microsoft	9%
Google	7%
New York Times	6%
Local News	5%
AOL	5%
Conservative Blogs/Websites	5%
Political Parties/Interest Groups	**4%**
Drudge Report	4%
Polling Websites and Aggregators	3%
Washington Post	3%
YouTube	2%
Huffington Post	2%
Liberal Blogs/Websites	2%
Politico	2%
BBC	2%
ABC	2%
Cable News Service Provider	2%
CBS	1%
Wall Street Journal	1%
Newsmagazines (Time, US News, Newsweek)	1%

Source: Pew Research Center for the People and the Press 2008.

Both the national political party committee and candidate Websites drew significant traffic in the five months prior to the first caucuses and primaries in 2012. In keeping with past patterns, candidate sites overall draw more visitors than party sites, but parties have been gaining ground. Table 10.2 provides analytic data from Quantcast comparing party and candidate Website visitors and rankings. On the Democratic side, Barack Obama's campaign site is one of the most popular political sites online, and had many more visitors—over 3 million per month—than the DNC site. However, the DNC Website still drew an average of over a half million visitors per month during this period, which compares favorably with traffic estimates in previous election cycles. With incumbent president Barack Obama certain to be the Democratic Party's nominee, the party site can complement the messaging and operational strategies of the campaign committee site (www.Barack Obama.com). During this time period, Obama's candidate site received a boost from publicity surrounding a makeover of the site in November as well as new features designed to generate precinct-level engagement with the platform. Highly publicized outreach efforts, such as a dinner with Barack Obama sweepstakes, also drove users to the candidate site (Dwyer 2011).

The Republican National Committee and Republican presidential candidate sites individually drew fewer visitors than the Democratic sites in the lead up to the 2012 nominating campaign. The one exception is the site of Herman Cain—a Republican candidate who suspended his campaign in early December—which attracted over a million visitors. The situation for the Republicans is complicated by the fact that their presidential nominee had yet to be selected at the time these data were collected. The RNC site, which drew just over 200,000 visitors per month, had to focus heavily on anti-Democrat and anti-Obama messages rather than on supporting a Republican candidate. The Republican contenders for the nomination vary

TABLE 10.2 Average Monthly Visitors to and Rankings of
Party and Candidate Websites

	Average Monthly Visitors (5 months)	Rank Among US Websites
Democrats.org	**577,800**	**3,244**
Barack.Obama.com	3,800,000	333
GOP.com	**206,300**	**8,967**
hermancain.com	1,200,000	1,326
michelebachmann.com	393,000	4,827
RonPaul2012.com	339,400	5,604
mittromney.com	277,100	6,859
newt.org (Gingrich)	121,200	14,500
ricksantorum.com	92,900	18,302
buddyroemer.com	11,100	119,850
jon2012.com (Huntsman)	10,500	125,767
rickperry.org	4,000	281,571

Source: Quantcast 2011. Data as of December 2011.

greatly in the extent to which they rely on their Web presence to get their message across. The two top contenders at the end of 2011, Mitt Romney and Newt Gingrich, had fewer visitors to their sites than Michele Bachmann and Ron Paul, candidates with Tea Party connections who were doing poorly in the polls. As we will discuss below, Tea Party candidates make a point of rejecting mainstream media in favor of their own digital media platforms. Rick Perry, who had a short stint as a favored candidate before dropping precipitously in the polls, had the fewest visitors to his campaign site.

The characteristics of visitors to the DNC and RNC Websites are depicted in Table 10.3. More women than men use the DNC Website, while the opposite is the case for the RNC site. Visitors to the DNC site skew slightly

TABLE 10.3 Audience Characteristics of Visitors to the Democratic and Republican National Committee Websites

	Democrats.org	*GOP.com*
Sex		
Male	45%	53%
Female	55%	47%
Age		
Under 18	4%	8%
18–34	28%	32%
35–49	31%	30%
50+	38%	31%
Race		
Caucasian	76%	84%
African American	11%	5%
Asian	4%	2%
Hispanic	9%	8%
Other	1%	1%
Education		
No College	32%	36%
College	47%	44%
Graduate School	21%	33%
Income		
0–$30,000	19%	14%
$30,000–$60,000	26%	25%
$60,000–$100,000	27%	28%
$100,000+	28%	33%
Family		
No Kids	69%	61%
Kids	31%	39%

Source: Quantcast 2011. Data as of December 2011.

younger than visitors to the GOP site. Thirty-two percent of visitors to the DNC site are under age thirty-five, while 38 percent are over fifty, while 40 percent of RNC site visitors are under thirty-five and 31 percent are over fifty. The vast majority of users of both sites are Caucasian; however a higher percentage of African Americans visit the DNC site. About two-thirds of visitors to both sites have at least a college degree, and many users have a graduate education. People with higher incomes are more inclined to visit the DNC and RNC sites than those with lower incomes. Finally, more than 60 percent of visitors to national party Websites have no children, perhaps indicating that they have fewer family commitments and can take the time to engage with online political media.

Parties' Digital Media in Post-2008 Era

Social media were an integral part of the Obama campaign's game-changing grassroots effort to mobilize the electorate in 2008. The Obama organization built a complex, multifaceted infrastructure that used Web-based strategies to spark offline grassroots mobilization. The public became integrally involved in the process by contributing to the creation and distribution of media messages through social media and video-sharing Websites (Plouffe 2009; Heilemann and Halperin 2010). While in office, President Obama continued to develop his grassroots social media network. By 2011 he had accumulated 19.3 million Facebook fans to whom he could readily reach out about issues and events (Preston 2011).

In the post-2008 election era, parties have become more assertive with their digital media strategies. The Democratic Party was more advanced in their use of digital technology for campaigning than the Republican Party in the immediate aftermath of the 2008 presidential election, as its association with the Obama campaign gave them an edge. The Republicans, recognizing the potential of social media, caught up with the Democrats during the 2010 midterm contests. Social media contributed to Republican victories in a number of House and Senate races (Preston 2011).

The national parties use e-mail and text messaging to make donating and engaging in campaigns easier for voters. The DNC and the RNC use their Facebook pages and Twitter to post content related to candidates, the electoral process, issues, and events, including ads. One goal of using these approaches is to appeal to voters, but there are few people actively engaged through these media. Most Facebook posts to national party pages generate one or two hundred comments, and Twitter messages may be retweeted, especially during events like debates. However, the larger goal of much of the social media activity of party organizations is to gain pickup by other media sources that reach much larger audiences. The national parties have been experimenting with ways to attract larger media attention through social media. The DNC, for example, initiates nightly hashtags on Twitter designed to reflect negatively on opposition candidates during the 2012 campaign. They spread hashtags aimed at Republican candidate Mitt Romney like #Questions MittLikes and #YoungerThanMittsPoliticalCareer, which they hope will trend and be picked up as story lines by television and other media.

New Media and Alternatives to the Major Parties

The mainstream media reinforce the major parties' dominance in the political process. The Republican and Democratic party organizations and their candidates receive the lion's share of coverage by established news platforms. Minor parties have difficulty attracting press attention. They generally lack the resources to air television ads, and their candidates are often excluded from participating in televised debates. The mainstream press covers minor party candidates when they make good copy for being outspoken or outlandish, and often they are treated as a sideshow rather than as serious contenders (Paletz, Owen, and Cook 2011).

Early in the evolution of the political Internet, scholars and political observers speculated that third parties would benefit disproportionately from the ability to establish an online presence, especially through Websites. They assumed that the Web would provide an opportunity for minor parties to build an organizational infrastructure that would allow them to widely disseminate their policy platforms and garner supporters (Corrado and Firestone 1997; Rash 1997). Online media would help close the awareness gap between major and minor parties that was in part attributable to unequal mainstream press coverage. There was some evidence that third parties were a notable presence on the Web during the 2000 presidential election, as the Libertarian Party had more links to its site than either the Republican or the Democratic parties, and the Green Party and the Natural Law Party had sites that attracted a good number of visitors (Gibson et al. 2003). However, these overly optimistic expectations were tempered by the realization that building and maintaining a quality Web presence is costly, and driving people to visit sites requires resources. The two major political parties were able to develop and publicize sophisticated Websites far more effectively than minor parties, and by 2004 the major party Web presence dwarfed that of minor parties.

Democratic political consultant Joe Trippi, who was behind Howard Dean's Web campaign in 2004, predicts that social media will radically change politics to the extent that, "It will be the end of the two parties." He argues that social media will enable an underdog third party candidate to come out of nowhere to upset a presidential front-runner by using digital tools to raise a billion dollars and running against the two parties perhaps as soon as 2012 (Zapler 2011). While Trippi's prediction may be overstated, public opinion polls indicate that Americans are amenable to a viable option other than the Democratic and Republican parties. A Gallup poll taken during the 2010 midterm elections found that 58 percent of the public favors a third party, which is the highest level in almost a decade. Only about 35 percent of the public believes that the two major parties do an adequate job (Jones 2010).

The Tea Party

The Internet and digital media are suited to oppositional politics and grassroots insurgencies due to their decentralized structure (Rhoades 2009; Willey 2011a). The Tea Party, which emerged on the political scene in 2009 as protestors organized against government "tax and spend" policies, is in many ways a product of the new media era. Whether the Tea Party formally constitutes a political party or is instead a grassroots, conservative-leaning social movement is a matter of debate. The Tea Party's decentralized structure, lack of clear leadership, and oppositional approach to politics is in contrast to the organization, identifiable leadership network, and policy-oriented approach typical of American major and third parties (Armey and Kibbe 2010; Lepore 2010; Willey 2011a; Zernicke 2010). The Tea Party is not a single entity, but instead is a loose mixture of disparate factions, such as the Tea Party Nation, Tea Party Patriots, and state and local groups, some of which are at odds with one another. However, the Tea Party conforms to Epstein's definition of a political party. The Tea Party gained attention during the 2010 midterm elections as Republican congressional candidates ran under the Tea Party label. Forty-five Tea Party–backed candidates gained national office, and others, such as

Christine O'Donnell and Sharron Angle, were unsuccessful, but received a great deal of national media attention. The Tea Party remained relevant in the 2012 election, as Republicans contesting for the presidential nomination were pressed to embrace or reject the Tea Party. A televised Republican presidential candidate debate was cosponsored by the Tea Party Express and CNN in September 2011.

Politicians identifying with the Tea Party publically reject the mainstream media in favor of social media, which they believe are more populist mechanisms for reaching their constituents. Tea Party activists distrust the mainstream media, which they maintain has a strong liberal agenda and supports big government, which they vehemently oppose. The Tea Party uses new media to circumvent mainstream media gatekeepers and get their message out. They have developed a strong Internet presence with Websites and Facebook pages. They rely on online videos that they hope will go viral, rally supporters, and generate media coverage. Tea Party activists are heavy users of Twitter and microblogging sites, like Tumblr. Tea Party groups regularly used e-mail to reach supporters directly and spread their antiestablishment rhetoric (Lepore 2010). The Tea Party employs social media for fund-raising far less frequently than the major parties, as they fear that asking for money may be inconsistent with their anti-tax-and-spend rhetoric (Willey 2011b).

Despite the fact that a cornerstone of their rhetoric is a suspicion of the mainstream media, the Tea Party relies fundamentally on the press to publicize their objectives, get behind their candidates, and provide momentum for the movement. The Tea Party's social media drives much mainstream media coverage, which is gleaned from blog posts, tweets, and videos. Colorful public figures with Tea Party ties, like former Alaska governor Sarah Palin and South Carolina senator Jim DeMint, decry the mainstream media while basking in its coverage. During elections, mainstream media coverage, especially television news, helps the Tea Party to build its base and bring national attention to state and local candidates (McGrath 2010; Lepore 2010; Willey 2011a).

Virtual Political Party Alternatives

A new class of alternatives to the two major political parties has emerged that is made possible by digital media. Virtual political party alternatives are nonpartisan and bipartisan organizations anchored by Websites that take advantage of the interactive features of the Internet that facilitate organizing, discussion, and the formation of online communities. They vary in their specific goals, structures, and functions, but are united in their belief that there should be more options than the two major parties. Some of these platforms can be characterized as "third party advocate groups" that seek to provide a new type of political organization for people who want to be connected to politics, but are not enamored of the Democratic or Republican parties (Cillizza 2011). Others seek to link voters on the basis of their policy views in an effort to organize the policy agenda.

One of the first of these organizations appeared in 2008 when a group of former election officials and wealthy individuals formed Unity08 (www .unity08.com) as a challenge to the party system. The organization faced legal challenges and shut down. Virtual party alternatives have proliferated in the 2012 election cycle in reaction to the public's high levels of disaffection with political institutions. A July 2011 Washington Post/ABC News poll, for example, found that 80 percent of the public was either angry or dissatisfied with the way that Washington works.

Americans Elect is the most visible digital alternative to political parties in the 2012 election, and is a direct descent of Unity08. The well-funded organization combines offline grassroots tactics, such as creating an active network of campus volunteers, holding publicity events, and sponsoring a nationwide bus tour, with digital methods, like e-mail, establishing a Facebook page and Twitter feeds, and posting videos, to drive traffic to their Website, where the first online primary election will be hosted. According to their Website, "Americans Elect is a secure, online nominating process that combines our oldest values with our newest technologies" (www.americanselect.org). The organization brokers a process that allows the public to select a presidential and vice presidential candidate ticket. Citizens of all political stripes can nominate candidates without participating in the Democratic or Republican primaries or caucuses. Elliot Ackerman, the group's chief operating officer, states: "The questions, the priorities, the nominations and the rules will all come from the community, not from two entrenched parties" (Friedman 2011, SR5). The ticket that emerges must include candidates who have different partisan leanings, such as a Republican presidential nominee running with a Democrat or an Independent. Hypothetically, if Republican John Huntsman were to run with Democrat Joe Biden, each would abandon their major party labels and run as Americans Elect candidates. People who are interested in participating as Americans Elect delegates register on the site and fill out a questionnaire identifying their issue priorities. Over 300,000 people had registered to become delegates as of December 2011. The organization brings together like-minded delegates, prominent politicians, and potential candidates in online forums where they discuss their views. Delegates can either draft a candidate or support one who has already been nominated. The nominees must meet all constitutional requirements and accept the offer. Some potential nominees, such as former secretary of state Condoleeza Rice, have been mentioned as Americans Elect candidates, but are not interested in running. Celebrities, such as Donald Trump, have shown interest in Americans Elect. Nominees will be screened by Americans Elect to ensure that they are serious contenders with appropriate credentials, and "not Lady Gaga" (Friedman 2011, SR5). Delegates also contribute questions to which the Americans Elect candidates respond either in writing or by video on the site. The candidate choices will be winnowed down to six possibilities through an online voting process, and an online convention will be held in June 2012 to determine the final slate. Americans Elect has gained ballot in states so that the candidates can automatically run under their label. Prior to January 2012, the organization had collected 2.55 million of the 2.9 million signatures that they needed to achieve ballot access in all fifty states (Harris 2011). Americans Elect received significant media coverage, and has been both praised as an exercise in digital democracy and vilified as being a secretive front for moneyed interests (Hansen 2011; Callahan 2011). Their Website—the heart of their operation—has been the target of numerous cyberattacks by people seeking to shut them down (Harris, 2011).

Other organizations have less ambitious electoral goals than Americans Elect, although they engage in some party functions. Votocracy is an online organization with the slogan: "Now you can run for any political office in America . . . or support those who do" (www.votocracy.com). The Website provides a mechanism for polling, fund-raising, and recruiting volunteers. No Labels is a bipartisan movement that seeks to "make Congress work" by monitoring and tracking the activities of members of congress "to ensure they are not playing hyper-partisan games" (www.nolabels.org/). Ruckus (www.ruck.us) is a social network for political organizing that helps connect people outside the two-party system. The network's slogan is: "No parties. Just People." The platform, which is similar to an online dating service for politics, connects liked-minded people digitally and helps them to become involved in elections on their own terms. Votifi is a nonpartisan, peer-to-peer network that uses opinion polling responsibly to inform the public, encourage debate, and empower citizens to take action (www.votifi.com).

Conclusion

New developments in the media landscape have precipitated changes in the way campaigns are waged. The two major American political parties are adaptive institutions that have responded to the new media environment with a renewed sense of their electoral purpose. They continue to court the mainstream media through both tried-and-true and new media methods. Gearing up for the 2012 election, the parties have upgraded their Websites and improved their social media strategies. They have become more aggressive in the ways in which they use digital communication to influence the press, raise money, and organize volunteers. The Democratic Party, in particular, has rather seamlessly coalesced its media presence and activities with those of the Obama campaign. The greater unity of party organization and campaign committee objectives may revitalize parties' electoral influence, which had waned in the broadcast media era.

Their enhanced new media strategies have the potential to provide numerous benefits to the two major party organizations. Professional journalists must work with fewer resources for reporting on stories. They have come to rely less on conventional sourcing and investigative techniques and spend more time consulting Websites, social media, and online video for content. Parties can become more aggressive agenda setters, as they provide an increasing amount of material to mainstream and new media entities. With sophisticated and aggressive outreach to communication outlets, parties can have a bigger say in how their organizations and candidates get covered.

New media also have made possible a broad array of virtual political party alternatives. The proliferation of these digital organizations mirrors the public's discontent with the entrenched two party system. It also demonstrates that citizens have a desire to communicate with one another and organize in new ways. It is likely that many of these online entities will not survive beyond the 2012 election, as they lack legitimate backing or business models to sustain their existence. However, others may thrive, develop stable constituencies, and assume some of the communication and organization functions of parties.

References

Armey, Dick, and Matt Kibbe. 2010. *Give Us Liberty: A Tea Party Manifesto*. New York: William Morrow.

Barr, Andy. 2009. "New RNC Website Stumbles Out of Gate." *Politico*. November 14. http://www.politico.com/news/stories/1009/28253.html.

Bennett, W. Lance. 2005. "The Twilight of Mass Media News." In *Freeing the Presses*, edited by Timothy E. Cook. Baton Rouge, LA: Louisiana State University Press.

Bimber, Bruce, and Richard Davis. 2003. *Campaigning Online*. New York: Oxford University Press.

Callahan, David. 2011. "A New Party Won't Necessarily Be More Pure Than Our Existing Two." Reuters. http://blogs.reuters.com/great-debate/2011/11/24/a-new-party-won%E2%80%99t-necessarily-be-more-pure-than-our-existing-two/.

Chalif, Rebecca. 2011. "Political Media Fragmentation: Echo Chambers in Cable News." *Electronic Media & Politics* 1, 3: 46–65.

Chomsky, Noam. 1997. "What Makes Mainstream Media Mainstream?" *Z Magazine*. October. http://www.chomsky.info/articles/199710—.htm.

Cillizza, Chris. 2011. "Voters' Renewed Anger at Washington Spurs Formation of Third-Party Advocate Groups." *Washington Post*, July 24. http://www.washingtonpost.com/politics/voters-renewed-anger-at-washington-spurs-formation-of-third-party-advocate-groups/2011/07/24/gIQAts3KXI_story.html.

Corrado, Anthony, and Charles M. Firestone, eds. 1997. *Elections in Cyberspace: Toward a New Era in American Politics*. Washington, DC: The Aspen Institute.

Davis, Richard. 1999. *The Web of Politics*. New York: Oxford University Press.

Davis, Richard, and Diana Owen. 1998. *New Media and American Politics*. New York: Oxford University Press.

Druckman, James N., Martin J. Kifer, and Michael Parkin. 2009. "The Technological Development of Candidate Web Sites: How and Why Candidates Use Web Innovations." In *Politicking Online*, edited by Costas Panagopoulos, 21–47. New Brunswick, NJ: Rutgers University Press.

Dwyer, Devin. 2011. "Obama Campaign Website Gets Makeover." *ABC News*. November 18. http://abcnews.go.com/blogs/politics/2011/11/obama-campaign-website-gets-makeover/.

Epstein, Leon D. 1989. *Political Parties in the American Mold*. Madison, WI: University of Wisconsin Press.

Falcone, Michael. 2008. "Obama Campaign Builds Rumor Debunking Site," The Caucus, http://thecaucus.blogs.nytimes.com/2008/06/12/obama-campaign-builds-rumor-debunking-site/.

Farmer, Rick, and Rich Fender. 2005. "E-Parties: Democratic and Republican State Parties in 2000." *Party Politics* 11, 1: 47–58.

Farrell, David M., and Paul Webb. 2000. "Political Parties as Campaign Organizations." In *Parties Without Partisans: Political Change in Advanced Industrial Democracies*, edited by Russell J. Dalton and Matin P. Wattenberg, 102–128. Oxford: Oxford University Press.

Foot, Kirsten A., and Steven M. Schneider. 2006. *Web Campaigning*. Cambridge, MA: MIT Press.

Friedman, Thomas L. 2001. "Make Way for the Radical Center." *New York Times*. July 23: SR5.

Gibson, Rachel K., Michael Margolis, David Resnick, and Stephen J. Ward. 2003. "Election Campaigning on the WWW in the USA and UK: A Comparative Analysis." *Party Politics* 9, 1: 47–75.

Gibson, Rachel K., and Andrea Rommele. 2001. "Political Parties and Professionalized Campaigning." *The Harvard International Journal of Press/Politics* 6, 1: 31–43.

Gibson, Rachel K., and Stephen J. Ward. 2000. "A Proposed Methodology for Studying the Function and Effectiveness of Party and Candidate Websites." *Social Science Computer Review* 18, 4: 301–319.

Green, Donald P., and Alan S. Gerber. 2004. *Get Out the Vote! How to Increase Voter Turnout.* Washington, DC: Brookings.

Hamilton, James T. 2004. *All the News That's Fit to Sell.* Princeton, NJ: Princeton University Press.

Hansen, Richard. 2011. "A Democracy Deficit at Americans Elect?" *Politico.* http://www.politico.com/news/stories/1111/67965.html.

Harris, Paul. 2011. "Americans Elect: Internet-Based Group Gaining Steam Ahead of Election." *The Guardian.* December 9. http://www.guardian.co.uk/world/2011/dec/09/americans-elect-group-gaining-steam?newsfeed=true.

Hart, Roderick P. 1999. *Seducing America.* Thousand Oaks, CA: Sage Publications.

Heilemann, John, and Mark Halperin. 2010. *Game Change.* New York: HarperCollins.

Holcomb, Jesse, and Kim Gross. 2011. *How Mainstream Media Outlets Use Twitter.* Washington, DC: Project for Excellence in Journalism and the George Washington University's School of Media and Public Affairs.

Horowitz, Jason. 2008. "Power of 'MYBO': Obama's Web Site Surmounts News." *New York Observer.* July 23. http://www.observer.com/2008/politics/power-mybo-obama-s-web-site-surmounts-news?show=all.

Jamieson, Kathleen Hall, and Joseph N. Cappella. 2008. *Echo Chamber.* New York: Oxford University Press.

Jarvis, Sharon E. 2001. "Imagining Political Parties: A Constructionist Approach." In *Communication in US Elections: New Agendas,* edited by Roderick P. Hart and Daron R. Shaw. Lanham, MD: Rowman and Littlefield.

Jones, Jeffrey M. 2010. "Americans Renew Call for Third Parties." *Gallup.* September 17. http://www.gallup.com/poll/143051/americans-renew-call-third-party.aspx.

Kerbel, Matthew Robert. 2002. "Political Parties in the Media: Where Elephants and Donkeys Are Pigs." In *The Parties Respond,* L. Sandy Maisel, 198–207. Boulder, CO: Westview Press.

Koger, Gregory, Seth Masket, and Hans Noel. 2009. "Partisan Webs: Information Exchange and Party Networks," *British Journal of Political Science* 39, 4: 633–653.

Lepore, Jill. 2010. *The Whites of Their Eyes: The Tea Party's Revolution and the Battle over American History.* Princeton, NJ: Princeton University Press.

Lutz, Monte. 2009. *The Social Pulpit: Barack Obama's Social Media Toolkit.* Washington, DC: Edelman Public Affairs.

McChesney, Robert W. 2004. *The Problem of the Media.* New York: Monthly Review Press.

McGrath, Ben. 2010. "The Movement: The Rise of Tea Party Activism." *The New Yorker.* February 1. http://www.newyorker.com/reporting/2010/02/01/100201fa_fact_mcgrath.

Mustafaraj, Eni, and Metaxas Panagiotis. 2010. "From Obscurity to Prominence in Minutes: Political Speech and Real-Time Search." In *Proceedings of the WebSci10: Extending the Frontiers of Society On-Line,* April 26–27. Raleigh, NC: US.

Negrine, Ralph, and Stylianos Papathanassopoulos. 1996. "The 'Americanization' of Political Communication: A Critique." *Press/Politics* 1, 2: 45–62.

Norris, Pippa. 2005. *Political Parties and Democracy in Theoretical and Practical Perspectives.* Washington, DC: National Democratic Institute for International Affairs.

Owen, Diana. 1991. *Media Messages in American Presidential Elections.* Westport, CT: Greenwood Press.

_____. 2011. "Media: The Complex Interplay of Old and New Forms." In *New Directions in Campaigns and Elections,* edited by Stephen K. Medvic, 145–162. New York: Routledge.

_____. 2012. "New Media and Political Campaigns." In *The Oxford Handbook of Political Communication Theories,* edited by Kate Kenski and Kathleen Hall Jamieson, Chapter 53. New York: Oxford University Press.

Paletz, David L., Diana Owen, and Timothy E. Cook. 2011. *American Government and Politics in the Information Age.* Irvington, NY: FlatWorld Knowledge Press.

Pasley, Jeffrey L. 2001. *The Tyranny of Printers: Newspaper Politics in the Early American Republic.* Charlottesville, VA: University of Virginia Press.

Patterson, Thomas E. 1980. *The Mass Media Election.* New York: Praeger.

_____. 1994. *Out of Order.* New York: Knopf.

_____. 2002. *The Vanishing Voter.* New York: Random House.

Pew Research Center for the People and the Press. 2008. October Political Survey. November 2008 Reinterview Survey. Washington, DC: Pew Research Center (Q.45).

Plouffe, David. 2009. *The Audacity to Win.* New York: Viking.

Preston, Jennifer. 2011. "Republicans Sharpening Online Tools for 2012." *New York Times.* April 19: A13.

Project for Excellence in Journalism. 2010. *The Year in News 2010.* Washington, DC: Project for Excellence in Journalism. http://www.journalism.org/analysis_report/year_news_2010.

Quantcast. 2011. Quantcast data pages for: Democrats, Barack Obama, GOP, Herman Cain, Michele Bachmann, Ron Paul, Mitt Romney, Newt Gingrich, Rick Santorum, Buddy Roemer, Jon Huntsman, Rick Perry. Available at www.quantcast.com. All data current as of December 2011.

Ranney, Austin. 1983. *Channels of Power.* New York: Basic Books.

Rash, Wayne. 1997. *Politics on the Nets: Wiring the Political Process.* New York: W. Freeman.

Rhoads, Christopher. 2009. "Playing Catch-Up, the GOP Is All Atwitter About the Internet." *Wall Street Journal.* January 30: A1.

Rommele, Andrea. 2003. "Political Parties, Party Communication and New Information and Communication Technologies." *Party Politics* 9, 7: 7–20.

Rubin, Richard L. 1981. *Press, Party and Presidency.* New York: W. W. Norton.

Sartori, Giovanni. 1976. *Parties and Party Systems: A Framework for Analysis.* London: Cambridge University Press.

Scammell, Margaret. 1997. *The Wisdom of the War Room: US Campaigning and Americanization.* Research Paper R-17. Cambridge, MA: The Joan Shorenstein Center, Harvard University.

Schudson, Michael. 1998. *The Good Citizen.* New York: The Free Press.

Stein, Sam. 2010. "DNC Reveals New Website, Logo." *Huffington Post.* September 15. http://www.huffingtonpost.com/2010/09/15/dnc-unveils-new-website-l_n_717687.html.

Stroud, Natalie Jomini. 2011. *Niche News.* New York: Oxford University Press.

Ward, Stephen, Diana Owen, Richard Davis, and David Taras, eds. 2008. *Making a Difference: The Internet and Elections in Comparative Perspective.* New York: Lexington.

Willey, J. Scott. 2011a. *The Decentralized Social Movement: How the Tea Party Gained Relevancy in the New Media Era.* MA Thesis. Washington, DC: Georgetown University.

_____. 2011b. "Don't Ask: The Tea Party Nation's E-Mail Strategy." *Electronic Media & Politics* 1, 5: 89–107.

Xenos, Michael, and W. Lance Bennett. 2007. "The Disconnection in Online Politics: The Youth Political Web Sphere and US Election Sites, 2002–2004." *Information, Communication & Society* 10, 4: 443–464.

Zapler, Mike. 2011. "Joe Trippi: Social Media Will Kill Two-Party System." *Politico*. March 14. http://www.politico.com/news/stories/0311/51234.html.

Zeigler, Todd. 2008. "The Evolution of Barack Obama's Campaign Website." *The Bivings Group*. January 7. http://www.bivingsreport.com/2008/the-evolution-of-barack-obamas -campaign-website/.

Zernicke. 2010. "Tea Party Disputes Take Toll on Convention." *New York Times*. January 25: A12.

11

Congressional Parties and the Policy Process

SEAN THERIAULT
JONATHAN LEWALLEN
University of Texas

In summer 2011, Washington, DC, and financial markets around the world became consumed with talk of the United States government reaching its debt ceiling, which would force the government to default on several of its loans. By June 1, 2011, members of Congress had introduced 131 different pieces of legislation to address the budget deficit or debt. Some efforts were taken more seriously than others. In the spring and early summer, most attention was focused on the Senate's Gang of Six, an informal bipartisan group who offered the most comprehensive attempt at a solution.

Between June 1 and July 15, members introduced an additional forty pieces of legislation to address the impending crisis. As time dragged on, it became clear that a solution was not likely to rise up through the rank and file members or even through the normal committee process, so party leaders in Congress became increasingly involved. At first, the leaders picked representatives to meet with Vice President Joe Biden to hammer out an agreement. When the talks broke down in late June, the responsibility for avoiding default ultimately fell on President Barack Obama and Speaker John Boehner (R-Ohio). They negotiated the details of an agreement to raise the federal debt ceiling and cut spending in a series of high-level talks with very limited participants. Congressional leaders met with their respective party member-ships, but these sessions were more informational and designed to make these members feel as if their input was being acknowledged. Indeed, one proposed measure had to be removed from House floor consideration close to the scheduled vote because Republican leaders had not convinced enough of their members to support the bill. Few of the committees that deal with tax and spending matters were involved in the process of crafting the final deal; instead, Speaker Boehner, Senate Majority Leader Harry Reid (D-Nev.), and Senate Minority Leader Mitch McConnell (R-Ky.) were the primary leg-islative players in reaching an agreement.

Little time existed between when the final agreement was reached on July 31, 2011, and when default would take effect. The normal legislative process needed to be accelerated to pass the legislation. The rule governing floor de-bate in the House provided for no amendments and only allowed for an hour of debate. On the following day, the Senate approved the agreement and the president signed it into law. In less than two days, the agreement became law.

The 2011 debt-ceiling story vividly shows the growing importance of party leaders in the contemporary Congress. In this chapter, we outline the processes that were at work to make the leaders so powerful vis-à-vis com-mittee chairs and rank-and-file members. In the first part, we describe the goals of congressional parties. In the second part, we show the conditions that fostered the growth of the party leaders' powers. In the third section, we outline these powers before concluding in the final section.

Party Goals in Congress

With 535 individuals representing the far corners of the American map, pre-dicting congressional action is a tricky business. Political scientists have uti-lized two features of Congress to make the task more manageable. First, the Constitution dictates and the chambers have developed rules, structures, and institutions that prescribe a more systematic pattern. Second, Richard Fenno (1973) and David Mayhew (1974) have provided analytic leverage for predicting legislative outcomes by outlining the goals of individual mem-bers. Mayhew in particular asserted that the easiest way to understand Con-gress was by starting with the proposition that members of Congress were "single-minded seekers of reelection." Even if they have other concerns, these authors reasoned that members of Congress need to secure reelection before even addressing their other goals of passing good public policy and gaining prestige within the institution.

Mayhew and Fenno were developing these arguments as the political parties in Congress were an ideological mess. Most analyses of party polarization in Congress suggest that the parties of the early 1970s were less distinct than at any time since Reconstruction and, quite likely, years before (McCarty, Poole, and Rosenthal 2006; Sinclair 2006; Theriault 2008). While George Wallace's quip that "there wasn't a dime's worth of difference between the parties" was a bit of an exaggeration, the divide between the parties less than thirty years later would reveal more veracity behind the claim than the parties he was criticizing would have thought possible at the time. As the time since Wallace made his famous remark has passed, members' individual goals are now most easily satisfied through their political parties. In fact, Rohde and Aldrich (2010) advocate a fourth goal to Fenno's list: being a member of the majority party.

We think it's helpful to not only appreciate these member goals, but to develop goals for political parties in hope of understanding the actions that Congress takes and the structures—both formal and informal—it implements. In this section, we outline two goals that the political parties in Congress have: solving public policy problems and achieving majority status.

Solving Public Policy Problems

Fenno developed his argument for members' goals in the beginning of a book that analyzes the congressional committee system. At the time, his focus made sense. In order to pass good public policies, members needed to work through their committees to develop solutions that would then be presented to the floor. Gaining prestige within the institution during that period implicitly meant becoming a committee leader. If members succeeded in climbing the rungs of the committee system ladder, they could both exercise their influence and achieve good policy. Both actions would presumably help them secure their reelection.

In the years after Mayhew's and Fenno's seminal studies, members passed a number of reforms that ultimately struck at the core of the committee-based problem solving structure (Shepsle 1978; Sinclair 2002). First, full committees were mandated to share their staffing and lawmaking powers with subcommittees. Second, the Speaker was given the right to refer bills to multiple committees, which forced committees to either act on legislation or give up their right to affect it. Third, committee leaders were prohibited from exercising the proxies of their fellow committee members who were not in the room at the time of committee votes. Fourth, party leaders established task forces to insure action on particular issues. And, finally, the committee leaders became subject to appointment by the party leaders.

Party leadership was either the repository of the power relinquished by committees as a result of these reforms or it was the cause of the reforms themselves. Regardless of the path chosen, parties are now the primary avenue by which members expect to fulfill their goal of passing good public policy. While committee or member initiatives still play an important role in the process, Congress, in addressing public policy problems, frequently chooses from two alternatives—the Democrats' proposed solution and the Republicans' proposed solution. These alternatives and the institution's track record of adopting them are woven into the parties' reputations that become the currency of elections.

At the broader level, Congress as a body often finds itself unable to ignore particular policy problems. The volume and complexity of national issues has increased over time, leading to increased demands from constituents to pursue more of these issues (Smith 1989). Many government programs are authorized only temporarily, so that committees and the floor take up these issues on a recurring basis (Dodd and Schott 1979; Hall 2004). Party leaders thus must regularly find space for these issues in their chamber's agenda and the relative costs and benefits of these temporary authorizations are not always predictable (Cox 2004).

Achieving Majority Party Status

The development of party platforms, their contestation during elections and their implementation are the means by which voters cast their ballots in congressional elections (Kiewiet and McCubbins 1991). The economic, military, and social conditions of the country also cast a significant shadow on those contests (Hibbing and Alford 1981; Stimson 2004), as does the record of the majority party in running the institution (Parker and Davidson 1979; Patterson and Magleby 1992). As the victors of individual seats accumulate on election day, a majority party is determined.

Obtaining majority status, of course, is only the first step toward maintaining it. In addition to the conditions beyond their control, majority parties are evaluated on their stewardship of Congress. Elections do not determine which specific policies will become law, but rather serve as opportunities to approve or reject political leaders (Weissberg 1976). Citizens often are asked whether they have confidence in congressional leaders (Lipset and Schneider 1983; Patterson and Caldeira 1990; Patterson and Magleby 1992). Other studies have asked respondents to evaluate the "management of the legislative environment" (Parker and Davidson 1979) or to compare the contemporary institutional leadership with their predecessors (Davidson and Parker 1972). Public evaluations of Congress may be negative when the majority party is ideologically dissimilar from an individual (Jones and McDermott 2009). This is particularly true as elections have increasingly been decided by national factors beyond district concerns (Hibbing and Alford 1981; Stimson 2004; Erickson and Wright 2005; Jones and McDermott 2009), and evaluations of Congress can in turn predict an individual's feelings about her own representative (Born 1990).

In addition to facing public judgment, party leaders also are responsible for ensuring that rank-and-file members are satisfied with congressional outcomes, often pulling them in competing directions. Party leaders often make decisions based on building majorities in the short term (Cox and McCubbins 1993; Binder 1996). Such a strategy, however, can create or exacerbate internal party tensions that lead to negative future consequences for leaders (Sinclair 1983).

While the public charges Congress with solving public problems, passing major legislation that addresses these problems does not come without costs. First, research shows that major enactments can actually decrease levels of congressional approval (Durr, Gilmour, and Wolbrecht 1997). The record from the 111th Congress (2009–10) shows that the passage of major bills, including the stimulus package, health-care reform, and financial services overhaul, contributed to the Democrats' demise in the 2010 elections. Second, passing bills—even those that enjoy popular support—often requires members of the majority party to cast uncomfortable votes. The very nature of American elections means that some members are safer than others, and majority parties sometimes need their most vulnerable members, who represent a majority of constituents from the other party, to cast votes that they would rather not. The danger for both the vulnerable majority party member and her party leaders is that the public also responds negatively to majorities that do not pass legislation.

The Electoral Conditions for Party Leadership in Congress

The tension between the parties' dual goals of offering solutions to public policy problems and comprising the chamber's majority was so great that it prevented the Democratic majority from pursuing an explicit party strategy on many issues for much of the post–New Deal era. As conditions changed, however, the incentives for developing a party strategy inside Congress grew. It is to those conditions that we now turn.

Unified Constituencies

As the United States was recovering from the Great Depression and World War II, the Democrats were forging an electoral coalition—which would come to be known as "the New Deal Coalition"—that included white southerners, union members, Catholics, African Americans, and urban dwellers. In helping to bring about the 1932 realigning election, this coalition became the dominant electoral paradigm that delivered both the White House and Congress to Democrats for much of the next fifty years. Even as the New Deal Coalition began breaking down in presidential contests, it remained unified behind Democrats until the Civil Rights Act of 1964 and the Voting Rights Act of 1965 forced such internal tensions within the coalition that the ideological fissures between the disparate groups became increasingly pronounced.

As Lyndon Johnson was winning election as president in 1964, Democrats captured more seats in the House (295) and Senate (68) than they would in any Congress since. As a consequence of their greater than two-to-one majority in both chambers, the Democrats were representing a broadly diverse set of constituencies. In fact, Johnson's Republican opponent Barry Goldwater received a higher percentage of the two-party vote in states represented by Democrats in the Senate than in states represented by Republicans. Furthermore, Goldwater did less than one percentage point better in Republican representatives' districts than he did nationwide and approximately four percentage points worse in Democratic representatives' districts.

The 1966 House elections provided even more puzzling results for the partisanship of the constituencies than the 1964 elections. The Democrats lost forty-seven seats, but those losses primarily came in the North where Goldwater was trounced; the party remained dominant in the South where Goldwater had performed better. The partisan difference between the Democratic and Republican representatives' districts became even smaller.

To systematically measure the underlying partisanship of members' districts and senators' states, we calculate the Republican presidential vote advantage (RPVA). This statistic, which is sometimes called the normalized vote, measures the difference between the Republican presidential candidate's two-party vote in the district and the candidate's nationwide percentage. For example, 2008 Republican presidential candidate John McCain received 67 percent of the vote in Wyoming but only 47 percent of the vote nationwide, making Wyoming's RPVA 20 percent.

Figure 11.1 shows the underlying partisan tilt of the districts represented by Democrats and Republicans in the House of Representatives since the 89th Congress (1965–66). In the 1960s, Democrats represented districts where, on average, the Republican presidential candidate performed about five percentage points worse than they performed nationwide. Republicans, on the other hand, represented districts where they did about five points better. Within thirty years, both numbers doubled.

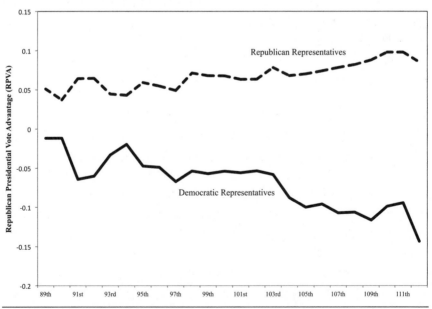

FIGURE 11.1 **Partisanship of Congressional District by Party, 89th–112th Congresses (1965–2012)**

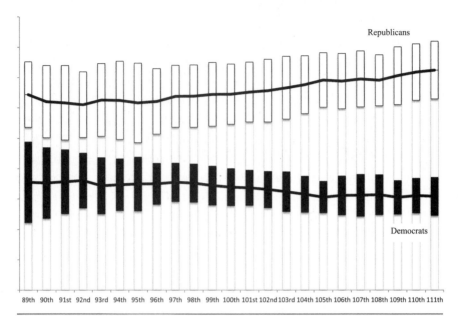

FIGURE 11.2 **Partisanship of State by Party, 89th–112th Congresses
(1965–2012)**

The Senate's data is presented in Figure 11.2. In the two congresses after the Senate passed the Civil Rights Act of 1964, Democratic senators came from more Republican states than did Republican senators. Only since President Bill Clinton's election have the differences between the senators' constituencies varied in a meaningful way.

Over time, the constituencies represented by Republicans and Democrats have become increasingly distinct. In the 112th Congress (2011–12), House Republicans represent districts that are 23 percent more Republican than the districts represented by Democrats. The difference in the Senate is about half as much. Figure 11.3 shows how the partisan differences between the constituencies have changed over time for both the House and Senate.

Political scientists have pointed to a number of reasons why the constituencies represented by Democrats and Republicans are increasingly distinct, including the design and implementation of partisan redistricting plans (Hirsch 2003; Carson, Crespin, Finocchiaro, and Rohde 2007), the geographic sorting of constituents into like-minded neighborhoods (Oppenheimer 2005; Bishop 2008), the ideological sorting that has occurred within parties (Fiorina 2005), and the extremism of party activists (Fiorina 2005; Brady, Han, and Pope

FIGURE 11.3 The Partisan Difference Between Democratic and Republican
Constituencies, 89th–112th Congresses (1965–2012)

2007). The disputes between the proponents of these arguments, while illuminating, are immaterial for our purposes in this article—all of these studies agree that the districts are becoming increasingly distinct.

The growing gap between the two major party constituencies not only tell an electoral story but also can provide clues to an institutional story. If the constituencies that Democrats represent are increasingly distinct from the constituencies that Republicans represent, the members' decisions to side with their constituents or their parties are increasingly rare. If members' partisan identification and constituencies' partisan tilt point in the same direction, so, too, do their primary voting considerations, thus decreasing the number of difficult votes they face and lessening the tension between the majority party goals (Rohde 1991; Aldrich 1995; Aldrich and Rohde 2001).

Intense Party Competition

As the Democratic and Republican constituencies become increasingly distinct, the margins between the number of Democratic and Republican representatives has become smaller. In the 1964 election, the Democrats had 130 more seats in the House and 30 more seats in the Senate than did the Republicans.

While these margins are particularly large, they are similar to the margins that the Democrats enjoyed as late as the 1970s.

But for two Congresses—the 80th (1947–48) and 83rd (1953–54)—the Democrats were a majority in the House and Senate from 1933 until 1980. With the Democrats safely in the majority representing an ideologically diverse set of constituencies, Republicans understood that the way they could most influence policy making in Congress was to constructively engage the majority. Because Democrats had so many conservative members and because the Republicans had so many moderate-to-liberal members, Republicans frequently found ideological counterparts in the majority party to help work their will. So long as the Republicans did not mind not being chairs of the committees, policy making in Congress did not regularly decay into partisan warfare.

Republicans achieved majority party status at different times in the different chambers. Heading into the 1980 election, most pundits thought the presidential election between the incumbent, Jimmy Carter, and his Republican challenger, Ronald Reagan, would be exceedingly close. No one thought that the Republicans had a prayer of becoming a majority party in either the House or the Senate. From the 89th to the 96th Congresses (1965–1980), the Democrats, on average, held a twenty-seat margin over the Republicans in the Senate. When Americans awoke on the day after the 1980 election, Reagan's landslide not only delivered him forty-four states in the electoral college but delivered twelve Senate seats to his party, enough to give Republicans a six-seat majority (see Figure 11.4 for the margin size of the majority party in the Senate).

Prior to 1994, the Democrats' lock on the House had been as great as it was on the Senate before the 1980 election. From the 89th to the 103rd Congress (1965–1994), the Democrats held an average of 263 House seats—an average margin of ninety-one seats. Only a handful of people in the United States thought that the Republicans could win a House majority in 1994 and most of them worked for House Minority Whip Newt Gingrich (R-Ga.). Gingrich's national strategy—embodied by the Contract with America—paid off as the Democrats went from a majority of eighty-two seats to a minority of twenty-six seats in what became known as the Republican Tsunami of 1994. Figure 11.5 shows the majority party size in the House of Representatives from 1965 to 2012.

Since the Republicans became competitive in each chamber, the majority size for either party has been almost two-thirds smaller in both chambers. In

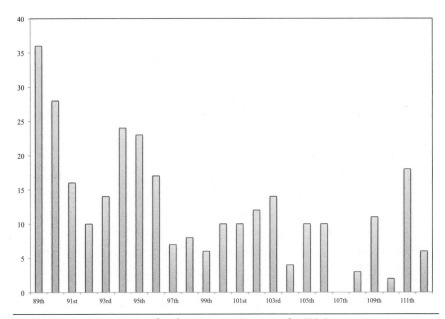

FIGURE 11.4 Margin Size for the Majority Party in the US Senate,
89th–112th Congresses (1965–2012)

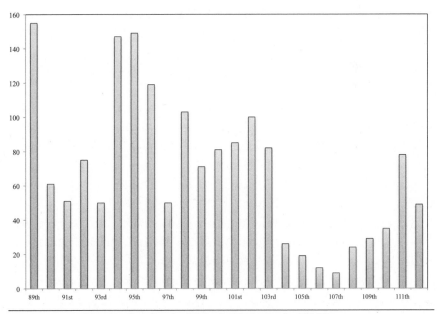

FIGURE 11.5 Margin Size for the Majority Party in the US House,
89th–112th Congresses (1965–2012)

the sixteen congresses since the Republicans became a majority in the Senate (1981–2012), the majority has held, on average, fewer than fifty-four seats. In the nine congresses since the Republicans became a majority in the House (1995–2012), the majority has held an average of 233 seats, a thirty-one-seat majority. With perhaps only the 2008 election as an exception, the future majority party in both chambers of Congress was never in doubt on the day of the election.

While the American electoral landscape may be shrinking over time (Shaw 2006), the stakes have drastically risen for the districts and states that remain in play on election day. This phenomenon not only has consequences for electoral politics, but also for how Congress operates internally. The race for majority party status has frequently eclipsed the desire for Congress to solve real problems. The legislative process and the chamber floors have increasingly become arenas for electoral politics. Congress's declining approval numbers are only one consequence of this transformation in the legislative process.

Wave Elections

Electoral competitiveness breaks down into two periods—though with a different date of demarcation—in both the House and Senate. The three most recent election cycles have been distinct. The 2006, 2008, and 2010 elections are all considered "wave" elections, in which the wind has been at the back of one of the parties—two Democratic waves (2006 and 2008) followed by a Republican wave (2010).

These three elections present a stark contrast to the other elections since 1994. In the 1996–2004 elections, one party or another gained fewer than three seats on average in the Senate and fewer than four seats in the House. In the last three elections, first the Democrats (in 2006 and 2008) and then the Republicans (in 2010) gained, on average, more than six seats in the Senate and thirty-nine seats in the House.

Wave elections are not rare in American politics. Since 1964, nine elections have resulted in a swing of greater than twenty seats in the House and a different set of nine elections resulted in a seat swing of at least five in the Senate. The 2006, 2008, and 2010 elections are unique by their inclusion in both sets of elections and that they are the only elections that happened back-to-back-to-back.

Wave elections are not only interesting electorally but also for the effect that they have on the internal dynamics of Congress. More so than other types of elections, waves are typically harder on moderates. Status quo elections may see a moderate Republican beat a moderate Democrat or vice versa, but wave elections see more than a few conservative Republicans beating moderate Democrats or liberal Democrats defeating moderate Republicans. Successive wave elections have decimated moderates in Congress.

The Effects on Congress

The interplay of members' goals and the conditions under which they operate have fundamentally changed how Congress functions as an institution. In this final section, we describe how polarized the political parties are inside the House and Senate. As members are becoming more ideological, they are also ceding more power to their leaders who are exercising it in a number of different ways (Rohde 1991; Aldrich 1995; Aldrich and Rohde 2001).

Polarized Parties

The 2008 elections brought about the most polarized Congress since at least the early 1900s, and there is nothing in the first year of the 112th Congress (2011–12) that suggests it will be any less so. We analyze DW-NOMINATE data in this section to show how polarized the parties have become. These data, which are generated from all nonconsensual roll-call votes in both the House and the Senate, range from -1 (extreme liberal) to +1 (extreme conservative).[1]

The congresses after the 1964 election and into the 1970s were some of the least polarized in modern history. The mean House Democratic DW-NOMINATE during these congresses, which is depicted as the black line running through the black bars of Figure 11.6, was about 0.5 away from the mean Republican DW-NOMINATE, which is depicted as the black line running through the white bars. The black (white) bars show one standard deviation on either side of the mean for the Democrats (Republicans). Beginning in the mid-1970s, the parties' means started to separate. The partisan divergence was only slightly less pronounced in the Senate (see Figure 11.7).

By the 111th Congress (2009–10), the divergence between the parties had almost doubled in the House to 0.97 and increased by more than 50 percent to 0.82 in the Senate. Not only have the means separated, but the parties have become much more internally cohesive. The infusion of Tea Party members in the 112th Congress and the Blue Dog Democrat losses in 2010 will likely only exacerbate the divide between the parties. The Blue Dog Coalition, which

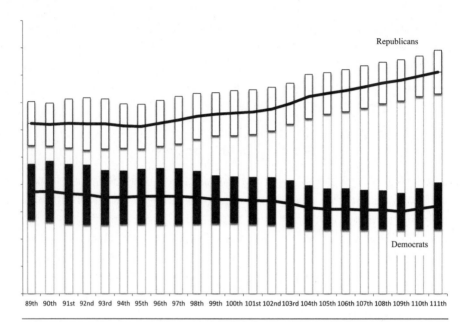

Republicans

Democrats

89th 90th 91st 92nd 93rd 94th 95th 96th 97th 98th 99th 100th 101st 102nd 103rd 104th 105th 106th 107th 108th 109th 110th 111th

FIGURE 11.6 Ideology by Party in the US House, 89th–112th Congresses
(1965–2012)

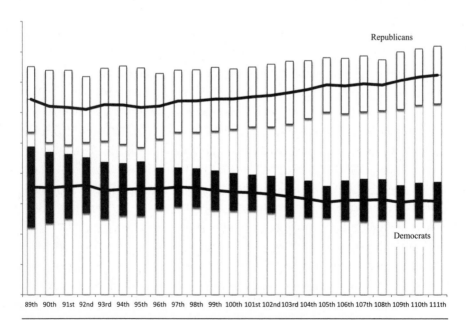

Republicans

Democrats

89th 90th 91st 92nd 93rd 94th 95th 96th 97th 98th 99th 100th 101st 102nd 103rd 104th 105th 106th 107th 108th 109th 110th 111th

FIGURE 11.7 Ideology by Party in the US Senate, 89th–112th Congresses
(1965–2012)

was formed during the 104th Congress to increase the visibility of moderate and conservative Democrats, represented 21 percent of the House Democratic Caucus during the 111th Congress, but just 13 percent of House Democrats following the 2010 elections.

Powerful Leadership

Congressional party leaders have several ways to manage their twin goals of addressing policy problems and maintaining or achieving majority party status. Over time leaders have gained more authority in assigning members to committees. In the House, this includes the powerful Rules Committee, which sets the terms of floor debate. Senate leaders also have become more involved in managing filibusters and the cloture process, allowing them to manage the floor schedule and exert greater control over who speaks and who may offer amendments to pending legislation.

Committee Assignments

A traditional view of parties in Congress is that they tend to be more important in structuring floor debate than they are within committees (Ripley 1967). Because the majority party leaders in Congress have an interest in showing that the institution is dealing with salient public problems, they are increasingly involved in committee deliberations. Congressional committees are critical in the flow of information in legislatures (Porter 1974; Sabatier and Whiteman 1985). They are where public problems are defined, policy alternatives are first debated, and hearings are held to explore new issues (Sheingate 2006). The congressional committee system allows for multiple points of access for interest groups and experts (Baumgartner and Jones 1993), and allows Congress to engage in parallel processing, whereby multiple issues are dealt with at the same time (Workman, Jones, and Jochim 2009). Furthermore, committees are responsible for "reporting" bills to their parent chambers. If the committee process breaks down or runs counter to the wishes of the party leaders, neither party goal in Congress can be achieved.

One way in which committee agendas can shift and respond to new issues is through changes in membership (Adler 2002). Party leaders have a great deal of authority over the committee assignment process, which has been called a "giant jigsaw puzzle" (Goodwin 1970; Shepsle 1978). Leaders can use committee assignments to reward certain members, bargain with others, and strengthen their positions within the party (Masters 1961), though leaders use this power selectively (Ripley 1967). Former Speaker Nancy Pelosi (D-Calif.) called the 110th Congress's freshman class her "Majority Makers," giving them prime committee assignments and legislative responsibilities to the frustration of some more senior Democrats (Leahy 2007).

Party leaders also may use their authority to bypass the seniority system and appoint (or have elected) committee chairs more closely aligned with their goals. Figure 11.8 lists the number of committee chair "seniority violations" from the 104th to the 110th Congresses.

After gaining control of the House in the 104th Congress, the Republican Conference adopted a party rule that seniority would no longer be the sole criterion for naming committee chairs. They also adopted term limits, preventing any member from serving more than three consecutive congresses as chair of a particular standing committee. While seniority is still the primary factor in determining committee chairs, fund-raising and party loyalty are now also taken into account.

The Republicans' changes were not necessarily new; Democratic majorities have committed seniority violations to ensure that committee chairs worked

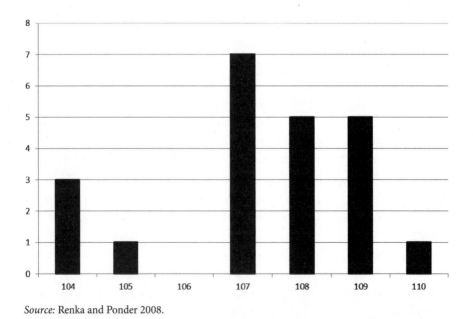

Source: Renka and Ponder 2008.

FIGURE 11.8 **Number of Committee Chair Seniority Violations, 104th–110th Congresses**

to advance collective party interests. Rep. Les Aspin (D-Wis.) successfully challenged House Armed Services Committee Chairman Melvin Price (D-Ill.) in
the 99th Congress, gaining control of that committee on promises that he
would more vigorously oppose President Ronald Reagan's defense initiatives
(Smith and Deering 1984). More recently, the Democratic Caucus voted in
2008 to replace House Energy and Commerce Committee Chairman John
Dingell (D-Mich.) with Pelosi ally Henry Waxman (D-Calif.). Dingell had been
the senior Democrat on that committee for three decades, but Waxman was
seen as more willing to work with Democratic President-elect Barack Obama
on energy legislation (Kane 2008). Still, after the Republican revisions to the
committee system, party unity and donations to the party's congressional campaign funds became the most significant determinants of gaining the nomination to chair a committee (Deering and Wahlbeck 2006; Cann 2008). Parties
and party leaders can advance their collective interests through the placement
of committee chairs, not just the assignment of rank-and-file members to particular committees.

The Power of Party Leaders During Floor Debates
The House Rules Committee has long been considered a position from which
members can increase their levels of prestige within the institution (Fenno
1973). The Rules Committee is responsible for setting the terms of debate in
the House, including the length of time a bill will be on the floor, the number
of amendments allowed, and which members will be permitted to offer those
amendments. Over time, the Rules Committee has become an arm of the
Speaker, as a way to fulfill multiple goals and manage the tension between
solving problems and serving the needs of party members. Limiting the number of floor amendments allowed on a particular piece of legislation reduces
uncertainty for the majority party about what alternatives might be proposed,
shapes the chamber's policy decisions, and reduces the probability of defeat
(Bach and Smith 1988).

In response, the minority party has become more creative in responding
to the increasing restrictions on their ability to alter legislation on the floor.
Even under closed rules (where no floor amendments are allowed), the minority party is traditionally allowed to offer a "motion to recommit" a bill back to
committee with the understanding that the committee would then make specific changes to the bill. The motion to recommit has become a vehicle for the
minority party to force cross-pressured majority party members into tough

votes. During a March 2007 debate over a bill to grant the District of Columbia greater representation in Congress, the Republican minority offered a motion to recommit that would have added a provision allowing DC residents to own handguns, in opposition to city ordinances. Many conservative Democrats were inclined to vote in favor of the motion, and Democratic party leaders pulled the bill from the floor rather than force their members to vote against the National Rifle Association's position.

Power in the Senate is more decentralized, and Senate party leaders are traditionally thought to have less control over floor outcomes than their House counterparts. The Senate majority leader, in consultation with the minority leader, has the burden of developing Unanimous Consent Agreements, which act as the Senate's counterpart to House Rules. As the Senate floor has become less manageable, UCAs have increasingly become intricate agreements between the leaders, specifying even the most minute procedures for establishing the parameters of floor debate (Gold 2008).

As the floor organizers for their parties, the leaders have also taken the primary responsibility for organizing and squashing filibusters. Although filibusters are traditionally viewed as the providence of individual senators whose intensely held preferences or constituent support for a particular position lead them to obstruct the consideration of legislation (Wawro and Schickler 2006), Senate leaders over time have taken a larger role in driving the filibuster-cloture process. Table 11.1 lists the percentage of cloture petitions filed by the Senate majority leader in each congress since 1971. Not only have these figures risen sharply over the past forty years, they likely underemphasize the majority party's role in the cloture process because many of the other cloture petitions filed are often done so by the majority whips. In the apparent aberration of the 107th Congress, for example, Democratic Whip Harry Reid filed more cloture petitions (38) than did Democratic Majority Leader Tom Daschle (23). Including Reid's activity in that congress's calculation reveals that the majority party leadership initiated 90.1 percent of the cloture petitions during the 107th Congress, in line with the historical trend.

Increased party leader involvement in the filibuster-cloture process serves several purposes. Some senators may be more likely to support the cloture petition out of party loyalty or solidarity with the leadership (Lee 2009). A leadership-driven cloture effort also elevates attention to the issue and potentially the level of support for a proposal. Leaders have an interest in cloture efforts because the majority is interested in enacting its broader legislative

TABLE 11.1 **Percentage of Cloture Petitions Filed by Senate Majority Leaders**

Congress	Majority Leader	Percentage of Petitions Filed
92	Mike Mansfield, D-Mont.	21.7
93	Mike Mansfield, D-Mont.	38.6
94	Mike Mansfield, D-Mont.	23.1
95	Robert C. Byrd, D-W.Va.	87
96	Robert C. Byrd, D-W.Va.	86.7
97	Howard H. Baker Jr., R-Tenn.	54.8
98	Howard H. Baker Jr., R-Tenn.	70.7
99	Robert Dole, R-Kan.	61
100	Robert C. Byrd, D-W.Va.	90.7
101	George J. Mitchell, D-Maine	73.7
102	George J. Mitchell, D-Maine	78.3
103	George J. Mitchell, D-Maine	67.5
104	Robert Dole, R-Kan./Trent Lott, R-Miss.	65.9
105	Trent Lott, R-Miss.	52.2
106	Trent Lott, R-Miss.	83.1
107	Trent Lott, R-Miss./Thomas A. Daschle, D-S.D.	40.8
108	William H. Frist, R-Tenn.	71
109	William H. Frist, R-Tenn.	73.5
110	Harry M. Reid, D-Nev.	88.4
111	Harry M. Reid, D-Nev.	95.6

Source: US Senate 2011.

agenda, so initiating a cloture petition allows members to have a better idea of the floor schedule and how many agenda items (and of what variety) the chamber will be able to process at one time.

Filibuster and cloture efforts also are costly to members in terms of time spent gathering supporters, managing the floor effort (either in support of or opposition to a proposal), and whipping votes on either side of the cloture petition. Because party leaders are already expected to undertake these tasks for nonfilibustered legislation and have the staff resources to do so, the costs for leaders to initiate filibuster and cloture efforts are much lower than they are for rank-and-file senators. The continuous communication that typically occurs between Senate party leaders may be used to schedule cloture votes at times convenient for members of both parties. Lowering the cost of filibusters and cloture efforts for rank-and-file senators not only increases the likelihood of support or opposition to a filibuster (Wawro and Schickler 2006; Koger 2010), it also allows other senators to use that time to develop legislation, perform constituent service, or work toward their other goals that help secure reelection. Increased involvement in the filibuster-cloture process provides yet another way for congressional parties to solve collective action problems for their members (Aldrich 1995).

Conference Committees and Negotiations Between Chambers

If the House and Senate pass different versions of the same bill, party leaders in each chamber typically appoint members to a joint conference committee to reconcile those differences and provide a single piece of legislation to be voted on (subject to chamber approval of a motion to appoint conferees). The only restriction on these appointments is that a majority of conference committee members must generally support the bill under consideration, and as such most members appointed to conference committees also sit on the original committee of referral. Committee members can thus use the deference afforded their position and influence over the conference process to shape final legislative outcomes. This power to shape the legislation at the final stage is often more important than a committee's ability to provide the initial legislative proposal considered on the floor (Shepsle and Weingast 1987). Conferees also often are advocates for their respective chamber's desired policy over their own personal preferences (Kiewiet and McCubbins 1991), and majority party leaders can use the fact that conference reports are not subject to amendment to achieve outcomes that favor the party instead of a particular committee.

Party leaders also are taking a more direct role in avoiding conference committees altogether by negotiation between the floors of each chamber. The number of public laws that were subject to conference committee negotiations dropped steadily from 13 percent in the 103rd Congress to 5 percent in the 109th Congress. Instead, one chamber will simply adopt the other's version of a bill, or a bill will be amended by each chamber in turn until a final agreement is reached. This development has decreased the committees' abilities to shape the final legislation. Engaging in this "ping-pong" strategy also allows majority party leaders to avoid filibusters in the Senate and House motions to instruct conferees, which could potentially advise or require House conferees to adopt certain negotiating positions contrary to the majority's wishes (Oleszek 2009).

Other Examples of Legislative Authority

Party leaders can play a direct role in policy debates by sponsoring high-profile legislation themselves rather than relying on committee chairs or other members to initiate. During the debate over raising the federal debt ceiling in 2011, Speaker of the House John Boehner took the lead in proposing and negotiating the terms of an agreement with the Senate despite a policy background primarily in education and labor issues (he had previously served as chair of the House Education and Workforce Committee). He did so in part because the House Republicans' budget proposal authored earlier in the year by Budget Committee chair Paul Ryan (R-Wis.) had been controversial for its spending cuts, particularly to entitlements such as Social Security and Medicare, and had been rejected by a Democratic-controlled Senate.

Boehner experienced difficulty keeping his caucus unified in voting on the debt ceiling legislation. The initial House vote was postponed because Republican leaders could not convince enough of their party's members to vote in favor of Boehner's proposal. After finally reaching the 218 votes needed for passage, the bill was again tabled by the Senate. Boehner, Senate Majority Leader Harry Reid, and President Obama finally negotiated the terms of an agreement that received bipartisan support in the House. Despite his initial struggles to keep the Republican caucus unified, Speaker Boehner's lead role allowed him greater latitude to negotiate with other political leaders and find a solution that would allow the US government to continue operating. Failure to do so likely would have severely damaged the House Republicans' reputation for effective governance.

Party leaders also can prioritize specific pieces of legislation that address salient issues. Beginning with the 106th Congress (1999–2000), the Speaker of the House has had the authority to assign specific legislation to the bill numbers HR 1–10, and this was later expanded to allow the minority leader to designate legislation to HR 11–20. A similar authority exists in the Senate, though in keeping with that chamber's character the practice is more informally determined and the number of bills subject to such designation may change from congress to congress. In the 110th Congress, Speaker Pelosi used this authority to mirror her party's "Six for '06" electoral platform and prioritized legislation on the 9/11 Commission's recommendations, raising the minimum wage, stem cell research, and energy policy. When Republicans obtained the majority in the 112th Congress, Speaker Boehner designated legislation that would repeal the major health-care law previously enacted by Democrats, prohibit federal funding for abortion, and limit health-care product-liability lawsuits. Leaders typically do not reserve these important pieces of legislation for themselves. Rather, they aim to highlight committee

TABLE 11.2 Bills Reserved for the Speaker, 106th–112th Congresses

Congress	Bills Reserved	Party Leader Sponsor	Committee Chair Sponsor	Rank and File Sponsor
106th	10	1	3	6
107th	8	1	3	4
108th	8	4	2	2
109th	6	1	3	2
110th	6	0	5	1
111th	2	0	1	1
112th	6	1	1	4
Total	46	8	18	20

Source: Library of Congress 2011.

leaders or other members to take the lead in these efforts (see Table 11.2 for the sponsors of these reserved numbers from the 106th to the 111th Congresses). Such an exercise of discretion only increases the leaders' power.

Party leaders in Congress have recently found other avenues for influencing the policy process. In order to further highlight her party's position on energy policy, Speaker Pelosi created a Select Committee on Energy Independence and Global Warming in 2007. House Energy and Commerce chair John Dingell objected to what he saw as an intrusion on his committee's jurisdiction, so the select committee was not given any legislative authority; its role was purely advisory. Still, this move allowed Pelosi and the Democratic Caucus to expand the scope of information it received on energy and environment issues, and the House Resolution creating the select committee also called for the standing committees (including Energy and Commerce) to produce energy legislation by a certain date. Because the select committee was authorized in legislation separate from the House Rules that are adopted at the beginning of each congress, Speaker Pelosi was given the authority to name all of the committee's members, giving her further power to decide who participated in House deliberation and decision making on those issues.

A similar authority arose in the 112th Congress. Legislation enacted in 2011 to raise the federal debt ceiling created a Joint Select Committee on Deficit Reduction that was charged with making formal recommendations on how to reduce the federal deficit by $1.5 trillion over the ensuing ten years. The committee was comprised of three members from each party in each chamber who were directly appointed by each chamber's party leaders. As seen in Table 11.3, the leaders managed to strike a balance between serving the needs of their respective parties and solving the problem of deficit reduction by selecting a mixture of members with leadership ties and committee chairs and members with experience processing finance and budget issues.

TABLE 11.3 Balance Between Party and Expertise on the
Joint Select Deficit Reduction Committee

Member	*Relevant Position, 112th Congress*
House	
Republicans	
Co-chair Jeb Hensarling, R-Texas	House Republican Conference Chairman
Dave Camp, R-Mich.	House Ways and Means Committee Chairman Joint Taxation Committee Chairman
Fred Upton, R-Mich.	House Energy and Commerce Committee Chairman Served in Office of Management and Budget under President Ronald Reagan
Democrats	
Rep. James Clyburn, D-S.C.	Assistant House Democratic Leader
Rep. Xavier Becerra, D-Calif.	Vice chair, House Democratic Caucus Member, House Ways and Means Committee
Rep. Chris Van Hollen, D-Md.	Ranking member, House Budget Committee Former chair, Democratic Congressional Campaign Committee
Senate	
Democrats	
Co-chair Patty Murray, D-Wash.	Senate Democratic Conference Secretary Chair, Democratic Senate Campaign Committee Member, Senate Budget Committee
Max Baucus, D-Mont.	Senate Finance Committee Chairman Joint Taxation Committee Vice Chairman
John Kerry, D-Mass.	Member, Senate Finance Committee
Republicans	
Jon Kyl, R-Ariz.	Senate Republican Whip Member, Senate Finance Committee
Rob Portman, R-Ohio	Member, Senate Budget Committee Former Office of Management and Budget director under President George W. Bush
Pat Toomey, R-Pa.	Member, Senate Budget Committee

Fund-Raising

Party leaders are assuming a larger role in raising money for congressional campaigns. As individuals they tend to be prolific fund-raisers, but because they also tend to be electorally safe, their fund-raising prowess is usually on behalf of their more vulnerable colleagues. Increasingly, leadership PACs have been used to distribute money throughout their caucus. Table 11.4 lists the amount of money raised by congressional party leaders for their leadership political action committees during the 2010 election cycle, rounded to the nearest ten thousand dollars.

Party leaders also often have institutional prerogatives that allow them to recruit and help elect new members, work to reelect incumbents, and achieve other electoral goals. The chairs of the Democratic Congressional Campaign Committee (DCCC) and Democratic Senatorial Campaign Committee (DSCC) serve as members of the party leadership and are directly appointed by the highest ranking party leader in their respective chambers. The National Republic Campaign Committee (NRCC) and the National Republican Senatorial Committee (NRSC) chairs are elected by the chamber's party membership with significant input from party leaders. These committees

TABLE 11.4 Fund-Raising by Congressional Leadership
Political Action Committees (2010)

Member	Position	Leadership PAC Receipts (in millions of dollars)
Eric Cantor, R-Va.	House Minority Whip	$4.41
John Boehner, R-Ohio	House Minority Leader	$3.15
Steny Hoyer, D-Md.	House Majority Leader	$2.81
James Clyburn, D-S.C.	House Majority Whip	$1.59
Jon Kyl, R-Ariz.	Senate Minority Whip	$1.22
Nancy Pelosi, D-Calif.	Speaker of the House	$1.21
Mitch McConnell, R-Ky.	Senate Minority Leader	$1.17
Harry Reid, D-Nev.	Senate Majority Leader	$1.0
Pete Sessions, R-Texas	NRCC Chair	$0.99
John Cornyn, R-Texas	NRSC Chair	$0.97
Chris Van Hollen, D-Md.	DCCC Chair/Asst to the Speaker	$0.92
Bob Menendez, D-N.J.	DSCC Chair	$0.88
Dick Durbin, D-Ill.	Senate Majority Whip	$0.56

Source: Center for Responsive Politics 2011a.

raise a substantial amount of money, which can then be targeted to close and important races, determinations of which also are made by party leaders (see Table 11.5 for the amount of money these campaign committees have spent in each election cycle since 2000).

Heading these committees also can serve as a stepping stone for those who hope to ascend to more powerful positions within their caucus. Both Mitch McConnell (R-Ky.) and Bill Frist (R-Tenn.) served as SRCC chair before being elected to the party's chamber leadership (majority whip and majority leader, respectively), and Senate Democrats created a special leadership position for Chuck Schumer (D-N.Y.) once his term as DSCC chair expired (Raju 2010).

TABLE 11.5 **Party Campaign Committee Spending Since 2000 (in millions of dollars)**

Election Cycle	DCCC	NRCC	DSCC	NRSC
2000	$107	$148	$105	$95
2002	$104	$204	$147	$127
2004	$93	$186	$88	$79
2006	$141	$178	$122	$90
2008	$177	$118	$163	$94
2010	$164	$132	$129	$68

Source: Center for Responsive Politics 2011b.

Conclusion

In the 1950s, the American Political Science Association (1950), in entering the real world of politics, bemoaned the lack of internal coherence and consistency within the congressional political parties. The voters, the report argued, did not have clear choices when they cast their ballots and, as a consequence, could not hold their members or the institution of Congress accountable for the decisions that they made. Stronger parties would clarify the elections and make democracy function more smoothly in the United States.

What the report asked for became reality (Sinclair 2002). The role of parties inside Congress has grown tremendously since the 1950s and nothing in the current Congress or in the conditions outside Congress suggests that that trend will change in the short term. As the districts and states represented by the respective parties have become more homogenous and as the wave elections have drowned a disproportionate number of moderates, party leaders have grown ever more powerful, which helps them simultaneously pursue the party goals of addressing public problems and achieving majority status. The close margins that currently divide majority parties from minority parties only exacerbate this cycle. The end result is party polarization and a transformation of the legislative arena into an electoral battlefield.

   The American public now has coherent parties and they have rendered their verdict—an abysmal approval rating for Congress. How Congress sorts itself out as it tries to resurrect its sagging numbers remains unclear. What is clear is that the party leadership will play an instrumental role in either raising the public's affection for Congress or driving the final nails in the coffin of an institution in disrepute.

References

Adler, E. Scott. 2002. "New Issues, New Members: Committee Composition and the Transformation of Issue Agendas on the House Banking and Public Works Committees." In *Policy Dynamics*, edited by Frank R. Baumgartner and Bryan D. Jones. Chicago: University of Chicago Press.

Aldrich, John H. 1995. *Why Parties? The Origin and Transformation of Political Parties in America*. Chicago, IL: University of Chicago Press.

Aldrich, John H., and David W. Rohde. 2001. "The Logic of Conditional Party Government: Revisiting the Electoral Connection." In *Congress Reconsidered*, edited by Lawrence C. Dodd and Bruce I. Oppenheimer. 7th ed. Washington, DC: CQ Press.

American Political Science Association. 1950. "The Need for Greater Party Responsibility." *American Political Science Review* 44: 15–36.

Bach, Stanley, and Steven S. Smith. 1988. *Managing Uncertainty in the House of Representatives*. Washington, DC: Brookings Institution Press.

Baumgartner, Frank R., and Bryan D. Jones. 1993. *Agendas and Instability in American Politics*. Chicago, IL: University of Chicago Press.

Binder, Sarah A. 1996. "The Partisan Basis of Procedural Choice: Allocating Parliamentary Rights in the House, 1789–1990." *American Political Science Review* 90: 498–508.

Bishop, Bill. 2008. *The Big Sort: Why the Clustering of Like-Minded America Is Tearing Us Apart*. New York: Mariner Books.

Born, Richard. 1990. "The Shared Fortunes of Congress and Congressmen: Members May Run from Congress, but They Can't Hide." *The Journal of Politics* 52: 1223–1241.

Brady, David W., Hahrie Han, and Jeremy C. Pope. 2007. "*Primary Elections and Candidate Ideology: Out of Step with the Primary Electorate?*" *Legislative Studies Quarterly* 32, 1: 79–106.

Cann, Damon M. 2008. "Modeling Committee Chair Selection in the U.S. House of Representatives." *Political Analysis* 16: 274–89.

Carson, Jamie, Michael H. Crespin, Charles J. Finocchiaro, and David W. Rohde. 2007. "Redistricting and Party Polarization in the U.S. House of Representatives." *American Politics Research* 35, 6: 878–904.

Center for Responsive Politics. 2011a. "Leadership PACs." http://www.opensecrets.org/pacs /industry.php?txt=Q03&cycle=2010.

_____. 2011b. "Political Parties Overview." http://www.opensecrets.org/parties/index.php.

Cox, Gary W., and Mathew D. McCubbins. 1993. *Legislative Leviathan: Party Government in the House.* Berkeley, CA: University of California Press.

Cox, James H. 2004. *Reviewing Delegation: An Analysis of the Congressional Reauthorization Process.* Santa Barbara, CA: Praeger Publishing.

Davidson, Roger H., and Glenn R. Parker. 1972. "Positive Support for Political Institutions: The Case of Congress." *The Western Political Quarterly* 25: 600–612.

Deering, Christopher J., and Paul J. Wahlbeck. 2006. "Determinants of House Committee Chair Selection." *American Politic Research* 34: 1–20.

Dodd, Lawrence C., and Richard L. Schott. 1979. *Congress and the Administrative State.* New York: Wiley.

Durr, Robert H., John B. Gilmour, and Christina Wolbrecht. 1997. "Explaining Congressional Approval." *American Journal of Political Science* 41: 175–207.

Erickson, Robert S., and Gerald C. Wright. 2005. "Voters, Candidates and Issues in Congressional Elections." In *Congress Reconsidered,* edited by Lawrence C. Dodd and Bruce I. Oppenheimer. 8th ed. Washington, DC: CQ Press.

Fenno, Richard. 1973. *Congressmen in Committees.* Boston, MA: Little, Brown and Company.

Fiorina, Morris P. 2005. *Culture War? The Myth of a Polarized America.* New York: Pearson Longman.

Gold, Martin B. 2008. *Senate Procedure and Practice.* 2nd ed. Lanham, MD: Rowman and Littlefield.

Goodwin, George, Jr. 1970. *The Little Legislatures.* Amherst, MA: University of Massachusetts Press.

Hall, Thad E. 2004. *Authorizing Policy.* Columbus, OH: Ohio State University Press.

Hibbing, John R., and John R. Alford. 1981. "The Electoral Impact of Economic Conditions: Who Is Held Responsible?" *American Journal of Political Science* 25: 423–39.

Hirsch, Sam. 2003. "The United States of Unrepresentatives: What Went Wrong in the Latest Round of Congressional Redistricting." *Election Law Journal* 2 (Nov.): 179–216.

Jones, David R., and Monika L. McDermott. 2009. *Americans, Congress and Democratic Responsiveness.* Ann Arbor, MI: University of Michigan Press.

Kane, Paul. 2008. "Detroit Automakers Lose Staunch Ally as Waxman Ousts Dingell on Key Committee." *Washington Post.* November 21.

Kiewiet, D. Roderick, and Mathew D. McCubbins. 1991. *The Logic of Delegation.* Chicago, IL: University of Chicago Press.

Koger, Gregory. 2010. *Filibustering: A Political History of Obstruction in the House and Senate.* Chicago, IL: University of Chicago Press.

Leahy, Michael. 2007. "House Rules." *Washington Post Magazine.* June 10.

Lee, Frances E. 2009. *Beyond Ideology: Politics, Principals and Partisanship in the U.S. Senate.* Chicago, IL: University of Chicago Press.

Library of Congress. 2011. 106th–112th Congresses. THOMAS database. http://thomas.loc .gov/home/LegislativeData.php.

Lipset, Seymour Martin, and William Schneider. 1983. *The Confidence Gap: Business, Labor and Government in the Public Mind.* New York: The Free Press.

Masters, Nicholas A. 1961. "Committee Assignments in the House of Representatives." *American Political Science Review* 55: 345–357.

Mayhew, David. 1974. *Congress: The Electoral Connection*. New Haven, CT: Yale University Press.

McCarty, Nolan, Keith T. Poole, and Howard Rosenthal. 2006. *Polarized America: The Dance of Ideology and Unequal Riches*. Cambridge, MA: MIT Press.

Oleszek, Walter J. 2009. *Congressional Procedures and the Policy Process*. Washington, DC: CQ Press.

Oppenheimer, Bruce I. 2005. "Deep Red and Blue Congressional Districts." In *Congress Reconsidered*, edited by Lawrence C. Dodd and Bruce I. Oppenheimer. 8th ed. Washington, DC: CQ Press.

Parker, Glenn R., and Roger H. Davidson. 1979. "Why Do Americans Love Their Congressmen So Much More Than Their Congress?" *Legislative Studies Quarterly* 4: 53–61.

Patterson, Kelly D., and David B. Magleby. 1992. "The Polls–Poll Trends: Public Support for Congress." *Public Opinion Quarterly* 56: 539–551.

Patterson, Samuel C., and Gregory A. Caldeira. 1990. "Standing Up for Congress: Variations in Public Esteem Since the 1960s." *Legislative Studies Quarterly* 15: 25–47.

Porter, H. Owen. 1974. "Legislative Experts and Outsiders: the Two-Step Flow of Communication." *The Journal of Politics* 36: 703–730.

Raju, Manu. 2010. "Harry Reid Creates Special Leadership Job for Chuck Schumer." *Politico.com*. November 15.

Renka, Russell D., and Daniel E. Ponder. 2008. "Committee Seniority Violations in the House–104th Through 110th Congresses, 1995–2008." Paper presented at the annual meeting of the Western Political Science Association, March 20–23.

Ripley, Randall B. 1967. *Party Leaders in the House of Representatives*. Washington, DC: Brookings Institution Press.

Rohde, David W. 1991. *Parties and Leaders in the Postreform House*. Chicago, IL: The University of Chicago Press.

Rohde, David, and John Aldrich. 2010. "Consequences of Electoral and Institutional Change: The Evolution of Conditional Party Government in the U.S. House of Representatives." In *New Directions in American Political Parties*, edited by Jeffrey M. Stonecash, 234–250. New York: Routledge.

Sabatier, Paul, and David Whiteman. 1985. "Legislative Decision Making and Substantive Policy Information: Models of Information Flow." *Legislative Studies Quarterly* 10: 395–421.

Shaw, Daron R. 2006. *The Race to 270: The Electoral College and the Campaign Strategies of 2000 and 2004*. Chicago, IL: University of Chicago Press.

Sheingate, Adam D. 2006. "Structure and Opportunity: Committee Jurisdiction and Issue Attention in Congress." *American Journal of Political Science* 50: 855–859.

Shepsle, Kenneth A. 1989. "The Changing Textbook Congress." In *Can the Government Govern?* edited by John E. Chubb and Paul E. Peterson. Washington, DC: The Brookings Institution.

Shepsle, Kenneth A. 1978. *The Giant Jigsaw Puzzle: Democratic Committee Assignments in the Modern House*. Chicago, IL: University of Chicago Press.

Shepsle, Kenneth A., and Barry R. Weingast. 1987. "The Institutional Foundations of Committee Power." *American Political Science Review* 81: 85–104.

Sinclair, Barbara. 1983. *Majority Leadership in the U.S. House*. Baltimore, MD: Johns Hopkins University Press.

_____. 2002. "The Dream Fulfilled? Party Development in Congress, 1950–2000." In *Responsible Partisanship? The Evolution of American Political Parties Since 1950*, edited by John C. Green and Paul S. Herrnson, 181–200. Lawrence, KA: University Press of Kansas.

_____. 2006. *Party Wars: Polarization and the Politics of National Policy Making*. Norman, OK: University of Oklahoma Press.

Smith, Steven S. 1989. *Call to Order: Floor Politics in the House and Senate*. Washington, DC: Brookings Institution Press.

Smith, Steven S., and Christopher J. Deering. 1984. *Committees in Congress*. Washington, DC: CQ Press.

Stimson, James A. 2004. *Tides of Consent: How Public Opinion Shapes American Politics*. New York: Cambridge University Press.

Theriault, Sean M. 2008. *Party Polarization in Congress*. New York: Cambridge University Press.

US Senate. 2011. "Senate Action on Cloture Motions." http://www.senate.gov/pagelayout /reference/cloture_motions/clotureCounts.htm.

Wawro, Gregory J., and Eric Schickler. 2006. *Filibuster: Obstruction and Lawmaking in the U.S. Senate*. Princeton: Princeton University Press.

Weissberg, Robert. 1976. *Public Opinion and Popular Government*. Englewood Cliffs, NJ: Prentice Hall.

Workman, Samuel, Bryan D. Jones, and Ashley E. Jochim. 2009. "Information Processing and Policy Dynamics." *Policy Studies Journal* 37: 75–92

Endnote

1. Poole and Rosenthal (1997) generate these data so that they are comparable across congresses within party systems. More care should be used in comparing these scores across chambers.

12

Partisan Presidential Leadership
The President's Appointees

G. CALVIN MACKENZIE
Colby College

Introduction

Politics is about control. Who controls the policy-making process and to what end? In a democracy, the legitimate exercise of political power falls to those who win free elections. One of the benefits of victory is the authority to control appointments to those executive offices that are not filled by election but which contribute substantially to the determination of public policy.

Throughout much of American history, political parties have served as wholesalers in this democratic process. In choosing a president, the American people also choose a political party to run the executive branch. From 1800, when Thomas Jefferson's election signaled a transfer of power from the Federalists to the Democratic Republicans, until 2008, when Barack Obama's election ended eight years of Republican control, parties have been a primary conduit for the translation of electoral victories into public policies. As the election of Jefferson portended the appointment of Democratic Republicans and their policy preferences, so the election of Barack Obama heralded the appointment of Democrats and their policy preferences.

To the casual observer, not much has changed. The tides that sweep into government after each election are party tides, carrying in the new president's copartisans, carrying out the copartisans of the old. But that surface appearance masks a set of important changes in the role that political parties now play in the staffing of presidential administrations and in appointments to the federal judiciary. While party is still the glue that seems to hold administrations together, its consistency is much thinner than ever before and its holding power is greatly reduced. What endures is the party label; what has changed is the meaning of the label and the influence of the party organizations in presidential personnel decisions. Elections are still about control but, now more than ever, they are about policy control not party control.

This chapter will examine the changes that have occurred in party impacts on federal executive staffing in the past century.[1] It begins with a look at the pre–New Deal experience. The New Deal and postwar evolution are then explored. That is followed by an effort to illuminate the reasons for the change in party role and influence, and to explain the impact of that change on the governing process.

Parties in Government: Staffing the Executive Branch

The Birth of Parties

The Constitution, and the debates from which it sprang, anticipated no role for political parties in staffing the government. In fact, of course, the framers of the Constitution did not very seriously contemplate the emergence of political parties, nor did they envision a government of such size that positions could not be filled by the president's personal acquaintances. There was little need for them to worry about the details of the appointment process for they had not worried very much about the details of the executive or judicial branches.

The framers seemed to believe that a single person—the president—would make wiser personnel choices than any collective body sharing the appointment power. And, while they established the Senate's right of advice and consent as a check against defective appointments, they thought they had created a process that the president would dominate. As Alexander Hamilton pointed out in the 76th *Federalist*, that was their clear intent.

One man of discernment is better fitted to analise and estimate the peculiar qualities adapted to particular offices, than a body of men of equal, or perhaps even of superior discernment.

The sole and undivided responsibility of one man will naturally beget a livelier sense of duty and a more exact regard to reputation. He will on this account feel himself under stronger obligations, and more interested to investigate with care the qualities requisite to the stations to be filled, and to prefer with impartiality the persons who may have the fairest pretensions to them. . . . In every exercise of the power of appointing to offices by an assembly of men, we must expect to see a full display of all the private party likings and dislikes, partialities and antipathies, attachments and animosities, which are felt by those who compose the assembly. The choice which may at any time happen to be made under such circumstances will of course be the result either of a victory gained by one party over the other, or of a compromise between the parties. . . . In the first, the qualifications best adapted to uniting the suffrages of the party will be more considered than those which fit the person for the station. In the last the coalition will commonly turn upon some interested equivalent—"Give us the man we wish for this office, and you shall have the one you wish for that." This will be the usual condition of the bargain. And it will rarely happen that the advancement of the public service will be the primary object either of party victories or of party negociations. (Cooke 1961, 510–511)

In filling appointive positions, George Washington relied—about as the framers had anticipated—on people of whom he had personal knowledge. Thomas Jefferson, Henry Knox, Edmund Randolph, and Alexander Hamilton filled the cabinet slots; Thomas Pinckney was appointed ambassador to Great Britain and Gouverneur Morris to France; John Jay became the first chief justice. Washington's circle of acquaintances was large and the number of positions he needed to fill was small.

When required to fill federal positions of primarily local importance, like customs collectors or postmasters, he found it convenient to defer to the judgment of senators from the relevant states. This practice quickly acquired the veneer of custom when the first Senate rejected Washington's appointment of Benjamin Fishbourn to be naval officer for the port of Savannah, Georgia. Fishbourn was fully qualified for the post, but the two senators from

Georgia preferred another candidate and succeeded in convincing their colleagues to reject the Fishbourn nomination (Mackenzie 1981, 93). Hence was born the concept of "senatorial courtesy" by which senators are granted significant influence over presidential appointments within their home states. (When parties later emerged, the courtesy was usually granted only to senators of the president's party.)

While most of Washington's appointees shared his views on important issues of the day, there was little sense of them and him as members of the same political party. Even as disagreements began to emerge on policy matters—the Jay treaty and the financing of state debts, for example—they produced cleavages that only slowly formed into lasting factions. Washington sought men of experience and judgment to aid him in running the government. He paid some attention to geographical balance. But any political litmus test he might have applied was informal and primitive.

That changed rather rapidly, however, after Washington's retirement and the election of John Adams. With Washington gone, politics became more bare-knuckled and political factions hardened. Adams's appointees took on a clearly defined political coloration: only Federalists need apply. On the eve of his departure from government and the transfer of power to the Jeffersonians, Adams sought to pack the government with Federalist appointments to many lower-level positions. Jefferson and his secretary of state, James Madison, tried to block these midnight appointments. The Supreme Court, in the great case of *Marbury v. Madison*, permitted them to do so. The battle was joined, and appointments would forever after be a chief prize of partisan politics.

The Spoils System

Partisan control of presidential appointments reached its zenith with the election of Andrew Jackson in 1828. His approach to appointments came to be known as the "spoils system," following the old adage that "to the victor belong the spoils." In the case of victors in presidential elections, the primary "spoils" were federal jobs.

In truth, Jackson did not invent the spoils system, nor was he the first president to put it into practice, nor were the vast majority of federal positions subjected to it. But he was so vigorous in using his appointment powers to place his own loyalists in visible government offices and so brazen about doing so that Jackson's presidency has usually been marked as a watershed in the development of federal personnel practices. It was all the more noteworthy, perhaps, because it resulted in a significant change in the kinds of people who staffed the federal government. Earlier presidents, in seeking fit candidates for office, had often turned to members of the country's wealthier families, and through the first six presidencies there was a distinct upper-class cast to the executive branch. The turn toward popular democracy that Jackson's election signified found expression in his appointees, many of whom had little wealth or education.

To political observers of the time, this suggested not only that Jackson intended to sweep out incumbent officeholders in favor of his own supporters but that political loyalty was to be the principal measure of fitness for office. Jobs in government began to be viewed as rewards for political services to the successful candidate.

Not coincidentally, this was a period of intense partisanship in American politics. Parties were becoming national political organizations and began to hold quadrennial national nominating conventions. Connections among partisans at local, state, and national levels were becoming tighter. The trickle of immigration was also just beginning and would soon turn into one of the great floods in human history. As politicians sought the support of these new groups, increasing numbers of recent immigrants were finding work in government offices or party organizations. Before long, pressure began to build to expand the number of government jobs and to make as many of them as possible available for political appointment. The state and local political machines were growing and they developed hearty appetites for government jobs (see Fish 1904; Van Riper 1958; White 1954).

One consequence of these political developments was that government jobs were becoming an increasingly valuable currency. Political leaders and members of Congress began to contest with the president for control over the appointment process. Presidents came to realize that a well-timed appointment of a political supporter of a member of Congress or a party boss could often produce votes for legislation in Congress. Trading of this sort took place in earnest.

This was also a time when United States senators were chosen by their state legislatures, not by direct election. Since most of those senators were beholden for their offices to the leaders of their party, not to the people directly, they were eager to assist in whatever way they could to acquire federal government jobs for party members in their states. This only added to the pressure to treat the appointment process as a supplement to party politics rather than a mechanism for attracting the country's most talented people into the public service. Political credentials were usually more valuable in seeking a federal job than talent or administrative experience.

Not surprisingly, the quality of the federal service during most of the nineteenth century was, at best, uneven. A great many positions were filled by appointees—sometimes called "spoilsmen"—who lacked any apparent substantive qualifications. The government survived this, in part at least, because it was not engaged in many activities that required significant technical or management skills. In fact, most of the technical specialties that now exist in government agencies were unknown in the nineteenth century: astrophysics, econometrics, environmental analysis, and so on.[2] The principal preoccupations of government in the nineteenth century were the conduct of a small number of routine functions that required little skill or experience: delivering the mail, collecting customs duties and taxes, building roads and canals. In many cases, a political hack could do these jobs about as well as anyone else. What was good for the party, therefore, was not always terrible for the government.

Nevertheless, the spoils system began to produce the seeds of its own destruction. The principal failing, of course, was that many of the people employed by the government were not the most talented nor the most qualified available. In many cases, in fact, they were totally without qualifications other than their political connections. The spoils system was also a hungry monster, a constant source of pressure for the creation of new government jobs, which provided for more political appointments and lightened the burden on officeholders so that they could devote more of their time to political activities.

The spoils system also invited corruption of all sorts because appointees were constrained by no sense of the honor of public service nor confined by any ethical notions of holding a public trust. They had their jobs because their party won an election and attained political power. And, as long as they held that power, there were few real limits on how they could exercise it. Knowing that their horizon only extended to the next election, appointees were also driven to take advantage of their offices as hastily as they could for they might soon be out of a job. If the sun was to shine only briefly, they felt compelled to make hay all the more quickly.

Another troubling aspect of the spoils system was the pressure it put on the president to devote substantial amounts of time to filling low-level positions in the federal government. Presidents in the nineteenth century had none of the elaborate White House staff structure that exists today. There was no one to whom they could delegate responsibility for handling patronage matters. Thus many hours were consumed brokering conflicting demands for appointments to individual offices. A story about President Lincoln suggests the plaguelike quality of these pressures. The White House was a public building for much of the nineteenth century and there were few restrictions on access to the main lobby. Job seekers often came there hoping for a moment or two with the president to plead their case. Lincoln found it very uncomfortable to pass through the lobby on the way to his office because that often set off a flurry of such pleading. Once when he was suffering from a bad cold, he said to his secretary as he was about to enter the lobby, "Now, at last, I have something I can give them."

The Creation of the Civil Service

Efforts to reform the personnel staffing process of the federal government appeared as early as the 1850s. They gathered steam after the Civil War. Rutherford B. Hayes was elected president in 1876, having campaigned for civil service reform. He made little headway against congressional resistance, however, during the next four years. His successor, James A. Garfield, had been a supporter of reform while serving in Congress. He was assassinated four months after his inauguration—in the legend of the time, by a "disappointed federal job-seeker"—and reformers used his slaying as evidence of the rottenness of the spoils system and the acute need for reform. Two years later, in 1883, Congress passed the Pendleton Act, which created the federal civil service system.

This was hardly the death of the spoils system. Civil service protection spread slowly among government jobs. The majority remained subject to political appointment for years yet to come. Some categories continued to be filled through political appointment until well into the twentieth century. Local postmasters, for example, remained political appointees until 1970. And even the most vigorous of the reformers recognized that some positions would always be political in character and thus could never be blanketed under the coverage of a merit-based civil service. But a significant change had begun in 1883, and it would continue to spread in the century that followed, as Table 12.1 indicates.

TABLE 12.1 Growth of the Federal Civil Service System

Year	Total Civilian Employment	Percentage Under The Merit System
1821	6,914	
1831	11,491	
1841	18,038	
1851	26,274	
1861	36,672	
1871	51,020	
1881	100,020	
1891	157,442	21.5%
1901	239,456	44.3
1911	395,905	57.5
1921	561,142	79.9
1931	609,746	76.8
1941	1,437,682	68.9
1951	2,482,666	86.4
1961	2,435,804	86.1
1971	2,862,894	84.1
1981	2,947,428	58.7
1991	3,138,180	56.4
2001	2,719,529	50.4
2007	2,715,395	48.6

Source: Stanley and Niemi 2009, 252–253.

Note: Under the Postal Reorganization Act of 1970, postal employees were moved from the merit system to "excepted service." In 2007, there were 684,762 postal employees, according to the Annual Report of the Postmaster General.

    The Pendleton Act and its subsequent refinements accomplished several things. First, it set the principle that government jobs should be open and available to all citizens and should be filled by those who successfully demonstrate that they are best qualified for the position. Second, it established the policy that examinations were the best and most objective way to determine those qualifications. Third, it provided civil servants with protections against political removal and established a pattern of continuity: civil servants would continue in office even as the presidency changed hands. And, fourth, to supervise this system and protect its neutrality from politics, the Act created a Civil Service Commission whose membership would have to reflect a degree of partisan balance.[3]

    Growing out of this success of the reform movement was a new question, one that has continued to be debated into our own time. Once the principle was established that some positions in the government should be filled on the basis of merit not politics, then arguments ensued about where the line should be drawn. Which positions should be granted civil service protection and which should continue to be treated as political appointments? The spread of civil service protection indicated in Table 12.1 suggests that a steadily growing percentage of federal offices have been placed outside of the political stream. But what of those left unprotected by the merit system? How were they to be filled? And by whom? That is the topic of the rest of this chapter.

Presidential Appointments in the Twentieth Century

1900–1932

Except that a slowly increasing number of government jobs were coming under the coverage of the civil service, the appointment process in the first third of the twentieth century varied little from what it had been in the second half of the nineteenth. The positions outside the civil service were still filled by a process in which political parties played an important role, and appointments were still viewed as a reward for political services.

This is not to suggest that all presidential appointees lacked substantive qualifications for federal service. Many of those who had been party activists had also built impressive records of public service and would have merited high-level positions even without party sponsorship. Names like Charles Evans Hughes and William Jennings Bryan would have appeared on most lists of highly qualified eligibles for cabinet or other top positions in government. And presidents also retained the latitude to select some appointees who had no significant record of party service, whose primary qualification was their talent or experience. In this category were people like Josephus Daniels, Andrew Mellon, and Henry Stimson.

But partisan pressures in the appointment process were ever present. In putting together their cabinets, for example, presidents felt constrained to select people who represented different factions or regional elements in their party (Fenno 1959, 78–88). In this sense, Woodrow Wilson's cabinet was not very different from Abraham Lincoln's. Though strong-willed and independent leaders, both felt compelled to respect partisan concerns in staffing the top positions in their administrations. In many ways this remains true today as well, at least for positions at the very top.

Throughout this period, the national party organizations played an important role in identifying candidates for presidential appointments. It was quite common, in fact, for the head of the president's party to hold a position in the cabinet, usually as postmaster general. This made sense, not only because the post office department was the principal consumer of patronage appointments, but also because a cabinet post provided a vantage point from which the party leader could work with the president and other cabinet secretaries to ensure a steady flow of partisan loyalists into federal posts throughout the government.

The party role was critical to government operations because there was at the time no alternative source of candidates for appointment. Each cabinet secretary had his own acquaintances and contacts, but few of them knew enough politicians to fill all the available positions in their departments with people who would be loyal to the administration, pass muster with appropriate members of Congress, and satisfy the political litmus tests of party leaders in the states and cities where they might serve. The party could help with all of that.

Many of the appointees who came through the party channel were skilled and qualified, not merely party hacks. More important, partisan control of this process usually guaranteed the construction of an administration that was broadly representative of the elements of the president's party and thus, in some important ways, in touch with the American people it was intended to serve. Equally important, the parties served as an employment agency upon which the government was heavily reliant. They provided a steady stream of politically approved candidates for federal offices. That was a function of no small significance in a government that lacked any other tested means of recruitment for positions outside the civil service.

1933–1952

Following the pattern of his predecessors, Franklin Roosevelt appointed James Farley, the leader of the Democratic Party, to serve as postmaster general and superintend the selection of lower-level appointments in the first Roosevelt administration. Farley directed a patronage operation that bore close resemblance to those of the previous half century.

Despite the familiar look of FDR's patronage operation, however, changes were set in motion by the New Deal that would have lasting consequences for the staffing of presidential administrations. Three of those deserve attention here.

The first was the very nature of the politics of the New Deal. The coalition that brought Franklin Roosevelt to office was composed of a broad diversity of groups and views. It provided FDR a sweeping victory by drawing support from Americans who disagreed with each other about important matters, yet agreed on the need to elect a president of their own party. But the New Deal coalition soon proved as useless for running a government as it had been useful for winning elections. Even with the most delicate kind of balancing act, it was no small task to construct an administration of intellectuals and union members, northern liberals and southern conservatives, progressives and racists. The task was complicated all the more by the intensity of the new administration's efforts, not merely to redirect, but to reconstruct public policy in the United States. It simply could not be reliably assumed that appointees would fully support all the dimensions of the president's program simply because they were Democrats.

Hence Roosevelt and his senior advisers began increasingly to end-run the Democratic Party patronage system in filling key positions in the government. More and more the people closest to the president—James Rowe, Louis Howe, Harry Hopkins, and others—began to operate their own recruitment programs. Typically they would identify bright young men already serving in government or anxious to do so and cultivate them with the kind of ad hoc assignments that prepared them for more important managerial positions. While these were either lifelong or recently converted Democrats, they often were not people with any history of party activism. It was the passions of the time and their commitment to the New Deal that inspired their interest in politics, not a pattern of service to local or state political machines.

The need for such people grew increasingly apparent as the consequence of a second change wrought by the New Deal. The government was growing. Total federal employment was 604,000 in 1933. It nearly doubled by the end of the decade. The New Deal seemed to spawn new agencies and programs almost daily. This created a voracious need not merely for people to fill newly created slots, but for skilled managers and creative program specialists to attend to problems at least as complicated as any the federal government had ever before tackled.

This, too, had the effect of diminishing the importance of the party patronage system as a source of appointees. It became increasingly apparent that the party faithful did not always include the kinds of people required to operate technical agencies like the Securities and Exchange Commission and the Agriculture Adjustment Administration. So Roosevelt turned to other sources, even occasionally risking the wrath of party leaders in so doing.

A third change in the New Deal years fed the momentum of the first two. That was the growing importance of the White House staff. As the energy of the federal government came to be centered in the presidency—and it did dramatically during the New Deal—the need for more support for the president became increasingly apparent. In 1936, Roosevelt appointed a committee headed by his friend Louis Brownlow to study the organization of the executive branch and make recommendations. The report of the Brownlow Committee described the need for vigorous executive leadership to make a modern democracy work. But it also pointed out that "the President needs help" in this enterprise. It went on to recommend that presidents have authority to appoint a small personal staff to assist in the management of the government (US President's Committee on Administrative Management 1937). In 1939, the Congress approved the appointment of six personal aides to the president and established executive reorganization authority that allowed Roosevelt to create an Executive Office of the President (EOP).

In the past, presidents had had little choice but to rely on their party's patronage operation because they lacked the staff necessary to run a personnel recruitment operation of their own. With the creation of the EOP that began to change. Embedded in the recommendations of the Brownlow Committee was a philosophy of public management that also threatened the importance of party patronage. Political control of the government, in the view of Brownlow and his many supporters in the schools of public administration, had come to mean policy control, not merely party control. It was no longer enough for a president to staff his administration with members of his own party and let them work with copartisans in Congress to superintend the routines of government. Instead, the president needed managerial support through broader control of the budget, government organization, and personnel selection to move public policy in the direction that he set and that had earned the endorsement of the American electorate.

This gradual evolution in management philosophy clearly suggested the need for the president and his personal staff to play a larger role in recruiting appointees who supported his policy priorities and who possessed the skills and creativity necessary to develop and implement them. In that scheme, government jobs could not be viewed primarily as rewards for party loyalty, and recruitment could not be left primarily to party patronage operations.

None of these changes took place overnight, but they slowly found their way into the operations of the presidency. Loyal Democrats continued to claim positions in the Roosevelt and later the Truman administration. The pressure to fill vacancies with the party faithful did not abate. The Democratic National Committee continued to operate a full-service employment agency. But few of the appointments to important positions came via this route any longer.

The strains on the patronage operation grew more acute after Roosevelt's death. Truman found himself in an odd position. Though a Democrat like Roosevelt, he needed to forge his own identity as president. Members of his party often had difficulty transferring their loyalties from the dead president to the new one, especially since many of them thought Truman several cuts below Roosevelt in stature.

The 1948 election campaign widened the fissures in the Democratic Party all the more. The southern wing of the party split off to support then Democratic Governor Strom Thurmond of South Carolina. The so-called Progressive wing had its own candidate in Henry Wallace. After winning reelection, Truman found that he had to temper his faith, slender as it had already become, in the ability of the Democratic Party to provide candidates for appointment who were certain to be loyal to him and the important policies of his presidency.

Truman did what any reasonable leader would have done under the circumstances. He relied less heavily on candidates recommended by the party and built his own recruitment process. The latter never passed much beyond the primitive stage and the former continued to play an important role. But change was under way, and its full impacts would emerge in the administrations that followed.

1952–1968

Dwight Eisenhower was the least partisan president of the twentieth century, and he came to office with fewer debts to his party than any of his predecessors. Though Republicans had not controlled the presidency for twenty years, Eisenhower's election did not signify the beginning of a flood of oldline Republican loyalists into federal offices. Eisenhower's chief of staff,

Sherman Adams, reported that the president was often indignant at what he considered to be political interference in his appointments and that he "avoided giving the Republican National Committee any responsibility for the selection of government officials, a duty the committee would have been happy to assume" (Adams 1961, 125).

Charles F. Willis Jr., an Eisenhower aide who worked on personnel matters, has said that the president "seemed to react against intense political pressure, more than anything else that I noticed, adversely, and I think that his appointments and the people he surrounded himself with at the top level reflected that he considered quality rather than political know-how" (Willis 1968, 28).

Eisenhower did intend to oust as many New Dealers and Fair Dealers as he could, but he sought to replace them with people who subscribed to his own brand of Republicanism. Being a Republican, even a lifelong member of the party faithful, was not enough to get a job in the Eisenhower administration—as soon became evident to Republicans across the country.

While the new administration worked closely with Republican National Committee Chairman Leonard Hall and did in fact place a number of party loyalists, appointments to top-level positions were much more heavily influenced by a group of the president's close friends. During the 1952 transition, Lucius Clay, Herbert Brownell, and Harold Talbott commissioned the New York consulting firm of McKinsey and Company to do a study identifying the most important positions in the government. Then, and in the years that followed, they were an important source of suggestions and advice to Eisenhower on matters of government staffing.

The composition of the Eisenhower administration quickly came to reflect the diminished role of the president's party as a source of senior-level personnel. A majority of Eisenhower's first cabinet had no significant history of Republican Party activism. The subcabinet looked much the same, drawing heavily on the practical talents of the business and legal communities, with only a scattering of officials whose primary credentials were partisan or political (Mann 1965, 293).

Eisenhower's second term marked an even more important turning point in the transition away from party dominance of the appointment process. The Twenty-Second Amendment, limiting presidents to two terms in office, had been ratified in 1951. Eisenhower was the first president to whom it applied, and his reelection in 1956 made him the first president ever to enter a term as a lame duck. Since he could not run again for reelection, there was less incentive for Eisenhower to be making appointments with an eye to building partisan electoral support: he was freer than ever to distance himself from patronage pressures.

That freedom was reflected in the significant initiatives that developed in Eisenhower's second term for management of the personnel function in the presidency, not the party. The Eisenhower White House was the first to respond to a modern president's need for centralized control over executive branch personnel by seeking to construct procedures and organizational structures to serve that objective. The position of Special Assistant for Personnel Management was created and the first elements of a systematic recruitment operation were put in place (Kaufman 1965, 66; Weko 1995).

This momentum toward centralized presidential control of the appointment process and away from reliance on party patronage accelerated in the Kennedy and Johnson administrations. Kennedy, like Eisenhower, had won the presidential nomination by setting up his own organization and capturing the party. His was not a life of deeply committed partisanship, nor did he grant the Democratic Party organization much credit for his narrow victory in the 1960 election. So Kennedy felt little compulsion to staff his administration with party loyalists to whom he might have had any debt or obligation. From the very start, he and his staff operated their own personnel recruitment operation.

After Kennedy's assassination, Lyndon Johnson continued the practice of operating a White House personnel office. He designated John Macy, then chairman of the Civil Service Commission, to handle presidential appointments as well. Macy expanded the personnel office and began to systematize its procedures, even employing computers to maintain records on thousands of potential appointees.

Under both Kennedy and Johnson, the White House personnel office worked with the Democratic National Committee, in varying degrees of cooperation. But the participation of the party was clearly subsidiary. Most of the time the National Committee's role was to determine that candidates for appointment selected by the White House would not incur the opposition of party leaders in their home states. The White House also conducted checks with home state Democratic senators and members of Congress to avoid opposition from them. But, as Dan H. Fenn Jr., an assistant to Kennedy on personnel matters, said, "The kind of people we were looking for weren't the kind of people who were active in party activities" (Fenn 1976).

These checks came to be known as clearances and they emerged as a routine of the appointment process, providing a role for the party, albeit a limited one. While party officials were a steady source of suggestions of potential nominees, genuine control over personnel selection had shifted to the White House. This process had begun in the early days of the New Deal; it accelerated as the size of the White House staff grew. The party ceased to have an initiative role in the appointment process and clearly no longer operated that process as it once had. The party had become a checkpoint and, with but few exceptions, not much more. As Hugh Heclo has indicated, its influence was reduced to the exercise of "'negative clearance'; that is, nursing political referrals and clearing official appointments in order to placate those political leaders in Congress and in state, local, or other organizations who might otherwise take exception" (Heclo 1977, 71). The party no longer drove the appointment process, but its disapproval of an appointment could bring that process to a temporary halt. It is, however, important to note here that even as presidents were consolidating the control of appointments under their own auspices, they were still overwhelmingly appointing members of their own parties to executive branch posts.

1969 and Beyond

The movement to centralize control over presidential appointments reached new levels of sophistication and success in the administration of Richard Nixon and those that followed. Nixon himself never had much interest in personnel selection, but the people to whom he delegated that task tended to be experienced professional managers who saw personnel selection as a critical ingredient in efforts to establish control over the executive branch.

In the years after 1969, the White House Personnel Office (later called the Presidential Personnel Office) became an important component of the White House Office and grew in size. It now routinely employs more than twenty-five people, and often swells to more than fifty at particularly busy times. Appointment procedures have been systematized and routinized. Computers play an important role in tracking the progress of appointments. And clearances with leaders of the president's party, with relevant members of Congress, with officials in the agency to which an appointment is to be made, and with policy specialists in the administration are regular features of almost every appointment decision (Bonafede 1987; Mackenzie 2001; Weko 1995).

But the most important characteristic of the modern appointment process, and the one that most critically affects the influence of political parties, has been the creation of a genuine and aggressive recruitment or outreach capability within the White House staff. Party influence in appointments remained significant as long as the White House lacked the ability to identify qualified candidates on its own. Then the president and his staff had little choice but to respond to recommendations and suggestions that came in, as the terminology of the time had it, "over the transom." It is an iron law of politics that "you can't beat someone with no one," and of football that "the best defense is a good offense." Both apply in the appointment process as well.

The thrust of most of the contemporary development of White House personnel operations has been to grasp the initiative, to relieve presidents from reliance on external sources for their appointees. Primary among those sources historically was the president's own political party organization, but the successful establishment of a recruiting capability in the White House has left the parties with little remaining control over a function they once dominated.

Parties and Presidential Leadership: An Accelerating Evolution

The years after World War II have been a time of diminishing influence for the national party organizations in the operations of the presidency. This was a trend with prewar antecedents, but its pace accelerated after the war. There is no simple explanation for the change. In fact, it resulted from a confluence of other changes occurring both inside and outside the government in those years. The most important of those are summarized here.

The Game Changed

Party influence was always largest on appointments to positions outside Washington. When an appointee was to serve as customs collector for the port of Philadelphia or postmaster in Butte, local party officials generally had a determining influence in choosing the person to fill the slot. Even though this was technically a presidential appointment, presidents readily deferred to the leaders of their party in the local area. Until relatively recent times, there were tens of thousands of such positions and they were a significant part of the political rewards system for party workers. A person who had spent years as party organizer, poll watcher, and minor officeholder could reasonably expect to cap a political career with an appointment to a sinecure as a local official of the federal government.

But after World War II, largely at the behest of an increasingly vocal public service reform movement, many of these positions were taken out of the patronage stream and placed under some form of civil service coverage. What was good for the party was increasingly bad for the delivery of government services. And the reform movement thought the solution was to take some of the politics out of appointments to these administrative offices.

The Number of Important
Presidential Appointments Grew

From the beginning of the New Deal onward, the number of senior level positions in the federal government grew. New cabinet departments and independent agencies were added. Old ones expanded as hordes of new programs were created. The bureaucracy thickened and new administrative layers were added to the federal government. Departments that might have had two or three presidential appointees before World War II now have a dozen or more. The Department of Defense, which came into being after World War II, has fifty-one senior positions filled by presidential appointment. The Department of Education, created in 1979, has sixteen[4] (Plum Book 2008). The broader picture is indicated in Table 12.2.

TABLE 12.2 Growth in Top-Level Executive Branch Positions
in Cabinet Departments, 1960–2004

Position	1960	1992	2004
Secretary	10	14	15
Deputy Secretary	6	20	24
Under Secretary	15	32	53
Assistant Secretary	87	225	256
Deputy Assistant Secretary	78	518	535
Total	196	809	883

Source: Light 2008, 62–63.

Many of these new positions required appointees with a high level of technical or scientific competence because they bore responsibility for complex government programs: the Under Secretary of Commerce for Oceans and Atmosphere, the Director of Defense Research and Engineering, the Director of the Office of Energy Research, for example. The kinds of people needed to fill these positions were unlikely to be found hanging out at party headquarters on election night.

As a consequence of the growth and increasing sophistication of the government's senior appointive positions, presidents needed to develop their own personnel recruitment operations. It became apparent during the New Deal that party channels would not be adequate to provide the number and kinds of skilled appointees that an increasingly active government required.

That inadequacy grew larger in the years that followed. In response, successive administrations developed and then refined their own systems and procedures for staffing the senior levels of the executive branch. Parties had once played a central role in this process. By the end of the second decade after World War II, their role was essentially peripheral. Members of the president's party continued to fill most of the appointed positions, but their identification, selection, and recruitment were conducted at some distance from the formal organization of the president's party.

The Power Situation Changed

As the federal government came to play a larger role in American life, appointees who developed and implemented programs became more powerful. Consider the contrast between 1932 and the present. The federal government in 1932 did *not* provide aid to education, run a national pension system, provide health care for the elderly, fund the national highway system, regulate financial markets, shoot rockets into space, or serve as democracy's policeman around the world. It does all of those things and many more today, and it spends more than $3 trillion each year doing them.

Management of those programs and of the distribution of the funds they involve affords a great deal of power to presidential appointees. Decisions on who fills those positions matter more than ever before. And the groups in American society affected by the choices made by these appointees have become increasingly unwilling to leave them to purely patronage appointees. They have sought instead to put pressure on presidents to select appointees with the necessary technical skills and experience and with particular policy views. Party loyalty and service have been largely irrelevant to these calculations.

As appointments became more important, parties became less important in filling them. For much of American history, the principal contests for power were outside of government, in elections where the parties were strongest. With the beginning of the New Deal, the power struggle increasingly took place within government, in the modern bureaucratic state where the parties were weakest. When the terrain shifted, the locus of power shifted as well.

Changes Outside the Appointment Process

Nothing in government occurs in a vacuum. In fact, government is a great social mirror: what happens there usually reflects what is happening elsewhere in society. That is certainly true of the changes that took place in the appointment process during the twentieth century. Parties could claim a dominant role in presidential appointment decisions only as long as they were able to control the candidate nominating process. Once parties lost this control, presidents increasingly took control of the appointment process and placed it within their own personal organizations.

Simultaneous with the loss of party control of presidential nominations was an explosion in the number of national special interest groups. Counting the number of national interest groups is no small task, but most estimates put the number of politically active special interest groups at more than 10,000. In 2010, there were nearly 13,000 registered lobbyists in Washington, and registered lobbyists are just the tip of the lobbying iceberg (Center for Responsive Politics 2011).

These groups were both much more substantive and much more focused than the major political parties. Typically, they were concerned with a relatively narrow set of policies and they represented the people most directly affected by the shape of those policies (Berry and Wilcox 2009). This permitted them to concentrate their attention and political influence on the small number of presidential appointments that mattered most to them. It also allowed them to work closely with the congressional committee and subcommittee chairs who were most interested in those programs and who controlled their appropriations. These were often politically potent combinations that generated considerably more influence over presidential appointments than broad-based, coalition parties were able to generate. In the competition for influence over appointments, interest groups became increasingly successful, often at the expense of the political parties.

In recent years, identity groups—women, racial minorities, gays and lesbians—have also assumed a more influential role in appointment decisions. Democratic Presidents Carter, Clinton, and Obama have been especially sensitive to the demands of these groups for a seat at the table. President Clinton's first administration took shape very slowly, in part because of his desire to satisfy what came to be known as the "EGG standard." He wanted an administration, as he said, that "looked like America," with appointments that amply represented the ethnic, gender, and geographical diversity of the country (Twentieth Century Fund 1996, 68–71; Weko 1995, 100–103). The first few months of George W. Bush's administration indicated that Republicans, too, had acquired a substantial sensitivity to the diversity of their appointments. Bush's initial cabinet appointments included three women, two African Americans, two Asian Americans, and one Hispanic—a long way from Richard Nixon's first cabinet in 1969, which was composed entirely of white males.

The decentralization of power in the Congress also worked against the interests of the parties in the appointment process. During the early decades of the twentieth century, real political power in Congress was concentrated in the hands of a relatively small number of institutional party leaders and committee chairs. Local political bosses and national party leaders regularly worked with them to influence the president's appointment decisions. If the leader of the Democratic National Committee or the mayor of Chicago called Sam Rayburn, the Speaker of the House, and asked him to try to get the president to appoint a particular Democrat to the Federal Communications Commission, it was hard for the president to deny the request. Sam Rayburn was a key factor in determining the fate of the president's legislative program. Keeping him happy was usually much more important than any particular appointment.

But increasingly after midcentury, the party leaders and committee chairs lost their grip on power in Congress. Younger members generated reforms that spread power around, to the subcommittee level in the House and to individual members in the Senate. The political calculus became much more complex and it was increasingly difficult for local bosses or leaders of the national party organization to use the congressional lever to influence presidential appointment decisions. Individual members of Congress were less beholden and less connected to the national party in any case, having built their own personal political organizations and developed their own sources of campaign funds. Their interest in presidential appointments was much more ad hoc and personal in character: they sought appointments for their friends and supporters and staff members, not for traditional party workers. As parties became less important to the job security of members of Congress, incentives diminished for members to use their influence in the appointment process for purposes broader than their own personal objectives.

So the political landscape underwent broad transitions after World War II. Senior-level appointments were growing more important as national political power moved to Washington. Lower-level appointments were transferred in large numbers to the civil service. The presidency was becoming a larger and increasingly sophisticated institution with management capabilities that had never before existed. The electoral process was no longer the sole realm of political party organizations. Interest groups were springing up everywhere and rapidly gaining political potency. A decentralized Congress was less able and less willing to serve purely partisan interests in the appointment process. Individually and collectively, these changes all served to erode the influence that parties once exercised on the staffing of the executive branch of the federal government.

The Continuing Problem of Political Control

A defining characteristic of the twentieth century with regard to the executive branch of the federal government was the steady and successful effort to isolate public employment from political pressure, to create a federal workforce that is "protected" from the tides of political passion in the country and the electorate. At the beginning of the twentieth century, there were 240,000 federal civilian employees. Of these, more than half were political appointees of one form or another. At the beginning of the twenty-first century, there are 2.7 million federal civilian employees. Of these, only a few thousand are actually filled by political appointment.

This suggests a peculiar but familiar reality: that Americans are suspicious of politics and parties. For many of them, politics is a dirty business, something that can easily mess up government. Hence there has been substantial public support for efforts to depoliticize the personnel selection process in government, to eliminate all the pejoratives: cronyism and nepotism and the spoils system.

But Americans are also highly skeptical of bureaucrats and so they respond positively to campaigning politicians who bash bureaucrats and promise to put government back into the hands of the people. The most popular American politician of recent times, Ronald Reagan, was a master of this. "Government," he said, "is the problem, not the solution."

Hence there exists a kind of public schizophrenia that deeply complicates the task of presidential leadership. Americans want a government that is isolated and protected from the worst aspects of partisan politics. But they also want a government that is not controlled by "faceless bureaucrats," but by elected leaders who will keep it responsive to popular concerns. Those are contradictory goals. How is it possible to have a government that is simultaneously free of politics and under political control? The answer, of course, is that it is not possible. And, as a consequence, conflict between these competing objectives constantly pervades the personnel process.

When parties were the dominant influence in presidential personnel selection, the notion reigned that getting control of the government meant establishing partisan control. The way to implement the will of the electorate was to fill as many positions as possible with members of the president's party. By filling all, or a large number, of federal offices with the president's copartisans, the government would move in the directions he laid out.

It wasn't a bad theory, except that it didn't work in practice, especially after 1932. It didn't work for two reasons primarily. First, it couldn't work in the United States because of the nature of American political parties. The large national parties whose candidates won presidential elections were constructed of fragile coalitions. They rarely offered the electorate a very detailed or refined set of policy objectives. Their primary task was to win the elections, and to do that they clung to the center, trimming specifics to develop the broadest possible mass appeal. Even in the most intense periods of party conflict in the United States, it was difficult for most voters to perceive very broad *policy* differences between the parties. Parties provided few meaningful clues to what exactly the government would do if their candidate were elected.

There was thus little reliability in the notion that staffing the government with members of the same party would provide a unified sense of direction under presidential leadership. In fact, members of the same party often disagreed with each other, and with their own president, on a great many matters of policy. In many cases, all they shared was a party label. The spoils system and its successors were a very shaky foundation for getting control of the government through coherent policy leadership from the White House.

Even if American political parties had been more ideologically and substantively unified, the theory would have failed in implementation. Partisan domination of the appointments process was never viewed by party leaders as a system for aiding the president in establishing policy leadership. It was treated as a vehicle for party, not presidential, purposes. In suggesting party candidates for appointment, the principal goal was to sustain the vigor and the regional and ideological balance of the party, not to find loyal or effective supporters of the president's program. Many presidential appointments, as indicated earlier, were controlled by the local party organizations who had little interest in national policy. They sought to get federal jobs to reward their own faithful servants and to prevent the federal government from upsetting their local control.

For both these reasons, party participation in presidential appointments failed to serve the purpose of aiding the incumbent administration in establishing policy leadership over the government. And as we have seen, American presidents began to reject that participation. Slowly but steadily they found ways to construct their own appointment processes, increasingly distanced from party influence. In the past few decades, party influence on appointments has faded almost to the vanishing point.

Presidents still struggle to "get control of the government." Few of them fully succeed. But no recent American president has sought significant help from their formal party organizations in accomplishing this critical objective. And for good reason. American political party organizations were rarely very helpful in this critical task, and American presidents have found ample reason to centralize this process within their own personal organizations as much as possible.

References

Adams, Sherman. 1961. *Firsthand Report.* New York: Harper and Brothers.
Berry, Jeffrey M., and Clyde Wilcox. 2009. *The Interest Group Society.* New York: Longman.
Bonafede, Dom. 1987. "The White House Personnel Office from Roosevelt to Reagan." In *The In-and-Outers*, edited by G. Calvin Mackenzie. Baltimore, MD: Johns Hopkins University Press.

Center for Responsive Politics. 2011. "Lobbying Database, 2011." http://www.opensecrets
.org/lobby/.
Cooke, Jacob E., ed. 1961. *The Federalist.* New York: Meridian.
Fenn, Dan H., Jr. 1976. Interview with the author. Waltham, Massachusetts, March 26.
Fenno, Richard F. 1959. *The President's Cabinet.* New York: Vintage.
Fish, Carl R. 1904. *The Civil Service and the Patronage.* Cambridge, MA: Harvard University
Press.
Heclo, Hugh. 1977. *A Government of Strangers.* Washington: Brookings.
Kaufman, Herbert. 1965. "The Growth of the Federal Personnel System." In *The Federal Gov-
ernment Service,* edited by Wallace S. Sayre. 2nd ed. Englewood Cliffs, NJ: Prentice-Hall.
Light, Paul C. 2008. *A Government Ill Executed.* Cambridge, MA: Harvard University Press.
Mackenzie, G. Calvin. 1981. *The Politics of Presidential Appointments.* New York: Free Press.
Mackenzie, G. Calvin, ed. 2001. *Innocent Until Nominated: The Breakdown of the Presidential
Appointment Process.* Washington, DC: Brookings.
Mann, Dean E. 1965. *The Assistant Secretaries: Problems and Processes of Appointment,*
Washington, DC: Brookings.
Plum Book. 2008. See US Senate. 2008.
Stanley, Harold W., and Richard G. Niemi. 2009. *Vital Statistics on American Politics 2009–
2010.* Washington, DC: CQ Press.
Twentieth Century Fund Task Force on the Presidential Appointment Process. 1996. *Obstacle
Course.* New York: Twentieth Century Fund Press.
US President's Committee on Administrative Management. 1937. *Report of the President's
Committee on Administrative Management.* Washington, DC: Government Printing Office.
US Senate. 2008. Committee on Homeland Security and Governmental Affairs. *Policy and
Supporting Positions.* Washington, DC: Government Printing Office. http://www.gpo
access.gov/plumbook/2008/index.html. Cited in text as Plum Book 2008.
Van Riper, Paul P. 1958. *History of the United States Civil Service.* New York: Harper and Row.
Weko, Thomas J. 1995. *The Politicizing Presidency: The White House Personnel Office, 1948–
1994.* Lawrence, KS: University of Kansas Press.
White, Leonard D. 1958. *The Jacksonians.* New York: Macmillan.
Willis, Charles F., Jr. 1968. Oral history interview with John T. Mason, Jr. Columbia Univer-
sity, March 15.

Endnotes

1. Partisanship in judicial appointments will not be discussed in this chapter because of space constraints. Interested readers are referred to the excellent work that Prof. Sheldon Goldman and others have done on this topic.

2. It should be noted that a few technical specialties had begun to emerge in the nineteenth century. Many of those were in public health and in agriculture. Even at the height of the spoils system, these positions were often treated as exceptions and were filled by the same people from one administration to the next, without regard to political loyalties.

3. In 1979, the Civil Service Commission was abolished and replaced by two new agencies: the Office of Personnel Management and the Merit Systems Protection Board.

4. The numbers in this paragraph refer to so-called PAS appointments: presidential appointments that require Senate confirmation.

13

American Political Parties in an Age of Polarization

ALAN I. ABRAMOWITZ
Emory University

Polarization is today the dominant feature of the American political system. The deep ideological divide between the Democratic and Republican parties pervades almost every aspect of American politics. Over the past forty years, the gap between the two parties in Congress has steadily increased across a wide range of policy issues. According to a statistical analysis of voting patterns in the House and Senate, since the 1960s the Republican Party has moved sharply to the right while the Democratic Party has moved, if not quite as dramatically, to the left (Poole and Rosenthal 2009). Liberal Republicans and conservative Democrats who exercised considerable influence in their respective parties during the 1950s and 1960s are now almost extinct (Sinclair 2005; Dodd and Oppenheimer 2005).

In 2010, the most recent year for which data were available, the ideological gap between the average Democrat and the average Republican in both chambers was greater than at any time in the previous hundred years. However, the gap may be even larger in the Congress that took office in 2011. Most of the Democrats who lost their seats in the 2010 midterm election were moderates representing swing states and districts, but their replacements were generally very conservative Republicans, many elected with the support of the Tea Party movement. In fact, the House Republicans elected in 2010 appear to be considerably more conservative as a group than those who served in the House under Newt Gingrich in 1995–96. They may well be the most conservative group of House Republicans since the end of World War II (Abramowitz 2011). Meanwhile, with the loss of many of their moderate members, the remaining House Democrats were considerably more liberal than those serving in the previous Congress. And while the changes in the makeup of the Senate were not as dramatic as those in the House, the divide between the two parties in the upper chamber appeared to be at least as great as in the previous Congress, as indicated by the straight party-line vote on the repeal of health-care reform.

Polarization in recent years has by no means been limited to the House of Representatives and Senate. There have also been sharp differences between the party nominees for president on a wide range of policy issues including health care, taxes, financial regulation, abortion, stem cell research, gay rights, and the war in Iraq. And while these differences were perhaps most accentuated during the nomination campaigns when the candidates were appealing to their parties' primary voters, they were clearly visible during the fall general election campaigns as well. There was little evidence, for example, that either Barack Obama or John McCain tried to move toward the center after winning their party's nominations in 2008. In fact, McCain's most important decision after securing the Republican nomination was to choose Alaska governor Sarah Palin as his running mate—a decision clearly aimed at energizing his party's conservative base rather than appealing to moderate swing voters (Heilemann and Halperin 2010).

Regardless of who wins the 2012 Republican presidential nomination, it is certain that the general election campaign will present voters with a clear choice between candidates offering widely diverging policies for addressing the challenges facing the country. As President, Mr. Obama, while hardly the radical socialist regularly castigated by right-wing talk show hosts and Republican leaders, has advanced an activist agenda including, in addition to health-care reform, an $800 billion economic stimulus package, stricter environmental regulations including regulation of greenhouse gases, tougher rules governing major financial institutions, increased federal aid to education, and repeal of the controversial Don't Ask, Don't Tell policy restricting the ability of gays and lesbians to serve openly in the US military. Meanwhile every one of the leading Republican presidential candidates, in addition to opposing all of these initiatives, has endorsed a budget plan proposed by Wisconsin Representative Paul Ryan that envisions drastic cuts in domestic spending, elimination of capital gains and estate taxes, and replacing traditional Medicare with vouchers requiring senior citizens to purchase healthcare plans from private insurance companies (Catanese 2011). The Ryan Medicare plan, in particular, proved to be highly controversial, with several polls showing strong public opposition. However, when one Republican presidential candidate, former House Speaker Newt Gingrich, dared to question the advisability of the proposed Medicare changes, he was sharply attacked by conservative pundits and politicians and forced to take back his comments (Liasson 2011).

Growing polarization has also been evident in recent years at the state level. Traditionally, political parties in the United States have been highly decentralized, with Democratic and Republican state parties often taking positions on major issues at variance with those of their national counterparts. Democratic state parties in the South were typically much more conservative than the national Democratic Party, and Republican state parties in the Northeast were generally much more liberal than the national Republican Party. While there is still some ideological variation among Democratic and Republican state parties, the differences are generally much smaller than in the past.

Today the ideological divide between the parties in the states is very similar to the ideological divide between the national parties. In fact, since the 2010 elections some of the sharpest ideological confrontations between the parties have been taking place at the state level as newly elected conservative Republican governors and state legislative majorities have sought to implement controversial policies including sharp cuts in spending on social programs and curbs on the benefits and bargaining rights of public employees. In states from Wisconsin to Florida and Michigan to New Jersey, public employees and their Democratic allies have fought back against legislation proposed by conservative Republicans with actions ranging from walkouts and mass demonstrations to recall elections (Tolan 2011). In Minnesota, a confrontation between the Democratic governor and the Republican state legislature over the state budget resulted in a partial government shutdown reminiscent of the one that affected the federal government during the 1990s (Hohmann 2011).

The Debate: Elite versus Mass Polarization

There is general agreement among political scientists and other observers of American politics that partisan polarization has substantially increased among political leaders and activists over the past several decades. Almost everyone agrees that Democratic and Republican elites—public officials, candidates, party leaders, and campaign activists—are much more sharply divided along ideological lines today than at any time in the recent past. It might be necessary to go back to the years immediately preceding the Civil War to find a time when the two major parties were as polarized as they are today. However, there is considerable disagreement about whether and to what extent polarization has also increased among the large majority of Americans who are not deeply involved in the political process—the mass public.

According to one school of thought, represented most prominently by political scientist Morris Fiorina and his coauthors, polarization in the United States is almost exclusively an elite phenomenon. They have forcefully argued that among the vast majority of Americans who are not actively involved in politics, polarization has not increased (Fiorina, Abrams, and Levendusky 2011; Fiorina and Levendusky 2006). In their view, ordinary Americans today, much like their counterparts forty or fifty years ago, are not very interested in politics and not very informed about the ideological debates that preoccupy officeholders. Moreover, in contrast to members of the political elite, their opinions tend to cluster around the center of the ideological spectrum. Very few ordinary citizens take consistently liberal or conservative positions on major policy issues.

Fiorina and his coauthors claim that there is a growing "disconnect" in American politics between an increasingly polarized political elite and a largely centrist public (Fiorina and Abrams 2009). Ordinary citizens, they argue, are turned off by the relatively extreme positions of both parties. As a result, a growing number of Americans consider themselves Independents and many prefer to stay at home on Election Day rather than choose between two extreme alternatives. In their words, "Americans are closely divided, but we are not deeply divided, and we are closely divided because many of us are ambivalent and uncertain, and consequently reluctant to make firm commitments to parties, politicians, or policies. We divide evenly in elections or sit them out entirely because we instinctively seek the center while the parties and candidates hang out on the extremes" (Fiorina, Abrams, and Levendusky 2011, xv).

The elite theory of polarization has found considerable favor among pundits and political commentators. It is an appealing line of argument because it absolves the large majority of Americans of any responsibility for the dysfunctional condition of our political system. According to this theory, it is the political elites—officeholders, candidates, and a small group of activists—who are to blame for hyperpartisanship and gridlock. The rest of us are merely victims. We are, in effect, trapped in a polarized party system that we had nothing to do with creating.

Despite its appeal, however, a careful examination of the arguments and the evidence indicates that the elite theory of polarization suffers from several major shortcomings. First, the theory fails to explain why ambitious political leaders would adopt extreme positions that are far out of line with the preferences of those who elect them. According to the well-known median voter theorem, in a centrist electorate, politicians seeking to win elections should adopt centrist positions (Downs 1957, chapter 8). Taking extreme positions in a centrist electorate would appear to be a recipe for political oblivion, as Barry Goldwater and George McGovern discovered in their disastrous presidential bids. Even if candidates were forced to adopt relatively extreme positions to appeal to their party's primary voters, one would expect them to move back toward the center during the general election campaign. The fact that this does not seem to be happening suggests that the general election voters are themselves more polarized than in the past.

Second, the claim that the political beliefs of the American public have changed little since the 1950s seems rather implausible in light of the dramatic changes that have affected American politics and society over the past six decades. These changes have included an ideological and regional realignment of the two-party system that has resulted in much clearer differences between the ideological positions of Democratic and Republican officeholders and candidates, rising levels of education within the public, the changing structure of the mass media, the increasing salience of cultural issues, and growing racial and ethnic diversity. It is hard to believe that these sweeping changes have had no impact on the way ordinary Americans think about politics.

Finally, and perhaps most important, broad generalizations about the low level of ideological sophistication of the American public ignore the enormous diversity that exists within the public with regard to political engagement. While many Americans have little or no interest in politics, ignore news about government and politics, and rarely vote or participate in politics in any way, many others care a great deal about politics, follow news about government and politics closely, vote regularly, talk about politics with their friends and neighbors, and donate time and money to candidates and political parties. Few Americans are political junkies whose lives revolve around politics, but few are totally apolitical.

Political engagement varies widely within the American public and we will see that this fact goes a long way toward explaining polarization among political elites. That is because political engagement is strongly related to polarization. The more engaged Americans are in the political process—the more they care about politics, they more they know about politics, and the more they participate in politics—the more partisan and the more polarized they tend to be. In the twenty-first century the ideals of democratic citizenship are best exemplified by those Americans with the strongest partisan and ideological convictions. In contrast, it is among the uninterested, the uninformed, and uninvolved that political independence and moderation flourish (Abramowitz 2010).

Contrary to the claims made by Fiorina and his coauthors, there is no "disconnect" between political elites and the public. Instead, the evidence presented in this book shows that political elites represent the views of the politically engaged segment of the public. Moreover, the politically engaged segment of the public has been growing in size in response to the increasing polarization of the parties. Voter turnout has been increasing since 1996. In 2008 turnout was higher than in any presidential election since the franchise was extended to include eighteen- to twenty-year-olds in 1972.

And it wasn't just voting that increased in 2004 and 2008. According to data from the American National Election Studies, in both 2004 and 2008 the percentage of Americans who cared a great deal about the outcome of the election, displayed a yard sign or bumper sticker, and tried to persuade a friend or neighbor to support a candidate was higher than at any time since the beginning of the ANES surveys in 1952. Rather than being turned off by polarization, as Fiorina and his coauthors have claimed, Americans actually have been energized by a choice between party nominees taking sharply contrasting policy positions (Abramowitz 2010, chapter 2).

Explaining the Rise of Mass Polarization

How did we get to this point? What happened to transform Converse's 1950s public in which ideological thinking was rare and partisan conflict was muted (Converse 1964; Campbell, et al. 1960, chapter 9) into the twenty-first century public in which ideological thinking is much more prevalent and partisan conflict is much more intense?

A number of changes in American politics and society have contributed to the rise of mass-based polarization since the 1950s. One of the most important changes in American politics during this period has been the ideological and regional realignment of the American party system. A prominent feature of the American party system during the 1950s and 1960s was the ideological diversity of the leadership of the two major parties. This ideological diversity was, in turn, closely related to the regional diversity of the party coalitions. The Democratic Party, though leaning toward the liberal side of the ideological spectrum, included a large and influential conservative wing based mainly in the South. The Republican Party, though leaning toward the conservative side of the ideological spectrum, included a large and influential moderate-to-liberal wing based mainly in the Northeast.

In the American electorate of the 1950s, the most important political cleavages were based on class, region, and religion. After capturing the presidency for the Democratic Party in 1932 in the midst of the worst economic crisis in American history, Franklin Roosevelt forged a coalition that dominated American politics for more than three decades. Roosevelt's New Deal policies resulted in a dramatic expansion in the role of the federal government in many areas of American life. Yet from the standpoint of the average voter, the appeal of the Democratic Party during those years was based less on an ideology of governmental activism than on the concrete benefits that the New Deal provided to those who had been hard hit by the Great Depression—benefits such as public works projects, rural electrification and agricultural price supports—and the association of Republicans with hard times and the Democrats with prosperity.

More than two decades after Roosevelt's first election, in surveys conducted by the American National Election Studies (ANES) between 1952 and 1960, the twin themes of group benefits and the goodness or badness of the times dominated Americans' responses to a series of open-ended questions asking what they liked or disliked about the two major parties. In contrast, references to the parties' ideological positions or policies were relatively rare (Campbell, et al. 1960, chapter 10).

Despite Republican Dwight Eisenhower's decisive victories in the 1952 and 1956 presidential elections, Roosevelt's New Deal coalition remained largely intact. Democrats enjoyed a large advantage in party identification in the national electorate during those years. According to the ANES surveys, Democrats and Independents leaning toward the Democratic Party made up 54 percent of the electorate during the 1950s while Republicans and Independents leaning toward the Republican Party made up only 39 percent.

The Democratic advantage was much larger among voters belonging to the three groups that formed the core of Roosevelt's electoral coalition: southern whites, northern white Catholics, and northern white blue-collar voters. According to the ANES data, during the 1950s Democrats and Democratic-leaning Independents outnumbered Republicans and Republican-leaning Independents by 75 percent to 19 percent among southern whites, by 68 percent to 24 percent among northern white Catholics, and by 59 percent to 33 percent among northern white blue-collar voters.

Ideological Realignment and the Demise of the New Deal Party System

The first cracks in FDR's coalition began to emerge not long after his death in 1945. Not surprisingly the issue that produced those cracks was race. In 1948, South Carolina governor J. Strom Thurmond led a walkout of southern delegates from the Democratic National Convention over the adoption of a fairly mild civil rights plank introduced by Minneapolis mayor and liberal firebrand Hubert Humphrey. Rather than endorse Roosevelt's successor, Harry Truman, Thurmond and his followers formed the States Rights or Dixiecrat Party with Thurmond as its standard-bearer, taking thirty-nine electoral votes in the Deep South from the Democrats.

It was probably inevitable that a coalition including groups with as widely diverging policy preferences as southern segregationists and progressive trade unionists would eventually break apart. Truman won the 1948 presidential election despite the defection of the Dixiecrats, but over the next

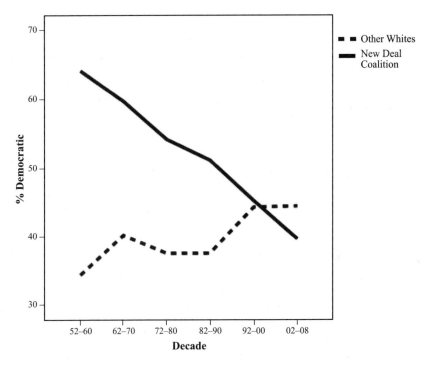

Source: ANES 2011.

FIGURE 13.1 Decline of the New Deal Coalition: Democratic Identification
Among White Voters Since the 1950s

several decades the cracks in the New Deal coalition would continue to expand as Republican politicians from Richard Nixon to Ronald Reagan
sought to win over traditional Democrats dissatisfied with their party's liberal national leadership and policies. Sensing an opportunity to expand their
party's electoral coalition, Republican leaders beginning with Richard Nixon
assiduously courted the support of traditional conservative Democrats in
the South and elsewhere who were upset about their party's embrace of civil
rights and other liberal causes (Phillips 1969). They were largely successful,
and later were able to expand the Republican base to include religious conservatives opposed to legalized abortion, bans on school prayer, and gay
rights. Ultimately, however, the GOP's growing conservatism sparked a
backlash among moderate-to-liberal Republicans in the Northeast and elsewhere. The end result of this realignment was a party system in which the

ideological differences between the parties were much sharper and the regional bases of the two parties were reversed. By the end of the twentieth century the conservative South had become a Republican stronghold while the liberal Northeast had become the most strongly Democratic region of the nation (Black and Black 2007).

Figure 13.1 displays the trends in party identification between the 1950s and the first decade of the twenty-first century of voters belonging to any of the three groups that had formed the core of Roosevelt's New Deal coalition— southern whites, northern white Catholics, and northern white blue-collar workers. Among voters belonging to these three groups, the data show a steady and dramatic decline in Democratic identification that began during the 1950s and has continued into the 2000s.

By the first decade of the twenty-first century, Democratic identification among northern white Catholics and northern blue-collar workers had fallen below 50 percent and southern whites had become one of the most Republican voting blocs in the electorate. In the 2008 presidential election, according to exit poll data, Barack Obama won only 30 percent of the vote among southern whites. In several states in the Deep South including Alabama, Mississippi, and Louisiana, Obama won barely a tenth of the white vote.

The decline of the New Deal coalition was part of a broader transformation of the American party system since the 1950s. Over several decades, a party system in which attachments to political parties were based primarily on membership in concrete social groups has been replaced by a party system in which attachments to political parties are based primarily on policy preferences and ideology. While supporters of the two major parties continue to differ in terms of their social characteristics, those differences are largely by-products of differences between the ideologies and policy preferences of members of various social groups. Group membership itself is no longer the prime determinant of party identification in the United States.

In addition to the growing ideological divide between the parties at the elite level, rising levels of education among the American public meant that the voters themselves were better able to understand the ideological cues that they were receiving from officeholders and candidates. In his research on ideological thinking in the American public in the 1950s, Converse found that education was a powerful predictor of ideological sophistication—college graduates were much more likely than those with only a grade school or high school education to understand ideological concepts and to take consistent positions on issues. And in the half century since Converse conducted his research, there has been a dramatic change in educational attainment in the American public. Between the 1950s and the first decade of the twenty-first century, according to data from American National Election Studies surveys, college graduates increased from only 8 percent of the voting-age population to 26 percent while those with only a grade school education fell from 34 percent of the voting-age population to only 3 percent.

Based on the growing clarity of party differences at the elite level and rising levels of education, one would expect the level of ideological sophistication of the public to have increased considerably over the past half century. In addition to these changes, however, one other trend has undoubtedly contributed to both increased awareness of party differences and growing ideological polarization among the public—the changing structure of the mass communications media. With the rise of cable television, talk radio, and the Internet, Americans now have easy access to a much greater variety of political information sources than in the past. And many of these sources provide information with a strongly partisan and ideological coloration. While the proportion of Americans regularly reading a daily newspaper or tuning in to a network evening news broadcast has fallen considerably over the past several decades, the proportion listening to talk radio, reading liberal or conservative blogs on the Internet, or watching ideologically tinged cable television programs has increased dramatically (Mutz 2006; Prior 2007).

The dramatic shifts in the party loyalties of social groups such as southern whites, northern white Catholics, and northern white blue-collar voters since the 1950s have been driven primarily by ideology. This is evident in Figure 13.2, which displays the trends in Democratic identification among liberals, moderates, and conservatives belonging to these three traditionally Democratic groups over the past four decades. Unfortunately it is not possible to trace these shifts back earlier than the 1970s because the ANES surveys did not include an ideological identification question before 1972. We therefore cannot capture the rather substantial shifts in party identification that occurred between the 1950s and 1970s. Nevertheless, the results displayed in Figure 13.2 are very revealing. The decline in Democratic identification between the 1970s and the 2000s was concentrated disproportionately among conservatives. Among this group, Democratic identification fell from 40

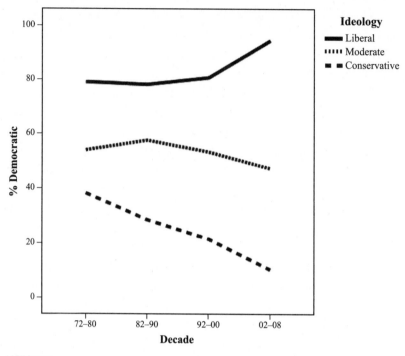

Source: ANES 2011.

FIGURE 13.2 **Ideological Realignment of the New Deal Coalition: Trend in Democratic Identification by Ideology**

percent in the 1970s to just over 10 percent in the 2000s. In contrast, there was only a modest decline in Democratic identification among moderates and an increase in Democratic identification among liberals.

A Growing Racial Divide

Perhaps the most important long-term trend contributing to the rise of polarization in the twenty-first century is the growing racial and ethnic diversity of the American population. Between 1992 and 2008 the nonwhite share of the US electorate doubled from 13 percent to 26 percent. Moreover, according to the 2007 Current Population Survey, nonwhites now make up close to half of the US population under the age of five compared to less than 10 percent of the population over the age of seventy. Latinos make up about a quarter of the under-age-five population today compared with less than 5 percent of the over-age-seventy population. So regardless of future trends in immigration, the nonwhite, and especially the Latino share of the population and the electorate is certain to continue growing over the next few decades. In fact, by 2050, Census Bureau projections indicate that nonwhites, including Latinos, will constitute a majority of the US population as they already do in the two most populous states in the nation—California and Texas.

The growing racial diversity of the US population has had profound consequences for American politics and American elections. For one thing, increased racial diversity made it possible for someone like Barack Obama to be elected to the presidency. If the racial composition of the American electorate in 2008 had been the same as the racial composition of the American electorate as recently as 1992, based on his share of the vote among various racial groups, Obama would have lost decisively to John McCain. Beyond the impact on the 2008 presidential election, growing racial diversity has also contributed to the rise of polarization in American politics. That is because the growing nonwhite share of the US electorate has led to a growing racial divide between the Democratic and Republican electoral coalitions, and this growing racial divide has been a major factor contributing to the growing ideological divide between the Democratic and Republican electoral coalitions.

Figure 13.3 displays the trends in the nonwhite percentages of Democratic and Republican voters over the past six decades based on data from the American National Election Studies. Over this time period, the nonwhite share of Democratic voters has increased dramatically, going from only 7 percent in the 1950s to 36 percent in the 2000s. Meanwhile, the nonwhite share of Republican voters has increased only slightly, going from 3 percent in the 1950s to 10 percent in the 2000s. As a result, the racial divide between supporters of the two parties has widened from a very narrow gap in the 1950s to a yawning chasm in the twenty-first century.

The data from the 2008 national exit poll confirms these trends. Nonwhites made up 39 percent of Obama voters versus only 10 percent of McCain voters. Most strikingly, African Americans made up 23 percent of Obama voters compared with only 1 percent of McCain voters. Despite the efforts of Republican leaders to expand their party's appeal beyond its white

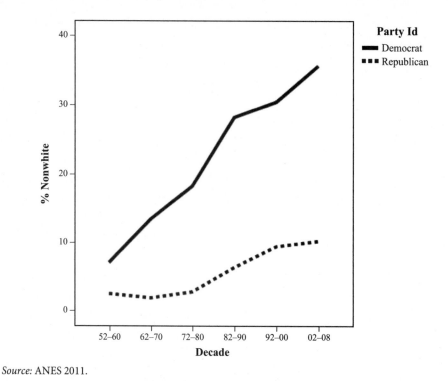

Source: ANES 2011.

FIGURE 13.3   The Growing Racial Divide: Trend in Nonwhite Share of
Democratic and Republican Electoral Coalitions

base and to place members of minority groups in highly visible leadership
positions, including the chairmanship of the Republican National Committee, the two major parties in the United States today present a stark contrast
in terms of their racial profiles. As anyone who has attended or watched
party conventions or campaign rallies in recent years knows, supporters of
the two parties look very different. In twenty-first century America we have
a two-party system that consists of a racially diverse Democratic Party and
an overwhelmingly white Republican Party.

Not only is the racial divide between supporters of the two major parties
now enormous, it is likely to grow even larger over the next several election
cycles. That is because the racial divide between the parties' electoral coalitions is much larger among younger voters than it is among older voters, as

evidence from the 2008 national exit poll makes clear. While nonwhites were much more prevalent among Obama voters than among McCain voters in every age group, the gap between the candidates' supporters was far greater in the youngest age group than it was in the oldest age group. Among voters over the age of sixty-five, nonwhites made up 26 percent of Obama voters compared with 7 percent of McCain voters. But among voters under the age of thirty, nonwhites made up 49 percent of Obama voters compared with 13 percent of McCain voters.

Latinos are now the fastest growing segment of the US electorate. According to data from the American National Election Studies, the Latino share of the US electorate grew from less than 1 percent in 1972 to 7 percent in 2008. In the southwestern states, including Texas and California, Latinos already comprise by far the largest minority voting bloc. According to state exit polls, Barack Obama would not have carried Nevada or New Mexico without the overwhelming support of Latino voters, and his margin in Colorado would have been very narrow. And over the next twenty to thirty years, the Latino share of the US electorate is expected to continue growing. By 2016, if not sooner, Latinos will probably comprise a larger voting bloc than African Americans.

The continued growth of the Latino electorate and the close balance of support between the Democratic and Republican parties in the nation mean that the outcomes of future national elections in the United States will depend heavily on Latino votes. In the past, both major parties have actively courted Latino voters. Traditionally Latinos, while leaning Democratic, have divided their votes between the two major parties much more evenly than African Americans, with a third or more sometimes supporting Republican candidates. As recently as 2004, according to data from the national exit poll, George W. Bush won well over 40 percent of the Latino vote.

The political diversity of the Latino electorate reflects, in part, the economic and cultural diversity of the Latino population in the United States (Abrajano and Alvarez 2010). For example, Cuban Americans in Florida have traditionally supported Republican candidates at the state and national level, based on a strong legacy of anti-Communist sentiment, while Mexican Americans in California have generally tilted strongly Democratic. Similarly, affluent Latinos have been more likely to vote Republican than lower-income Latinos. However, the steady rightward drift of the Republican Party, and especially the Party's increasingly hard-line position on the issue of immigration, are now threatening to undermine future Latino support for the GOP. According to data from the 2008 American National Election Study, more than two-thirds of Latino voters support comprehensive immigration reform, including a path to citizenship—a position rejected by almost all prominent Republican leaders and by nearly two-thirds of white Republican voters. Moreover, among the large majority of Latino voters who consider immigration reform a very or extremely important issue, over 80 percent favor comprehensive reform including a path to citizenship.

The growing size of the nonwhite electorate and the steady rightward drift of the Republican Party almost guarantee that the nonwhite share of Democratic electoral base will continue to grow over the next several election cycles. And this trend should, in turn, continue to drive conservative and racially resentful whites into the Republican camp, thereby pushing the GOP even further to the right. In fact, we don't have to wait to see evidence of this trend— we have already seen this dynamic at work in the rise of the Tea Party movement following the 2008 election (Williamson, Skocpol, and Coggin 2011). The growing racial and ethnic diversity of the electorate has had major consequences for American politics. Without this shift, Barack Obama would never have become the nation's first African American president. In 2008, Obama lost the white vote by a margin of more than 11 million votes, but won the nonwhite vote by a margin of more than 20 million votes. More fundamentally, the movement of nonwhite voters into the Democratic Party and the corresponding movement of conservative white voters out of the Democratic Party and into the Republican Party have transformed both party coalitions and contributed to ideological polarization. The Democratic electoral coalition today is dominated by nonwhites and white liberals who strongly support activist government; the Republican electoral coalition is dominated by white conservatives who strongly oppose activist government, especially activist government that is seen as primarily benefiting nonwhites.

A Growing Cultural Divide

The issues that divide the parties have also changed over the past half century. Along with the traditional issues involving the role of government in regulating economic activity and providing a social safety net for those left behind by the normal operation of a capitalist economy, differences over the role of the United States in the world and especially the use of American military power have increased since the end of the Cold War. At the same time, a new set of issues has emerged in American politics in recent decades. These are issues that were rarely if ever discussed by candidates and party leaders during the 1950s and 1960s, such as abortion and gay marriage, that divide Americans along religious and cultural lines rather than along economic or class lines (White 2003).

For many Americans today, cultural issues have a stronger influence on party identification and voting decisions than economic or foreign policy issues. Over time, the party divide on these issues has become sharper as the positions of party leaders have become more consistent across different issue domains. Today almost all prominent Democratic leaders are both cultural and economic liberals while almost all prominent Republican leaders are both cultural and economic conservatives.

The cultural divide was very evident in the results of the 2008 presidential election, despite the fact that the election took place in the midst of a major economic crisis and neither major party candidate focused much attention on cultural issues during the campaign. One of the strongest predictors of candidate choice among white voters in 2008 was frequency of church attendance. The data from the 2008 national exit poll show that the more time white voters reported spending in church, the more likely they were to cast a Republican ballot. Among whites who never attended religious services, fewer than 40 percent voted for the Republican presidential candidate, but among those who attended religious services more than once a week, almost 80 percent voted for the Republican candidate.

Religiosity is now a powerful predictor of party identification and candidate preference among white voters in the United States—more powerful in many elections than characteristics traditionally associated with party affiliation and voting behavior such as social class and union membership. Thus, data from the 2008 national exit poll show that among white voters the impact of church attendance on candidate choice was much stronger than the impact of either family income or union membership. The difference in support for Obama between whites who attended church more than once a week and those who never attended church was a stunning forty-five percentage points. In contrast, the difference in support for Obama between whites with family incomes below $30,000 and those with family incomes above $150,000 was a meager six percentage points. And despite the strong support that he received from organized labor in the general election, the difference in support for Obama between whites in union households and those in nonunion households was only nine percentage points.

Regardless of income or household union membership, religious whites voted overwhelmingly for the Republican presidential candidate in 2008. Thus, whites with family incomes below $50,000 who attended religious services more than once a week voted for John McCain over Barack Obama by better than a two-to-one margin. And despite the strong support of union leaders for the Democratic ticket, whites from union households who attended religious services more than once a week voted for McCain over Obama by close to a three-to-one margin.

On the other hand, regardless of income or household union membership, secular whites voted overwhelmingly for the Democratic presidential candidate in 2008. Whites with family incomes above $100,000 who never attended religious services voted for Obama over McCain by better than a two-to-one margin, and whites from nonunion households who never attended religious services voted for Obama over McCain by better than a three-to-two margin.

The deep partisan divide between religious and nonreligious whites is a relatively recent development in American politics. In the years following World War II, the most significant religious divide among white voters in the United States was that between Protestants and Catholics. White Catholics were strongly Democratic, while white Protestants outside of the South were almost as strongly Republican. In the 1960 presidential election, for example, according to data from the American National Election Study survey, 82 percent of white Catholics voted for Democrat John F. Kennedy, while 71 percent of white Protestants in the North voted for Republican Richard M. Nixon.

Since the 1960s, the partisan divide between white Catholics and Protestants has gradually diminished as a result of the ideological realignment of the American party system. Conservative Catholics have gravitated toward the Republican Party while liberal Protestants have moved into the Democratic camp. By 2008, according to the ANES survey, the 46 percent of white Catholics who voted for Barack Obama was almost identical to the 45 percent of northern white Protestants who voted for Obama. However, as the Catholic-Protestant split has diminished, a new religious divide has emerged among white voters—a divide between the religious and the nonreligious.

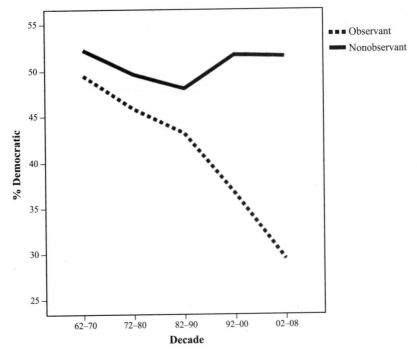

Source: ANES 2011.

FIGURE 13.4 **The Growing Cultural Divide: Trend in Democratic
Identification by Church Attendance Among White Voters**

Figure 13.4 displays the trend in party identification among white voters
between the 1960s and the first decade of the twenty-first century based on
frequency of church attendance. Voters were classified as "observant" if they
reported attending religious services every week or almost every week and
as "nonobservant" if they reported attending religious services only a few
times a year or never. On average, about 40 percent of white voters fell into
each of these two categories. About 20 percent of white voters who reported
attending religious services "a few times a month" are left out of the graph.
Their party identification generally falls right in the middle of the "observant" and "nonobservant" groups.

The data in Figure 13.4 show that between the 1960s and the 1980s Democratic identification (which includes Independents leaning toward the Democratic Party) declined among both observant and nonobservant whites, with

the gap between the two groups only growing slightly. Since then, however, the gap has widened considerably due mainly to a sharp drop in Democratic identification among observant whites. During this more recent period, Democratic identification has increased modestly among nonobservant whites. As a result, by the 2000s the religious divide among white voters had reached an all-time high. Slightly over 50 percent of nonobservant white voters identified with or leaned toward the Democratic Party compared with less than 30 percent of observant white voters. To put this in perspective, the twenty-two-point gap in Democratic identification between observant and nonobservant whites was considerably larger than either the thirteen-point marriage gap or the seven-point gender gap among white voters.

A Growing Geographic Divide

In his keynote address to the Democratic National Convention in 2004, Barack Obama famously minimized the differences between Americans living in the red states and blue states:

> The pundits like to slice-and-dice our country into red states and blue states; red states for Republicans, blue states for Democrats. But I've got news for them, too. We worship an awesome God in the blue states, and we don't like federal agents poking around in our libraries in the red states. We coach Little League in the blue states and yes, we've got some gay friends in the red states. . . . We are one people, all of us pledging allegiance to the stars and stripes, all of us defending the United States of America.

Obama was widely praised in 2004 for trying to move the nation past the bitter divisions of the Bush years. Indeed, the speech put Obama on the national political map and paved the way for his successful presidential campaign four years later. Yet Obama's own election in 2008 produced the deepest divisions between red states and blue states in recent history. The data in Table 13.1 show that there were fewer closely contested states and more landslide states in 2008 than in any other nationally competitive presidential election in the past half century including the 2000 and 2004 elections. Only six states were decided by a margin of less than five percentage points, while twenty-six states plus the District of Columbia were decided by a margin of at least fif-

TABLE 13.1 Distributions of States and Voters by State
Competitiveness in Presidential Elections

	1960	1976	2000	2004	2008
STATES					
Competitive	20	20	12	11	6
Lean D, R	14	11	10	10	9
Solid D, R	7	9	6	8	9
Safe D, R	9	11	23	22	27
VOTERS					
Competitive	52%	59%	28%	24%	19%
Lean D, R	30	20	22	29	13
Solid D, R	8	11	22	16	19
Safe D, R	11	10	34	31	49

Source: Leip 2011.

Note: Competitive = 0-4.99%, Lean D, R = 5-9.99%, Solid D, R = 10-14.99%, Safe D, R = 15% plus.
District of Columbia included in 1976-2008 results.

teen percentage points. In contrast, in 1960, twenty states were decided by a margin of less than five percentage points and only nine were decided by a margin of at least fifteen percentage points, and in 1976, twenty states were decided by a margin of less than five percentage points and only eleven plus the District of Columbia were decided by a margin of at least fifteen percentage points. Moreover, the decline in closely contested states and increase in landslide states represented a continuation of a long-term trend. There were far fewer closely contested states and far more landslide states in both 2000 and 2004 than in 1960 or 1976. But the 2008 results set a new standard for geographic polarization in the modern era.

Not only have there been fewer closely contested states and more landslide states in recent presidential elections than in earlier nationally competitive elections, but several of the most populous states with the largest blocs of electoral votes have been decided by landslide margins in recent years. In earlier nationally competitive elections, almost all of the populous states were presidential battlegrounds. In 1960, for example, seven of the eight most populous states were decided by a margin of less than five percentage points and the only exception, New York, was decided by just over five percentage points. And in 1976, all eight of the most populous states were battlegrounds: California, New York, Texas, Florida, Illinois, Ohio, Pennsylvania, and Michigan were all decided by fewer than five percentage points. In contrast, in 2000 and 2004 only Florida, Ohio, and Pennsylvania were decided by fewer than five percentage points, and in 2008 only Florida and Ohio were decided by fewer than five percentage points. As a result, the percentage of the nation's voters in battleground states has declined from 52 percent in 1960 and 59 percent in 1976, to 28 percent in 2000, 24 percent in 2004, and only 19 percent in 2008. At the same time, the percentage of voters in landslide states has grown from only 11 percent in 1960 and 10 percent in 1976, to 34 percent in 2000, 31 percent in 2004, and a remarkable 49 percent in 2008. Almost half of the nation's voters in 2008 resided in states where the presidential election was decided by a landslide margin.

Explaining the Red-Blue Divide

The deepening divide in presidential voting between red states and blue states is itself a reflection of important differences between the social characteristics and political beliefs of voters in these two types of states. In 2008, Barack Obama carried twenty-four states by at least five percentage points, and John McCain carried twenty states by at least five percentage points. The twenty-four blue states included 45 percent of voters in the 2008 ANES, while the twenty red states included 35 percent of voters in the 2008 ANES.

Perhaps the most politically significant differences between the social characteristics of voters in the red states and voters in the blue states involved their religious orientations. Americans in the blue states may "worship an awesome God," as Barack Obama stated in his 2004 keynote address, but they appear to worship that God less frequently and less fervently than Americans in the red states. According to the evidence from the 2008 American National Election Study, voters in the red states were much more likely than voters in the blue states to describe themselves as born-again or evangelical Christians and much more likely to report attending religious services every week. And these differences are even larger when we compare white voters in the red states and blue states. For example, 61 percent of white voters in the red states described themselves as born-again or evangelical Christians compared with only 33 percent of white voters in the blue states. Given the strong relationship between religious beliefs and partisanship among white voters, these differences go a long way toward explaining the red state–blue state divide in partisanship and presidential candidate preference. According to the ANES data, only 23 percent of whites who described themselves as born-again or evangelical Christians voted for Barack Obama, compared with 51 percent of other whites.

The political attitudes and behavior of voters in red states and blue states also differed fairly dramatically. According to the 2008 ANES, 67 percent of voters in the blue states cast their ballot for Barack Obama, compared with only 41 percent of voters in the red states. And the difference between white voters in the blue states and red states was even more dramatic—only 25 percent of white voters in the red states supported Obama compared with 58 percent of white voters in the blue states. Given the overwhelming support of nonwhite voters for Barack Obama, the fact that an outright majority of whites in the blue states voted for the Democratic candidate guaranteed that he would easily carry most of these states.

The candidate preferences of voters in the red and blue states were consistent with their underlying partisan and ideological orientations as well as their views on major campaign issues. Voters in the blue states were much less likely than their counterparts in the red states to identify with the Republican Party or to describe themselves as conservatives. They were also much more likely to describe themselves as pro-choice on abortion, to support same-sex marriage, and to favor the creation of a single-payer health-care system.

Again, the differences between white voters in the red states and blue states were generally even larger than the differences between all voters in these two sets of states. For example, only 40 percent of white voters in the blue states identified with the Republican Party compared with 63 percent of white voters in the red states; only 38 percent of white voters in the blue states described themselves as conservative compared with 57 percent of white voters in the red states; and only 27 percent of white voters in the red states were pro-choice on abortion compared with 55 percent of white voters in the blue states.

When it comes to political geography, Americans today are not only closely divided, they are also deeply divided. Whether one focuses on states, House districts, counties, or just about any other geographic unit, it is clear that by any reasonable standard the partisan divide is much deeper today than it was thirty or forty years ago. There are far more solidly red and solidly blue states, congressional districts and counties than there were in the past and far fewer closely divided states, congressional districts, and counties. Moreover, these differences in party affiliation and voting behavior reflect differences in fundamental beliefs about religion, morality, and the role of government in American society.

The result of this growing red-blue divide is that general elections have become less competitive, primary elections have become more important in choosing elected officials, and incentives for bipartisan cooperation and compromise have been eroded. And because this trend is not a result of partisan gerrymandering but of important changes in American politics and society, it is unlikely to be reversed any time soon.

Polarization and American Democracy: Is Gridlock Inevitable?

Whether the 2012 elections result in unified Democratic control of Congress and the presidency, unified Republican control, or some type of split party control, the deep ideological divide between the two major parties will remain a significant obstacle to any meaningful bipartisan compromise on major policy issues. Even under unified party control, it is almost certain that the minority party in the Senate will control considerably more than the forty-one votes needed to block legislation by using the filibuster. And neither party has shown any hesitation in recent years about using the filibuster along with holds and other delaying tactics to thwart the will of the majority. During 2009–10 when Democrats controlled both chambers of Congress and the White House, Republicans routinely used filibusters and holds to block Democratic legislation and President Obama's nominees to the courts and key administrative positions. There is little doubt that Senate Democrats would use the same tactics to obstruct the will of a Republican president and Congress if they found themselves in the minority after the 2012 election.

The fundamental problem is that the American political system, based on the Madisonian principles of separation of powers and checks and balances, was not designed to work under conditions of intense partisan polarization. Political parties in their modern form did not exist at the time of the founding, of course. Indeed, the founders viewed parties as dangerous fomenters of conflict. But modern political parties quickly developed during the first half of the nineteenth century with the expansion of the franchise and the need to mobilize a mass electorate. Today, parties are generally considered essential for the effective functioning of representative democracy, providing a link between candidates and elected officials and the public, and clarifying the choices for voters in elections.

Within government, parties also play a vital role in the American political system by organizing the legislative process and helping to bridge the separation of powers by creating a bond of self-interest between the president and members of his party in the House and Senate. For the bond of self-interest to work, however, the president and both chambers of Congress must be controlled by the same party. When that is not the case, and divided party control of the White House and at least one chamber has been much more common since World War II than previously, the result is either bipartisan compromise or gridlock and—as we have seen since the 2010 midterm election produced the most conservative House of Representatives in decades—the deeper the ideological divide between the parties, the greater the likelihood of gridlock.

There are two formulas for overcoming gridlock. One involves bipartisan compromise, which is the preferred solution of many editorial writers and pundits. They wonder why Democrats and Republicans cannot get together and move past their parties' entrenched positions to "do what is in the best interest of the country." The answer is that Democrats and Republicans today profoundly disagree on what is in the best interest of the country. In fact, their ideas about what should be done to address the nation's biggest problems are fundamentally incompatible. Democrats, for example, believe strongly that the best way to create jobs and grow the economy is to increase government spending in order to stimulate demand for goods and services, while Republicans believe just as strongly that the best way to create jobs and grow the economy is to reduce government spending and regulation and cut taxes on corporations and upper-income Americans in order to increase incentives for investment in the private sector. And when it comes to cultural issues like abortion, the divide is even deeper. It is almost impossible to reconcile the view of most Democrats, that women have a fundamental right to choose whether to continue a pregnancy, and the view of most Republicans, that abortion is immoral and should be banned or allowed only under extraordinary circumstances.

As long as these fundamental differences between Democrats and Republicans continue to exist, and there is little reason to expect them to disappear any time soon, bipartisan compromise is going to be very difficult. And simply urging an end to partisan infighting, as many pundits and editorial writers have done, is not going to accomplish anything. The diverging positions of Democratic and Republican elected officials and candidates reflect the diverging positions of those who put them in office.

A more plausible formula for overcoming gridlock under these circumstances is party government. Under party government, a system that exists in some countries with a parliamentary political system, the party that wins an election gets to carry out the policies it campaigned on until the next election, at which point the voters get to choose whether to keep that party in power or replace it with the opposition party. But this system requires unified party control of the executive and legislative branches for a long enough time period to allow the majority party's policies to be implemented and work, a requirement that midterm elections frequently interfere with. And party government would also require an end to antimajoritarian rules like the Senate filibuster that allow the minority party to frustrate the will of the majority. Party government is a risky approach to policy making because it requires the minority party to accept the right of the majority party to implement its preferred policies no matter how much the minority party dislikes those policies. But the fact that the majority party is likely to find itself in the minority at some point in the near future can act as a check on abuses of power or ideological overreach. And in a polarized political system, the alternative to party government is not bipartisan compromise—it is continued gridlock.

References

Abrajano, Marisa A., and Alvarez, Michael R. 2010. *New Faces, New Voices: The Hispanic Electorate in America*. Princeton, NJ: Princeton University Press.

Abramowitz, Alan I. 2010. *The Disappearing Center: Engaged Citizens, Polarization and American Democracy*. New Haven, CT: Yale University Press.

_____. 2011. "Expect Confrontation, Not Compromise: The 112th House of Representatives Is Likely to Be the Most Conservative and Polarized House in the Modern Era." *PS: Political Science and Politics* 44 (April): 293–296.

ANES (American National Election Studies). 2011. http://electionstudies.org/studypages /download/datacenter_all.htm.

Black, Earl, and Black, Merle. 2007. *Divided America: The Ferocious Power Struggle in American Politics*. New York: Simon and Schuster.

Campbell, Angus, Philip E. Converse, Warren E. Miller, and Donald E. Stokes. 1960. *The American Voter*. New York: John Wiley and Sons.

Catanese, David. 2011. "Paul Ryan Budget Becomes Litmus Test for GOP Primaries." *Politico*. June 3. http://www.politico.com/news/stories/0611/57678.html.

Converse, Philip E. 1964. "The Nature of Belief Systems in Mass Publics." In *Ideology and Discontent*, edited by David Apter. New York: Free Press of Glencoe.

Dodd, Lawrence C., and Bruce I. Oppenheimer. 2005. "A Decade of Republican Control: The House of Representatives, 1995–2005." In *Congress Reconsidered*, edited by Lawrence C. Dodd and Bruce I. Oppenheimer. 8th ed. Washington, DC: CQ Press.

Downs, Anthony. 1957. *An Economic Theory of Democracy*. New York: Harper and Row.

Fiorina, Morris P., with Matthew S. Levendusky. 2006. "Disconnected: The Political Class Versus the People." In *Red and Blue Nation? Characteristics and Causes of America's Polarized Politics, Volume One*, edited by Pietro S. Nivola and David W. Brady. Washington, DC: Brookings Institution.

Fiorina, Morris P., with Samuel J. Abrams and Matthew S. Levendusky. 2011. *Culture War? The Myth of a Polarized America*. 3rd ed. New York: Longman.

Fiorina, Morris P., with Samuel J. Abrams. 2009. *Disconnect: The Breakdown of Representation in American Politics*. Norman, OK: University of Oklahoma Press.

Heilemann, John, and Mark Halperin, 2010. *Game Change: Obama and the Clintons, McCain and Palin, and the Race of a Lifetime*. New York: HarperCollins.

Hohmann, James. 2011. "Minnesota Mean at Heart of Government Shutdown." *Politico*. July 3. http://www.politico.com/news/stories/0711/58260.html.

Leip, David. 2011. *Atlas of US Presidential Elections*. http://uselectionatlas.org/.

Liasson, Mara. 2011. "Gingrich Backpedals on Medicare Comments in Iowa." National Public Radio. May 20. http://www.npr.org/2011/05/20/136467767/gingrich-backpedals-medicare -comments-in-iowa.

Mutz, Diane E. 2006. "How the Mass Media Divide Us." In *Red and Blue Nation? Characteristics and Causes of America's Polarized Politics, Volume One*, edited by Pietro S. Nivola and David W. Brady. Washington, DC: Brookings.

Phillips, Kevin. 1969. *The Emerging Republican Majority*. New Rochelle, NY: Arlington House.

Poole, Keith, and Howard Rosenthal. 2009. *Ideology and Congress*. New York: Transaction Books.

Prior, Markus. 2007. *Post-Broadcast Democracy: How Media Choice Increases Inequality in Political Involvement and Polarizes Elections*. New York: Cambridge University Press.

Sinclair, Barbara. 2005. "The New World of US Senators." In *Congress Reconsidered*, edited by Lawrence C. Dodd and Bruce I. Oppenheimer. 8th ed. Washington, DC: CQ Press.

Tolan, Tom. 2011. First Round in Senate Recall Elections Draws Near. *Milwaukee Journal-Sentinel*. July 2. http://www.jsonline.com/news/statepolitics/124925369.html.

White, John Kenneth. 2003. *The Values Divide: American Politics and Culture in Transition*. New York: Chatham House.

Williamson, Vanessa, Theda Skocpol, and John Coggin. 2011. "The Tea Party and the Remaking of Republican Conservatism." *Perspectives on Politics* 9 (March): 25–44.

About the Editors and Contributors

Mark D. Brewer is Associate Professor of Political Science at the University of Maine, and received his PhD in political science from Syracuse University. His research interests focus generally on political behavior, with specific research areas including partisanship and electoral behavior at both the mass and elite levels, the linkages between public opinion and public policy, and the interactions that exist between religion and politics in the United States. He is the author of *Party Images in the American Electorate* and *Relevant No More? The Catholic/Protestant Divide in American Electoral Politics*, and coauthor of *Diverging Parties, Split: Class and Cultural Divides in American Politics, Dynamics of American Political Parties,* and *Parties and Elections in America,* now in its 6th edition. He has published articles in *Political Research Quarterly, Political Behavior, Legislative Studies Quarterly,* and *Journal for the Scientific Study of Religion.* He is currently working on a study of the place of personal responsibility in American politics with Jeffrey M. Stonecash.

L. Sandy Maisel is William R. Kenan Jr. Professor of Government and director of the Goldfarb Center for Public Affairs and Civic Engagement at Colby College. Former president of the New England Political Science Association and former chair of the Legislative Studies and the Political Organizations and Parties sections of the American Political Science Association, Maisel is the general editor of *Political Parties and Elections in the United States: An Encyclopedia* and of *Jews in American Politics;* coauthor of *Parties and Elections in America,* now in its 6th edition, and author or coauthor of dozens of journal articles and book chapters.

Alan I. Abramowitz is the Alben W. Barkley Professor of Political Science at Emory University in Atlanta, Georgia. He received his BA from the University of Rochester in 1969 and his PhD from Stanford University in 1976. Dr. Abramowitz has authored or coauthored five books, dozens of contributions to edited volumes, and more than fifty articles in political science journals dealing with political parties, elections, and voting behavior in the United States. Dr. Abramowitz's most recent book, *The Disappearing Center: Engaged Citizens, Polarization and American Democracy*, was published in 2010 by Yale University Press.

Nathaniel Birkhead is a PhD candidate at Indiana University specializing in legislatures, representation, and electoral behavior. His dissertation evaluates the effects that partisan-ideological sorting and geographic sorting have on legislative extremism.

Diana Dwyre is Professor of Political Science at California State University, Chico, where she coordinates the political science major and directs the internship program. She was the 2009–2010 Fulbright Australian National University Distinguished Chair in American Political Science at Australian National University in Canberra, Australia. She has coauthored two books on campaign finance, *Legislative Labyrinth: Congress and Campaign Finance Reform* (2001) and *Limits and Loopholes: The Quest for Money, Free Speech and Fair Elections* (2007), and has written numerous articles and book chapters on political parties and campaign finance.

Beth C. Easter is a PhD candidate in the Department of Political Science at Indiana University. She holds a Juris Doctorate from Emory Law School and is a licensed member of the Michigan Bar. Her research interests include judicial politics, elections, political parties, and interest groups. Her dissertation examines the participation of political parties and organized interests in state Supreme Court elections.

Paul S. Herrnson is Director of the Center for American Politics and Citizenship, Professor in the Department of Government and Politics, and Distinguished Scholar-Teacher at the University of Maryland. His interests include political parties and elections, money and politics, and voting technology and ballot design. He has published numerous articles and books, including *Congressional Elections: Campaigning at Home and in Washington* and *Voting Technology: The Not-So-Simple Act of Casting a Ballot.* Herrnson has served as President of the Southern Political Science Association and as an American Political Science Association Congressional Fellow. He has advised the US Congress, the Maryland General Assembly, and the Federal Election Commission, as well as numerous government agencies and nongovernmental organizations, on matters pertaining to campaign finance, political parties, and election reform.

Marjorie Randon Hershey is a professor of political science at Indiana University. She is the author of *Party Politics in America*, now in its 15th edition, and a number of other books, articles, and book chapters. She specializes in political parties, elections, and media coverage of campaigns.

Jonathan Lewallen is a graduate student at the University of Texas-Austin. His work focuses on relationships between congressional committees and party leaders.

Trevor C. Lowman received his BA degree from the University of California, Davis, with honors in Political Science, College honors, and Phi Beta Kappa. He was awarded a Research Experiences for Undergraduates supplementary grant from the National Science Foundation to assist with the UC Davis Congressional Election Study, and explore the effects of voter sophistication in the context of congressional elections. His interests include elections and voting behavior, and public opinion.

G. Calvin Mackenzie is The Goldfarb Family Distinguished Professor of Government at Colby College where he has taught since 1978. He is a graduate of Bowdoin College and has a PhD in Government from Harvard. Mackenzie's professional work focuses on governance and public policy, with a special interest in presidential transitions and the politics of presidential appointments. He has often been a consultant to presidential personnel staffs and congressional committees on those matters. He was Senior Advisor to the Brookings Presidential Appointee Initiative and to the National Commission on the Public Service chaired by Paul Volcker. His many books on presidential appointments include *The Politics of Presidential Appointments, America's Unelected Government, The In-and-Outers, Innocent Until Nominated: The Breakdown* *of the Presidential Appointments Process*, and *Scandal Proof: Can Ethics Laws Make Government Ethical?* In 2004, he was elected a Fellow of the National Academy of Public Administration.

Barbara Norrander is a Professor in the School of Government and Public Policy at the University of Arizona. She has written about presidential nomination politics since the 1980s, covering such topics as participation levels, voters' choices, and candidate exits. Her most recent book is *The Imperfect Primary: Oddities, Biases and Strengths of U.S. Presidential Nomination Politics*.

Diana Owen is Associate Professor of Political Science and Director of American Studies at Georgetown University, and teaches in the Communication, Culture, and Technology graduate program. She is a graduate of the George Washington University, and received her doctorate in Political Science from the University of Wisconsin-Madison. Diana has been an American Political Science Association Congressional Media Fellow. She is the author, with Richard Davis, of *New Media and American Politics* (Oxford, 1998) and *Media Messages in American Presidential Elections* (Greenwood, 1991), editor of *The Internet and Politics: Citizens, Voters, and Activists*, with Sarah Oates and Rachel Gibson (Routledge, 2006), and editor of *Making a Difference: The Internet and Elections in Comparative Perspective*, with Richard Davis, Stephen Ward, and David Taras (Lexington, 2009). Her most recent book is *American Government and Politics in the Information Age*, with David Paletz and Tim Cook (FlatWorld, 2011). She has published numerous scholarly journal articles and book chapters in the areas of American government, mass political behavior, political communication, media and politics, political socialization, civic education, and elections and voting behavior. Her most recent work focuses on digital media in American politics and elections, and the intersection of civic education and political engagement.

Nicol C. Rae (DPhil, Oxford University) is Professor of Political Science and Senior Associate Dean for Liberal Arts at Florida International University, Miami, Florida. His most recent book (coedited with Timothy Power) is *Exporting Congress: The Influence of the US Congress on World Legislatures* (University of Pittsburgh Press, 2006). Other books include *Impeaching Clinton: Partisan Strife on Capitol Hill* (with Colton Campbell); and *Conservative Reformers: The Republican Freshmen and the Lessons of the 104th Congress*.

Professor Rae has also written numerous journal articles and book chapters on American and European politics and government. He was chosen for an American Political Science Association Congressional Fellowship in 1995–1996, and was Gwylim Gibbon Prize Research Fellow at Nuffield College Oxford from 1985–1988.

Daniel M. Shea is a Professor of Political Science and director of the Center for Political Participation at Allegheny College. He has written or edited a number of books and articles on American government. His two most recent books include, *Let's Vote: The Essentials of the American Electoral Process* (Pearson 2012) and, with coeditor Morris Fiorina, *Can We Talk: The Rise of Rude, Nasty, Stubborn Politics* (Pearson 2012).

Walter J. Stone is a Professor of Political Science at the University of California, Davis. He served as chair of the department from 2001 to 2006 and currently is directing the UC Davis 2006–2010 Congressional Election Study (http://electionstudy.ucdavis.edu/). He has authored and coauthored numerous books and dozens of articles in journals such as the *American Political Science Review*, *Journal of Politics*, *American Journal of Political Science*, *Political Research Quarterly*, and many others.

Jeffrey M. Stonecash is Maxwell Professor of Political Science specializing in American political parties. His recent publications are: *Counter Realignment: Political Change in the Northeast* (with Howard L. Reiter, Cambridge, 2011); *New Directions in Party Politics*, Editor (Routledge, 2010); *The Dynamics of the American Party System* (with Mark D. Brewer, Cambridge, 2009); *Reassessing the Incumbency Effect* (Cambridge, 2008); *Split: Class and Cultural Divisions in American Politics* (with Mark D. Brewer, CQ Press, 2007); *Parties Matter: Realignment and the Return of Partisanship* (Lynne-Rienner, 2006); *The Emergence of State Government: Parties and New Jersey Politics, 1950–2000* (Fairleigh Dickinson University Press, 2002); *Diverging Parties: Social Change, Realignment, and Party Polarization* (with Mark D. Brewer and Mack D. Mariani, Westview Press, 2003); and *Class and Party in American Politics* (Westview Press, 2000). He has just completed *Party Pursuits and the Presidential-House Election Connection, 1900–2008.* He is now working with Mark Brewer on a book about the divide over personal responsibility in American politics.

J. Cherie Strachan is Director of Women and Gender Studies and Associate Professor of Political Science at Central Michigan University. In addition to local political processes, her research interests include the role of civility in public deliberation and politics, as well as college level civic education efforts.

Sean M. Theriault is an Associate Professor at the University of Texas. He is the author of *The Power of the People, Party Polarization in Congress*, and a number of articles on a variety of topics. Professor Theriault has earned numerous teaching awards.

Michael R. Wolf is an Associate Professor of Political Science at Indiana University–Purdue University Fort Wayne. Wolf has published numerous articles and book chapters on political behavior and political party dynamics of the United States and other advanced industrial democracies.

Index